Human Relations in Industry:

People at Work

Human Relations in Industry:

People at Work

JAYNE P. CROLLEY

Horry-Georgetown Technical College

Prentice Hall, Englewood Cliffs, New Jersey 07632

Crolley, Jayne P.
  Human relations in industry.

  Includes index.
  1. Psychology, Industrial. 2. Personnel management.
  3. Psychology, Industrial—Case studies. 4. Personnel
  management—Case studies. I. Title.

HF5548.8.C66   1989   658.3   88-19512

Editorial/production supervision and
  interior design: **Anthony Calcara**
Cover design: **Baldino Design**
Manufacturing buyer: **Ed O'Dougherty**
Cover photo: **Dick Luria, FPG**

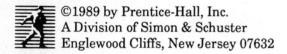
Printed in the United States of America
10 9 8 7 6 5 4 3 2 1

ISBN 0-13-445685-8

Prentice-Hall International (UK) Limited, *London*
Prentice-Hall of Australia Pty. Limited, *Sydney*
Prentice-Hall Canada Inc., *Toronto*
Prentice-Hall Hispanoamericana, S.A., *Mexico*
Prentice-Hall of India Private Limited, *New Delhi*
Prentice-Hall of Japan, Inc., *Tokyo*
Simon & Schuster Asia Pte. Ltd., *Singapore*
Editora Prentice-Hall do Brasil, Ltda., *Rio de Janeiro*

For John and Margie

Contents

Preface

The one third of our lives spent at work should be as meaningful as possible. There is a human side to the work world, and good human relations skills of working with, through, and for other people are essential for career success.

While this book doesn't promise to solve all human relations problems, it blends theory and application in such a way that anyone who needs information on being successful at work, gaining understanding of self and others, getting along better with boss and co-workers, and achieving increased job satisfaction will not be disappointed. People studying a variety of career fields will find the information practical, relevant, and appropriate, whether the person is a novice in the working world or someone more experienced who is making a career change.

Most texts of this nature cover the standard topics of morale, motivation, leadership, communication, and prejudice. This book goes a few steps farther and adds information on relationships at work career decisions, good work habits, personality development, and personal problems. If you want to learn about handling stress, managing time, or getting a job, this is the book for you.

While similar texts focus on management, especially white collar management, this text is for the person who may or may not have management aspirations. Although the subjects of supervision, management fundamentals, and organizational behavior are broached, the book was designed to meet the needs of human relations courses in junior colleges, technical colleges, and community colleges.

Although the book has a strong research base, it stresses the real world and doesn't follow a complex, excessively theoretical approach. Readers soon learn that psychological concepts and models really do apply to daily experiences.

Features

Throughout the text the focus is on applications of principles being taught. Self-quizzes, learning activities, and case studies bridge the gap between theory and practice by providing an opportunity to learn and to use the information. Some activities are to be done alone, for example, "Rate Your Boss as a Leader," while others, for example, "Using 'I' Messages," require interaction with others. Each case study relates to the content of that specific chapter and encourages the student to read, ponder, and discuss the cases, which were taken from life experiences.

To show that reading and learning don't have to be dull, timely boxed-in information on topics ranging from secretarial burnout to quality circles is included. Cartoons, contemporary photographs, and relevant line drawings are used to reinforce the material visually.

There are objectives at the beginning of each chapter that indicate competencies that readers will acquire after reading and studying the material. Throughout the chapter are margin notes that consist of the key ideas being presented. At the end of each chapter are case studies, additional activities, summaries, key terms, review and discussion questions, and endnotes. A glossary of definitions is at the end of the text.

Organization of the Text

The book is divided into five parts, the first of which is "Applying Psychology to the Work Life." Many community college students take a human relations course with a psychology prefix, and they want to know what psychology is, what psychologists do besides work with people with "problems," and how a study of psychology can apply to their lives. Their questions are answered tin Chapter 1. Chapter 2 includes an overview of the history of the human relations movement from the time of the Industrial Revolution up to the present, including a description of the changing nature of work and of the work force.

Part Two concerns "Building Relationships," and the overriding theme is that effective communication is essential for human relations success. One of the communication chapters focuses on communication patterns at work while the other has both work and personal applications. The intent of both chapters is to help the reader improve interpersonal communication by recognizing common barriers to communication, understanding nonverbal communication, and improving listening skills.

Chapter 5 ties in with the communication chapters by emphasizing that since no one works in a vacuum, interpersonal skills are just as important to career success as are technical or job-related skills. The final chapter in this section explores personality in the hopes that the reader will find answers to such questions as "Who am I?" "Why does Ella act the way she does?" and "Am I normal to feel this way?"

Nearly every day you hear the offhand remark that most people hate their jobs. Not so. The fact is that most people like their jobs though they are dissatisfied with some of its elements. The third part, "Improving the Quality of Work Life," focuses on the nature of motivation (theory and application), morale and job satisfaction, and leadership. Although this is not a how-to book for supervision, readers with and without leadership aspirations who study this section will better understand the motivational process, know how to assess and improve morale, and become familiar with leadership styles and theories.

The fourth part, "Developing Career Success," was written because many students aren't aware of the variety of occupations available to them, what their own vast possibilities might be, or how to go about the job hunt. This material is helpful and needed whether the reader is looking for the first "real" job, making a midlife career change, or looking for something satisfying to do after retirement. Mature adults are often just as befuddled about career information as younger people.

The first chapter of this section, Chapter 10, encourages the reader to consider seriously the impact of vocational choice and to get involved in assessing individual aptitudes, interests, and values when choosing a career. The next chapter stresses effective resume writing and employment interview skills. To enlighten individuals who think that such virtues as hard work, perseverance, attendance, and punctuality are all that it takes to move ahead and be successful on their jobs, Chapter 12 gives advice on setting goals, managing time, accepting challenges, continuing to learn, playing politics, and looking the part.

The fifth and final part of the text is entitles "Meeting Personal and Organizational Challenges." Although stress, burnout, depression, drug use, and prejudice, the topics in this part may seem strictly personal, they all have organization ramifications. An individual under stress that he or she cannot handle is not as productive as is one who knows about causes, effects, symptoms, and ways of coping. A depressed employee may not be able to concentrate on work and will consequently make more mistakes. A prejudiced employee unaware of civil rights legislation who discriminates against someone in protected group could be depriving that someone of a job, a promotion, or a career opportunity.

Since stress, depression, burnout, drug use, and prejudice are both personal and organizational challenges, causes, effects, and "cures" of each are explored in the three final chapters of the text.

Acknowledgments

Many besides the author are involved in the creation and production of a book. My thanks go to Catherine Rossbach and Sue Jacob, part of the editorial team at Prentice Hall, and Sally Ann Bailey, the copy editor. Anthony Calcara, production editor, deserves special appreciation for his patience, calm assistance, and technical guidance.

While it would be impossible to recognize all of those who have assisted me at various stages of the "project," there are a few colleagues to whom I am especially grateful. Their assistance was as varied as their talents and ranged from making suggestions on parts of the manuscript to providing material for case studies. Thanks to Tony Atkins, Ella Boyd, Barbara Brittain, Gloria Gasque, Teresa Hilburn, and Dennis Murphy for your encouragement, insightful comments, and contributions.

To Frankie, Carrie, Elizabeth, and Paul, a special thanks. The undertaking would have been impossible without your support and understanding.

chapter 1

Psychology as a Science

After reading and studying this chapter, you will be able to:

1. Describe the scientific method.
2. Recognize scientific questions.
3. Discuss ways in which psychologists gather information.
4. Tell how psychological data can be applied to real life situations.
5. Differentiate between what different psychologists do.
6. Contrast four major psychological perspectives
7. Explain how a knowledge of psychology can help individuals in their work and personal lives.

The most successful single ingredient in the formula of success is knowing how to get along with people.

Theodore Roosevelt

Most work-related problems from poor communication to low morale reflect human relations failings. Human relations consists of all interactions between people, whether they're engaged in conflict or cooperation. Psychology, though it offers no foolproof explanations, predictions, or solutions, does offer behavioral concepts that you can use in your life, both on and off the job.

In this chapter, you'll explore psychology as a science and take a peek at the various fields of psychology and the major psychological perspectives. Many people are not aware that psychologists are involved in work that affects nearly every aspect of their lives. Psychologists do a lot more than counsel people with emotional problems, and they have widely different explanations for behavior.

HOW MUCH DO YOU KNOW ABOUT PEOPLE?

To get you off to a good start, read and think about the following statements. Are they true or false?

1. Rewards and punishments can change behavior.
2. Communication consists of more than mere words.
3. Money doesn't always motivate a worker.
4. A happy worker is not necessarily a productive one.
5. Stress can make a person physically sick.
6. Behavior is often determined by motives known only to the unconscious mind.
7. Perfectionists are more likely to fall short of their high expectations and become depressed.
8. People who believe that they are in control of whether they receive reinforcement make higher grades.
9. Excessive stress on the job can result in poor concentration and the inability to make sound decisions.
10. Sexism is discrimination based on gender.

Since observation, personal experience, and common sense tell you that the foregoing statements are all true, why should you study psychology in a classroom? After all, you've been a student of human relations since the day you were born (literally). Unfortunately, your astute observations, unique experiences, and perceptive common sense do not ensure success on the job. As Voltaire said, "Common sense is not so common." If it were, there would be fewer problems and fewer problem people.

WHAT IS PSYCHOLOGY?

Psychology is the scientific study of human and animal behavior.

Psychology isn't such a mysterious word. It's the combination of two Greek words, *psyche* meaning "soul" or "spirit" and *logos* meaning "study of." Psychology is defined as the scientific study of human and animal behavior. Behavior of organisms, whether human or animal, can be observable or nonobservable, mental or physical. With such a definition of behavior, an industrial psychologist might study the effect of noise on productivity, the relationship of stress to disease, or the correlation of alcohol consumption and work injuries.

Human behavior has always held a certain fascination for other humans. While many people attempt to satisfy their curiosity by casual observation or by consulting the neighborhood guru, psychologists prefer a more scientific approach.

THE SCIENTIFIC METHOD

The goals of psychology are to describe, explain, predict, and control behavior.

Psychology is a science that employs the scientific method to help describe, explain, predict, and possibly control behavior. True, it's not as exact a science as biology or chemistry. After all, people can't be put into test-tubes or under microscopes. They're much too complex for that. Human behavior is dynamic and changing, not static and unchanging. Still, by using the scientific method, psychologists have discovered valuable information to help us improve the quality of our lives.

The scientific method can be reduced to three steps, which are:

1. Formulate a hypothesis.
2. Gather and analyze data.
3. Apply the research.

Formulate a Hypothesis

A hypothesis is a statement or assumption about behavior believed to be true.

To formulate a hypothesis, a statement or assumption about behavior, a psychologist must have some question in mind that warrants investigation. All research begins with questioning. A good scientific question is one that can be answered by empirical means, those means emphasizing observation and experimentation. Value questions are taboo. They're grounded in our emotions, beliefs, opinions, and morals and can't be answered by seeking the facts.

Am empirical question can be answered by controlled observation, survey methods, correlational research, or experiment.

Questions using such terms as good, bad, right, wrong, should, or should not are avoided by psychologists. For example, the question "Is it wrong for employees to use sick days for blue Monday?" is not answerable by observation. Is it *wrong*? Your *opinion* is as good as mine. An empirical question, one answered by controlled observation or experiment, would be, "What proportion of American's work force is absent on Monday?" As a matter of fact, General Motors' management asked this question and discovered that on Mondays and Fridays the absenteeism rate increased to 10 percent compared to 5 percent on the other three workdays.[1]

Gather and Analyze Data

There are many ways in which psychologists collect facts. The methods used most often by industrial psychologists include naturalistic observation, surveys, experiments, and correlational methods.

Naturalistic observation involves simply observing the organism in his or her natural environment. While observation is a fascinating pastime (Don't you enjoy people watching?) and certainly offers some advantages, at least two difficulties are involved.

Naturalistic observation is a scientific form of people watching.

One involves the observer, the other involves the observee. Observer bias occurs when the observer is not as objective, detached, and scientific as the situation requires. Having preconceived ideas about a person, place, or thing can prevent an observer from seeing things the way they really are. People see exactly what they expect to see.

Since everyone comes from different backgrounds and has had different experiences, no two people perceive the same situation in exactly the same way. To avoid preconceived judgments and observer bias, having two or more people observe the same situation or people is a good idea. Afterward the observers can pool their notes and arrive at a more objective consensus about what really took place.

As noted, there may be problems with the observee as well. For instance, since some people aim to please, they will actually change their behavior to meet observer expectations if they're aware of being watched. They don't want to appear uncooperative, stupid, or unsophisticated. When the observee knows of the observation, the research can actually become worthless and invalid. Psychologists should keep a low profile and be as unobtrusive as possible. Otherwise, observing behavior actually changes the behavior itself.

A population is a group of people being investigated.

A *survey* is a type of scientific investigation in which people are questioned about anything from satisfaction with salaries to the brand of cereal preferred. Since it is virtually impossible to survey every single person, curious scientists question a representative sample of the target population. A population is a group of people being investigated.

A survey takes the form of either a personal interview, sometimes called a poll, or a questionnaire. There are a few disadvantages of each. For instance, sometimes you just can't believe what people tell you. Sometimes they misrepresent themselves accidentally or purposely. Maybe they want to ingratiate themselves with the surveyor, especially if the survey is not anonymous and could affect the relationship with the boss.

A survey can be either an interview or a questionnaire.

Some people see a questionnaire as an avoidable annoyance, and if they don't toss it into the trashcan, man's second best friend, they will answer it quickly and without much thought. Also, since all people don't respond to a mailed out questionnaire, a psychologist has to ask herself whether the surveyed who respond differ significantly from those who do not. For instance, perhaps those who took time to answer the survey are more conscientious than those who did not.

In the case of a personal interview, there could be a clash between the interviewer and the interviewee. Still the personal interview reveals more information than the questionnaire and probably could be used more often if the interview process weren't so time consuming and costly.

With all the disadvantages, you might ask why psychologists use surveys. Gordon Allport, a personality psychologist, provides one answer: "If we want to know how people feel: what they experience and what they remember, what their emotions and motives are like, and the reasons for acting as they do—why not ask them?"[2]

Many psychologists prefer conducting *experiments* to other means of gathering information. Why? Because not only can the experimenters observe what happens, but they can also control the experiences of the people or animals involved.

Suppose a psychologist wants to know whether flexible working hours affect job satisfaction and productivity. He can divide workers (subjects) into two groups with both groups being as equal as possible in terms of age, sex, education, and years with the company. Members of one group would be given the treatment, also known as the independent variable. The group who receives the independent variable is called *the experimental group* while the group who receives no special treatment is the *control group*.

An independent variable is the treatment given to the experimental group.

In this experiment, the treatment or independent variable would be flexible working hours. If, after a trial period, one group outperformed and outproduced the other group, you might suspect that flexible working hours had made a difference. The improved performance, the outcome of the experiment, is known as the dependent variable. The variable depends on the effect of the independent variable on the experimental group.

As a matter of fact, Christopher Orpen, a human relations researcher, conducted just such an experiment to determine the effects of flexible working hours on job satisfaction, productivity, and performance.[3] Flexitime features flexible starting and quitting times for employees and has already been adopted by some businesses and industries.

This experiment took place in South Africa. Arrival times for the 72 female clerical workers in Orpen's experiment ranged from 7:30 to 10:30, and departure times varied from 3:30 to 6:30. All employees had to be present during the core time of 10:30 to 3:30. Women randomly assigned to the experimental group were given flexible hours while those in the control group had fixed hours. Before and after the experiment, the employees completed a job satisfaction survey.

The findings were interesting. Before your boss adopts flexitime, maybe you should fill her in on the results of Orpen's experiment. Briefly, morale and satisfaction improved among the women with flexible hours, but performance and productivity did not. Furthermore, their job satisfaction (as measured by the survey form) was higher than that of the women in the control group. The implication is that if your boss likes seeing happy workers, then introduce her to flexitime. If performance and productivity are her top priorities, forget mentioning the idea.

Are you sold on the scientific merits of this experiment? Consider the following:

1. The experiment took place in South Africa, not North America. Such an experiment undertaken in Kansas might turn out differently.
2. The subjects were all female, not male. Men might be more or less impressed with the possibility of flexible working hours.
3. The women were clerical workers, not nurses or machinists.

Correlational research is a method of scientific investigation that identifies and studies the relationship between variables. It implies but doesn't show cause and effect since no experimental treatment is used. For example, in the chapter on stress you will read that stress is linked to physiological ailments such as headaches, asthma, heart disease, and even the common cold. Psychologists didn't cold-heartedly and deliberately make a person's life full of change, anxiety, and conflict and then sit back to observe the effects. They simply discovered that sick people have more stressers, stress producing people or events, in their lives. A relationship, or correlation, between stress and illness was determined though no cause and effect experimental design was utilized.

Applying the Information

Some research is *pure research* and is performed just for the sake of adding to the body of scientific information. On the other hand, *applied research* is applied to real life situations in order to improve the quality of our social, personal, and work lives. Perhaps some examples of applied research will convince you of its usefulness.

1. In *Passages*, Gail Sheehy writes that women enter midlife at around 35, five years earlier than men do at 40. This time pinch sets off a last chance urgency to do certain things. Not surprisingly, 34 is the average age at which married women re-enter the work force.[4] What's the message here for a manager? For a 34-year old woman?

2. Physical exercise actually makes you more resistant to disease and more mentally alert. Joggers reportedly have lower levels of depression and anxiety, so jog before clocking in.

3. When done correctly, positive reinforcement improves productivity. Using appropriate methods of reinforcement means considering several things including:

   * Rewards should be contingent on performance.
   * Too much reinforcement shouldn't be given; it's almost as bad as none at all.
   * Reinforcement is a personal thing so what reinforces one worker might actually turn another off.
   * Reinforcement should be given as soon as possible after the desired performance so the employee will be more likely to associate the reinforcer with the performance.[5]

4. Clothes make the man—and the woman. When meeting someone new, you make an impression even before you speak, and those impressions have a tendency to persist in spite of later evidence to the contrary. Emily Cho writes, "Clothes telegraph your economic class, your educational level, your social position, your level of sophistication, your trustworthiness, your hopes, your fears, your savvy (or lack of it), your state of mind, and your joie de vivre."[6] Clothing is

laden with symbolism that provides cues about "social and occupational standing, sex-role identification, political orientation, ethnicity and esthetic priorities."[7] Invest in some new clothing before that important job interview.

5. Once a need has been satisfied, it ceases to motivate. If your salary allows you to live a comfortable life, then you need some other incentive to spur you on. Some appreciation for a job well done is nice. So is a chance to participate in decisions that affect your life.

RESEARCH METHODS

Here are several hypotheses that need to be tested. From your reading of the chapter, which method of gathering research would be most appropriate. Survey? Naturalistic observation? Experiment? Correlational research? Some statements can be researched in more than one way.

1. Obese people eat more sweet foods than do normal weight individuals.
2. Smoking marijuana decreases motivation.
3. Drinking cola drinks makes children hyperactive.
4. Depression can be successfully treated with drug therapy.
5. Onions and apples taste the same.
6. High blood pressure can be controlled by medication.
7. Cigarette smokers smoke more when under stress.
8. Women tend to conform to group pressure more than men do.
9. Men are more likely to interrupt others than are women.
10. Males have greater math and spatial abilities than women do.
11. High noise levels can raise blood pressure.
12. Extreme temperatures (very hot or very cold) can negatively affect performance and activity levels.
13. Employees under stress have more job-related accidents.
14. Most people work primarily to satisfy their basic needs for food and shelter.
15. Students who study in spaced periods of two hours each make better grades than do those who study for six hours straight.

Discuss answers with class members. Why did you decide that a certain hypothesis could be better answered one way than another? How would you actually carry out your research? Be specific.

WHAT PSYCHOLOGISTS DO

Many people have an image of a psychologist as being a "shrink," someone who works with people who are sick, mentally ill, or disturbed. Actually, psychologists don't "shrink"; instead they try to expand a person's growth and self-image. Some psychologists serve as therapists, but others are involved in other areas which touch your life daily.

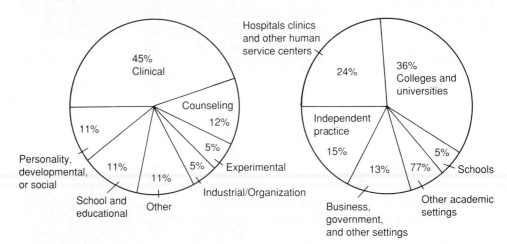

MAJOR SPECIALTIES OF PSYCHOLOGISTS   WHERE PSYCHOLOGISTS WORK

Psychiatrists have a medical degree.

Clinical psychologists help people to adjust to the demands of life. They counsel individuals who are depressed, frustrated, or anxious over marriages, jobs, and relationships or who have personal problems relating to drug and alcohol abuse. *Psychiatrists* do similar work. The difference is that they have a medical degree and often look for physical causes of disorders. They went through medical school and decided to specialize in diseases of the mind instead of the heart, skin, or eye. Since psychiatrists are medical doctors, they can prescribe drugs.

Experimental psychologists often work at a university and combine research and teaching.

Experimental psychologists conduct experiments. Research methods are used to investigate the basic psychological process, usually in a laboratory setting. Often an experimental psychologist works at a university to combine research and teaching.

Developmental psychologists are concerned with the growth and develpment of a person from conception until death. Whether the development is physical, emotional, motor, moral, cognitive, or social, it's within the domain of developmental psychologists. For example, one developmental psychologist might study the effects of maternal use of alcohol on an unborn child while another researches the factors involved in a midlife crisis.

Developmental psychologists study human behavior from the cradle to the grave

Chances are that you brushed your teeth this morning with Crest, Colgate, or some other leading brand of toothpaste instead of baking soda. If so, *consumer psychologists* were again successful in influencing consumer behavior. They study consumers and their buying patterns and then attempt to influence them.

Educational psychologists try to optimize the classroom experience.

Educational psychologists have optimizing the classroom situation to facilitate learning as their goal. They want to increase the efficiency of learning in schools, and they concentrate on course planning, curriculum development, and instructional method.

Social psychologists are concerned with ways in which people are influenced by other individuals and groups. Interpersonal attraction, conformity, and obedience to authority are examples of topics addressed by social psychologists. Can you see applications of social psychology in

Social psychologists study interpersonal attraction, conformity, and obedience to authority.

Physiological psychologists study the biological mechanisms that influence behavior.

the workplace? What is there about your best friend that attracted you to him or her? Are your friends more similar than dissimilar?

Environmental psychologists study how behavior is influenced by the physical environment. The effects of noise, air pollution, temperature, extremes in weather, crowding, and color interest environmental psychologists since they believe it's difficult to understand behavior without understanding the environment in which it occurs.

Physiological processes relate to behavior, and that relationship is of interest to *physiological psychologists* who study the biological mechanisms that influence behavior. The brain and the nervous system, the endocrine system, and the contribution of heredity to personality,

Industrial psychologists conduct research that will aid in improving efficiency, productivity, motivation, and job satisfaction.

mental illness, and intelligence are some areas investigated by physiological psychologists.

This text is primarily concerned with your work life. *Industrial psychologists* conduct research relating to nearly every aspect of your career, from techniques of selection and training to fundamentals of supervision. They study such topics as motivation, morale, efficiency and productivity, communication, group behavior, and stress. Industrial psychologists apply their psychological expertise to improve working conditions, enhance productivity and motivation, decrease absenteeism and turnover, and counsel employees with personal problems.

MAJOR PERSPECTIVES

What makes people do the things they do? Why are some people depressed more often than others? Why do some people have greater problems with alcohol and drug abuse than others? What makes learning so easy for certain individuals? Is mechanical ability inborn? What about personality? How does it develop? Can leadership ability be learned?

Psychologists don't profess to know the answers to all these questions, but they do claim to have some theories that aid in understanding people and behavior. No one theory is more right than another. All have their value and look at behavior from a different viewpoint. Let's take a brief look at four of the major perspectives of human behavior.

Psychoanalytic

Psychoanalytic theorists believe that people are influenced by unconscious motives.

Sigmund Freud, an Austrian physician, is considered to be the father of the psychoanalytic school of thought. The unconscious mind is of utmost importance in Freud's scheme of things. Hidden impulses, particularly sexual and aggressive, influence behavior and feelings. Repressed memories, fears, and drives are more important than is conscious

thought in understanding an individual's personality and motivation. People think, do, and say things for reasons beyond their awareness.

Behavioristic

John Watson is the founder of American behaviorism.

John Watson, founder of American behaviorism, totally disagreed with Freud. It's impossible actually to observe the conscious mind, much less the unconscious mind. Watson didn't deny that people have dreams, feelings, thoughts, and ideas, but he believed that psychology should be the science of observable behavior since all that can be actually observed about a person is his or her public behavior.

Behavior is primarily caused by the environment. People are a little like robots, Watson believed, and can be understood by studying the ways in which environment shapes behavior. Simply stated, behaviorists believe that acts followed by rewards are repeated and acts followed by punishment are abandoned.

Operant conditioning theory was developed by B. F. Skinner.

B. F. Skinner is a contemporary behaviorist who is best known for his theory of operant conditioning, a type of learning in which behavior is strengthened if followed by a reward and weakened or suppressed if followed by punishment. Like Watson, he believes people are a composite of their biological makeup and their reinforcement histories. Positive and negative reinforcement, terms similar to reward and punishment, are important words in operant conditioning. Many people see using operant conditioning as manipulative, but few can discount the importance of rewarding a job well done.

Humanistic

Humanism is the "third force" in psychology.

Abraham Maslow and Carl Rogers are two well-known humanistic psychologists representing the "third force" in psychology. Basically, they believe that people are neither controlled by unconscious, animalistic im-

pulses nor are they at the mercy of external forces in the environment. Humanists assert that people have an inner drive to fulfill their potential. They are conscious, creative, and unique free agents, not robotlike machines controlled totally by external forces in their environment. Finally, humanists emphasize human potential and growth, not mental discord and the darker, negative side of a person's nature.

Biological

Psychologists with biological slant focus on how the body and brain work together to create emotions, behavior, and sensory experience.

The biological perspective focuses on how the body and brain work together in creating emotions, behavior, and sensory experience. Theorists study how messages are transmitted within the brain, how body chemistry is linked to moods and motives, and how heredity affects personality, intelligence, and even mental illness. They look at the endocrine system and the nervous system as being responsible for thoughts, dreams, feelings, and fantasies.

What are some of your feelings about behavior, your own or that of your family, friends, co-workers, or boss? Is the mysterious, hidden unconscious responsible for a sour disposition? Does the person's reinforcement history hold the key? Perhaps the humanists are correct in their assumption that such an unhappy person needed more unconditional positive regard. Then again, physical causes might explain mood and action. Whatever the behavior, there's a reason, and psychological theories aid in understanding those reasons.

PSYCHOLOGY AND YOUR LIFE

What can psychology do for you? It can help you learn more about yourself and help you cope with personal problems. It can help you communicate with co-workers, a boss, or a next door neighbor. It can show you ways to alleviate stress, improve your morale, develop leadership potential, understand your motivations, and assess your strengths and weaknesses when setting goals, whether those goals are personal or career related.

Psychology, the science of human and animal behavior is tied into nearly every aspect of your daily life, and an understanding of some of its basic principles will help you to enjoy a fuller, more abundant life. Skim through the book and read a few passages that look appealing to you. As you sift through the information in your mind and relate it to your experiences, you'll see that psychology offers new ways of looking at issues, topics, and people.

SCIENTIFIC QUESTIONS

Would you recognize a scientific question if you saw one?

Here are 20 questions: Some are scientific questions and can be answered empirically by the methods discussed in this chapter; others cannot. Can you tell the difference between the two? Circle the questions you think are answerable scientifically.

1. Should mothers stay home with their children or put them in day care centers?
2. What are the psychological differences between children in day care centers and children who stay home with their mothers?
3. Is premarital sexual intercourse wrong?
4. What is the relation between premarital intercourse and later marital sexual adjustment?
5. Is it wrong for bosses to show favoritism?
6. How does favoritism and unfair supervision affect employees?
7. Should people who are mentally disturbed be given drugs even if they do not want them?
8. What is the effect of drug therapy on the severity of psychotic symptoms?
9. Should alcoholic workers be forced to participate in a drug rehabilitation program?
10. What proportion of alcoholics are able to return to work after participating in an employee assistance program?
11. Is it better to be an introvert or an extrovert?
12. What are the personality traits of an introvert?
13. Is snorting cocaine wrong?
14. What are the physiological effects of cocaine use?
15. Is capital punishment wrong?
16. What is the effect of capital punishment in deterring would-be criminals?
17. Is it better to be self-employed or work for a major corporation?
18. What are some variables a person should consider in career choice?
19. Is there something crazy about someone who always wants to do more and more in less and less time?
20. What are some of the characteristics of a Type A personality?

If you circled the even numbered questions on this little quiz as being scientific, you show great promise of being a budding psychologist. The odd-numbered questions are value questions and imply right and wrong, good and bad. Such questions have to do with our morals, opinions, and beliefs. No matter how strongly you feel about one of them, none can be answered by research methods discussed in this chapter.

SUMMARY

Psychology, the scientific study of human and animal behavior, offers behavioral concepts that individuals can use to enhance their lives, both on and off the job.

Since psychology is a science, psychologists employ the scientific method to help describe, explain, predict, and control behavior. The scientific method can be reduced to three steps: formulating a hypothesis, gathering and analyzing data, and applying the findings.

A hypothesis is a statement about behavior believed to be true. All research begins with questioning. Since good scientific questions are answered by the scientific method, questions that deal with concepts of right and wrong or imply a value judgment are not used.

Psychologists gather their data in several ways. Industrial psychologists primarily use naturalistic observation, surveys, experiments, and correlational methods.

Some research is pure research, research performed merely to add to the body of scientific knowledge. Applied research is applied to real life situations to improve the quality of our social, personal, emotional, and work lives.

Although many people think of psychologists primarily as those who with individuals who are mentally disturbed, they are actually involved in quite a diversity of activities, activities which affect our lives daily. For example, a developmental psychologist studies human growth and development throughout the life span while a social psychologist is concerned with ways in which people are influenced by other individuals and groups. The thrust of this text is on the work of industrial psychologists whose work touches aspects of careers from selection and training to motivation and leadership.

There are several perspectives of psychological thought and all have a slightly different explanation for behavior. The psychoanalytic school of thought founded by Sigmund Freud stresses the unconscious mind while John Watson, B. F. Skinner, and the other behaviorists insist that cognitive processes are unobservable and hence cannot be studied empirically. Instead the behaviorists focus on observable behavior and the reinforcement of such behavior as keys to understanding a person. The humanists, including Abraham Maslow and Carl Rogers, stress the uniqueness of each person and see potential and growth as primary determinants of behavior. Those theorists of the biological school emphasize the brain and the nervous system, the endocrine system, and genes and chromosomes as keys to understanding behavior.

Psychology can help you learn more about yourself and increase your understanding of others. It can also help you learn to cope with personal problems, communicate with obnoxious co-workers, alleviate stress, improve morale, develop leadership potential, set goals, and understand your motivations.

KEY TERMS

Psychology
Hypothesis
Scientific Method
Naturalistic Observation
Survey
Experiment
Independent Variable
Dependent Variable
Control Group
Experimental Group
Pure Research
Applied Research
Positive Reinforcement
Correlational Research
Sigmund Freud
John Watson
B. F. Skinner
Abraham Maslow
Carl Rogers

REVIEW AND DISCUSSION QUESTIONS

1. What are the four goals of psychology? How can they be applied to a work related situation? Be specific.

2. What are four methods used by industrial psychologists to gather information? What are advantages and disadvantages of each?

3. Differentiate between pure and applied research. Give examples of each from your own experiences and studies.

4. What is your image of what psychologists do? How does it compare with that in the chapter?

5. After reading the major perspectives of psychological thought, compare them as to their explanations of a particular behavior. For example, how might the different viewpoints interpret causes of a co-worker's poor attitude?

ENDNOTES

[1] JEFFREY L. SHELER, "Why So Many Workers Lie Down on the Job," *U. S. News & World Report*, April 6, 1981, p. 71.

[2] GORDON ALLPORT, "The Trend in Motivational Theory", *American Journal of Orthopsychiatry*, 23 (1953), 107–119.

[3] CHRISTOPHER ORPEN, "Effect of Flexible Hours on Employee Satisfaction and Performance: A Field Experiment," *Journal of Applied Psychology*, February 1981, pp. 113–115.

[4] GAIL SHEEHY, *Passages* (New York: E. P. Dutton), p. 309.

[5] DEAN R. SPITZER, "30 Ways to Motivate Employees to Perform Better," *Training/HRD*, March 1981, p 51.

[6] EMILY CHO AND HERMINE LUEDERS, *Looking, Working, Living Terrific 24 Hours a Day* (New York: G. P. Putnam, 1982), p. 29.

[7] MICHAEL R. SOLOMON, "Dress for Effect," *Psychology Today*, April 1986, p. 20.

chapter 2

Human Relations, Past and Present

After reading and studying this chapter, you will be able to:

1. Identify Frederick Taylor and discuss his contribution to scientific management.
2. Identify Frank and Lillian Gilbreth.
3. Discuss the significance of the Hawthorne studies.
4. Trace the human relations movement from the Depression until today.
5. Relate how both the work force and the nature of work have changed.
6. Understand why human relations knowledge and skill are necessary for any worker's success.

I don't think we need to make a choice between individual happiness and pride, and mass production and objective materialism. I think the answers lie in combining both of them, and that is a tremendous task for the future.

Taylor Caldwell, This Side of Innocence

Human relations is a modern development. In the "good old days," things weren't necessarily that good. Fringe benefits? Forget it. Positive reinforcement in the form of praise or recognition? Unheard of! Flexible working hours? What a foolish idea! It wasn't until the mid-1880s that the human relations movement took a few faltering steps. Industrialism and scientific management preceded human relations as we know it today.

Human relations is a process in which both management and workers are brought into contact with the organization in such a way that the objectives of each are achieved. The concept implies a concern for employees without losing sight of overall objectives. People aren't mollycoddled but are treated with dignity and respect as they attempt to meet organizational and personal goals.

THE INDUSTRIAL REVOLUTION

Before the Industrial Revolution in the late 1880s most work was performed by skilled craftworkers who more or less set their own pace. Each worker saw his or her own product through from beginning to end, whether it was a shoe, a bookcase, or a dress. Certainly, the work was hard and laborious, but it was stamped with individuality and allowed people to feel pride in the accomplishment of a finished product. The individual's sense of importance and belief in his or her own value counted for something.

With the advent of the Industrial Revolution, things changed. Farmers left the land and flocked to the cities, the industrial and manufacturing centers, in hopes of improving their lives. In fact, at the turn of the century farmers made up one-third of the labor force compared to the 3 percent they constitute today.[1]

Factory owners used a paternalistic style of managing people.

After coming from down on the farm, the ex-farmer and ex-craft worker were viewed right along with time, raw materials, and capital as items considered in the marketing equation, no more, no less. They were simply articles of commerce. Since there was plenty of labor, management had a "like it or leave it" attitude. Most workers, however, had nowhere to go. To make matters worse, factory owners knew very little about managing people and relied heavily on a paternalistic style of management. Some exploited workers for efficiency and profit, workers who were having a difficult time just adjusting to the monotonous, confining factory work.

Cities became increasingly congested with available workers so the labor supply was cheap and plentiful. Why should management concern itself with safety, well-being, motivation, and development of potential? Factory owners didn't even worry about health or sanitary conditions, much less job satisfaction. Hours were long, and pay was low. Take a look at a list of rules posted in a Boston office in 1872.

RULES FOR OFFICE EMPLOYEES

1. Office employees each will fill lamps, clean chimneys, and trim wicks. Wash windows once a week.
2. Each clerk will bring in a bucket of water and a scuttle of coal for the day's business.
3. Make your pens carefully. You may whittle nibs to your individual taste.
4. Men employees will be given an evening off each for courting purposes, or two evenings a week if they go regularly to church.
5. After 13 hours of labor in the office, the employee should spend the remaining time reading the Bible and other good books.
6. Every employee should lay aside from each payday a goodly sum of his earnings for his benefit during his declining years so that he will not become a burden on society.
7. Any employee who smokes Spanish cigars, uses liquor in any form, or frequents pool and public halls or gets shaved in a barber shop will give a good reason to suspect his worth, intentions, integrity, and honesty.
8. The employee who has performed his labor faithfully and without fault for five years will be given an increase of five cents per day in his pay, providing profits from business permit it.

TAYLOR'S SCIENTIFIC MANAGEMENT

Frederick Taylor, a mechanical engineer, and other researchers introduced the concept of scientific management around the turn of the century. Jobs were broken down into isolated, specialized tasks in hopes of maximizing efficiency. Taylor broke down tasks so that they could be completed in the shortest time possible. For example, he believed that people should avoid zig-zag motions of their hands and that a completed motion should begin and end with both hands simultaneously.

Reductionism is referred to as the specialization of work.

The efficiency methods extended into every aspect of the workplace, including the layout of machines and the flow of work. Taylor watched and studied the workers in an attempt to increase ways of working more efficiently. The specialization of work, also called Taylorism and reductionism, coincided with mass production and helped to pave the way for the assembly line. It became quite popular with management, but alas, the poor worker was treated even more as a commodity, a dehumanized cog in the production process.

Frederick Taylor is the father of scientific management.

Taylor, referred to as the father of scientific management, felt that people could be made to operate as efficiently as machines. He actually stood over the workers with a stopwatch as he studied and streamlined tasks. Taylor's primary goal was improving worker efficiency and productivity, and he consequently changed procedures, laid off excess employees, or changed the tools and implements needed to accomplish the tasks.

As you might imagine, some workers were resistant to what they perceived to be unrealistic standards. Some were concerned that they would be fired if they didn't reach the higher standards; others feared that if they did achieve the high standards, then even higher ones would be imposed. What a dilemma. Taylor himself wasn't immune to worker attitudes and is quoted as saying, "It's a horrid life for any man to live not being able to look any work man in the face without seeing hostility there, and a feeling that every man around you is your virtual enemy."[2] Suffice it to say that Taylor didn't win any popularity contests through his research. Just for the record, however, let it be noted that he is credited with first giving workers an unheard of rest break.

Taylor also advocated high wages for workers in the belief that optimal productivity could be achieved only through the cooperative efforts of management and labor. Having a genuine concern for workers, Taylor contended that contributors should have a share of the profits. However, Taylor's concern for workers was obscured by his emphasis on efficiency. Employers weren't eager to increase wages or improve working conditions, but they were eager to increase productivity.

Frank and Lillian Gilbreth pioneered the use of time and motion studies.

From Taylor's studies and his application of a scientific approach to management, the concept of time and motion studies was developed. A husband and wife team, Frank and Lillian Gilbreth, pioneered the use of time and motion studies and contributed greatly to the expansion of worker potential. Interestingly, Gilbreth's first job as a bricklayer opened his eyes to wasted time and motion. As a bricklayer's apprentice, the young Gilbreth noticed the diversity of his fellow workers' job actions and was struck by the inefficiency of wasted effort. He took it upon himself to develop a system to increase efficiency of laying bricks and handling materials. Lower costs and higher wages were by-products of Gilbreth's interest.

Later the Gilbreths conducted laboratory studies to determine the most efficient methods to operate machines. They observed workers to discover more efficient ways for them to do their jobs. From their scientific observations, the Gilbreths developed time study into an exact science.

THE HAWTHORNE STUDIES

The so-called "Hawthorne experiments" marked the beginning of an approach emphasizing human relations. The study began as an attempt by engineers at the Hawthorne Western Electric plant near Chicago to increase efficiency and productivity. In 1927, Elton Mayo, an industrial sociologist from Harvard, was called in to aid in these landmark studies.

The intention was to study the effects of variables such as light, ventilation, and fatigue on workers. Twenty-four different working conditions were altered, some for the better and some for the worse. No matter what change was made, productivity increased. For example, one of the highest levels of output was recorded when the light was scarcely brighter than that of the full moon! Workers had to rely on their sense of touch to perform their job tasks.

Another group of employees was given increasingly longer breaks, a shorter workday, piecework, and even hot snacks. Predictably, productivity improved. Instead of assuming that the positive changes brought about the increase in productivity, the experimenters took away all the goodies to see what would happen. Workers put in a 48-hour workweek with no rest periods and no hot snacks, and amazingly, productivity hit an all time high.[3]

From conducting the experiments and from talking to the employees, Mayo made some important discoveries with implications for today. When people are paid attention to, treated like human beings instead of machines, given feedback on their performance, and given greater freedom from supervisory control, their motivation, morale, and productivity increase. The changes in attitude and motivation were due largely to friendly supervision and a cooperative, nonthreatening environment.

The Hawthorne effect refers to any improvement in worker performance that is the by-product of attention and feelings of self-worth.

The Hawthorne effect today refers to any improvement in worker performance that is the by-product of attention and feelings of self-worth. Mayo's research made it obvious that the average worker is a complex combination of needs, attitudes, values, and beliefs who desires attention and feedback. The studies set the pace for research of the 1940s and 1950s which emphasized the influence of informal groups in organizations and the role of the supervisor.

Both Taylor and Mayo were concerned with increasing productivity, but their approaches were vastly different. Taylor concentrated on the individual and Mayo on the group. Taylor tried to minimize informal social contacts at work since he believed that such contacts hampered production. Mayo, on the other hand, recommended the informal contacts between employees. He contended that workers should be provided membership in a group and that they should be allowed to communicate with co-workers. Mayo realized the importance of the social forces within a group and that output was often determined by informal group norms. For instance, anyone working too hard for the group's satisfaction was considered a rate buster and was ridiculed or scorned until falling within acceptable group standards. The division of labor advocated by Taylor fostered social isolation that led to lost efficiency and output. Regardless of the approach used, Taylor and Mayo pioneered the way for the human relations movement.

THE DEPRESSION

Many significant improvements in the treatment of workers began in times of great change or upheaval within society itself, and the Depression is no exception. During the Depression, unions increased their efforts to organize workers and to force employers to rectify deplorable working conditions. The unions fought for shorter working hours, more pay, and child labor protection. Business and government both fought the establishment of unions, sometimes violently. It's estimated that more than 100 workers were killed between 1933 and 1936 while fighting for union recognition.

During the late 1930s the federal government altered its position and supported the right of workers to join unions and to bargain collectively with their employers. When Congress passed the Wagner Act in 1935, businesses were required to negotiate contracts with union representatives. In the 1930s labor laws prohibited child labor and reduced the number of hours women worked. In addition, many industries instituted a minimum wage, created safer working conditions, and paid fringe benefits.

WORLD WAR II TO TODAY

During World War II and afterward, the interest in human relations at work gained momentum. Papers were written. Experiments were conducted. Surveys were given. Abraham Maslow, noted humanist psychologist, came forward with his well-known hierarchy of needs. Douglas McGregor introduced the X and Y theories of management, and in more recent years, William Ouchi wrote of Theory Z, a hybrid of Japanese and American leadership principles. Frederick Herzberg devised a two-factor theory of motivation. These theories of motivation and management will be examined later, in Chapters 7 and 9.

Time marched on, and human relations research began to concentrate more on human interaction and personal awareness. Concepts developed by B. F. Skinner, Carl Rogers, and Sigmund Freud which focused on positive reinforcement, personality development, interpersonal communication, and the unconscious mind were introduced to the working world. Chapter 6 will introduce these men and concepts to you since they are so applicable to work and social life.

Since World War II, expectations concerning the treatment of physically and mentally disabled, minorities, women, aging, and other disadvantaged groups have increased. During the 1950s human relations training for supervisors and managers was practically a fad. Managerial and organizational success was based on being people oriented. A concern for the worker is still important, but training today also emphasizes objective investigation using research methods of the behavioral sciences. Employers believe that attention to the needs of employees and to the influence of informal groups is vital.

HOW MUCH DO YOU KNOW ABOUT THE ATTITUDES AND BEHAVIOR OF PEOPLE AT WORK?

You might be surprised at how well your personal knowledge corresponds to the outcomes of research on attitudes and behaviors of people in the workplace. To see if you can determine what psychologists have found, answer the questions below. Do this by indicating whether you believe an item is mostly true or mostly false by writing "True or False" in the space provided.

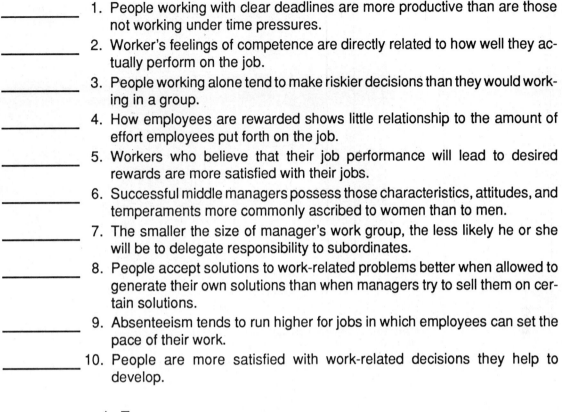

_____ 1. People working with clear deadlines are more productive than are those not working under time pressures.

_____ 2. Worker's feelings of competence are directly related to how well they actually perform on the job.

_____ 3. People working alone tend to make riskier decisions than they would working in a group.

_____ 4. How employees are rewarded shows little relationship to the amount of effort employees put forth on the job.

_____ 5. Workers who believe that their job performance will lead to desired rewards are more satisfied with their jobs.

_____ 6. Successful middle managers possess those characteristics, attitudes, and temperaments more commonly ascribed to women than to men.

_____ 7. The smaller the size of manager's work group, the less likely he or she will be to delegate responsibility to subordinates.

_____ 8. People accept solutions to work-related problems better when allowed to generate their own solutions than when managers try to sell them on certain solutions.

_____ 9. Absenteeism tends to run higher for jobs in which employees can set the pace of their work.

_____ 10. People are more satisfied with work-related decisions they help to develop.

1. T
2. T
3. F
4. F
5. T
6. F
7. T
8. T
9. F
10. T

From Anthony F. Grasha, *Practical Applications of Psychology*, 3rd ed., p. 43. Copyright © 1987 by Anthony F. Grasha. Reprinted by permission of Scott, Foresman and Company.

THE PRESENT

Human relations, the study of all interactions among people, has progressed significantly since the mid-1800s. In most cases, the worker is now recognized as a complex, unique human begin with the desire and potential for growth. The whole-person concept has attained acceptance. A sound mixer is more than a sound mixer. He's a composite of skills, needs, experiences, fears, and ambitions that he doesn't discard when he comes to work.

Changing Nature of the Work Force

The individual is not the only impetus behind the human relations movement. The character of the work force itself is changing. Need evidence? Read the following and judge for yourself.

Today's workers are more educated and demand more from their employers and from their jobs.

1. Today's workers are more educated and have higher expectations. In 1984, Americans had completed a median of 12.6 years of school compared to 10.6 years in 1960.[4] The numbers of individuals attending and completing college are also increasing. These better educated workers demand more from their employers and from their jobs.

2. The average worker is more protected by the courts and is more aware of his rights, something that certainly wasn't true before the 1930s. There are increasing numbers of suits filed against employers because of sexual harassment, hazardous working conditions, and discrimination because of age, sex, race, national origin, or handicap.

Worker compensation laws which provide financial coverage for employees disabled by industrial accidents have previously been limited to physical injury. Things have changed. Since 1960, court decisions have forced many states to allow worker compensation payments in job-related cases of anxiety, depression, and other mental and emotional disorders. For instance, the Michigan Supreme Court upheld a compensation award to a machine operator who claimed that daily work on the assembly line caused his mental illness. A New York secretary won a $7,000 award for emotional distress caused by her boss's continual criticism and prying questions about her family life.[5]

Adjustment is a personal thing. Some people are less resistant to mental problems than are others. In any case, the courts have established that an employer can be held liable for a worker's mental illness if it has been "aggravated, accelerated, precipitated, or triggered" by the conditions of the job.[6]

A few examples of employment legislation are the Equal Pay Act requiring equal pay for men and women performing similar work, the Age Discrimination in Employment Act prohibiting discrimination against individuals aged 40 to 70, and the Rehabilitation Act promoting employment of the handicapped. Important also is the landmark Civil Rights Act of 1964 protecting minorities from discrimination.

3. The composition of the work force is vastly different from what it was 20 years ago. The numbers of women, racial and ethnic minority groups, and senior citizens who are gainfully employed have risen to tens of millions.

According to the U.S. Bureau of Labor Statistics, over one-half of all American women are working outside of the home. In fact, in 1900, about 5 percent of married women worked outside the home, and today 60 percent of all women between 25 and 55 are working at outside jobs.[7] Additionally, many women are entering nontraditional fields such as welding, drafting, bus driving, and even brick masonry. The sweeping influx of women in the work force over the past 20 years has been described "as the single most outstanding social phenomenon of the century."[8]

Greater numbers of employed Blacks, Hispanics, Asians, native Americans, and other ethnic groups make a sensitivity to cultural differences not just important, but imperative. "We have moved from the myth of the melting pot to a celebration of cultural diversity," writes John Naisbett, author of *Megatrends*.[9] In the past, it seemed that Americans put new immigrants through an imaginary blender until they came out as homogenized Americans with little remaining of their former heritage. That is not the case now. People are proud of their ethnic and racial origins, and as a result, this country has a high level of cultural diversity. Uniformity is probably impossible—and even undesirable. Can you imagine life without pizza, tacos, and egg rolls?

For the first time in history there are more Americans over 65 than there are teenagers.

Finally, people are living and working longer. In 1982, the life expectancy was 70.8 years for men and 78.2 for women.[10] By the year 2000 some forecasters predict that 33 percent of the American population will be over age 60. For the first time in history there are more Americans over 65 than there are teenagers, and one out of every four Americans is over 50.[11] Many of these senior citizens are healthy and vigorous, and

they want to be productive and employed.

Older and younger workers often have different attitudes toward the value of work, a topic examined in the chapter on morale, Chapter 8. All of us need to be more aware of potential problems caused by sexual, cultural, and age differences among employees.

4. In general, people have different attitudes toward work and leisure. They want more than a paycheck and a means of filling 40 hours a week. They want recognition, an opportunity to participate in work decisions, a sense of achievement, and a feeling of pride. In short, they need to feel the pride of equipment operator, Hub Hillard.

> There's a certain amount of pride—I don't care how little you did. You drive down the road and you say, "I worked on this road." If there's a bridge, you say, "I worked on this bridge." Or you drive by a building and you say, "I worked on this building." Maybe it don't mean anything to anybody else, but there's a certain pride knowing you did your bit.
>
> That building we put up, a medical building. Well, that granite was imported from Canada. It was really expensive. Well, I set all this granite around there. So you do this and you don't make a scratch on it. It's food for your soul that you know you did it good. When somebody walks by this building you can say, "Well, I did that."[12]

Changing Nature of Work

The nature of work has changed too. Technological advances affect what we do, where we do it, and with whom we interact. How we relate to others has changed. A couple of examples of technological changes are robots and electronic cottages.

A robot is really just a sophisticated machine tool that gets its orders from a computer. William C. Byham calls the robot the steel-collar

---

QUALITY CIRCLES

Many American businesses and industries are experimenting with quality circles, a means of employee participation popularized in Japan. These circles are designed to improve communication between workers and management and make employees feel more involved in company affairs. Usually a circle consists of a small group of workers doing similar work who meet and discuss work-related problems. "Histories of successful QWL [quality of work life] programs demonstrate that they can improve product quality and productivity, reduce absenteeism and turnover, and increase job satisfaction for workers."[13]

Honeywell had more than 1,000 active circles as of August 1983, more than any firm outside Japan. Insisting that the quality circles are not a quick fix or a short-term program to increase profits, Jim Wiltfildt, formerly of Honeywell, is quoted as saying, "Quality circles is a philosophy of management that assumes employees can creatively contribute to solving operational problems."[14]

QUALITY CIRCLES: FROM AMERICA TO JAPAN AND BACK AGAIN

The QC technique actually began in the late 1940s with H. Edwards Deming, an American who lectured in post-World War II Japan about statistical methods for quality control. He stressed that production quality must involve both workers and management; the Japanese combined Deming's ideas with a philosophy of bringing workers together in groups to solve problems. At the heart of the Japanese program was the assumption that the person who performs a job is the one who best knows how to identify and correct its problems.

Post–World War II American workers who were better educated and more financially secure than their older colleagues began demanding a greater say in decisions that affected their work and jobs that were more psychologically rewarding. In November 1973, the Lockheed Corporations sent six employees to Japan to study QCs. They were impressed by how the QC technique led to major improvements and by the excitement and involvement of Japanese workers in QC meetings and in their jobs. The Lockheed people brought the Japanese technique back to the United States and established the first QCs in America one year later.

The International Association of Quality Circles has grown in membership from 100 in 1978 to more than 7,000 in 1985. QCs are now found in virtually every sector, from transportation, entertainment, and finance to the military and government, and involve workers of all types and shades of color.

"Quality Circles: From America to Japan and Back Again," *Psychology Today*, March 1986, p. 44.

worker, and while he concedes that the installation of these steel-collar workers has not been smooth, he feels that the robotization of industry is inevitable.[15] Although many individuals associate robots primarily with automobile assembly plants, robots are used in a variety of companies from upholstery factories and candy makers to plastics moldlers and novelties companies.

There are several reasons for the resistance to robots. Supervisors and workers alike fear the loss of their jobs, and while it is true that many people will require retraining, the newly created jobs are more interesting and challenging. Workers can't socialize as much with steel-collar workers around, and supervisors suffer a reduced self-image from machine tending, but the advantages of robots outweigh the disadvantages. For instance, some unhealthy or hazardous jobs may be completely automated—coal mining, for example. Robots will handle the danger and dirt, and humans will be free to learn more challenging work.

In discussing changes for the decade ahead, Bolles predicts a continued move toward the electronic society. He forecasts a growth in home offices linked by computer to a central work office or offices, the growth of self-employment comprised of several contract jobs, the expansion of totally new industries based on research and development now being done in the energy field, and the increased number of hospices and other alternatives to hospitals. Productivity experts, machine tool workers, and secretaries should have no problem finding a job, and people will al-

ways need "good auto mechanics to fix our cars, good doctors to assist us in maintaining our body health, and good mailpersons to get our bills to us."[16]

WORKPLACE CHANGES

Reading material about the changes in the workplace and in the labor force is one thing, but sometimes reading is not enough to get a real feeling for the rapid and sometimes dramatic changes that have occurred in the past few years. To appreciate these changes fully, try a little scientific surveying of your own.

1. Interview employees at all levels (entry-level jobs all the way to the head honcho) about changes that have occurred in their place of employment. These employees can be people who work where you want to work one day, or they can simply be your friends and relatives.

2. Be specific with your questions to make sure the interviewees will be specific with their answers. For example, if you want to know how management practices have changed, ask that. If you want to know about what technological changes have come about, ask about what they are and how those changes have affected work routines.

3. Ask what future changes they expect. For instance, what might robotics do to the assembly-line workers? What other skills will such an employee need? For work force changes, you might ask how the increasing numbers of women and minorities in the labor force will affect policies and practices? How will older people fit into the scheme of things?

4. After everyone has had an opportunity to interview at least one person, share your findings with the class. Were you surprised with the results? Pleased? Frightened?

5. What are some of the implications of the findings for your career?

Many researchers see the electronic cottage as a prospective technological change. Creating, processing, and distributing information by use of a computer terminal and/or word processor is called telecommuting. Telework was originally thought of as a way to save gas and electricity, but then other benefits became apparent. Organizational benefits include improved productivity, greater employee retention, greater staffing flexibility and cost control, and office space control. There are also advantages for the employee such as fewer work interruptions, a sense of control over work, and savings on transportation.[17] Parents can stay at home and mind the kids while working, and creative employees whose bright ideas strike late at night have the computer at home.

Will telecommuting become widespread? Some people say they feel isolated from the juicy office gossip and the warm interaction with friends. There are still certain advantages—no rush-hour traffic, no dressing for success, no nine-to-five supervisor keeping time tabs. You can work at 3:00 A.M. or 3:00 P.M. as long as you get the work done. Most people, however, want work-related contacts to be animate, breathing, and gossiping, not inanimate objects.

Telecommuting isn't for everyone. For example, young singles and older workers who miss the office social life, dieters who can't resist the refrigerator, or those whose family lives are full of conflict would be better off facing the rush-hour traffic. As for being electronically hooked to the office while staying at home being billed as a solution for working parents, "anyone who has ever tried to accomplish a 20-minute task while responsible for the activities of one or more young children can tell you it ain't going to fly."[18]

Still telecommuting is a technically feasible option, say the editors of *HRD/Training*, and they believe that it will proliferate. Companies that are trying it include J. C. Penney, American Express, Blue

Cross/Blue Shield, and Apple Computer. "By 1990 if current trends continue, we expect between ten and fifteen million corporate employees regularly telecommuting from home or satellite offices with their companies' full knowledge and support."[19]

What About Today?

Human relations at work has progressed a lot since the first industrial psychology book, *Psychology and Industrial Efficiency*, was authored by Hugo Munsterberg and published in 1913. The industrial psychologist today has to think not only about motivation, communication, and job satisfaction, but also about equal opportunity employment, alcohol and drug abuse, and employee rights. With the many different backgrounds and experiences that people bring to the workplace, managers and industrial psychologists are constantly challenged to enhance the quality of work life while maintaining efficiency and productivity.

Things have changed for the better for the American worker. Most people receive a decent salary and fair, sometimes lavish, fringe benefits. In December 1986, Wells Fargo Bank gave its workers an extra day off and a coffee mug reading "Take a Break." These employees also got a $100 bonus and an extra week's paid vacation in 1987. Some progressive employers go a step farther and try to make jobs meaningful, interesting, and challenging for the employee. Employees are making decisions affecting their work lives ranging from when to take a yearly vacation to what hours are most suitable.

Human relations and its counterpart, industrial psychology, are not absolute. There are no pat answers or magic formulas to ensure continuous harmonious relationships, clear communication, high morale, motivation, and job satisfaction. Many individuals suffer from the so-called "Good Fairy syndrome," an attitude that all our problems can somehow be swept away if only we can find the right Good Fairy to wave the magic wand.[20] Everyone is disappointed when the fairy fails to turn the pumpkin into a golden coach, when all of the problems with people and production don't disappear. Nevertheless, research has yielded concepts which, if applied correctly, can aid in increasing cooperation and decreasing conflict in business and industry.

CASE STUDY

Matichuk's Manager

Jay Matichuk has a problem. 12 weeks out of the year his job becomes a nightmare. During those 12 weeks, not only does his relationship with his supervisor change, but his supervisor himself changes. No, it's not a Jekyll and Hyde transformation but a change of job duties and supervisors.

Jay is employed by Lakeside Development, a huge apartment complex which features tennis courts, a swimming pool, and a nine hole golf course for residents. Jay's job is on the golf course. He's the assistant superintendent, and his responsibilities include directing and participating in the construction and maintenance of golf course tees, greens, fairways, roads, and paths. He also supervises the maintenance and repair of motorized and mechanical equipment and participates in the maintenance of irrigation and drainage systems.

Jay's superintendent, Gene Modjeski, is a good leader who communicates well with the golf course workers regardless of their position. He treats the day laborer with the same respect as the assistant superintendent and is able to convey a genuine concern for the individual workers. Modjeski uses a participative style of management by encouraging upward communication in the form of ideas, suggestions, and complaints from the employees. From experience, Modjeski realizes that cleaning traps and changing cups is not that fulfilling or challenging and strives to think of ways to motivate employees and maintain high group morale.

Because of the severe winters, the course is closed 12 weeks out of the year, and during that time, Jay has to work for Gary Dreisbaugh, a retired military man. Dreisbaugh is the maintenance supervisor for the entire apartment complex, excluding the golf course. If there is a heat or air conditioning problem, Dreisbaugh is in charge of repairs. If equipment malfunctions, then Dreisbaugh is responsible for getting the equipment operational. If there's a leak, he finds someone to plug it up. Jay's duties now include doing whatever suits Dreisbaugh's whim.

Dreisbaugh's leadership style contrasts sharply with Modjeski's. He's an autocrat who prefers to control and direct employees by barking out orders and threatening employees with dismissal or loss of pay. He is convinced of his infallibility and resents any upward communication. Dreisbaugh refuses to listen to ideas that the "lowly employees" might suggest.

Even when Jay notices things that Dreisbaugh does that are completely stupid, he isn't able to express his feelings. For instance, the supervisor is always complaining about food wrappings and crumbs, drink cups and spills, and cigarette butts and smoke in the shop area. He constantly gets Jay to sweep and clean the area even though it's not Jay's job. As a supervisor, Dreisbaugh could just request that people do their eating, drinking, and smoking in another area. Jay was getting pretty tired of cleaning up other people's trash while at the same time listening to the supervisor complain about the pigsty. He tactfully tried to suggest making a no eating, drinking, or smoking policy, but the supervisor exploded. Before Jay got the words out of his mouth, Dreisbaugh reminded him that he made the rules, not Jay.

Although this is just one little incident, it is typical of Dreisbaugh's opinionated, arrogant attitude and Jay's dilemma.

Questions:

1. Based on what you know about human relations, do you think that Jay really has a problem? Is he expecting too much from Dreisbaugh after working for Modjeski?

2. Can you think of any guidelines for getting along with a boss that might be helpful to Jay? If not, look ahead to Chapter 5, Relationships at Work.

3. How would you handle the situation if you were Jay? What are his alternatives?

SUMMARY

Human relations, a modern development, is a process in which both employees and management work together to achieve individual, group, and organizational objectives. The term implies concern and caring for employees with the realization that objectives of the organization have to be met. Factories, firms, schools, and hospitals still have to make money, but not at the expense of exploiting workers.

There are basically three stages in the human relations movement: industrialization, scientific management, and behavioral management.

With the advent of the Industrial Revolution, the labor supply was cheap and plentiful as workers flocked to the cities in hopes of a better life. Management was concerned with efficiency and productivity, not safety, well-being, motivation, or job satisfaction. Managers knew little about the science art of management and used primarily a paternalistic style of leadership.

At the turn of the century, Frederick Taylor, known as the father of scientific management, broke down tasks so that they could be completed in the shortest time possible. These efficiency methods extended to every aspect of the workplace and paved the way for the assembly line. Although Taylor advocated high wages for workers, his concern was obscured by his emphasis on efficiency and by the employers' emphasis on profits.

Taylor's study and subsequent application of a scientific approach to management led to the development of time and motion studies. These studies were pioneered by a husband and wife team, Frank and Lillian Gilbreth.

Behavioral management as we know it today began somewhat unofficially with the Hawthorne experiments conducted at the Hawthorne Western Electric Plant near Chicago. The purpose of the study was to measure the effects of variables such as lighting, ventilation, and fatigue on the productivity of workers. The surprising discovery was that when people are paid attention to, given feedback on their performance, and given freedom from supervisory control, their motivation, morale, and productivity increase.

While Taylor and Mayo were both concerned with increasing productivity, their approaches were vastly different. Since Taylor believed that social contacts at work hampered production, he sought to minimize such contacts. Mayo, however, realized the importance of social forces within a group. Both men were instrumental in the development of the human relations movement.

During the Depression unions increased their efforts to organize workers and to force employers to rectify deplorable working conditions. During the late 1930s the federal government supported the right of workers to join unions and to bargain collectively with their employers.

After World War II the human relations movement gained momentum as papers were written, experiments were conducted, and theories were espoused by such individuals as Abraham Maslow, Douglas McGregor, and Frederick Herzberg. Research began to concentrate more on personal awareness and human interaction. B. F. Skinner, Carl Rogers, and Sigmund Freud influenced the working world, with such concepts as positive reinforcement, interpersonal communication, and unconscious motivation.

The character and composition of the work force are ever changing. Workers are better educated and more aware of their individual rights. The numbers of women, racial and ethnic minority groups, and senior citizens who are gainfully employed have risen to tens of millions. These employees have attitudes and perspectives as diverse as their backgrounds.

The nature of work is changing too. Technological advances affect what we do, where we do it, and with whom we interact. Robot use is spreading rapidly beyond the automobile industry to be used in tasks ranging from candy making to plastics molding. Creating, processing, and distributing information by use of a computer terminal and/or word processor, known as telecommuting, is also gaining in popularity.

Much progress has been made since the first psychology text was written by Hugo Munsterberg in 1913. Today's industrial psychologist has to be concerned with motivation, communication, and job satisfaction in addition to problems with drug and alcohol abuse, employee rights, and equal opportunity laws. Enhancing the quality of work life while maintaining efficiency and productivity is a constant challenge in the workplace today.

KEY TERMS

Human relations
Frederick Taylor
Scientific management
Reductionism
Frank and Lillian Gilbreth
Elton Mayo
Hawthorne experiments
Quality circles
Telecommuting
Hugo Munsterberg
Good Fairy syndrome

REVIEW AND DISCUSSION QUESTIONS

1. How did the Industrial Revolution contribute to the development of the human relations movement?

2. What does the term "human relations" mean to you? How can a study of this help you in your work and personal life?

3. What is meant by reductionism? How did it pave the way for the assembly line?

4. Who were Frederick Taylor? Frank and Lillian Gilbreth? Elton Mayo? How do their approaches differ?

5. Describe the significance of the Hawthorne experiments.

6. When did the interest in human relations work really gain momentum? Give specific examples.

7. In what ways has the character of the work force changed? How do these changes make the work of managers and psychologists more challenging?

8. Give examples of the changing nature of work itself. How do these changes affect the worker?

ENDNOTES

[1]JOHN NAISBETT, *Megatrends* (New York: Warner Books, 1982), p. 14.

[2]J. A. C. BROWN, *The Social Psychology of Industry* (New York: Penguin Books, 1954), p. 302.

[3]Adapted from GARY DEEL, "Revelations at Hawthorne," unpublished research paper, 1985.

[4]U.S. BUREAU OF THE CENSUS, *Statistical Abstracts of the United States: 1986*, 106th edition (Washington, D.C.: U.S. Government Printing Office, 1985), p. 133.

[5]BERKELY RICE, "Can Companies Kill?" *Psychology Today*, June 1981, p. 81.

[6]Ibid., p. 81.

[7]KAREN PENNAR AND EDWARD MERVOSH, "Women at Work," *Business Week*, January 28, 1985, p. 83.

[8]GAY BRYANT, *Working Woman Report* (New York: Simon & Schuster, 1984), p. 13.

[9]NAISBETT, *Megatrends*, p. 244.

[10]DAVID B. BRINKERHOFF AND LYNN K. WHITE, *Sociology* (St. Paul, Minn.: West Publishing Company, 1985), p. 265.

[11]RICHARD STENGEL, "Snapshot of a Changing America," *Time*, September 2, 1985, p. 16.

[12]STUDS TERKEL, *Working* (New York: Avon Books, 1974), p. 54.

[13]"Quality of Work Life: Catching On," *Business Week*, September 2, 1981, p. 72.

[14]NAISBETT, *Megatrends*, p. 202.

[15]WILLIAM C. BYHAM, "HRD and the Steel-Collar Worker," *Training/HRD*, January 1984, p. 62.

[16]JOHN NELSON BOLLES, *What Color is Your Parachute?* (Berkeley, Calif.: Ten Speed Press, 1982), pp. 310–311.

[17]MARCIA M. KELLY, "The Next Workplace Revolution: Telecommuting," *Supervisory Management*, October 1985, pp. 2–7.

[18]JACK GORDON, CHRIS LEE, AND RON ZEMKE, "Remembrance of Things Passe," *Training/HRD*, January 1984, p. 38.

[19]KELLY, "The Next Workplace Revolution: Telecommuting," p. 6.

[20]GORDON AND OTHERS, "Remembrance of Things Passe," p. 23.

chapter 3

Communicating at Work

After reading and studying this chapter, you will be able to:

1. Discuss the importance of communication.
2. Define communication and distinguish between intrapersonal and interpersonal communication.
3. Outline the six steps in the communication process.
4. Contrast formal and informal channels of communication.
5. Differentiate between upward, downward, and horizontal communication.
6. Give ways to improve upward and downward communication.
7. Discuss the merits of the grapevine.

I know you think you understand what you think I said, but I'm not sure you understand that what I said is not what I meant.

Communication is essential for our survival. This may sound dramatic until you consider the importance that communication plays in our lives. It is the foundation of all interpersonal relationships, for without communication, how could we obtain a job and carry out our work responsibilities? How could we satisfy our emotional, intellectual, and social needs without relating to others? Speaking of others, how do we understand their wants and needs without communicating with them?

IMPORTANCE OF COMMUNICATION

Individuals spend 75–80 percent of their waking hours communicating with others.

From the time we are babbling babies, we use communication, verbal and nonverbal, to make ourselves understood and to understand others, and yet very little time and effort are spent actually studying the four communication skills of listening, speaking, reading and writing. This is unfortunate since estimates suggest that individuals spend 75–80 percent of their waking hours communicating with others.

This chapter, in an effort to enhance your communication skills, explores the communication process itself and the formal and informal communication channels operating in the workplace. Before yawning and saying to yourself, "Is this really important for me as a machinist, pipefitter, or pastry chef?" be aware that all sorts of problems–from absenteeism, sabotage, and low morale to inability to follow instructions can be linked to poor communication. Try to calculate the astronomical cost to the economy if each of the country's 100 million workers made just one $10 mistake because of poor communication skills; the price tag would be well over $1 billion annually.

So what is this process of communication? It's a dynamic process of transmitting information and understanding between individuals. All persons involved must understand what has been spoken, written, heard, or read in the same manner, or communication breaks down. A two-way connection must take place if communication is to be successful.

SELF-APPRAISAL SURVEY

The purpose of this survey is to determine your susceptibility to being a source of communication breakdown. Since no one but you will see the results of this questionnaire, it is in your best interest to answer the questions as honestly as possible. Respond not as you would like to be seen as a communicator but as you *really* are.

Indicate how frequently you engage in the following behaviors when communicating with another person or persons.

Use this scale to describe your behavior.

4—I always do this.
3—I often do this.
2—I sometimes do this.
1—I seldom do this.
0—I never do this.

_____ 1. When I have something to say, I am open and honest about my need to say it.

_____ 2. I communicate with an awareness that the words I choose may not mean the same thing to other people that they do to me.

_____ 3. I recognize that the message I receive may not be the same one the other person intended to send.

_____ 4. Before I communicate, I ask myself questions about who my receiver is and how that will affect his or her reception of my message.

_____ 5. As I communicate to someone, I keep a watchful eye and ear out for an indication that I am understood.

_____ 6. I make my messages as brief and to the point as possible.

_____ 7. I consciously avoid the use of jargon with those who may not understand it.

_____ 8. I consciously avoid the use of slang words and colloquialisms with those who may be put off by them.

_____ 9. I try not to use red-flag words that may upset or distract the receiver of my message.

_____ 10. I recognize that *how* I say something is just as important as *what* I say.

_____ 11. I analyze my communication style to determine what nonverbal messages I send and how well they conform to the meaning I desire to get across.

_____ 12. I carefully consider whether my message would be best understood by my receiver in a face-to-face meeting, over the telephone, or in writing.

_____ 13. I form opinions about what others say to me based on what I hear them saying rather than what I think of them as a person.

_____ 14. I make a genuine effort to listen to ideas with which I don't agree.

_____ 15. I look for ways to improve my listening skills.

[ ]   TOTAL SCORE

Total your responses and use the chart below to find out how effective you are as a communicator. Scores below 30 indicate that there's much room for improvement.

Score	Number of Students	Interpretations
50-60	[ ]	Are you sure you were honest? If so, you are an extremely effective communicator who almost never contributes to misunderstanding.
40-49	[ ]	You are an effective communicator who only infrequently causes communication breakdown. The goal of these exercises is to move everyone up to this level.
30-39	[ ]	You are an above-average communicator with occasional lapses. You cause some misunderstandings but less than your share.

DEFINITION OF COMMUNICATION

Interpersonal communication takes place between persons, and intrapersonal communication takes place within a person.

Communication can be both interpersonal and intrapersonal. *Interpersonal* communication takes place between persons, and *intrapersonal* communication takes place within a person. Interpersonal communication occurs when writing a letter, reading a blueprint, telling a joke, or listening to a co-worker give her interpretation of the latest sick leave policy. On the other hand, thoughts, dreams, ideas, and fantasies are all examples of intrapersonal communication. When you're taking a shower and planning your day, fighting the traffic and worrying about being late for work, or reading a book and visualizing a romantic scene, you are engaging in intrapersonal communication. We actually spend 100 percent of our waking hours communicating within ourselves or with others. While the examination of your own thoughts can be entertaining and rewarding, this chapter emphasizes interpersonal communication.

A COMMUNICATION MODEL

There are six steps in the communication process according to Keith Davis in *Human Relations at Work: The Dynamics of Organizational Behavior.*[1] While this model may appear to be an orderly sequence of events, the communication process itself is not orderly, logical, or static. People are receiving, sending, interpreting, and inferring information all at the same time. There is no fixed beginning and no fixed end. Still, this model is helpful in gaining a basic understanding of the communication process.

The Process

Develop an idea.

This step is also called ideation. Think before you speak. All the other steps are useless unless you have a worthwhile idea to communi-

cate. "The trouble with people who talk too fast is that they often say something they haven't thought of yet."[2]

Encode.

The connotation of a word is its subjective meaning; the denotation is the dictionary definition.

As the sender of the message, you must determine how to translate your thoughts or ideas into symbols for transmission. Symbols can be verbal or nonverbal. A word is a symbol, and so is a shrug. When encoding a message, always keep the other person foremost in mind. Common everyday words have different emotional and intellectual meanings for all of us. Often a word's denotation (dictionary definition) and connotation (subjective meaning) are different.

Mr. Webster defines love objectively, and yet because of personal experiences, we all attach somewhat different meanings to this abstract and subjective word. To demonstrate that the meanings of words exist in the person and not in the word itself, I asked a group of students to write anonymously the personal definitions of the word love. Two particularly memorable responses were "Love is just another four letter word," and "Love is a strong emotion requiring sharing and commitment." Do you think these two people would understand each other's meaning of those three little words "I love you"? I predict a communication failure.

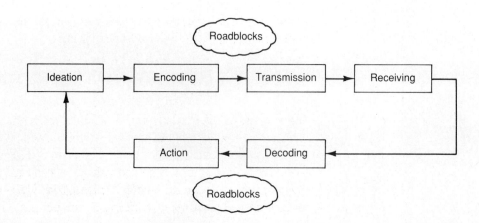

Transmit.

After you develop and encode an idea, you transmit it to the receiver. The channel of communication decided on, whether written or oral, should be free of interference. Noise, distracting mannerisms, interruptions, and illegible handwriting are examples of interference. Channels of communication include letters, memos, telephone conversations, and face-to-face talks.

Circumstances dictate which channel is more effective. Use a memo if a written record is needed or if a large number of people need to be informed. Since the average business letter costs approximately $6.00 to send, try using Ma Bell, especially if immediate feedback is desired. If a message is controversial, sensitive, or easily misunderstood, the people involved should talk it out face to face.

Receive.

If the channel is relatively free of interference, the reader or listener receives your message. Communication can break down at the receiving stage as easily as it can at any of the others. If writing is illegible, a reader cannot make sense of the scribbling. If a listener doesn't listen well to an oral message, the message is lost, not received. Reasons for poor listening and suggestions for improvement are found in the next chapter.

Decode.

Differences in perception and experience often cause misunderstanding at the decoding step.

When talking to someone, have you ever thought, "Am I getting through to Tom? If I am, then why do I feel so frustrated at the end of our conversations?" Perhaps Tom is not decoding your message accurately. The decoder must decode the message so that it is understood in exactly the same way it was sent. Sometimes even cooperative, sincere readers and listeners do not interpret the message in the manner intended because of a difference in perceptions and experiences.

Consider the varying interpretations of a simple statement such as, "Joan has a good job." What is a good job? One that pays well? One that has job security? Is a good job a stimulating job? Is the speaker facetiously insinuating that Joan has a good job while you do not? When the speaker is uncertain of the intended message, paying close attention to nonverbal signals is beneficial. If the speaker smirks while telling you about Joan's job, maybe he's being sarcastic.

Many communications failures occur during the decoding step. Have any of the following ever happened to you?

1. The speaker uses abstract or technical terms without explaining them. While a competent, knowledgeable secretary might know that a dot matrix is a type of printer, the average woman (or man!) on the street might not. An electronics wizard might know the meaning of pixel, a dot in an electronic image which is one-tenth the width of a human hair, but how many other people do?

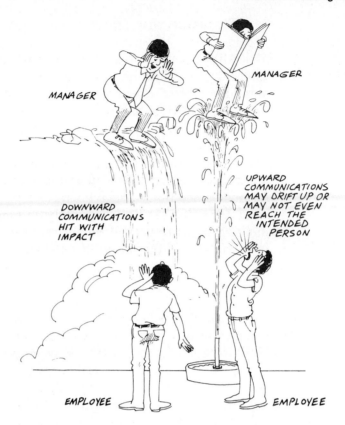

2. You mistrust the speaker's intention. Is your supervisor trying to manipulate you by commending your dedication and zeal or is the compliment sincere?

3. You're prejudiced against the speaker. A woman's place is in the home, not teaching you how to read blueprints, and your resentment interferes with your ability to listen and learn.

4. The speaker is too wordy. He or she adds irrelevant ideas and prolongs getting to the point.

5. Your interpretation of a message differs from that of the speaker. Hearing the word "math" is anxiety provoking (even bone chilling) for some people, while others feel neutral or even enthusiastic over the prospect of solving complex mathematical problems. A more detailed discussion of language barriers follows in the next chapter.

Satisfactory communication is more rare than we realize. We naively assume that since what we say is clear to us, it therefore will be equally clear to others. We fail to comprehend the fact that the speech signs we make have to be filtered through the nervous systems of other persons, on their way to minds made up of experiences different from our own.[3]

Use.

The acid test of communication effectiveness is whether your sender receives the desired response. The receiver must use the communication in some way. He can ignore it, carry out the job duty requested, respond to you verbally, shrug his shoulders, hug you, or simply store the information away. Whatever the response, it provides feedback to the sender, thereby completing the two-way communication process. The receiver's use of the communication and the action taken could even begin a new communication sequence.

Past, present, and future all blend together during the communication process.

Remember that these six steps are not static. During the communication process, past, present, and future all blend together. Some steps overlap and even occur simultaneously. You could receive a nonverbal message from a worried-looking person on the night shift that something is amiss and ideate, encode, and transmit a response all at the same time. Finally, the process could take only seconds to complete, or it could take months for a response to be made.

WIIO'S FIRST LAW OF COMMUNICATION

Take the six steps of the communication process seriously. In a humorous spoof of Murphy's Law, Osmo Wiio warns in his first law of communication that "Communication usually fails—except by chance." He adds that the general efficiency rate of the communication process is often under 5 percent. Wiio's corollaries to the first law of communication are:

1. If communication can fail—it will.
2. If communication cannot fail—it usually fails.
3. If communication seems to succeed in the way which was intended, it must be in a way which was not intended.
4. If you are satisfied that your communication is bound to succeed, then the communication is bound to fail.[4]

Don't be discouraged by Wiio's law. Just design your message for your receiver and don't take the communication process lightly.

FORMAL CHANNELS OF COMMUNICATION

All organizations have both formal and informal channels of communication.

All organizations, whether it's the Marriott Corporation or the Noe Appliance Repair Shop, have formal and informal channels of communication. Formal communication moves along both vertical and horizontal

By permission of Johnny Hart and News America Syndicate.

lines along official paths dictated by job function and the organizational hierarchy. Its three channels are downward, upward, and horizontal. Downward communication consists of information on policy, job duties, and expectations and travels from the top executive, the head honcho, down to the lowest-level employee. On the other hand, upward communication carries suggestions, complaints, or questions from workers at all levels to the top executive. Finally, horizontal communication occurs among co-workers, managers, departments, or divisions on the same level.

Downward Communication

Downward communication is primarily directive and informative without being condescending.

Although upward and downward communication share the same vertical pathway, the nature and content of the messages differ. Halloran compares their difference to the force of water: "Downward communication is like water streaming down from a waterfall or showerhead. It pours more easily with great force and wets a large area; upward communication is like a small spurt of water shooting up from a fountain against the pull of gravity. The higher it goes, the more it loses its force."[5] In short, downward communication is forceful and reaches a great number of people, while upward communication is weak and reaches few people.

Downward communication is primarily directive and informative without being condescending. Company rules, pay practices, promotion procedures, and actual job training are examples of downward communication. Whether downward communication should be written, oral, or both depends on the situation. For example, tender topics such as reprimands, firings, or arbitrating conflicts between workers are best handled face to face. Information carried "down the organization" consists primarily of job instructions, performance feedback, and just plain news.

Job instruction is anything an employee needs to know to carry out his or her work responsibilities. Instructions can be written or oral depending on the complexity of the task. A good rule of thumb is to use written instructions if a task requires precision, has more than five steps, and contains hard-to-remember details.

Downward communication in the form of performance feedback is important in that it lets employees know how well or how poorly they are performing. If performance is satisfactory or superior (think positively), self-esteem and morale may be enhanced; if performance is unsatisfactory, employees need to become aware of their shortcomings and of ways to improve.

Finally, news traveling the downward route helps workers to feel aware and informed and discourages rumor and speculation. In general, employees in the know feel better about their organization and are more loyal if they can participate in decisions about themselves and their jobs. Job posting, one of the most basic forms of downward communication, makes jobs that are available widely known so that all employees can compete for them.

The communication choices at our disposal are impressive, even mind boggling. A supervisor sends a message to employees by showing a film, providing a booklet, hiring a competent secretary, installing an intercom system, using a word processor, phoning a subordinate, or taking a listening course. It seems that sometimes there is an overemphasis on the use of expensive and often ineffective equipment that results in a one-way communication. Sadly, with all the elaborate possibilities, downward communication still occasionally falls short as illustrated in the following passage.

Horizontal or lateral communication with our own peers seems to be no great problem to us in our organizations. But vertical communication downward reveals an entirely different picture. If the chairman of the board calls in a vice-president and tells her something, on the average only 63 percent of the message is assimilated by the latter.

If the vice-president relays the same message to a general supervisor, 56 percent of it arrives. If the supervisor gives it to a plant manager, 40 percent arrives. If the plant manager passes it along to a supervisor, 30 percent is received. And if the supervisor gives it to the squad of workers who are her or his responsibility, only 20 percent of the original message will have passed down through five levels of authority to reach its ultimate receivers.[6]

Can a person in a supervisory position improve downward communication? Of course. How? Simple. She can try the following:

Demonstrate the importance of good communication.

Many managers profess to have a positive communication attitude, but their actions belie their empty words. What do you think about a supervisor's sincerity when he says, "I really care about my employees. In fact, I firmly believe that people are our most valuable resource," yet this person fidgets with his clothing and frequently glances at his watch while "listening" to you?

There are other suggestions for demonstrating the importance of good communication. One is to hold informal meetings of small groups to discuss common problems and solutions. Additionally, when employees are open enough to tell employers of concerns or complaints, the latter have to learn to respond to bad news without overreacting. If the boss goes berserk every time he or she receives less than positive feedback, employees will soon stop communicating upward. Now that is bad news! When employees are always shielding the boss from the unpleasantness of situations, soon the supervisor won't know what's going on. Finally, if employees contribute good ideas and suggestions, they should be recognized and rewarded. As an example, Maytag has an elaborate suggestion system accompanied by generous rewards. Employees evidently think the process is worthwhile since 94 percent of them participate.

Make all downward communication clear, specific, and understandable.

If a report is due in three days, the supervisor should say so instead of saying "soon." Saying that 75 percent of the sales force worked an average of two hours of overtime per week to reach the goal of 1,000 new accounts is more specific than is saying that most employees are making a tremendous effort to meet the quota.

A student was employed at a golf course as part of his hands-on work-study experience. Since he lived in a resort area with literally dozens of courses, the young man was aware of the job potential and was anxious to learn all aspects of the job. The superintendent who had been in the business for years assumed that the intern was more knowledgeable than he actually was and gave him little or no direction.

On the first day, the young man was told to change tees, and being anxious to work, he did so and did a superb job, but how often can one change tees? Afterward he had to guess what else to do by watching others. After three days the boss chewed him out for not carrying off several bags of trash. The intern didn't know he was supposed to carry it off, and when questioned replied that he thought someone would do it but didn't know he was supposed to. One day after digging up trees, the superintendent told him to put them on the back of the truck. The intern was industriously throwing the uprooted trees on the truck when the boss began yelling and screaming. It turned out that the trees were to be transplanted, not disposed of, and the young man was inadvertently damaging the root systems. These three experiences took place within one week; wouldn't the internship have turned out better for all parties if the superintendent had been more clear and specific with his assignments?

Use the KISS Formula (better known as "Keep it simple, Stupid!").

The message should be written or spoken in terms that the employee can understand. Most people are not able to process large amounts of new information at a time. Whether training a child, friend, or subordinate, others see things through a different window and don't have the knowledge and experience of the trainer or manager. Incidentally, the word stupid is a definite turn off for some people, so try "Keep it simple and straightforward" when working with them.

Develop trust along the vertical lines.

Trust is the basis for every good relationship.

According to Davis, when trust is lacking, information flow among people is reduced. "If employees suspect trickery, unfairness, or blindness to their ranks, they tend to react negatively and seize upon every opportunity to misinterpret what was said."[7] Trust is the basis for every good relationship.

Upward Communication

Employees withhold bad news, unfavorable opinions, and mistakes from their bosses.

Ideas, complaints, criticisms, problems, and suggestions are all examples of upward communication, communication sent upward from the lowest levels in an organization to and through the various supervisory levels. Some questions can be answered and some problems resolved by a first-line supervisor while others need to be sent to the "big boss."

There are more barriers to upward communication than downward communication. Employees withhold bad news, unfavorable opinions, and mistakes since they fear negative consequences like dismissal, demotion, or salary cuts. Consequently, upward communication is more protective. Some people don't communicate with their bosses because they feel that supervisors perceive upward communication as merely the healthy letting off of steam. Workers don't like having their concerns treated in so lightly a manner.

Workers in supervisory positions should encourage upward communication for a number of reasons. "When there is no means of learning what suggestions, complaints, or other information subordinates have relating to their work and other organizational matters, supervisors and managers necessarily must operate without the benefit of the feedback so vital to appraisal and revision of their own ideas, plans, and directives."[8]

Poor upward communication can lead to low morale, excessive absenteeism, rapid turnover, and even sabotage.

Even though complaints and suggestions from employees tend to be protective, upward communication gives feedback to employers about attitude and potential problems. The information conveyed is often guarded because employees are concerned with job security and group belongingness. Poor upward communication can lead to low morale. In turn, low morale can mushroom into other problems like psychosomatic illnesses, prolonged lunch hours, excessive absenteeism, rapid turnover, and even sabotage.

Timm and Peterson suggest several ways that a supervisor can encourage upward communication, and these methods can be applied in any organization, regardless of size. Three of these methods are the open-door policy, good downward communication, and sympathetic listening.[9]

Open-door policy

Practicing the open door policy is time consuming for all concerned.

Sounds like a good idea, right? The problem is that sometimes the open-door policy is just that—a policy and not a practice. Some managers say they have an open door when, in fact, they do not. Even if the supervisor is sincere in welcoming visitors, many employees are reluctant to come calling. Their friends might suspect them to trying to curry favor. The "middle man" may wonder if you're going over his head about something. Another drawback—it takes time on everyone's part.

By the time a toolmaker leaves his work area and arrives at the manager's office, much of his 10-minute break is gone. Since a pleasant but firm secretary screens visitors (especially those without appointments), the worker is further delayed. Having an open portal is time consuming for the manager too. If all supervisors left their doors ajar for every tissue technician, teacher, and clerical worker who wanted to chat, time for planning, organizing, staffing, directing, and controlling would be limited.

Some people in supervisory positions realize that the door opens both ways. They make it a common practice to walk out of the office to observe and talk to employees. Not only does this practice keep supervisors "in the know," but it also boosts employee morale. Many progressive managers boast of having a MBWA degree, which stands for management by walking around.

Roger D'Aprix shares a story that demonstrates both the simplicity and the complexity of the communication process. A client called in a management consultant to suggest ways in which management might communicate better with its work force. The company was about to spend almost $300,000 on what it perceived as the most up-to-date way to transmit messages to employees: closed-circuit television monitors scattered throughout the premises.

The consultant was dismayed and after getting the "feel" of the place, he suggested that the president join his people out in the corridor at a coffee bar. After much persistence, the president reluctantly agreed to try the reverse open-door policy. Here's an account of what happened.

> The first attempt was an abysmal failure. He didn't even know how to work the coffee machine. A bystander, seeing him fumble with the coins, walked over and told him the coffee was free. Red-faced, he took the cup in hand and looked for someone to begin a conversation with. No one approached him; employees were clustered in little groups quietly discussing their various concerns and glancing curiously at him. He drank his coffee and walked back into his office. At first the president was emphatic of his refusal to subject himself to such humiliation. Eventually he agreed to try it one more time, but with his coat off.

> This time he got his coffee without incident and screwed up the courage to break into the perimeter of a small gathering. After some conversation about the weather, he asked how things were going and heard some pleasantries from the group indicating that everything was fine.

The next day and the next the president went out to the corridor for his morning coffee. In time he found himself holding forth on all kinds of company issues with employees, who now felt comfortable enough to air their concerns. The kaffee-klatsches were working so well that he asked his senior staff to begin mingling with their people at coffee time. He also canceled the TV equipment in favor of the simpler and more effective technique of firsthand, face-to-face communication.[10]

Good Downward Communication

Downward communication which is clear, fair, and reliable can actually enhance upward communication since the two depend on each other. Not only does good downward communication make employees feel important and "in the know," but it also helps them do their jobs better.

Sympathetic Listening

Gerald Goldhaber believes that while employees need a greater opportunity to voice complaints and evaluate supervisors, they are threatened in doing so. "Sympathetic listening during the many day-to-day informal contacts within the department and outside the work place" can improve upward communication.[11]

Horizontal Communication

Problem solving, task coordination, and information sharing are some benefits of good horizontal communication.

Horizontal communication takes place between workers at the same level—welder to welder, nurse to nurse, night supervisor to day supervisor. Workers at all levels often interact to make certain that they all have the same information and that they all understand it in the same way. Problem solving, task coordination, information sharing, and conflict resolution are but a few of the uses of horizontal communication. Deterrents to good horizontal communication include rivalry and specialization. When co-workers are competing to get ahead, they might actually withhold information from each other.

INFORMAL COMMUNICATION

Unlike formal communication channels, informal patterns of communication are not found on an organization chart. Rather, these patterns emerge from social interactions of people who work together day after day. Such relationships can be complex and rapidly changing. Another major difference between formal and informal channels is that both work and social topics are discussed informally. A bank teller may discuss her mother-in-law's idiosyncrasies one moment and the correct procedure for a complicated transaction the next. Incidentally, good informal communication can contribute to worker efficiency, productivity, and cooperation.

The Grapevine

The grapevine is a normal, natural occurrence which moves along both vertical and horizontal lines.

A discussion of informal communication would be incomplete without a discussion of the infamous grapevine. The word "grapevine" hails from the Civil War era when telegraph wires were strung from tree to tree and had the appearance of a grapevine. Because the telegraph messages were often garbled and misunderstood, people tend to regard the grapevine as the source of unclear, ambiguous information.

The grapevine at work is a normal, natural occurrence that moves both vertically and horizontally. It is useful in that it helps to satisfy workers' social needs of belongingness and being in other things. Another useful function is that the grapevine helps to interpret and clarify formal communication.

Even though it might send shudders up some supervisory spines, the grapevine is a useful vehicle for disseminating information without meeting or memo. News travels fast, and surprisingly enough, three-fourths of the information conveyed about noncontroversial work matters is accurate.[12]

Since the grapevine cannot be eliminated, most managers use it to their advantage. They listen to it and feed it valuable information. One female supervisor concluded a departmental meeting with the words "Well, what's the latest on the grapevine? Anything I need to know about?" The subordinates were momentarily taken aback, but realizing her seriousness, they haltingly began to reveal little tidbits. Some information was totally erroneous, and the supervisor was able to correct some faulty thinking by sharing information she had picked up on the grapevine earlier that day.

Rumor is the grapevine's worst feature.

Of course, the grapevine would not have received its wicked reputation if it were always a reliable source of information. Sometimes information is distorted, exaggerated, and woefully inaccurate.

Rumor

Rumor is perhaps the grapevine's worst feature and probably deserves the evil reputation it holds. Supervisors, like plumbers, electricians, and salespersons, would do well to remember McGrait's law: "A rumor will travel fastest to the place where it will do the greatest harm." Facts combat rumor since many rumors get started simply because people misunderstand something or have been given incorrect information. Keeping all formal channels of communication open is an effective rumor squelcher. Withholding information from channels such as bulletin board notices and group meetings will start rumors spreading.

COMMUNICATION ROLE PLAY:
SAY WHAT YOU MEAN AND MEAN WHAT YOU SAY

Communicating is not as easy as it seems. People attach different meanings to seemingly easy, everyday words. By the time they discover their varying interpretations, sometimes problems have already occurred. In discussing the problem, emotions and past experiences all influence the parties' perception of the situation.

To illustrate the importance of communicating just the right message, choose two students to role play the following true situation. Although not always adhered to, the company's policy on leaves and tardies follows the description of the situation.

Employee's Role

You've been employed as a machine operator at Atkins Manufacturing for 11 years. Having always prided yourself on accepting responsibility and doing a full day's work for a full day's pay, you've missed only six days of work in those eleven years and have never been late! Lately, however, a long-standing family problem has worsened. Your spouse's persistent drinking has developed into alcoholism, and you've had to devote a great deal of time helping him recover while handling all household responsibilities, including the care of two young children.

Knowing ahead of time that these problems could conflict with your work schedule, you explained the situation to your supervisor and advised him that you might need to take a day's sick leave if the situation demanded it. Too, you explained that taking the children to school might mean an occasional tardy morning. He seemed to understand perfectly and indicated that things could be worked out as long as your absences and tardiness were not "excessive."

During the past two months you've taken three days' sick leave and have been late for work on six occasions. Considering the nature of your problem and your excellent past work history, you don't feel that your absences and tardiness have been "excessive."

The supervisor has left a message indicating that he wants to see you, and rumor has it that he's pretty fed up with parceling out your work to others on such a regular basis. Of special concern to the supervisor is the negative effect of your absences and tardiness on co-workers.

What will you say to him?

Supervisor's Role

You're a supervisor in the Production Department at Atkins Manufacturing Company. You've held this position for a little over a year and have developed a high level of dedication and morale in your department. About two months ago one of your best employees approached you about a personal problem and indicated the probability that the problem might require occasional days of sick leave and some tardiness.

This employee, who is very conscientious and reliable, has been working for the company for 11 years, much longer than you have. As a slightly older worker, she seems to have a stabilizing effect on some of the younger workers. Although the employee has no formal position power, she has a lot of personal power and is well respected by co-workers.

When approached about the problem, you readily agreed to work with the employee for a number of reasons: the low absentee rate in the past, the positive influence on the other workers, and the seriousness of the situation. Just to make sure that you understood each other you mentioned that the absences and tardiness shouldn't be "excessive."

You've recently had to write a reprimand to an employee who has been with the company for nine months because of his fourth tardy. This employee became irate, citing the absences of the 11-year person and emphasizing that the latter had not been reprimanded. Talk is beginning to spread in your department about the differences in treatment of the employees.

You've left a message for the older employee to come by your office, and the person will be in to see you in a moment.

What will you say?

Atkins Manufacturing Company Leave Policy

Annual Leave. The plant will close from July 1 until July 15th of each year. Except for administrative employees, all employees must take their annual leave during this period.

Sick Leave. Each employee shall accrue sick leave at a rate of 4 hours per month. An employee may not accrue in excess of 80 hours of sick leave. Sick leave may only be used for personal or family illness. Sick leave in excess of one working day (8 hours) must be supported by a doctor's certificate of illness.

Tardiness. Employees are expected to report to work on time and to put in a full workday. If an employee is late for work, he or she will receive a verbal reprimand for the first such occurrence. The second occurrence in one calendar year will elicit a written reprimand from the supervisor with a copy to personnel. A third occurrence in the same calendar year may be cause for dismissal.

CASE STUDIES

Construction Supervisor

A construction supervisor found that his authority was being repeatedly challenged by one of the carpenters. This employee had an outgoing personality, a charming manner, and an impressive joke-telling ability. The carpenter had become an informal leader because of his personal power, not his position power. The other workers liked to be entertained by their informal leader instead of hanging doors and building cabinets.

The supervisor knew that his authority not only was being under-mined but also that the building would not be completed on schedule if conditions stayed the same. Entertaining Eddie was warned to cut the jokes and get to work several times without results. In fact, the situation became worse. It was as if the carpenter dared the supervisor to fire him. Finally, the supervisor fired Eddie without informing his admiring audience of the facts, the real reason for the dismissal. This action was apparently fertile grounds for rumor growth. The workers began to speculate. Was Eddie fired because the company's going broke? Are we all going to lose our jobs? Does the boss have a grudge against Eddie? In-stead of working harder, the other carpenters became resentful and developed a poor attitude.

1. What is the reason for the poor attitude on the part of the employees?
2. Could this misunderstanding have been avoided? How?
3. Should the construction supervisor have told his employees why Eddie was fired (downward communication) and encouraged ques-tions and concerns (upward communication)? Why or why not?

Robinson and Sanchez

Two men are sitting at their desks feeling frustrated. They both just came from a meeting in which one offered the other a promotion which was turned down; then again, maybe it was and maybe it wasn't. Confused? So are they. Here's the story.

Phillip Robinson just offered what he considered to be the oppor-tunity of a lifetime to the office's top claims adjuster, Richard Sanchez, and he thinks, but isn't sure, that Sanchez turned him down. When Phil-lip outlined the new job for Richard, he closely watched his facial expres-sion for clues of excitement. There were none. Not even when Phillip told Richard of the generous raise and the challenge involved in moving into a new territory. Instead Richard had remarked that he had little ex-perience in management, that his family knew no one in the new area, and had even laughingly stated that money wasn't everything. "What's wrong with the man?" mused Phillip. "Doesn't he realize that an offer like this doesn't come along too often?"

Richard knew all too well of the career opportunity which had been surprisingly placed before him. The problem was that he was frightened, scared to death that he would not be able to meet the challenge and would disappoint his company, his family, and himself. Although Richard more than meets the qualifications for the new position and is very capable of managing his own office, he's not so sure. When he hesitated in Phillip's office, it was because he desperately needed reassurance, not because he was unwilling to tackle the challenge.

The two men perceive their conversation entirely differently. What Phillip sees as disinterest and lack of conviction is actually reluctance and fear of failure. Each is wondering if he missed something or said too much or too little.

1. What suggestions can you offer to overcome this communication breakdown?
2. Can you think of a similar situation on or off the job which left you and your fellow communicator feeling frustrated because you couldn't say what you wanted to say? Or maybe you said what you wanted to say but the other person didn't respond in the manner which you anticipated? What could have helped the situation?

SUMMARY

Communication is essential for our survival and is the foundation of all interpersonal relationships. It can be defined as a dynamic process of transmitting information and understanding between people.

Communication can be either interpersonal or intrapersonal. Interpersonal occurs between persons and intrapersonal takes place within an individual's mind.

The six steps in the communication process are ideation, encoding, transmission, reception, decoding, and usage. Far from being stable, the steps often overlap and sometimes even occur simultaneously.

Osmo Wiio's law of communication states that "Communication usually fails—except by chance" and asserts that the general efficiency rate of the communication process is often under 5 percent.

All organizations have formal and informal channels of communication. Formal communication moves along both vertical and horizontal lines by paths dictated by job function and organizational hierarchy. Its three channels are upward, downward, and horizontal.

Downward communication travels from the top executive down to the lowest-level employee and consists of information on policies, job duties, and expectations. Upward communication carries suggestions, complaints, or questions from workers at all levels to management. Horizontal communication occurs among co-workers, managers, departments, or divisions on the same level.

To improve downward communication, a supervisor can be clear and specific, use the KISS formula, develop trust along the vertical lines, use repetition, and ask for definite feedback. Suggestions for improving upward communication include trying the open-door policy, practicing good downward communication, and listening sympathetically to troubled employees.

When successful, horizontal communication can be helpful in problem solving, information sharing, and conflict resolution.

Informal communication channels are not found on an organization chart. Emerging from the social interaction of people who work together day after day, informal communication consists of both work and social topics. Good informal communication can contribute to worker efficiency, productivity, and cooperation.

The grapevine is a component of the informal channel and is a normal, natural occurrence. In spite of its evil reputation, the grapevine is useful in helping to satisfy workers' social needs and in disseminating information. Although sometimes its information is exaggerated and distorted, three-fourths of grapevine data is accurate.

KEY TERMS

Interpersonal communication
Intrapersonal communication
Communication process
Keith Davis
Osmo Wiio
Formal communication channels
Upward communication
Downward communication
Horizontal communication
KISS formula
Informal communication channels
Open-door policy
MBWA
Grapevine

REVIEW AND DISCUSSION QUESTIONS

1. Why is the communication process so important in our work and personal lives?

2. Differentiate between intrapersonal and interpersonal communication. Give examples of each.

3. What are the six steps in the communication process? Think of an instance in which communication broke down at one of these steps. Analyze the breakdown.

4. What are the three types of formal communication? What distinguishes formal from informal communication?

5. What can a supervisor do to improve upward communication?

6. What are some advantages and disadvantages of the open-door policy?

7. Can you remember a situation that could have turned out more positively if there had been more clear vertical communication? Be as specific as possible.

8. How can good horizontal communication help a person on the job? How can poor horizontal communication hurt someone?

9. What are some merits of the supposedly "notorious" grapevine? What is its worst feature? Why?

ENDNOTES

[1] KEITH DAVIS, *Human Behavior at Work: Organizational Behavior*, 6th ed. (New York: McGraw-Hill, 1981), pp. 400–402.

[2] JACK HALLORAN, *Supervision: The Art of Management* (Englewood Cliffs, N. J.: Prentice Hall, 1981), p. 63.

[3] GOODWIN F. BERQUEST, JR., ed. *Speeches for Illustration and Example* (Glenview, Ill.: Scott, Foresman, 1965), p. 5. Information first seen in Glenn R. Capp and G. Richard Capp, Jr., *Basic Oral Communication*, 2nd ed. (Englewood Cliffs, N. J.: Prentice Hall, 1976), p. 258.

[4] OSMO WIIO, *Wiio's Laws—and Some Others* (Espoo, Finland: Welin-Goos, 1978).

[5] JACK HALLORAN, *Applied Human Relations*, 2nd ed. (Englewood Cliffs, N. J.: Prentice Hall, 1983), pp. 60–61.

[6] ERNEST G. BORMANN AND OTHERS, *Interpersonal Communication in the Modern Organization* (Englewood Cliffs, N. J.: Prentice Hall, 1982), p.113.

[7] DAVIS, *Human Behavior at Work*, p. 423.

[8] FRED CARVELL, *Human Relations in Business* (New York: Macmillan, 1975), p. 38.

[9] PAUL R. TIMM AND BRENT D. PETERSON, *People at Work: Human Relations in Organizations* (St. Paul, Minn.: West, 1982), p. 307.

[10] ROGER D'APRIX, "The Oldest (and Best) Way to Communicate with Employees," *Harvard Business Review*, September–October 1982, pp. 30–31.

[11] GERALD M. GOLDHABER, *Organizational Communication*, 2nd ed. (Dubuque, Iowa: William C. Brown, 1979), p. 139.

[12] HALLORAN, *Applied Human Relations*, p. 71.

chapter 4

Improving Your Communication

After reading and studying this chapter, you will be able to:

1. Discuss the many language, emotional, and physical barriers to communication.
2. Define nonverbal communication and discuss its importance.
3. Discuss four types of nonverbal communication.
4. Explain how an understanding of nonverbal communication can increase your understanding of self and others.
5. Discuss the importance of listening.
6. List several ways to improve listening.

Know how to listen and you will profit even from those who talk badly.
Plutarch

A word is the skin of a living thought.

Justice Oliver Wendell Holmes

BARRIERS TO COMMUNICATION

Communication counts. It literally makes the world go 'round, and yet as Osmo Wiio humorously noted, "If a message can be understood in different ways, it will be understood in just the way it does the most harm." As mentioned in the preceding chapter, Wiio contends that the general efficiency rate of the communication process is often under 5 percent.[1] How can you improve those odds? Knowing some of the primary barriers to communication, becoming aware of the significance of nonverbal communication, and improving your listening skills are three ways to improve your personal communication efficiency.

Barriers to communication can result in disruptions in productivity, rifts in relationships, decline of motivation, and growth of hostility. Misunderstandings from these barriers, or roadblocks, can and should be eliminated. Most barriers can be classified as language, emotional or physical.

Language

As mentioned in the preceding chapter, words are merely symbols which stand for thoughts, feelings, and ideas. A word is simply an arbitrary arrangement of a few of the 26 letters of the alphabet. So what's in a word? Plenty!

Perceptions are the unique ways in which an individual views the world.

Individuals attach different meanings to their words according to life experiences which influence both perceptions and values. Perceptions are the unique ways in which an individual views the world, while a value system is an underlying set of beliefs about what is right and wrong, important and unimportant. To complicate the issue further, as a person grows and matures, her values and perceptions change. A 20-year-old and a 60-year-old differ both in the way they perceive the word "security" and in the way they value the concept it represents. Since no two people have exactly the same life experiences, values, or perceptions, a supervisor might interpret a message a little differently from what was sent. Everyone applies different labels or symbols (words) to his or her unique world.

Timm states that it is indeed ironic that language, the very basis of oral communication, poses as one of the most pervasive sources of misunderstanding in the communication process. He further suggests that it is amazing that people can communicate at all![2] How can language be such a bother? Just look at the possibilities.

1. Foreign words and phrases
2. Slang language
3. Technical jargon
4. Complex words
5. Connotation differences
6. Regional differences
7. Ambiguous terms

Foreign Words And Phrases

If you live in Florida, Arizona, Texas, New Mexico, or Southern California, you'd do well to brush up on your español since more than half of all Hispanic Americans live in those states. Even if you don't live in one of those locales, knowing a second language is a definite advantage at work and at play.

Because of the sharp increase in the number of foreign employees in American companies, an awareness of potential cross-cultural verbal and nonverbal communication breakdowns is increasingly important. Yet "in 1976 only four percent of American high school graduates had two years of foreign language training; in 1977 only nine percent of all college students were enrolled in a foreign language course—this is an era when one industrial job in eight depends on international trade."[3] Employees and supervisors alike express frustration over frequent misunderstanding that lead to performance errors and confusion on the job.

We are a nation of subcultures. In 1984 over 15 million Spanish-speaking people were officially recorded as residing in the United States, and several million additional Hispanics are believed to have entered without official documents.[4] Furthermore, there are approximately 2.5 million Asian-Americans living in the United States, many of whom do not speak English.[5] At our college there are several Vietnamese students who have difficulty with the English language. It is frustrating to try to explain a concept to these bright international students who are learning English as a second language. These men and women work in local industries and experience communication roadblocks there too.

A humorous incident illustrates this foreign language roadblock. An instructor left a test to be copied in the print shop. Following his instructions concerning the number of copies and the time he needed them, Mr. X added por favor before signing his name. The work-study student making the copies was completely baffled by this Spanish phrase meaning "please" and scurried around asking for help in deciphering and understanding the words.

Slang

Slang is faddish and
ages quickly.

Slang is vivid, forceful, and expressive. It enriches our language and aids in communicating just the right message. On the other hand, slang is faddish, ages quickly, and indicates a limited vocabulary when used excessively. "Its life is brief, intense, and slightly disreputable, like adolescence."[6] Use it but don't abuse it by overuse.

This colorful, popular language has its rightful place, but since slang develops within subgroups, those outside of your group may not understand your lingo. Subgroups develop according to profession, age, activity, interest, and ethnic group. For example, computer programmers have software, hardware, and even wetware (the brain); CB operators speak of handles, seatcovers, and green stamps; drug users "do" goofballs, yellow jackets, roaches, cubes, and speed to become stewed, fried, wired, and twisted; students flag tests, especially frosh, unless they're four or five pointers. Does this blow your mind? Subcultures use slang to promote a feeling of we-ness, and when other groups begin using the words, they are dropped since they no longer indicate group identity.

Test yourself. If you think a bean eater actually eats beans and an apple polisher actually shines apples, my friend, you're all wet. Good eggs and cream puffs won't make you a fat cat, and cribs are not just for babies. Don't get uptight over this Mickey Mouse mumbo jumbo because slang should be used only occasionally. Get my drift?

Technical Jargon

Specialists have specialized vocabularies. Sometimes, however, the words and phrases used by individuals are unknown to laypeople outside of the specialists' work or special interest group, and the specialists themselves are so accustomed to writing the technical terms that they erroneously assume that outsiders understand overseeding a golf course, cruising timber, troubleshooting, treating paranoid schizophrenia, and improving orthoepy. By all means, learn and use technical terms related to your career. Just remember that all people don't understand your words so a definition and/or alternative choice may be necessary.

Complex Words

Abraham Lincoln reportedly said, "Speak so that the most lowly can understand you, and the rest will have no difficulty," and that sage advice applies today. Adapt your choice of words to your listeners. Never use big words just to impress, and always use a simple word when available and appropriate.

If a man were to take a piece of meat and smell it and look disgusted, and his little boy were to say, "What's the matter with it, Pop?" and he were to say, "It is undergoing a process of decomposition in the formation of raw chemical compounds," the boy would be all in. But if his father were to say, "It's rotten," then the boy would understand and hold his nose. "Rotten" is a good Anglo-Saxon word, and you do not have to go to the dictionary to find out what it means.[7]

Say	Not
Learn	Ascertain
Drink	Imbibe
Try	Endeavor
Chew	Masticate
Cut	Lacerate
Buy	Purchase
Clothing	Apparel
Avoid	Eschew
Beauty	Pulchritude
Engaged	Betrothed

Incidentally, it pays to increase your vocabulary. Even though you may not speak or write words like perdurable or yammer, it's nice to understand them when used by others. Most of us have larger passive than active vocabularies. That is, you probably comprehend literally hundreds of words when you hear them spoken by others or when you read them in the newspaper, but you are unlikely to use those words in your speech and writing.

Connotation Differences.

A connotation is derived from the feelings and emotions a word represents.

The denotation of a word is its actual dictionary definition whereas its connotation is its definition derived from the feelings and emotions the word represents. Slim and skinny have the same denotation, but slim has a more positive connotation. Since we've all had different experiences, we attach different feelings to our words and need to keep that fact in mind when communicating with others. The following job titles illustrate connotation differences.

Housewife—Domestic engineer, homemaker
Grease monkey—Automotive technician
Garbage man—Sanitation engineer
Cop—Law officer, policeman
Boss—Supervisor
Broad—Woman

Regional Differences

Regional differences and colloquialisms vary from one locale to another. In the South, individuals use terms such as "Ma'am" and "Sir" when addressing their elders or superiors, and yet in other sections of the country the use of such titles indicates sassiness on the part of the speaker. Folks who live in mountainous "parts" speak of "walking a fur piece toting a poke of taters" while those from Palm Springs "carry a bag of potatoes."

As a final example, a visitor from Canada jokingly remarked that Americans speak American while Canadians speak Canadian. What's the difference? English is English, right? Wrong. At first we didn't understand what our Northern neighbor meant when she said that she'd like to "visit a washroom before going to the plaza." Washroom is the Canadian term for restroom, and a plaza is a mall.

Ambiguous Words

Many English words have more than one meaning. Even a teeny-tiny word like *run* can be confusing because of its multiple usages.

Sports enthusiasts can hit home *runs*, *run* a mile, and afterward *run* a warm bath.

At work you can be given the *run-around* by an evasive supervisor and *run around* with co-workers all at the same time. Then, of course, there's the new employee who needs a *rundown* on a job operation. Her supervisor can *run* through the steps of making a computer *run* with her.

Ever had a *run-in* with a disagreeable person? Was it a chatterer who liked to *run off* at the mouth?

In language, clarity is everything.

A speaker can *run into* trouble if he fails to give his speech a *dry run* ahead of time. A woman can get a *run* in her hose, an average garment is *run of the mill*, and an unpainted building appears *rundown*.

When communicating with others, never forget that language, though invaluable, can be a barrier. As Confucius said, "In language, clarity is everything." Being clear, simple, and direct has its rewards. "When communication is really working, the experience can range from thrilling to deeply satisfying. When someone really hears you, there is an exquisite sense of relief and warmth and closeness. What a reward!"[8]

Emotional Barriers

Emotional barriers are more difficult to remove than language barriers.

Emotional barriers are more difficult to remove than are language barriers since they are rooted deep within us and concern our more personal, private feelings. In fact, sometimes the feelings are so private that they're unconscious, and we are not even aware of our feelings of greed, envy, or prejudice. Take a deep, honest, probing look within yourself. Do any of these emotional roadblocks need removing?

Stereotyping
Hostility

Charisma
Preoccupation
Role expectations
Self-concept

Stereotyping

Stereotyping hinders communication by putting a distance between you and others.

All people are guilty of stereotyping others into neat little categories according to age, race, sex, or geographic area. This is unfortunate. All teenagers are not irresponsible, all Italians are not terrific lovers, all women are not scatterbrained, and all Southerners are not illiterate. Expecting Germans to be neat and orderly, Japanese to be polite, and Italians to be emotional is expecting a broad and diverse group to be homogeneous. When you put labels on people according to one of the groups to which they belong, it hinders your communication by putting a distance between you and them.

Hostility

This negative attitude hampers our ability to send and receive messages. It's difficult to listen to job instructions from someone toward whom you feel ill will and animosity. That's too bad because sometimes good ideas and useful information can come from someone we dislike. Perhaps it's the sex, the clothing, the manner, or even the physical appearance of an individual which arouses our hostile attitude.

A closed mind is unteachable.

Hostility is felt toward subjects as well as the people who discuss them. Sometimes we just don't want our ideas and opinions challenged, so we refuse to listen. A closed mind is unteachable. Try to rid yourself of fixed attitudes and become more flexible. Along the same lines, closing your mind to such topics as communism, homosexuality, or drunk drivers ensures only that you won't learn anything.

Charisma

Charisma is a magnetism that attracts others.

Charisma is a special quality that some people possess; it's a magnetism that attracts others. Charisma can be a positive force, and yet it can also interfere with healthy communication because it closes minds as readily as does hostility. A person's charm and manner can cause another to listen and accept ideas and "follow the leader" even when the information is potentially harmful. It's as if the listener is blinded by the charismatic person's light and can't think clearly for himself. Need some examples? Would you agree that Hitler had charisma? What about Jim Jones?

Preoccupation

People can listen at twice the rate they can speak.

Communication experts agree that while most people utter between 120 and 180 words per minute, we can listen at twice that rate, or more— 300 to 350 words per minute! This time lag allows us plenty of time to think about other things—to become preoccupied. One student might daydream about his plans for the weekend, while another worries about making financial obligations. A secretary "listens" to a co-worker while planning her evening meal.

Role Expectation

A role is a part played by a person on the stage of life. You play several roles. A role expectation is how we expect ourselves and others to act based on our perceptions of stenographer, machinist, grocery shopper, father, minister, or teacher.

Although expecting a certain communication style from someone can be helpful, it can be harmful in at least two ways. Role expectations don't always allow others to change roles or to take on new ones. Mike, an assistant grocery store manager who began his career as bagboy is still reacted to by some as a bagboy. Fellow workers, even young Mike's subordinates, might fail to take him seriously in his new role and ignore his instructions and suggestions.

Also role expectations negatively affect good communication when people use the role itself to relate to others. A restaurant manager might expect others to do as he says because he says so, because he's the boss, the ultimate authority. Ask no questions. Make no suggestions. Employees are stuck with one way communication. How frustrating.

Self-Concept

Self-concept is a mental picture of what we believe about ourselves.

All individuals form mental pictures of themselves. This mental picture, or self-concept, is what we believe about ourselves and is a controlling factor in our communication with friends, family, and co-workers. How we self-appraise ourselves is coupled with reactions and responses of others in forming our self-concept. Verderber suggests several communication functions served by our personal mental pictures three of which are predictors of behavior, filter of statements, and influences of word choice and tone of voice.[9]

Predictor of Behavior: Possessors of positive self-concepts are more likely to speak in ways which predict positive experiences and expectations, while those with lower self-concepts speak in ways which predict negative experiences. Speech soon shapes reality, and predictions come true. A salesman says to himself, "I'm not dynamic enough. I just know I'll blow this sale." Sure enough, his worry, negative thoughts, and prediction of failure produce failure, and the confident dynamo next door makes the sale.

Filter of Statements: Our ears hear, but sometimes we only really listen to those words that reinforce our self-concept. Imagine yourself as a female bookkeeper in a fairly large organization. You have a good head for figures but don't perceive your numerical ability as extraordinary. Suppose your supervisor commends you on your work and conscientious attitude and suggests that with your brilliant intellect and discipline, you would become an accountant with a four-year degree. What? An accountant? Brilliant intellect? This woman's self-concept forces her to seek messages that reinforce her view of herself and screen out those that don't. If her supervisor's comments get past the filter, change in self-concept will occur. Our bookkeeper with a mediocre private mental picture could blossom into a chief accountant!

Influencer of Word Choice and Tone of Voice: Combine a whiny voice with negative words like "never," "not," "regret," "sorry," "cannot," and you'll find a speaker or writer with a negative self-concept every time. "Continued use of self-criticism, weakness, and self-doubt is often a sign of low self-esteem. On the other hand a speech style that is characterized by confidence, honest effort, and probability of success is a sign of positive self-concept."[10]

Physical Barriers

Physical barriers to communication are probably the least complicated.

Physical barriers to communication are probably the least complicated. Noise, distance, poor hearing, furniture arrangement, and inefficient mailing systems are a few examples of physical barriers. All these roadblocks are readily recognized and can be easily removed. A manager who asks for suggestions to improve morale while standing 15 feet away from his employees shouldn't expect an overwhelming response. To get the desired feedback, this manager should reduce the distance between him or her and the employees. He or she might even try sitting down on the subordinates' level instead of towering over them in an upright, superior position.

Suppose you have a personal problem, and your supervisor professes to have a total-person concept of the worker. In other words, he or she sees you as a person with problems, fears, worries, dreams, and fantasies, not just another pipe fitter. Recognizing from your downcast expression and listless attitude that you have a problem, this "caring" supervisor asks you to come in and talk things over. When you arrive, you find him or her behind the desk expecting you to sit on the other side of the desk. How open will you be? How sincere is the supervisor in wanting to listen to your worrisome woes? The desk is a physical barrier to communication. The counseling role of this supervisor's job would be en-

hanced if a chair were placed beside the desk, a more informal furniture arrangement.

Consider noise for a moment. As a roadblock to communication, noise can usually be easily controlled. Shut the door. Turn off the whirring, roaring machine. Go to a quiet room. Don't just turn off that television. Unplug it!

Temperature, light, and color can all act as stimulants or deterrents to communication.

Verderber suggests that temperature, light, and color can all act as both stimulants and deterrents to communication, depending on the situation.[11] Since Americans are most comfy when the temperature is between 68 and 75 degrees, don't confess the details of your latest romance to a co-worker in a stuffy, overheated room. If he yawns, you'd get your dander up and assume that he's bored instead of just deenergized by the room temperature. Bright light encourages good listening while dim lighting encourages intimate conversation. Finally, the variable of color is important in determining behavior. Red, orange, and yellow are stimulating, exciting. It's almost impossible to read a technical report with concentration in a red room. Blue and green have a calming, soothing effect. Remember that fact whenever you have to give someone bad news.

NONVERBAL COMMUNICATION

Words convey 35 percent of a message while nonverbal signs convey 65 percent.

Nonverbal communication, or body language as it is more popularly called, is as important in getting a message across as is verbal communication—perhaps even more so. Mehrabian estimates that as much as 90 percent of the total message communicated is nonverbal. Other communication scholars suggest that words convey 35 percent of the meaning communicated, while nonverbal signs such as gestures, postures, and clothing convey the remaining 65 percent.

To illustrate further the importance of nonverbal communication, if there's a discrepancy (or contradiction) between what your words say and what your body says, well, actions really do speak louder than words. We can plan our speech, but as Julius Fast, author of *Body Language* contends, "Your body doesn't know how to lie." To prove his point, Fast tells a story in which a young woman told her psychiatrist that "she loved her boyfriend very much while nodding her head from side to side in subconscious denial."[12]

You've been observing and interpreting nonverbal communication all your life. However, you can improve your understanding of others' nonverbal messages by learning more about kinesics (body language), proxemics (distance), paralanguage (vocal cues), and object language (dress, hairstyle, etc.).

Kinesics

Kinesics consists of gestures, facial expressions, and posture.

Kinesics is more commonly referred to as body language and consists primarily of gestures, facial expressions, and posture. Although people worldwide smile when they feel pleasure and frown when they feel displeasure, there are very few absolutes in the science of kinesics. A smile can mean pleasure, but it can also mean amusement, sarcasm, or even apology. What the nonverbal message means depends upon the context, both cultural and physical, and upon the person's personality. Crossed arms can mean:

"Stay away."
"Help me, I'm locked in."
"I'm cold."
"Don't intrude on my private world."
"I'm afraid."

The meaning of nonverbal messages depends upon the context in which they occur and the person's personality.

Crossing one's arms across the body can mean simply that the person has to do something with the limbs, so don't jump to conclusions.

Cultural differences should be considered in an increasingly small world. Americans nod their heads up and down to indicate yes and from side to side to indicate no. In some societies in India just the opposite is true. Maintaining eye contact is a sign of respect and goodwill for most Americans. Some Hispanics feel that looking a superior in the eye, whether boss or parent, is a sign of disrespect. Many people assume that nonverbal communication is universal, and it definitely is not.

* Waving good-by is a good way to summon a Filipino.
* The typical thumbs-up gesture is offensive to Arabs.
* The left hand is considered unclean in many cultures (often relating to matters of hygiene); hence, eating with left hand is taboo in some places.
* In many cultures—China, for example—there is no inhibition against staring; most Americans are made uncomfortable by it.
* It is not uncommon or Arab men to walk hand-in-hand or to kiss each other when meeting or leaving; it is also in no way a form of sexual contact, although Americans instinctively react to it that way.[13]

The individual's personality should be considered when interpreting body language. Some people look glum and forlorn because of their nature, not because they had a bad day or because you hurt their feelings. Occasionally, the author has known students who smiled more frequently than the "norm." Smiling is generally perceived as positive, but there was something disconcerting about these smiles. In questioning the students about their amusement, it became obvious that smiling was just a natural expression of their happy, optimistic outlooks, not an expression of amusement or humor.

Categories of Nonverbal Behavior

A discussion of kinesics would be incomplete without a brief mention of the five categories of nonverbal behavior:[14]

1. *Emblems.* These directly suggest specific words or phrases. A beckoning gesture with the forefinger or entire hand means "Come hither."

2. *Illustrators.* These gestures and expressions reinforce the verbal message. A downward thrust of the hand means, "Don't bug me with that!"

3. *Affect Displays.* These are movements or expressions of the face that convey emotional meaning. If eyes are indeed the windows of the soul, then they can show love, hate, interest, or disinterest. In fact, the pupil of the eye dilates when one is aroused by a pleasant sight, be it a loved one, a sunset, an ice cream sundae, or a paycheck.

4. *Regulators.* These messages regulate the communication of others. Nodding your head indicates that you understand your supervisor's instructions and that you want him to continue. The boss looking at his watch indicates to you that his time is valuable.

5. *Adaptors.* These messages are the most difficult classification of cues to define because they change from person to person and from situation to situation. They're viewed as efforts to satisfy personal needs that arise as people relate to each other. Posture, facial expressions, gestures, and even eye contact vary as you communicate with different people.

Think about the body language of co-workers, friends, loved ones, and bosses. If a friend quickly removes his glasses when you are talking to him, it can signal displeasure. If you observe a woman fidgeting with her necklace or touching her neck, she could be showing anxiety and the need for reassurance.[15] According to Mehrabian, liking is expressed by leaning forward, a direct body orientation, greater closeness, a relaxed posture, open arms and body, positive facial expressions, and more eye contact.[16] Is this true for you? Power is expressed by more expansive gestures and less eye contact. Notice the way your employer reacts to you nonverbally.

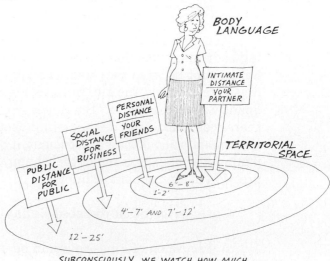

SUBCONSCIOUSLY WE WATCH HOW MUCH SPACE WE PUT BETWEEN OURSELVES AND OTHERS.

Proxemics

Proxemics refers to use of space.

Proxemics is a word coined by anthropologist Edward T. Hall and means the use of space.[17] Two concepts, territoriality and personal space, should be considered when studying proxemics.

Territory is one's own space and is generally immovable and usually separate from the person. Although their names are not branded on territory, people have their own parking spaces, seats in classrooms, and personal chairs at the dining room table. Have you ever seen a person walk into a cafeteria and distribute her newspaper, books, purse, coat, and other belongings on the table and on the surrounding chairs? She's simply marking her territory.

Edward Hall has determined four distances that people regularly use.

Personal space moves with you. It's like a 2-foot imaginary bubble surrounding you and keeping you at a distance from others. Hall has designated four distances that people regularly use. The *intimate* distance extends from touch to 18 inches and is reserved for close, private encounters. The *personal* distance is from 18 inches to 2 feet and includes a variety of conversations from personal to newsy, formal to informal. *Social* distance, 4 to 12 feet, is recognized as the appropriate space for people conducting business, while the *public distance*, over 12 feet, is used in public speaking situations.

As in the study of kinesics, there are several variables to consider when interpreting distance. What are the characteristics of the people involved? What about their cultural background? What is the nature of their relationship? This excerpt from Fast's *Body Language* illustrates the proxemics of people at work.

> The "big boss" will walk into his subordinate's office unannounced. The subordinate will wait outside the boss's office until he is permitted in. If the boss is on the phone, the subordinate may tiptoe off and come back later. If the subordinate is on the phone, the boss will usually assert his status by standing above the subordinate until he murmurs, "Let me call you back," and then gives the boss his full attention.[18]

Paralanguage

Paralanguage consists of the vocal cues that accompany the spoken word.

Paralanguage consists of all oral aspects of language except for the words themselves, the vocal cues that accompany the spoken word. Fast states that we all speak at least two languages—the words themselves and the meanings behind and within and around the words. Paralanguage is a type of communication that sometimes strengthens and sometimes weakens or sometimes even contradicts the words we use. Speakers use paralanguage to show irony, tenderness, sarcasm, sincerity, disgust, and anger. Variations in pitch, rate, volume, quality, and emphasis can supplement and even contradict the words we use.

Pitch is defined as the highness or lowness of a sound on the musical scale. In general, men have lower-pitched voices than do women. Changes in pitch indicate variations in meaning. For example, women tend to end declarative statements with an upward inflection, which suggests a question, not a declaration. Why do you think this is so?

Changes in pitch indicate variations in meaning.

How rapidly or slowly a person speaks is her *rate*. Be careful when interpreting a speaker's rate. Some people speak rapidly because it's characteristic of them, others because they're anxious to get the message out, and yet others because they're nervous. Speaking slowly in a low-pitched voice could signal fatigue or even depression, but then again, maybe the speaker is a man with a low-pitched Southern drawl.

Volume is the loudness or softness of sounds.

Volume is the loudness or softness of sounds. For example, when angry, we speak loudly, but when we are speaking tenderly to a loved one, our voices lower. Mothers worldwide calm their babies with identical soft, soothing sounds, and the babies get the message and are comforted whether actual words are spoken or not.

As an additional example of volume, Fast says that men often feel free to dominate women vocally and in return many women use a soft voice against this kind of domination. The meaning behind the softly spoken words is, "Don't attack me because I am helpless against the aggressive onslaught of your voice. I am lowering my own to show how defenseless I am."[19]

The pleasant and unpleasant characteristics of a voice combine to form vocal *quality*. There are whiny voices, bombastic voices, raspy voices, and all indicate something about the speaker's personality and mood. It's been said that the voice is an index of the speaker's character.

Finally, *emphasis* is also a paralanguage characteristic. The manner in which a person stresses or emphasizes a word or phrase can change the meaning of a sentence. Try saying, "Your friends are in the kitchen" and emphasize a different word each time.

Object Language

Object language consists of hairstyle, dress, cosmetics, and jewelry.

Object language consisting of hairstyle, dress, cosmetics, and jewelry makes a statement about an individual. Your object language gives a message to others about your personality, your age, your role, your socioeconomic status, and group membership. While men don't usually wear dresses in our society, they do have a variety of clothing from which to choose. What does wearing a business suit to a job interview instead of an open-necked shirt displaying several gold neck chains say about a man? What statement does a neat, conservative hairstyle make about a person? Does trendy, faddish clothing indicate anything about a woman's personality and taste?

LISTENING

Approximately 40 percent of your waking hours are spent listening.

Listening is more than a skill; it's an art. You spend more of your waking, working hours listening, approximately 40 percent, than speaking, reading, or writing, and yet most people listen inefficiently. Research indicates "that we operate at almost precisely a 25 percent level of efficiency when listening to a ten-minute talk."[20]

Importance of Listening

All our relationships can be enhanced by improving our listening skills. A person who listens attentively to job instructions can save herself and her supervisor time and effort. Good listening is especially important for a supervisor since keeping an open, receptive ear and mind helps this person understand motives and aspirations of employees. A manager who listens knows about morale, potential problems, worries, and concerns that a nonlistening manager is unaware of. Many employees equate a "caring" supervisor with a "listening" supervisor.

One Dozen Ways to Improve Listening

There are many techniques for improving listening. The following are a dozen designed to make you a good listener, the kind described by Nichols as "a sifter, a screener, a winnower of the wheat from the chaff. He or she is always trying to find something practical or worthwhile to store away in the back part of the brain and put to work for his or her own selfish benefit in the months to come."[21]

1. *Adopt a positive attitude*. You should want to listen. Someone once remarked that not only is a good listener popular everywhere he goes, but after a while, he learns something. Look at the other person—her face, gestures, expressions, and posture are all telling you something.
2. *Don't evaluate*. Arguing mentally with the speaker sets up a barrier between you and him. Don't pass judgment or be supercritical.
3. *Don't anticipate*. How can you really listen when anticipating the speaker's words?
4. *Act the part*. Sit up straight. Lean slightly forward. To demonstrate your interest, don't look at the floor or out the window but at the other person. "Eyes are the key nonverbal indicator. Eye contact indicates a desire for communication or feedback and friendliness. Lack of eye contact may indicate either dislike or lack of interest."[22]

   Encourage the speaker with appropriate gestures and expressions. Smiling helps. So does nodding. Acting the part is referred to as "giving feedback."
5. *Leave emotions behind*. Forget your worries, fears, doubts, stereotyped thinking, and other emotional barriers. Don't get so excited or overstimulated that you react unfavorably.
6. *Concentrate on the main points*. Examples, stories, statistics, and anecdotes are important only as they prove the main ideas. Good listeners remember the broader picture, not just facts and details.
7. *Stop talking*. How can you listen and talk at the same time? Don't interrupt with your comments even though it's a human tendency to want to jump right in. That's as rude as stepping on someone's toes.

8. *Share responsibility for communication.* The speaker is only partially responsible for getting the message across. Ask questions if you don't understand instead of imagining that the speaker can read your mind.

9. *Use the difference in rate to your advantage.* Since you can listen to and analyze 300 to 500 words per minute when a speaker speaks approximately 120 to 180 words per minute, shouldn't you use that lag time to your advantage? Think about what the speaker is saying and relate it to your experiences.

10. *Review what's been said from time to time.* Review what's already been spoken and tie the message together.

11. *Take notes* if appropriate. You can't remember everything. An old Chinese proverb says, "Even the palest ink is better than the best memory."

12. *Resist distractions.* Don't shuffle with papers, look at a third party, or wind your watch. Not only will it prevent you from listening well, but it might also discourage the speaker from telling you something valuable.

EXERCISE

Read the following list of words and try to think of adjectives with a more positive connotation.

Gabby
Sly
Stubborn
Plain
Picky
Skinny
Touchy
Obese

SAY IT ONE MORE TIME—WITH FEELING

As you know, how you say something is just as important as what you say. Paralanguage allows us to show disgust, frustration, excitement, sarcasm, joy, or sadness just by changing our tone of voice, pitch, volume, or rate. To get a little practice, follow these directions:

1. Say, "That's just terrific!" at least three different times to show the three distinctly different emotions of joy, sarcasm, and anger.

   Say, "I'm sorry," sincerely, sarcastically, regretfully, and finally resentfully.

2. Say, "I asked Kimberly to write the memo," several times and emphasize a different word each time. Does the shifting emphasis change the meaning of the statement?

   Do the same thing with, "Your mother is in the living room."

   And, finally, "Your son is in the spelling bee."

COMMUNICATION REGULATORS QUIZ
TEST YOUR NONVERBAL ABILITY

Simple observation has taught you a lot about nonverbal messages. You know what message is conveyed when someone shakes his or her head, smiles warmly at a friend, or looks away when asked embarrassing questions. Not content to call such behavior "body language," communication scholars have designated labels for different types of nonverbal expressions.

After reading the definitions of these communication messages, test yourself on your ability to differentiate among them. Match each of the following expressions with its appropriate label.

_____ 1. A stylized nonverbal gesture that serves as a substitute for words such as a wave.

_____ 2. Nodding your head rapidly at someone who's in the middle of an explanation of something you already know.

_____ 3. Folding your arms across your body when you disagree with a person's ideas.

_____ 4. Using your hands to describe the size of the fish that got away in the fishing tournament.

_____ 5. Pointing your finger at a book on a table while asking someone to bring it to you.

_____ 6. Smiling happily when seeing a loved one approach.

a. emblem
b. affect display
c. illustrator
d. regulator
e. adaptor

Answers

1. a   2. d   3. e   4. c   5. c   6. b

CASE STUDY

Neyle Wiggins

Neyle Wiggins, a branch manager of a savings and loan institution, has two very unhappy tellers in his office. He knows that, to a customer, the teller represents the bank itself, and he wants to get this problem cleared up pronto. Both women are practically seething with anger toward each other. In an effort to be fair and to get a true picture of whatever led to this ill will, Neyle has asked each employee to tell her side of the story.

Susan has been a teller in the bank for three years. Until four weeks ago she was head teller, but because of her upcoming marriage and relocation, she relinquished her position to Gloria Parker, a young woman Susan's age, 25. Gloria has worked at the savings and loan institution for two years, one year less than Susan. The rationale behind the job switch was that it would make the transition period following Susan's departure easier if she could train her own replacement, thereby giving the replacement time to fulfill her new responsibilities under the knowing eyes of an "old pro." In fact, the idea of stepping down was Susan's.

Although both women were efficient and competent, they had far different temperaments. Susan was relaxed and laid back. She never stood over the tellers while they balanced, or barked out orders, or went into a tizzy when something went wrong. If someone had a question, she answered it patiently. If someone occasionally needed to run an extra errand during the lunch hour, it was okay with Susan. Gloria, on the other hand, was energy plus, a real dynamo. She requested that the other tellers come in an extra ten minutes early every morning to be sure everything was shipshape. If someone failed to come in early and if later she happened to run out of deposit slips, coins, or suckers for the children, woe be unto her. Gloria would remind the teller by words and actions that she had "told her so." It's not that Gloria was a domineering taskmaster. She was really just a hard worker who wanted everyone else to be hard workers too.

The others tellers, especially Susan, resented this sort of management style, and matters had come to a head the afternoon before, at closing time. The bank had closed for business, and the tellers had balanced their machines and were preparing to leave. Susan was in a frantic hurry since she had to meet with the photographer about wedding photographs. As she was leaving, Susan heard Gloria say, "Hey Susan, check the vault!" Angry about Gloria's recent treatment of her and preoccupied with the photography session ahead, Susan retorted, "Check it yourself! It's your job!"

Gloria was flabbergasted by Susan's angry response. She claims that she *asked* Susan whether she had checked the vault, not *ordered* her to do it. Gloria remembers her comment being, "Hey, Susan, have you checked the vault?" and can't believe that Susan got so angry and upset. In fact, Gloria sees checking the vault as something only she, Susan, or Neyle could do and feels that it was a compliment to Susan to be asked.

1. If you were Neyle, what kind of a problem would you label this?
2. If it is a communication problem, what type is it? What is causing the misunderstanding among the women?
3. What action can be taken to correct this situation?

SUMMARY

Barriers to communicate can result in disruptions in productivity, rifts in relationships, decline of motivation, and growth of hostility. Three barriers to communication are language, emotional, and physical.

It is ironic that language, the basis of oral communication, is one of the most prevalent causes of misunderstanding. Foreign language, slang expressions, technical jargon, complex words, connotation differences, and ambiguous terms all hinder communication. To overcome language barriers, a person should communicate with an awareness that the words she uses might not mean the same to the listener as they do to her. Choosing words carefully and being clear and simple is good advice.

Emotional barriers concern our personal and private feelings and are more difficult to remove than are language barriers, especially since we are sometimes unaware of these feelings. Stereotyping, hostility, charisma, preoccupation, role expectations, and self-concept are some of the emotional barriers which hamper our ability to send and receive messages.

Since physical barriers to communication are the least complicated of the roadblocks, they are usually easily recognized and easily removed. A few examples of these barriers are noise, distance, temperature, and furniture arrangement.

Communication scholars suggest that nonverbal communication conveys as much as 65 percent of a message while words convey only 35 percent. Four types of nonverbal communication are kinesics, proxemics, paralanguage, and object language.

Kinesics is more commonly referred to as body language and consists primarily of gestures, facial expressions, and posture. Although some nonverbal behavior is universal, what a message really means depends on the context and on the person's personality. For example, maintaining eye contact is a sign of respect and goodwill for most Americans, but some Hispanics feel that looking a superior in the eye is a sign of disrespect.

Verderber has categorized nonverbal behavior as emblems, illustrators, affect displays, regulators, and adaptors.

Proxemics means use of space. Territoriality and personal space are key concepts of proxemics. Edward Hall has designated four distances that people regularly use when communicating with others: intimate, personal, social, and public.

Paralanguage consists of all oral aspects of language except the words themselves. Included in this category of vocal cues are pitch, rate, volume, quality, and emphasis. They can supplement and even contradict the words we use.

Object language consists of hairstyle, dress, cosmetics, and jewelry. It gives an unspoken message to others about your personality, age, role, and socioeconomic status.

Although we spend more of our waking hours listening than we do using any other communication skill, we listen rather inefficiently. All relationships can be enhanced by it. A few ways to improve listening are to adopt a positive attitude, leave emotions behind, review what's been said from time to time, and resist distractions.

KEY TERMS

Perceptions

Slang

Technical jargon
Emotional barriers
Language barriers
Physical barriers
Role expectation
Nonverbal communication
Julius Fast
Edward T. Hall
Kinesics
Proxemics
Paralanguage
Object language
Emblems
Illustrators
Affect displays
Regulators
Adaptors
Territory
Personal space

REVIEW AND DISCUSSION QUESTIONS

1. What are three of the primary barriers to communication? Give examples of each.

2. Why are emotional barriers more difficult to remove than language or physical barriers?

3. Discuss specifically how communication can be affected (influenced) by self-concept.

4. How can nonverbal communication communicate meaning? What are at least four areas of nonverbal communication?

5. How can object language affect a job interview? Be as specific as possible.

6. What are some advantages of improving listening?

7. What are at least eight ways to improve listening?

ENDNOTES

[1] ADAPTED FROM OSMO WIIO, *Wiio's Laws—and Some Others* (Espoo, Finland: Welin-Goos, 1978).

[2] PAUL R. TIMM, "The Way We Word," *Supervisory Management*, 23 (1978), pp. 20–26.

[3] DICK SCHAAF, "The Growing Need for Cross-Cultural and Bilingual Training," *Training/HRD*, January 1981, p. 85.

[4] JOHN T. KENNA, "The Latinization of the U.S.," *1983 Britannica Book of the Year* (Chicago: Encyclopedia Britannica, 1983), pp. 586–587.

[5] CHRISTOPHER BATES DOOB, *Sociology: An Introduction* (New York: Holt, Rinehart and Winston, 1985), p. 252.

[6] LANCE MORROW, "If Slang Is Not a Sin," *Time*, November 8, 1982, p. 91.

[7] JOHN R. PELSMA, *Essentials of Speech* (New York: Crowell, Collier, and Macmillan, 1934), p. 193.

[8] EILEEN MAZER, "How to Say What's Really on Your Mind," *Prevention*, September 1981, p. 121.

[9] RANDOLPH F. VERDERBER, *Communicate!* (Belmont, Calif.: Wadsworth, 1981), pp. 30–32.

[10] IBID., p. 32.

[11] IBID., pp. 64–65.

[12] JULIUS FAST, *Body Language* (New York: M. Evans, distributed in association with Lippincott, 1970), p. 9.

[13] SCHAAF, "The Growing Need for Cross-Cultural and Bilingual Training," pp. 85–86.

[14] PAUL EKMAN AND W. V. FRIESEN, "The Repertoire of Nonverbal Behavior: Categories, Origins, Usage, and Coding," *Semiotica*, 1 (1969), pp. 49–98.

[15] GERARD I. NIERENBERG AND HENRY H. CALERO, *How to Read a Person Like a Book* (New York: Hawthorne Books, 1971), p. 75.

[16] ALBERT MEHRABIAN, *Silent Messages* (Belmont, Calif.: Wadsworth, 1971), pp. 113–118.

[17] EDWARD T. HALL, *The Silent Language* (Garden City, N.Y.: Doubleday, 1959), pp. 163–164.

[18] FAST, *Body Language*, p. 48.

[19] JULIUS AND BARBARA FAST, *Talking Between the Lines* (New York: Viking Press, 1979), p. 29.

[20] RALPH G. NICHOLS, "Do We Know How to Listen: Practical Helps in a Modern Age," *The Speech Teacher*, 10:2 (March 1961), 120.

[21] ERNEST G. BORMAN AND OTHERS, *Interpersonal Communication in the Modern Organization* (Englewood Cliffs, N.J.: Prentice Hall, 1982), p. 124.

[22] WALTER D. ST. JOHN, "You Are What You Communicate," *Personnel Journal*, October 1985, p. 42.

chapter 5

Relationships at Work

After reading and studying this chapter, you will be able to:

1. State the advantages of good work relationships.
2. Explain the concept of group dynamics.
3. Describe specific ways of showing friendliness that aid in improved work relations.
4. Discuss components of communication often overlooked at work.
5. List ways of coping with worrisome behavior and conflict.
6. Elaborate on five conflict resolution styles.
7. Describe ways of improving your relationship with your boss.

I will pay more for the ability to deal with people than any other ability under the sun.

John D. Rockefeller

They come in all shapes, sizes, and colors. At times, they brag, complain, or argue. If that's not bad enough, they have irritating, obnoxious habits and mannerisms. One blows cigarette smoke in your face, another chatters incessantly, and a third slaps you on the back while telling off-color jokes. These are the people you work with, your co-workers and your boss.

Most of us have no control over our work partners or bosses. We're more or less stuck with an assortment of personalities for eight hours per day. Why not make the best of it? Getting along with your co-workers and boss can prove to be very productive for you in many ways. Nathaniel Stewart writes, "From factory workers to executives, workers express the need to be with people, make social contacts, and possibly build friendships."[1] A work relationship can stay just that or it can blossom into a meaningful part of your life. It's more likely that you'll become friends with those who live or work in close proximity, and even though co-workers are there because of accidental proximity, deep, genuine friendship often develops as this passage from *Winning Friends at Work* indicates:

> While he was modest and seldom talked about himself, I gradually came to learn from other co-workers about his wide range of interests. As a merchant seaman he traveled widely, was a certified meteorologist and navigator, knew the world of nature extensively and could discuss plant and animal life with great knowledge and devotion. In addition, he had been a pharmacist's mate aboard a ship, knew real estate and home-building, and had put three children through college. He would quote from literature and the arts. While he was a welder by trade, he far surpassed his college-bred children as an educated person. And, what a gifted conversationalist!
>
> I must confess that I deliberately sought him out as a friend so that I could learn from him. For all his modesty, most every workday was a stimulating day for me—and an educational one.[2]

ADVANTAGES OF GOOD WORK RELATIONSHIPS

To a degree, mental and physical health depends on the quality of relationships with others.

Some of the advantages of good work relationships include increased productivity, emotional support, improved communication, career success, high morale, increased knowledge, and cooperation. Work friends can help you meet deadlines, increase your self-esteem, stand up for you, help you solve problems, and lend a helping hand. To a degree, mental and physical health depends on the quality of relationships with others. Building and maintaining cooperative, interdependent relationships with others is often cited as a indication of physical health. Otherwise, people run the risk of being anxious, depressed, frustrated, and alienated.

You're with your co-workers at least 40 hours a week. You've everything to gain and nothing to lose from improving the quality of your relationships with others both individually and in a group. Maybe you don't want to become pals forever with everyone. You have a nodding acquaintance that satisfies your social needs at work. Fine. You don't have to build friendships to last throughout the ages with your workmates. You do have to work with, through, and for them, though, and it's nice to have their cooperation to benefit from another's knowledge and expertise in a given area. It's also gratifying to be in on things if there's something you need to know that affects your job.

GROUP DYNAMICS

Informal groups meet a variety of individual needs not met by the formal organization.

A knowledge of group dynamics and the social nature of workers is important. Small, informal groups arise in the workplace, groups that do not appear on organizational charts and yet strongly influence organizational effectiveness. The groups develop to meet a variety of individual needs that are not met by the formal organization. Group members identify with one another, influence one another's behavior, and contribute to mutual need satisfaction.

Research has identified a number of areas where informal groups meet the needs of their members:

* *Companionship.* Group affiliation provides an opportunity for close association with others which in itself is a source of satisfaction. It enables someone to avoid the pain of loneliness and the ego-crushing experience of rejection.
* *Reassurance and Support.* Just knowing that one other person is supportive may give someone the courage to express a conviction or take a stand on an important issue.
* *Reduction of Tension.* Informal groups often contribute to a reduction of internal tension through humor and horseplay that prevent members from taking themselves and their work too seriously.

WHEN YOU MEET
A PERSON WITHOUT
A SMILE, GIVE HIM
ONE OF YOURS.

* *Sense of Identity.* A group gives members a sense of personal identity, a sense of being somebody.
* *Improved Communications.* When workers are ignorant concerning actions that affect their welfare, informal groups often provide information.[3]

Behavior expectations are known as norms.

Groups also set standards of acceptable behavior and expect members to follow those standards. These behavior expectations are known as norms. Norms express the collective values of a group and provide guidelines for member behavior in achieving group and individual goals. An example of a group norm might be that one worker should not put out so much effort that the other workers look lazy and unproductive by comparison. This behavior is more likely to occur in a group of people whose jobs provide little chance for job satisfaction or promotion. Workers also understand that they are not to discuss anything derogatory about a co-worker with management. In a more competitive situation when promotion is possible and desirable, the norms might be different. For example, superior performance might be expected, and anything less than good quality work and high productivity is frowned on.

Since norms are usually unwritten and unspoken, they are not always obvious to a new worker.

Norms of an establishment are not always immediately apparent to a new worker. Since they are for the most part unwritten and undiscussed, a new hiree has to be observant and perceptive. What type of clothing do employees wear? How much time is really in a lunch hour? Do employees discuss salary and management decisions among themselves? If there is a work-related problem, do they talk to the immediate supervisor, resolve it themselves, or pretend that it doesn't exist?

GETTING ALONG WITH CO-WORKERS

Many people cling to unproductive, unskilled ways of reaching out to others. Getting along does require skill. It's not an innate, natural gift. However, there are some tried and proven methods of building and maintaining relationships which we'll explore in this chapter. These methods are not just contemporary means thought up by ivory tower psychologists. Some of them are borrowed from the lives and writings of such greats as Benjamin Franklin and Dale Carnegie.

Facets of Friendliness

Use positive reinforcement in the form of appreciation and praise.

Showing appreciation and giving sincere praise are methods of confirming another as an important, worthwhile, unique human being. "All of us are self-centered, suckers for a bit of praise, and generally like to think of ourselves as winners. We all think we're tops. We're exuberantly, wildly irrational about ourselves."[4] Since all people are somewhat self-centered, they hunger for appreciation, and it doesn't take much creativity to discover ways to make them feel important. Remember their birthday. Tell them they have handsome children (if they do). Compliment the lady who works next to you on her new haircut. Often people think positive things about others but are reluctant to speak up. Do it. It'll make the other person fell great. Mary Kay Ash, owner of Mary Kay Cosmetics says to imagine people wearing an invisible sign which reads, "MAKE ME FEEL IMPORTANT."[5]

Dale Carnegie, author of *How to Win Friends and Influence People*, was a great believer in the stupendous power of heartfelt appreciation. A phrase seen several times throughout his book is, "Be hearty in your approbation, and lavish in your praise."[6] This phrase was borrowed from Charles Schwab, president of Bethlehem Steel. Schwab believed that his greatest asset was his ability to develop what was the best in a person by appreciation and encouragement. B. F. Skinner, the renowned behavioral psychologist, asserts that positive reinforcement, in this case praise, is the basic concept for modifying behavior. Praise someone and his behavior will continue. Fail to do so and it might become extinct.

How often have you been quick to criticize or condemn a fellow worker for something? Have you ever let any opportunities go by when you could have complimented someone? Maybe you like the way your boss handles conflict. Tell her so. Perhaps you admire the diligence of the machinist next to you. Let him know. If you like the receptionist's new frock, speak up. Quit thinking so much of yourself. Think of the other person's good points and let him or her know about it. This advice applies to workers in offices, shops, schools, hospitals, markets, and factories. Never forget that your associates are human and hunger for appreciation.

Use a little empathy.

Empathy differs from sympathy. Sympathy means feeling sorry for someone, but empathy means feeling with someone. Before you condemn, judge, or criticize, try to see things from the other person's point of view. "People who can put themselves in the place of other people, who can understand the workings of their minds, need never worry about what the future has in store for them."[7]

Success in dealing with co-workers depends on an understanding of their viewpoints. Why does that braggart boast so of his accomplishments? What causes the fellow next to you to criticize others constantly? Why does your boss seem to delight in putting subordinates in their place? There's always a reason why a person acts and thinks as she does. Try to put yourself in her place, in her shoes, and see things from her perspective. The world looks totally different to all of us because of different experiences.

Be friendly.

You don't have to go overboard. Don't invite someone whom you can barely tolerate to go bowling with you. There's no sense in making yourself miserable just to get along with someone. On the other hand, speaking to someone by name and smiling are two practices that cost little but add a lot to another's feeling of self-esteem. These practices cause people to feel better about themselves. Most people are more interested in their own names than any other, and it's irritating to be called Jean when your name is June or Tom when your name is Don. It makes you wonder whether the other person is really interested enough in you to remember your name.

Paying attention to a person's features, size, and expression helps you to remember their names.

Many people claim that they can't remember another's name when the truth is that they're too lazy to take the extra few seconds to concentrate and memorize names. Most individuals are introduced to strangers and forget their names before the conversation is over. How can you improve your ability to remember names? Take a memory course

---

HELLO EUNICE

Remembering a person's name and using it really works in establishing good interpersonal relationships. Dale Carnegie provides an excellent example.

Ken Nottingham, an employee of General Motors in Indiana, usually had lunch at the company cafeteria. He noticed that the woman who worked behind the counter always had a scowl on her face. "She had been making sandwiches for about two hours and I was just another sandwich to her. I told her what I wanted. She weighed out the ham on a little scale, then she gave me one leaf of lettuce, a few potato chips and handed them to me."

The next day I went through the same line. Same woman, same scowl. The only difference was I noticed her name tag. I smiled and said, "Hello, Eunice'"and then told her what I wanted. Well, she forgot the scale, piled on the ham, gave me three leaves of lettuce and heaped on the potato chips until they feel off the plate."

Dale Carnegie, *How to Win Friends and Influence People* (New York: Pocket Books, 1981), p. 83.

if you want to invest the time and money. For now, just try to insert the name in your conversation several times. Try "Do you live around here, June?" or "What'd you think of the game, Don?" If the name is unusual, ask the person to spell it. Meanwhile, pay attention to your new acquaintance's features, size, expression, and overall appearance.

Greeting someone with a smile is another aspect of being friendly. Some individuals resent the way Americans greet each other by the ritual exchange that goes something like this:

"Hello, how are you?"
"Fine, and you?"
"Great."
"Have a good day."
"Yeah, you too."

Parallaction recognizes and acknowledges the presence of others.

Communication scholars scorn this exchange and call it *parallaction*, a term for pseudo interaction in which people appear to be having an exchange, and yet there is no involvement with each other. Parallaction means that the communication is parallel, and independent and has no intersection. The real purpose of this pseudo interaction is to recognize or acknowledge the presence of another. While communication scholars scoff and call parallaction a form of noncommunication, most people would rather be acknowledged and recognized than ignored or snubbed.

To make all exchanges more rewarding, try smiling. In the preceding chapter on communication (Chapter 4), you were reminded that actions speak louder than words, that nonverbal expressions communicate more meaning than words. A smile communicates warmth, pleasure, and happiness. It means, "I'm glad to see you today. You're a nice person to work with."

Parallaction

Smile at your spouse, your co-workers, your boss, the tax auditor, the highway patrolman. If it seems unnatural for you and against your nature, try it anyway. Force yourself to smile even when you don't feel like it. Since many psychologists believe that feeling follows action, that happy feeling might just follow action. Most of the time smiles and greetings will be returned, and the workplace will be much more pleasant. A smile conveys goodwill, liking, and a positive attitude. Besides, it improves your face value. Everyone benefits.

Show an interest in your co-workers.

"I" is the most frequently used word in the English language.

The most frequently used word in the English language has to be "I." "I" like carrots. "I" don't like your attitude. "I" had a rough night. "I" think "I'm" overworked. So what? How thoughtless it is to force another to listen to your accounts of personal preferences, activities, and interests. In the words of Benjamin Franklin, "A man wrapped up in himself makes a very small bundle."

Give the other person a chance to speak. Ask questions about his hobbies, grandchildren, or latest project. Get her involved in talking about her latest vacation, roses, or new career. Let people talk about themselves, and they'll think you're the greatest conversationalist around. People are interested in us when we are interested in them.

Try a little common courtesy.

It's often remarked that people treat family members with rudeness and discourtesy because they take them for granted. It's often the same

---

A MINI COURSE IN HUMAN RELATIONS

The Six Most Important Words
I admit I made a mistake.

The Five Most Important Words
You did a good job.

The Four Most Important Words
What is your opinion?

The Three Most Important Words
Will you please?

The Two Most Important Words
Thank you.

The Most Important Word
We

The Least Important Word
I

at work. You see work friends day in and day out, and you begin to take their presence and your relationships for granted. Don't allow that to happen. Take the time for simple courtesies. Open the door for a woman. Even if she's a liberated woman, she'll appreciate it. Say thanks to someone who explains a complicated diagram to you. Say please to your boss when you're asking for clarification of instructions.

Men, like bullets, go farthest when they are smoothest. Jean Paul Richter

Courtesy costs nothing but gains much, both for individuals and their companies, so be considerate of others, no matter what their position. If you're always inconsiderate of others, how can you expect them to be cooperative? To lend you a helping hand? To listen if you have a problem?

Components of Communication

Develop your listening skills.

Good listening is an art which most people don't come by naturally. They have to work at it. The chapter on communication offers guidelines to improve your listening skills. The most important technique to remember is to let your whole attitude convey, "I'm interested in what you have to say." For present purposes, let's look at ways in which listening to your co-workers and boss can improve work and personal relationships.

The workplace is filled with people experiencing every emotion known to man. At any given time some feel joy and others deep despair. Whatever the feeling, it needs to be shared. Lend an ear. Giving someone the opportunity to tell you about a rewarding experience, a funny incident, or a basic philosophy of life adds to their good humor and to yours. Encourage people to talk about themselves and their accomplishments since most are more interested in themselves than in anyone or anything else. A shin splint to a jogger is far more important at that moment than are all the hungry children in Africa.

Resist the impulse to judge or give advice while listening.

People who are blue, depressed, or worried can also benefit from your listening. Sometimes if a worried person has the opportunity to talk freely, she'll gain insight into her own problems, doubts, and fears. You don't have to do a thing but listen with empathy. Urge the speaker to continue with smiles and nods of encouragement. Resist the impulse to judge or give advice. Don't interrupt or contradict. It is acceptable, however, to get involved by active listening. Active listening means paraphrasing what the person says, asking questions, and making comments such as "And then?" or "Uh-huh" or "I see."

"If you cannot lift the load off another's back, do not walk away. Try to lighten it." Frank Tyger[8]

Be tactful and diplomatic.

If you must complain or criticize, do it appropriately. You don't want to gain the reputation of being an abrasive, dogmatic, opinionated person. There are always things that you have a legitimate reason to complain about. Relationships are not always harmonious. People annoy you. Someone chronically makes mistakes. The weather is too hot, too cold, too humid, too dry. Don't you have a right to voice your feelings? Sure you do, but there's a right way and a wrong way. Strive to say what you believe is true without arousing hostility.

Stating your feelings and opinions provisionally helps to maintain good relationships and a cooperative work environment.

Imagine that you and one of your co-workers have different political views. Instead of attacking his intelligence and self-esteem by telling him how wrong he is, try diplomacy. Say something like, "Well, you may have a point. I'd never thought of it that way, and yet here's the way I see it," or "I may not be right. I've been known to make mistakes before." This tactic, known as provisionalism, helps to maintain good relationships and a cooperative work environment.

Dogmatism develops defensiveness.

Telling someone that he or she is wrong, mistaken, ignorant, or stupid might make you feel good for a moment, but you run the risk of making an enemy, an adversary. You'll never convince someone against his or her will. Even if a person knows deep down inside that he is in error, he doesn't want to be told about it in an arrogant, superior manner. Consider what you want to communicate to the other person, and then carefully decide on your phrasing and overall tone. Remember, dogmatism develops defensiveness.

Benjamin Franklin who was once an opinionated, insolent youth developed into one of our country's most capable and diplomatic statesmen because of the advice given to him by a Quaker friend, advice that is just as timely today. The friend's tongue lashing went something like this:

> Ben, you are impossible. Your opinions have a slap in them for everyone who differs with you. They have become so offensive that nobody cares for them. Your friends find they enjoy themselves better when you are not around. You know so much that no man can tell you anything. Indeed, no man is going to try, for the effort would lead only to discomfort and hard work. So you are not likely ever to know any more than you do now, which is very little.[9]

Benjamin Franklin saw the truth in those words. He mended his ways by avoiding direct contradiction of another's ideas as well as positive assertion of his own. By doing so, he soon discovered that his conversations and relationships became much more pleasant. Yours will too.

Keep complaining to a minimum.

Complaining is unfair to others and virtually useless for you.

What's the use of complaining? It might make you feel relieved, but it annoys others to have to listen to your incessant moaning and groaning. Complaining that everyone makes more money than you do, that Henry goofs off without ever getting caught, or that the boss has it in for you is unfair to others and virtually useless for you. Think about what your gripe is and then realize that you are the only one who should be in control of your life. You made the choice to work where you work.

If you don't like the salary, lazy Henry, or the unfair supervisor, take action. How? Make your boss aware of the wage inequity—or make him aware that you're aware! You can't change Henry, so ignore him. Ask yourself whether your boss has really singled you out or if it's in your imagination. If you're convinced that you're being mistreated, review your work record. Could your boss be justified in his treatment of you? After objectively reviewing your work performance, if you are still convinced of unfairness, speak up. If nothing else works, resign. Get another job. If you aren't willing or able to do that, cease griping. Nobody wants to hear you complain if you aren't willing to change the situation.

Complaining is least appreciated whenever you tell someone that you are tired and whenever you tell someone that you don't feel well.

Wayne Dyer, author of *Your Erroneous Zones*, writes that there are two occasions when complaining is least appreciated: (1) whenever you tell someone that you are tired and (2) whenever you tell someone that you don't feel well. Complaining to even one poor soul about your tiredness is abusing that person and won't make you any less fatigued. Dyer says the same kind of logic applies to complaints of not feeling well. Why complain to someone about the state of your health if that person can do nothing about it?[10]

Maintain a positive attitude.

Your Attitude Is Showing maintains that working hard may have been enough to ensure success on the job 30 years ago but not today. Now you have to do the best possible job you can *and* get along with all people to the best of your ability. Your positive attitude toward your job, your company, and your life in general can help you move up the ladder of success and help you to be a happier person. Here are some suggestions for improving your attitude.

1. Build a more positive attitude in one environment, and you will be successful in another. The benefits of making an effort to be a more positive person in your social and personal life will spill over into your work life.
2. Talk about positive things. Instead of griping about the rain, talk about the boon to the farmers.
3. Look for the good things in the people you work with, especially your supervisors. Everyone has some redeeming qualities. Concentrate on those.
4. Look for the good things in your department. Do you like the hours? The physical surroundings? The people you work with? Nothing's ever perfect, but constantly dwelling on negative aspects brings you and your co-workers down.
5. Look for the good things in your company. Are there opportunities for promotion? What kind of wage and benefit package do you enjoy? Employees at a local industry recently went on strike to protest wage cuts, and one of the area newspapers ran an editorial aimed

at getting these union workers to think twice about their striking. The scathing editorial reminded them that they at least still had their jobs while other workers in the county had lost their jobs for some of the very reasons about which the strikers were protesting. The laid-off workers wanted more money and more benefits, but since that was an impossibility, the workers had eventually talked themselves out of a job.

6. Don't permit a fellow worker (or supervisor) who has a negative attitude to trap you into his or her way of thinking.[11]

Ways of Combating Worrisome Behavior and Conflict

Learn to cope with worrisome behavior.

People are funny, amusing, enjoyable, and entertaining. Co-workers can enrich our lives in many ways. They can also be obnoxious, abrasive, moody, flighty, worrisome, and clingy.

The following is a list of irritating behaviors, habits, and mannerisms. Are your co-workers guilty of any of them? How about you? Are you aware of any of your own behaviors that might rub acquaintances the wrong way?

Offensive Habits, Behaviors, and Mannerisms

Telling off-color stories
Using offensive or vulgar language
Making ethnic, racial, or sexual slurs
Talking excessively
Goofing off
Clockwatching
Clearing the throat
Dressing improperly for the job (too trendy, too skimpy, etc.)
Using poor grammar
Having a bothersome voice (whiny, loud, high-pitched, raspy)
Having a nervous laugh
Singing
Whistling
Humming
Having tics or other nervous mannerisms
Complaining chronically
Bumming cigarettes, gum, or money
Interrupting others
Belching
Having poor personal hygiene
Gossiping

Having a sloppy work area
Sniffling
Cracking knuckles

Some behaviors are tied in with basic personality traits and are unlikely to change.
What can you do to deal with undesirable behavior? First, accept the fact that some behaviors are tied in with basic personality traits and are unlikely to change. Sometimes, however, just making someone aware of an annoying habit helps. Many people honestly are not aware that they are irritating you or that they have a distracting mannerism. Tell them in a tactful way.

Don't attack or criticize. For example, a mechanic had the irksome habit of saying "you know," over and over and over again. He said it while telling stories to co-workers, explaining a process to a customer, or relating experiences to his wife. Finally, a fellow line mechanic smiled at him and said, "No, I don't know." The mechanic was confused at first but quickly realized what his friend meant. Thereafter, whenever he said, "you know," he looked at the co-worker with a "Oh no, there I go again," look. Before long, the meaningless phrase was eliminated from the mechanic's speech.

Try both direct and indirect approaches when dealing with undesirable behavior.
People are not always so cooperative. Try both direct and indirect approaches. Try more than one method. Try kidding them about whistling. Tell them firmly that you are offended by vulgar jokes. Make someone aware of good etiquette if that's what is needed. Get a third party involved. If all else fails, and the behavior is affecting your work, talk it over with your boss. She can take some action or offer you a different perspective of the situation.

Some people have abrasive personalities. "The abrasive personality is sarcastic, condescending, and opinionated with subordinates, peers, and superiors."[12] Many people avoid contact with him since he has a knack for jabbing someone in an irritating way. There are many approaches you can try with such a person. Talk it over with him and repeat your feelings and observations objectively and uncritically. Point out that he has to take others into account and consider their feelings. Even if such a person challenges you or accuses you of feeling hostility toward him, stay cool, calm, and collected.

Imagine a co-worker who always says, "Hey, Donna c'mere. I wanna show you something," in a domineering, demanding, superior tone, and it really irks you to be summoned in such a manner. You resent being beckoned. What are your options? Go see what the person wants while fuming inside? Stay right where you are and pout? Stay where you are and make her wonder if you're angry or deaf? Yell, "You come here if you want me, you lazy slob!"?

None of these tactics is very effective—unless you want a rift in your work relationship. Why not try an "I" message that will eliminate the tendency to blame or insult another person. When we send "you" messages, we risk damaging a relationship since the other person is likely to feel defensive and resentful. "I feel *angry* when you *call me over here all the time* because *it makes me feel manipulated*" will be better received than "You make me so mad!" It could be that your beckoner never thought of it that way, and using the "I" message opened her eyes and the lines of communication.

USING "I" MESSAGES

In reporting your feelings to someone, state the facts without criticizing, complaining, condemning, or judging. Send more "I" messages. An "I" message has three main parts:

1. State your feelings. How do you feel about the behavior anyway? Upset? Angry? Manipulated? Hurt? Left out?
2. State the specific behavior that brings about your feelings of anger, hurt, betrayal, or annoyance.
3. State why you feel the way you do when a person engages in such behavior.

I feel _____ when you _____ because
_____. Think of a conversation that occurred with another in which you could have communicated better if using an "I" message. Fill in the blanks using words that possibly would have produced a different outcome. Is there a situation in your life right now that could benefit from using a few "I" messages? If so, practice this technique.

I was angry with my friend:
I told my wrath, and my wrath did end.

I was angry with my foe:
I told it not, my wrath did grow.

William Blake, "The Poison Tree"

Be more assertive.

Assertiveness means standing up for yourself without violating the rights and/or feelings of others.

"Assertiveness" is a word stressed so much in the working world that a chapter on relationships would be incomplete without mentioning it. Being assertive simply means standing up for yourself, expressing your opinions and rights, and saying no when necessary without violating the rights and/or feelings of another person. A shy person lets others manipulate him, an aggressive person tries to manipulate others, and the assertive person fits neatly between the two. She neither lets others manipulate her, nor does she attempt to manipulate others.

The broken-record technique and fogging are ways of being assertive.

Some people are nonassertive because they've never been taught. Still others have low self-esteem. They don't feel that they're good enough, smart enough, or competent enough to express their thoughts and feelings. Whatever the reason, if you are nonassertive and want to remedy that, two suggestions are the broken-record technique and fogging.[13]

In the *broken-record technique,* simply be persistent and keep saying what you want over and over and over and over again without getting irritated or angry. Stick to the point and be calm and repetitive until you get what you want or until the other party agrees to a compromise.

A homemaker who wanted to return to college to take an introductory course in computers without enrolling in the entire curriculum successfully used the broken-record technique. She wanted to attend classes only two mornings a week, and she wanted to do so first thing in the morning and as early in the week as possible. Delighted to find a section available that suited her schedule perfectly, she was soon disappointed to find that particular section was one of the ones restricted to the computer technology majors. Although there were other sections of the same course, they met three times a week or in the middle of the day, and she was unwilling to change her substitute teaching plans or to drive the 15 miles three times a week when the class was offered twice a week.

When first the advisor and later a dean tried to explain to her about the restricted sections and about the other times available for people with her needs, she calmly and persistently said that the early class was the one she wanted, that she had other plans that would conflict with the other sections, and finally, that she would not take the course that particular term if the college couldn't cooperate with someone who only wanted to continue her education. Reluctantly, the dean allowed her in the restricted section, and since that time she has enrolled in the entire program. By sticking to the point, remaining calm, and being tactful, the homemaker achieved her goal, and the college benefited as well.

Fogging helps you cope with manipulative criticism without getting defensive or counter-attacking with criticism of your own. Respond as if you were in a fog bank. No one can see through a fog bank, and it offers no resistance to penetration. Fogging helps a person to cope assertively by offering no resistance or hard psychological striking surfaces. Read the next example, and you'll have a better idea of how fogging works.

Critic: Anyone who dresses like that obviously hasn't got much going for them.

Learner: You're right. I do have a lot of faults.

Critic: Faults! Is that what you call them? They are more like chasms. Your personality is one empty Grand Canyon.

Learner: You could be right. There are a lot of things I could improve.

Critic: I doubt if you are able to do a job effectively if you can't even dress properly.

Learner: That's true. I could improve my work on the job.

Critic: And you probably pick up your paycheck each week from the poor boss you are ripping off without feeling any guilt.

Learner: You're right. I don't feel any guilt at all.

Critic: What a thing to say. You should feel guilty!

Learner: You're probably right, I could feel a bit guiltier.

Critic: You probably don't budget the salary you cheat other people, hard-working people, not loafers like you, out of.

Learner: You're probably right, I could budget my money better, and I do loaf a lot.

> Critic: If you were smarter and had some moral sensibility, you could ask someone how to buy better clothes so you don't look like a bum.
> Learner: That's true, I could ask someone how to buy better clothes, and I certainly could be smarter than I am.
> Critic: You look nervous when I tell you things that you don't like.
> Learner: I'm sure I do look nervous.
> Critic: You shouldn't be nervous. I'm your friend.
> Learner: That's true, I shouldn't be as nervous as I am.[14]

Learn to handle conflict.

Conflict has constructive aspects.

You can practice all the techniques recommended for getting along with friends and acquaintances at work. Still, since most people are not always rational and logical, sooner or later disagreement and misunderstanding are bound to erupt. It doesn't matter how harmonious relationships are, people can be suspicious, petty, self-centered, and sensitive. Conflict is inevitable. Don't think of it as entirely negative, however, for a total lack of disagreement can signal growth or noncommunication. Conflicts in and of themselves aren't bad, but failure to resolve them is harmful on both an organizational and a personal level.

Have you ever considered these constructive aspects of conflict?

1. They make life interesting.
2. They make us aware of problems in our relationships that need to be resolved.
3. They increase motivation to deal with problems. Sometimes something can rankle you for months, even years, but you keep it within when bringing it out in the open could help the relationship and help you feel better about the person.
4. They help you understand what you're like as a person and can lead to personal growth.
5. They can actually deepen and strengthen a relationship.[15]

If you have a conflict with a co-worker, boss, spouse, child, or friend, never get caught in a win-lose situation. Even if you win the conflict, in the long run, you risk losing the friendship. Conflicts create feelings like anger, resentment, fear, frustration, and anxiety, but they are still possible to resolve if lines of communication are left open. Define conflict as a mutual problem to be solved, and both parties have a better chance of experiencing a win-win situation.

Gnawing on bones of contention provides little nourishment.
Arnold Glasow

There are at least five conflict resolution styles suggested by David Johnson in *Reaching Out*.[16] Instead of saying this strategy is better than that one, apply them as the situation calls for. Sometimes you need to be confrontive and other times you need to be soothing. At all times, effective and continued communication is of vital importance.

1. *Turtle* (withdrawing). Turtles withdraw into their shells to avoid conflicts. They give up their personal goals and relationships rather

than confront someone with whom they disagree. Turtles stay away from the area where the conflict is taking place and from the people with whom they are in conflict. They feel helpless and believe trying to resolve the conflict is hopeless.

2. *Shark* (forcing). Sharks try to overpower opponents by forcing them to accept their solution to the conflict. Their own goals are very important to them, and the relationship itself is of minor importance. Sharks want to achieve goals at all costs and aren't concerned with the needs of others. They want to win and attempt to do so by attacking, overpowering, overwhelming, or intimidating others. Winning gives the sharks a feeling of pride and accomplishment, and losing gives them a feeling of failure, weakness, and inadequacy.

3. *Teddy bear* (smoothing). To teddy bears the relationship is more important than their own goals. They want to be accepted and liked by others, and conflict is avoided in favor of harmony. Teddy bears are afraid that if a conflict continues, someone will get hurt, and that could ruin the relationship. They try to smooth over conflicts for fear of harming a relationship.

4. *Fox* (compromising). Foxes are moderately concerned with their own goals and relationships with others. They are willing to give up part of their goals and try to persuade others to do the same. They seek a solution to conflicts in which both parties gain something—a middle ground between two extreme positions.

5. *Owl* (confronting). Owls value goals and relationships and view conflicts as problems to be solved. They consequently seek a solution that achieves both their own goals and the goals of the other party. They are not satisfied until the solution is found that achieves the satisfaction of everyone's goals and that eliminates tension and negative feelings.

GETTING ALONG WITH YOUR BOSS

Are you interacting with your boss with the same care and attention that you give to your fellow workers and subordinates? Since your boss is a human being, many of the principles discussed for developing relationships with your co-workers can be applied to getting along with your boss. Showing appreciation, being friendly and courteous, and listening are all behaviors most bosses appreciate. Since your relationship with your supervisor is a subordinate one, however, there are additional means you can use to improve your relationship with him or her.

You and your boss are the two people most responsible for your success on the job.

The techniques discussed here are tried and proven methods of developing a good work relationship with your boss. Bootlicking and apple polishing aren't recommended since most people of average intelligence can spot an insincere phony a mile away. Playing politics in a sensible manner can do much to enhance your career. Besides you, your boss is probably the person most responsible for your success or failure on the job, and knowing and using strategies of impressing this person will help you.

Michael LeBoeuf, author of *The Greatest Management Principle in the World*, asserts that managing your boss is not just desirable, but absolutely essential since nobody makes it on his own in today's work world. A novel way of looking at boss management is that "you own 50 percent of your relationships with your boss and are 100 percent in control of your own behavior. The way you behave toward your boss teaches him how to treat you."[17] Treat him like an all-powerful parent, and he'll treat you like a child. Making work more enjoyable and productive for both of you is what boss management is all about since both of you have a mutual interest in seeing to it that each of you succeeds.

Do Your Job

The first thing you can do to impress your boss is to *do your job*. No amount of cooperation, courtesy, or communication compensates for poor job performance. Some people don't do their jobs well because of a lack of education, experience, aptitude, ability, or interest. If you like the job and desire to improve your performance, then do whatever it takes to do so. Take a course. Practice in your off hours. Observe others and learn from them. No matter how much you like working at ABC Widgets, your boss's bottom-line question is: "Is she doing her job?"

An employee and an employer have different perspectives of good work.

Your most profitable investment is to give your best to your employer. That advice applies to both sexes and all ages. Give your best, and if you can't or won't, don't be surprised when your boss fails to appreciate you. Make sure your work is really good enough to deserve recognition. An employee and an employer have different perspectives of good work. You might see your work as outstanding while your boss sees it as satisfactory.

Be Reliable

Two ways of demonstrating your reliability are to show up for work regularly and to be on time. Many students are surprised to find that what's permissible in an academic setting is simply not tolerated in a work environment. There have been innumerable instances of students at our technical college who habitually arrive at five or ten minutes after the hour instead of being on time for class. Some sheepishly make excuses—a drawbridge, a slow school bus, morning traffic, a stalled engine, misplaced car keys. Others saunter in nonchalantly as if coming to school late were the norm. What a rude awakening these students have when employers don't tolerate tardiness. As B. C. Forbes, editor of *Forbes*, eloquently states, "Punctuality, or the reverse, is a matter of habit. Somehow, I can't help questioning the ability, the efficiency, the dependability of any person who is habitually late. Don't handicap yourself by permitting this habit to fasten itself upon you."[18]

It's difficult for a supervisor to evaluate your performance positively if you don't show up for work on a regular basis. If you get into the habit of calling in sick whenever the spirit moves you to do so, you'll soon earn the reputation of being undependable. Be at work regularly—and punctually.

Get to Know Your Boss's Strengths and Weaknesses

You and your boss have a lot in common since both of you have a job to do and since you depend on each other to get it done. Gather as much objective information about your boss as you can. Get to know his blind spots, pet peeves, and sore spots. LeBoeuf suggests questions to ask yourself to help you learn a lot about your boss. Here are a few of them.

* What are your boss's major goals?
* How do you help him achieve them?
* What is he rewarded for?
* What is his boss like?
* Does he share or conceal information?
* What are the pressures of his job?
* Who are his allies and enemies?
* What do you like best about him?
* What do you like least?
* How could he help to make your work more satisfying?
* Does he like to delegate responsibility or keep a finger in every pie?
* At what time of day is he at his best?
* What things does he do best?
* What does he hate to do?
* Does he like to deal with one thing at a time or jump from task to task?
* What are his educational history and work experience?
* Does he have any special quirks or idiosyncrasies that you've noticed?[19]

Look to yourself too. Be honest. Look within as objectively as possible. Ask yourself what you want from your job, what part of it you like most and least, whether you require close supervision, whether you are a self-starter or need someone to get you going, and what kinds of jobs you put off.

If your boss is weak in one area, offer to help.

After assessing the best that both of you have to offer, try building on the strengths. If your boss is weak in one area, offer to help. If he likes public appearances, but hates writing speeches, offer to help him organize his thoughts on paper. If you're both morning people, confer about important things then. Build on the best that both of you have to offer and make adjustments to compensate for weaknesses.

Use Positive Reinforcement on Your Boss

You can't give her a raise, a promotion, or a challenging work assignment, but there are ways you can reward your boss. Praise her good points. From forepersons to top executives, all bosses have fears and uncertainties and need bolstering from time to time. They worry about rejection, authority, ridicule, criticism, and wrong decisions. If you think he or she did a good job handling a dispute between two quarreling workers, say so.

Show Loyalty

If you disagree with your boss, don't express your feelings publicly.

Let your boss and others know that you support him and his ideas, the department, and the entire organization. There are other ways to do this besides just giving lip service. For instance, you can use company products. A GM employee driving a Toyota is not displaying loyalty. A person who never attends company functions, balks at putting a company sticker on his car, or ridicules his or her boss's authority is not loyal.

ARE YOU IN OR OUT?

To determine whether you are in or out with your boss, answer the following questions:

1. Do you usually know where you stand with your boss? That is, do you know if the boss is satisfied with what you do?
2. Is it likely that your boss would use his or her power to help you solve work problems or "bail you out" of a jam?
3. Would you describe your working relationship with your boss as effective?
4. Would you be willing to defend your boss's actions if he or she were not present to do so?
5. Does your boss recognize your potential?
6. Does your boss ask you for your opinions and advice on work-related issues?
7. Could you influence your boss to take a particular course of action if you really wanted to steer him or her in a given direction?

People who are in with their boss generally answer "yes" to these questions, while people who are out tend to say "no." Although most people like to believe that they are in with their supervisor, the reality is that a certain segment of any work group is likely to be out.

Robert Vecchio, "Are You In or Out with Your Boss?" *Business Horizons*, November-December, 1986, p. 78.

Just because a person is in a supervisory position doesn't mean he doesn't make mistakes. Everyone makes mistakes. Even if you disagree with your boss's policies or decisions, you owe it to him or her not to broadcast your feelings publicly. If you really feel strongly about it, discuss it with your supervisor privately.

When you work for someone,
work for them all the way.

If you are in something,
get all the way in and if you can't get all the way in,
then get all the way out.[20]

Stay in Touch

Try to see and talk with your boss on a regular basis. Let him know of your accomplishments, hopes, and activities. Otherwise, how is he to know about your feelings and aspirations? Some people disagree with this strategy and call it "playing politics" when actually it's just an honest, upfront method of keeping your boss informed. Remember, he'll hear about your goof ups soon enough, so keep him informed about the things you do right.

Your boss is not a mind reader. He can't possibly know of everyone's interests, activities, and career goals without being told. If you're taking a course to improve your work, let him know. He might even want to take it himself. If you're interested in advancement, tell the boss that too. Otherwise, he might think you're perfectly content doing what you're doing. Toot your own horn—softly.

Communicate with Your Boss

Communicating is but another way of keeping in touch. Each of us is ultimately responsible for the success or failure of our relationships, and the foundations of all personal and professional relationships is communication. If you need help, ask your boss. It's better to ask for assistance in completing a job task than it is to flounder helplessly and risk failure when one little question could clarify things for you. The boss would rather that you ask for help than ruin materials or waste time. She probably isn't even aware that you're having a problem unless you say so. Besides, it's part of her job to help you and makes some bosses feel needed when they're asked for assistance or advice. Just don't overdo asking for help, or the boss might think you're incompetent.

Telling your boss of your activities and asking for assistance are only half of the communication process; listening is the other half. It's imperative that you listen to instructions and job related information from your boss. Too, sometimes she needs someone to listen to a new plan, proposal, or idea. Do both of you a favor and listen attentively.

Respect Your Boss's Authority

No one is asking you to demean yourself by kowtowing to your boss. Showing respect means realizing that while you might not always agree with what your boss says and does, you continue to respect his authority as your superior in the work environment. He's the boss, not you. Don't grovel or sacrifice your values, but do ask for advice and direction on work-related matters and follow through with that advice.

Many workplaces are informal and employees call the boss by his or her first name. In front of visitors, customers, or outsiders, using a title and last name demonstrates respect for your boss's position. Would you be impressed if your doctor's receptionist said, "Slim will be with you shortly"? Probably not. No matter how charming the nickname sounds, Dr. Walkup sounds better and more professional. Informal rules and customs vary from office to office, plant to plant. Mary Kay Ash of Mary Kay

Cosmetics insists on being called Mary Kay instead of Mrs. Ash, yet no one doubts who is in control of this multimillion-dollar industry.

Follow the Chain of Command

Failure to follow the chain of command is looked upon unfavorably.

A sure way to rub your boss the wrong way is to go over his or her head about a problem or complaint. Doing so lets her know either that you think she is incapable of resolving the situation or that you don't trust her judgment in the matter. Dubrin suggests that another possibility is that you are secretly launching a complaint against your boss. He adds that this boss bypass is looked upon so negatively that most experienced managers won't even listen to your problem unless you've already discussed it with your immediate supervisor.[21]

If you want to stay on the good side of your boss, go directly to him or her with problems. If she is unable or unwilling to help you, inform your supervisor diplomatically that you are going to approach the next in line for another opinion.

Consider Your Options

You can learn something from everyone, even an abrasive, intolerable boss.

What if your boss is unmanageable, critical, intolerable, bitter, sarcastic, abrasive, incompetent, or unfair. What if you've tried everything and your boss just can't be managed? What should you do then? There are several alternatives depending on how much you like the job, what your future plans are, and your other job options. For instance, you can quit, but sometimes that's inadvisable in the long run, especially if you can learn something from your boss.

Jimmy Carter endured his mentor, Admiral Hyman Rickover, and learned a lot from him. The former president said, "All the time I worked for him he never said a decent word to me. . . . If he found no fault, he simply looked, turned around and walked away. However, if I made the slightest mistake, in one of the loudest and most obnoxious voices I ever heard, he would turn around and tell the other people in the area what a horrible disgrace I was to the Navy and that I ought to go back to the oldest and slowest and smallest submarine from which I had come."[22]

If you can't learn anything from your boss but have no other options at the moment, grin and bear it. You can't fire an incompetent boss (or any other kind) so just keep doing the best job you can while trying to establish good communication with others in the organization so that your abilities will be distinguished from his inabilities. Maybe things will improve if you wait it out. Realize that a tough but manageable boss will be a real challenge. Such a person will keep you trying harder than you would otherwise. Besides, most bosses can be managed, provided that you do it with common sense, patience, and persistence. It takes time and continuing effort to build a long-term, mutually satisfying relationship.

All the techniques presented in this chapter for getting along with people and/or establishing relationships at work are useful. There are no shortcuts that work in gaining cooperation, loyalty, and respect from work acquaintances and friends, whether they are your subordinates, peers, or superiors. Winning and keeping friends takes continued time and effort. Remember the "three T" formula. *Things take time. Take the time.*

BOSS SPELLED BACKWARD IS DOUBLE SSOB. OR IS IT?

Sometimes in your career, you may feel victimized by a less than desirable boss. However, before blaming your woes on the one you report to, complete the following checklist. Then sit down with two other persons and get their feedback on each of the items. It might even be in your best interest to get feedback from your boss. Answer yes or no to these questions.

_____ 1. Are you doing the very best you can in your current position? Cite specific evidence to support your answer.

_____ 2. Is your best good enough for your organization?

_____ 3. Are you certain that you are not blaming your boss's attitude for your own weaknesses or lack of performance?

_____ 4. Are you described as professional?

      _____ Well disciplined?

      _____ Well groomed?

      _____ Pleasant to be around?

_____ 5. Is it clear to you what is expected of you?

_____ 6. Do you let your personal life interfere with your performance at work?

_____ 7. Is it clear to you what management's position is in your organization?

      _____ Does management have the reputation for being fair to employees?

      _____ Is management approachable, willing to listen?

      _____ Do you think that management in your organization would be willing to reprimand or dismiss a supervisor as well as a subordinate?

_____ 8. Have you fully assessed your boss's situation?

      _____ Is your boss perceived as credible by your organization?

      _____ Are there personal problems in your boss's life that could be affecting his or her performance as well as the relationship with you?

_____ 9. Do you feel that you are in a no-win position?

_____ 10. What are you willing to do to change your behavior to improve your relationship with your boss? _____

TELL 'EM HOW YOU FEEL

From the text, you've learned that "I" messages are a non-accusatory way of letting others know how you really feel about something. Another advantage is that saying, "I feel," instead of, "You make me feel," establishes that you own the feeling—it's all yours and not the other person's.

Even though most people agree that "I" messages are quite effective, people often have a difficult time using the technique because they aren't familiar with enough words that accurately describe their feelings. Generally speaking, people use the same old words over and over again—words like mad, sick, upset, frustrated, bad, and yucky. What does "yucky" really mean?

To give you some practice with describing feelings, read the following list of words. They aren't difficult or complex and yet they aren't used nearly enough. After familiarizing yourself with the words, read the statements that follow the words and write an appropriate "I" message to describe the feelings you have. Remember, you don't want to alienate the other person or hurt anyone's feelings.

abused	grateful	rejected
afraid	hopeful	repulsed
angry	humiliated	resentful
annoyed	hurt	sad
ashamed	impatient	shaky
awed (overawed)	inadequate	shy
baffled	inferior	silly
bitter	irritated	slighted
bored	jealous	snubbed
calm	lowly	tense
concerned	manipulated	thrilled
confident	mistreated	uncertain
exasperated	offended	unimportant
foolish	overwhelmed	used
giddy	puzzled	worried

1. Your child/spouse/roommate leaves belongings all over the house and you resent having to ask repeatedly to have the shoes, clothing, and books picked up. What's worse is that sometimes you end up picking them up yourself in order to clear the clutter and avoid a conflict. You're really steamed when you realize that this person thinks you'll probably clean up after him or her again.

2. Your boss tells you that the promotion you had worked so hard for is going to another person. To make matters worse, you helped to train this person who is now getting what should be your job!

3. Your spouse is spending more and more time at the office (plant, store, school) and less and less time with you. When with you, he or she seems distracted and restless.

4. Your friend drops in unexpectedly, and you have a big psychology test to study for and a research paper to outline. The person seems troubled, but then so are you.

5. A co-worker drops by your office to "chew the fat," and you're really pressed for time. This is a good friend but one who has a habit of complaining about work, salary, and the boss. This attitude really irks you.

6. Your boss makes more and more requests of you with no release from other duties or pay increase. It almost seems that you're being penalized for good work.

7. An acquaintance is pressuring you to give her a home permanent when you've made other plans for your leisure hours. The person is trying to make you feel guilty for not giving more selflessly to a "friend."

8. At a meeting a co-worker speaks up and takes credit for one of your ideas. It was a very good idea and could save the business a lot of money.

9. Your "sweetheart" complains that since you've been in school, you have no time for romance in your life. While it's true that you do have to "hit the books" pretty regularly, you wonder if this person is exaggerating just a bit.

10. You and a classmate are working together on a project to be presented in one of your classes. So far, you've done the research, made a poster, and are not writing the paper. The other person hasn't contributed anything yet except the idea itself and a list of excuses. He's pleasant enough, and yet. . . .

TRY FOGGING THEM

Are you controlled, manipulated, or unduly influenced by other people? Do you say yes when you want to say no? Do you let people run over you, boss you around, or make you feel guilty?

Put an end to this by fogging their statements. Respond as if you are in a fog-bank through which information, especially negative information, cannot penetrate. Agree partially or completely with whatever they say to you, and after a while, they'll tire of your pleasant agreeableness and change the way they treat you.

For example, a friend might say "If you were really serious about your career, you'd try to look more professional. Have you ever considered reading *Dress for Success*?"

To fog him or her, respond by saying, "You're probably right. I could be a little more image conscious, but it doesn't seem to matter to me very much right now."

Your turn now. What would you say to these statements?

1. "I'm really disappointed in you. I can't believe you won't donate even an hour of your time for such a worthy cause. I thought you were more compassionate."

2. "What! You've never given blood? You should feel ashamed of yourself. Think of all the people who are in desperate need of something a healthy person like you could so generously give."

3. "You're not as conscientious about your work as I imagined. Otherwise, you'd stay overtime and help us clear up this problem."

4. "Have you ever considered cutting your hair? Your present style is a little well, youthful for someone your age."

5. "This is a poorly written paper. You must not have spent much time on it. Obviously, this class is not important to you."

6. "I've been waiting here in this dreadful lobby for twenty minutes. You should feel guilty for making me wait so long."
7. "Judging from the way you're dressed, meeting my parents is not very important to you."
8. "If you really cared about me and my feelings, you'd call me more often."

CASE STUDIES

Shirley Huddy

Shirley Huddy is employed at a clothing manufacturing plant and annoys co-workers with her incessant complaining. Never an exuberant, happy person, she's become increasingly bitter and acerbic. It's as if her whole outlook on life has soured.

An examination of her personal life reveals possible reasons for her poor attitude. Her first husband had died some 20 years earlier when she was still a relatively young woman, leaving her with two teenaged children to raise. She didn't even know how to fill out a job application or write a resume. Having had no work experience, Shirley felt lost, afraid, and bitter.

As time passed, the children married, moved away, and tried to get on with their lives. Their mother was angry with the children and felt that they were uncaring and selfish for leaving her. In short, she was both alone and lonely, and being alone with few outside interests or activities gave her time to brood and to let problems become magnified.

Like sunlight from behind a cloud, love came into her life. The romance ended in marriage. Alas, marriage ended in divorce when in a few short months the bridegroom proclaimed his love for another. The scorned Shirley was infuriated, not just at her husband, but at life in general.

1. As a co-worker, is there anything you could do to help Shirley?
2. Relate some specific techniques for getting along with co-workers mentioned in this chapter and tell how they might help Shirley and her co-workers.

Ann Johnson

A school teacher, Ann Johnson, who had small children at home tried to get most of her schoolwork done before leaving the premises. Unfortunately, everyday two aides came into what was supposed to be a quiet work area to chitchat with each other about husbands, recipes, weather, TV stars—anything and everything. They disturbed the teacher who was trying to concentrate on grading papers and preparing lectures. Especially irksome to this conscientious teacher was the fact that these aides were supposed to be fulfilling other duties during this hour and often joked about getting away with goofing off.

Ann considered her alternatives. Should she report the aides, ask them to leave the work area, or rudely say "This is supposed to be a quiet planning area. Hush!" Having an awareness of human relations skills helped Ann to realize that any of these tactics would have angered the aides unnecessarily and made enemies of them. Besides, they were not even aware that their chattering was annoying her.

1. If you were Ann, what would you do?
2. Give an example of an effective "I" message.
3. Illustrate how the broken-record technique of assertiveness would work in this situation.

SUMMARY

Getting along with your co-workers and boss can prove to be productive for you in many ways. Some advantages of good work relationships include increased productivity, emotional support, improved communication, career success, high morale, and increased knowledge. To a degree, mental and physical health depend upon the quality of relationships with others.

Informal groups which develop in the workplace meet a variety of individual needs not met by the formal organization. Examples of these needs are companionship, reassurance and support, reduction of tension, and sense of identity.

Groups set standards of acceptable behavior called norms. These norms express the collective values of a group and provide guidelines for member behavior in achieving group and individual goals.

Building and maintaining relationships requires skill and effort. Strategies of getting along with others include using positive reinforcement practicing empathy, demonstrating friendliness, showing an interest in co-workers, and being courteous.

Components of communication include developing listening skills, being tactful and diplomatic, minimizing complaints, and having a positive attitude.

Since people are not always enjoyable and pleasant, we should also know and practice methods of combating worrisome behavior and conflict. We should be careful not to attack or criticize others and to use both direct and indirect approaches in dealing with their irksome behavior. Sending "I" messages are effective in that they eliminate the tendency to blame or insult another person.

Assertiveness means standing up for yourself and your opinions without violating the rights and feelings of someone else. Two methods that are particularly effective in being assertive are the broken-record technique and fogging.

When conflict develops, as it inevitably does, remember that it is not totally negative. Conflicts make life interesting, make us aware of problems in our relationships that need to be resolved, help you to understand what you're like as a person, and can actually deepen and strengthen a relationship.

There are at least five conflict resolution styles: withdrawing, forcing, smoothing, compromising, and confronting.

Besides you, your boss is probably the person most responsible for your success or failure, so knowing and using techniques of boss management are essential. These techniques include doing your job well, being reliable, getting to know your boss's strengths and weaknesses, displaying loyalty, letting him or her know of your accomplishments and activities, and following the chain of command. If the person remains unmanageable, critical, or unfair after you've tried all the principles of boss management, then it's time to consider your options.

KEY TERMS

Informal groups
Norms
Positive reinforcement
Dale Carnegie
Empathy
Parallaction
Wayne Dyer
Abrasive personality
"I" message
Assertiveness
Broken-record technique
Fogging
Conflict
Boss management
Michael LeBoeuf

REVIEW AND DISCUSSION QUESTIONS

1. What are some advantages to improved work relationships?

2. What are some areas in which informal groups meet the needs of their members?

3. List ways of showing friendliness in the workplace. How can these methods improve work relations?

4. List some of the components of communication that are often overlooked at work.

5. Discuss ways by which you can deal with worrisome or undesirable behavior of co-workers.

6. Think of an instance in which an "I" message would be very effective. How would you phrase it?

7. What are some advantages of being assertive? How could fogging work in dealing with a supercritical supervisor?

8. Are there any advantages to conflict? If so, what are they?

9. Think of your present or most recent job. What are some ways you can apply the material in your text on boss management?

10. How can getting to know your boss's strengths and weaknesses help you in your career success? Be specific.

11. Tell why good communication with your boss is important.

ENDNOTES

[1] NATHANIEL STEWART, *Winning Friends at Work* (New York: Ballantine Books, 1985), p. 26.

[2] Ibid., pp. 55–56.

[3] J. CLIFTON WILLIAMS AND GEORGE P. HUBER, *Human Behavior in Organizations* (Cincinnati: South-Western, 1986), pp. 153–154.

[4]THOMAS J. PETERS AND ROBERT H. WATERMAN, JR., *In Search of Excellence* (New York: Harper & Row, 1982), p. 55.

[5]MARY KAY ASH, *Mary Kay on People Management* (New York: Warner Books, 1984), p. 15.

[6]DALE CARNEGIE, *How to Win Friends and Influence People*, rev. ed. (New York: Pocket Books, 1981).

[7]OWEN D. YOUNG, "Thoughts on the Business of Life," *Forbes*, April 22, 1985, p. 180.

[8]FRANK TYGER, "Thoughts on the Business of Life," *Forbes*, July 6, l981, p. 196.

[9]DALE CARNEGIE, *How to Enjoy Your Life and Your Job* (New York: Pocket Books, 1970), p. 126.

[10]WAYNE DYER, *Your Erroneous Zones* (New York: Avon Books, 1977), p. 51.

[11]ELWOOD N. CHAPMAN, *Your Attitude is Showing*, 3rd ed. (Chicago: Science Research Associates, 1972), pp. 20–21.

[12]HARRY LEVINSON, "The Abrasive Personality at the Office," *Psychology Today*, May 1978, p. 81.

[13]MANUEL J. SMITH, *When I Say No, I Feel Guilty* (New York: Bantam Books, 1975), pp. 74, 104, 105.

[14]Ibid., pp. 107–109.

[15]DAVID W. JOHNSON, *Reaching Out*, 2nd ed. (Englewood Cliffs, N.J.: Prentice Hall, 1981), p. 196.

[16]Ibid., pp. 204–206.

[17]MICHAEL LEBOEUF, "You Can Manage Your Boss," *Success*, (May 1985).

[18]B. C. FORBES, "Thoughts," *Forbes*, March 26, 1984, p. 252.

[19]LEBOEUF, "You Can Manage Your Boss," p. 42.

[20]ZIG ZIGLAR, *See You at the Top* (Gretna, Calif.: Pelican, 1977), p. 99.

[21]ANDREW J. DUBRIN, *Human Relations for Career and Personal Success* (Reston, Va.: Reston, 1983), p. 161.

[22]LEVINSON, "The Abrasive Personality," p. 81.

chapter 6

Personality Development

After reading and studying this chapter, you will be able to:

1. Define personality.
2. Explain how an understanding of personality development can help in interpreting others' actions, attitudes, and feelings.
3. Discuss three theories of personality development which developed from three traditional schools of psychological thought.
4. Compare and contrast the psychoanalytic, behavioristic, and humanistic theories of personality development
5. Discuss trait theory.
6. Identify specific personality theorists.

A man who has been the indisputable favorite of his mother keeps for life the feeling of a conqueror, that confidence of success that often induces real success.[1]

Sigmund Freud

PERSONALITY

Marsha has a dynamic personality. Bill's a real charmer. And Tony? Well, Tony has "a lot" of personality. These descriptions should sound pretty familiar to you since laypersons usually use such terms when describing others. Psychologists, however, search for more scientific means of defining personality. Psychologists need a more conclusive, scientific definition to aid in their attempts to understand, predict, and control human behavior.

At work and elsewhere you are confronted with people and their little quirks and idiosyncrasies. Knowing something about personality will enhance your understanding of why people do the things they do and will increase your tolerance of individual differences. As John Watson said, "We are all dominated by our pasts and our judgments of other people are always clouded by difficulties in our own personality."[2] Whether someone is impulsive, generous, obnoxious, defensive, sweet, or overbearing, there's a reason. Also, as you learn more about your feelings, reactions and actions, motivation, likes and dislikes, you'll know more about your personality, the why of you.

Knowing something about personality will increase your tolerance of individual differences.

Everyone has a personality, and this chapter focuses on defining it, looking at major theories of personality development, and describing a healthy personality. If human behavior were fully understood we wouldn't need theories. Some theorists attempt to explain how personality develops while others are content with description, not explanation. An explanatory theory emphasizes development throughout the life cycle and interaction with others as major determinants of personality. A descriptive theorist simply describes typical traits and types of individuals but makes no effort to explain their development or presence.

What Is Personality?

Personality originally referred to the masks worn by theatrical players.

The word "personality" comes from the Latin word *persona*, which originally referred to the masks worn by theatrical players in ancient Greek dramas. Since it eventually came to mean the actor's role, not the mask worn, personality originally referred to a public personality. The public personality, the one most associated with someone, deals with superficial factors such as charm, popularity, and physical attractiveness.

The Three Faces of You

Holland states that all people have three different faces—a personal face, a social face, and a real face.[3] The social face is similar to the actor's role. It's the face you wear in public. It's the way you act around others, a public image that changes according to the impression you want to make. You use clothes, voice, cosmetics, and hairstyle to present this face just like an actor playing a role. Sometimes you appear smart and sophisticated, and at other times in different settings, you might appear casual and carefree.

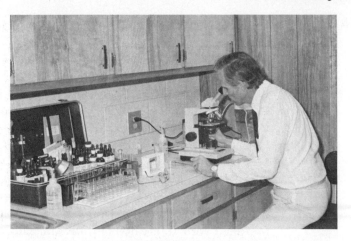

Your personal face is the way you see yourself. It can be positive or negative. If you see yourself as competent, likable, and intelligent, then you have a positive self-concept. How you feel about yourself and how others perceive you is not always the same. Because of a number of reasons, a girl may believe herself unattractive and unworthy while others see her in an entirely different manner.

Your personal face is the way you see yourself; your real face is the way you really are.

Finally, your real face is what you really are. It's how you would appear if you could see yourself clearly. People are prevented from seeing themselves clearly for a variety of reasons. Perhaps others' judgments have been taken too seriously. Perhaps people don't see themselves the way they really are because to do so would create anxiety.

So What Is Personality?

Personality can be defined as your enduring and unique pattern of behavior. Enduring is an important part of the definition because it means that your characteristic way of behaving will last. Jack Block of the University of California at Berkley found that basic personality stays much the same throughout the years. "Those who have been cheerful adolescents were cheerful adults. Those who behaved in self-defeating ways in high school—the boys who were always being hauled down to the principal's office, for example—were usually acting the same 30 years later, constantly at odds with their bosses or workers."[4] Do you know any such person? Don't give up on him or her since, according to some theorists, "typical" behavior of someone can be altered to meet the changing demands of life. Many psychologists think of personality in terms of interaction between people and situations; when situations change, people change.

Personalty is your enduring and unique pattern of behavior.

The word "unique" is equally important in describing personality since your uniqueness is what separates you from others. It's your specialness, your singleness, your oneness. A good definition of personality which concentrates on uniqueness is the "consistency in who you are, have been, and will become. It also refers to the special combination of talents, attitudes, values, hopes, loves, hates, and habits that make each person unique."[5]

Some people see personality, temperament, and character as synonymous, but they are not. Gordon Allport, a noted personality theorist, states that temperament is the raw material—along with intelligence and physique—out of which the personality is fashioned.[6] You were born with temperament, and people responded to you accordingly. For instance, some babies are "easy," and some are "difficult," and common sense tells you that its easier to respond positively and affectionately to an "easy" baby.

Temperament is the raw material from which the personality is fashioned.

Temperamental endowment is not unchangeable though it sets limits upon the development of personality. It can be altered somewhat by medical, surgical, and nutritional influences. Certain foods are now known to bring about behavioral changes. People become nervous, restless, hyperactive, or even lazy and lethargic depending on the food they consume. Since learning and life experience can also alter personality, temperament may change somewhat as personality evolves.

Character refers to a moral standard or value system against which your actions are evaluated.[7] Character is an ethical concept. Good character, in other words, implies moral excellence while good personality means that a person is socially effective.

THEORIES OF PERSONALITY

What accounts for the differences between people? From the major perspectives of psychological thought, many theories of personality have evolved. Bear in mind that the theories are just that—theories to increase our understanding of human behavior, not irrefutable facts. Since the theorists themselves are human and have widely different views on the nature of man, their basic assumptions affect their individual personality theories. Even though there are dozens of personality theories, we will concentrate on the major contributors to psychoanalytic (psychodynamic), behavioristic (social learning), and humanistic (self) theories. A personality theory based on traits will also be examined.

Psychoanalytic Theory

When psychoanalytic theory is discussed, Sigmund Freud's name appears. He's considered to be the father of psychoanalytic thought which focuses primarily on the unconscious mind. No one can deny that Freud was a dedicated theorist. Who could doubt the dedication of a man who said, "My life has been aimed at one goal only; to infer or to guess how the mental apparatus is constructed and what forces interplay and counteract in it."[8]

Sigmund Freud is the founder of the psychoanalytic theory of personality development.

Psychoanalytic theories concentrate on the inner workings of a person's mind, especially the unconscious mind. Because of the dynamic interplay and struggle within the unconscious mind, psychoanalytic theory is also referred to as the psychodynamic theory. Basically, Freud believed that there exist three levels of awareness, three structures of personality which are always engaged in a struggle, and five psychosexual stages that people go through as they mature and progress toward adulthood. The unconscious mind and the struggles among the three structures of personality—the id, ego, and superego—are emphasized.

From his own self-analysis and from his clinical research as a Viennese physician, Freud determined that the human mind was like an iceberg, the tip of which rises from the water while most of the iceberg stays hidden beneath the surface. He concluded this from speaking with patients who seemed to have little or no insight into their problems and maladies. Troubling and upsetting feelings and experiences appeared to be forgotten or repressed somehow and yet these feelings and experiences still had the power to make people feel doubt, shame, pain, fear, guilt, and insecurity.

Repressed feelings have the power to make people feel doubt, shame, pain, fear, guilt, and insecurity.

The "iceberg" or mind has three levels of awareness which are the conscious, preconscious, and unconscious mind. The conscious mind is like the tip of the iceberg. It's your present state of awareness and contains sensory information, your thoughts, and your daydreams. Your conscious mind contains whatever you're thinking about right at this moment.

The conscious mind contains sensory information, thoughts, and daydreams.

Your preconscious mind acts like a bridge between your conscious and unconscious. It contains information that is not in your present awareness but that you could readily retrieve. For example, if your birthday is July 10, you don't scratch you head and say. "Well, it's sometime in hot weather." You know when your birthday is, who the first president was, when Columbus discovered America, how to use a calculator, and what psychology is, but you can't go around with those tidbits cluttering up your consciousness all the time. This material is readily recalled when asked for or when the person is given an appropriate cue. For this reason, the preconscious is often referred to as a person's *available memory*.

The preconscious is often referred to as one's available memory.

Unconscious material is unavailable and includes unacceptable images, including past events, present impulses, and desires of which you are not aware. Your unconscious mind contains sexual and aggressive impulses as well as repressed (forgotten) memories, feelings, and emotions. This material remains unconscious because awareness of hidden thoughts could cause uneasiness, anxiety, shame, or guilt. Except

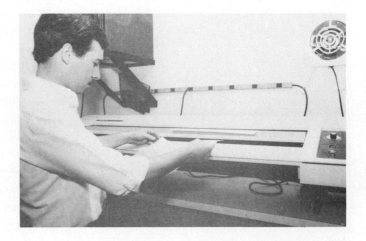

through dream analysis, free association (a psychoanalytic therapeutic technique), or hypnosis, this information remains hidden from most people. It's the part of the iceberg beneath the water, and yet it affects our behavior and emotions.

Sexual and aggressive urges and repressed memories and emotions are in the unconscious mind.

There's a resistance within the person to some thoughts ever becoming conscious. However, occasionally people will relax and make what is called a Freudian slip. It's a slip of the tongue which indicates an unconscious thought. For instance, if a newlywed introduces her bridegoon (Oops! I meant bridegroom) as Jerk instead of Jack, you might question the couple's wedded bliss. Have you ever been guilty of a Freudian slip? Have you ever called someone by the wrong name? Why? Could it have been because of an unconscious feeling or thought?

Behavioristic Perspective

Instead of examining unconscious thoughts or being concerned with the stages of life, the behaviorists concentrate on observable behavior. The radical behaviorists see people as machines, as robots acting and reacting according to the stimuli in their environment. The social learning theorists believe reinforcements in the environment to be important, but they look to cognitive aspects as well.

John B. Watson is the father of American behaviorism.

John B. Watson, the father of American behaviorism, emphasized observable environmental stimuli and the observable behaviors or responses that occurred in the presence of such stimuli. Since behaviorism has to do with stimuli and responses, many people call it S-R psychology. Others call it "black box" psychology since Watson believed the mind to be a mysterious black box whose contents could not be examined objectively. Behaviorists contend that since you can't see a conscious thought, much less an unconscious one, the mind is not to be studied.

What can be observed is behavior, so it should be studied and measured, not remain as some unseen and undetectable mental structure. Behavior, just like personality, is learned. According to the operant principle, behaviors are learned and continue to be displayed when they are positively reinforced or rewarded; those not reinforced or punished are extinguished. Someone performs an act or expresses an opinion, gets reinforced for it, and consequently performs the same act or expresses the same opinion again.

Behavior, like personality, is learned and continues when reinforced or rewarded.

Whether it's an attitude, a value, an act, an interest, or a feeling, it's all learned. "Personality is the sum of activities that can be discovered by actual observation of behavior over a long enough time to give reliable information. In other words, personality is but the end product of our habit system."[9]

Furthermore, whatever has been learned can be unlearned and relearned. Consequently, personality is not static and unchanging, but adapting and evolving as situations change. People act to receive certain rewards, and since available reinforcements change throughout life, it stands to reason that personality changes according to rewards or reinforcements available in the environment.

Behaviorists believe that conditioning is responsible for the development of personality. They see no use in speculating about internal motives, traits, or hidden conflicts since behavior is determined by outside events. Watson said that if you were to give him a dozen healthy, well-formed infants, that he could make them into doctors, lawyers, and yes, even the proverbial beggarmen thieves by using conditioning techniques. Commenting on the importance of the environment, Watson states, "It is what happens to individuals after birth that makes one a hewer of wood and a drawer, another a diplomat, a thief, a successful business man or a far-famed scientist."[10]

Responsible for operant conditioning principles, B.F. Skinner is said to be one of the most influential psychologists of the century.

A present-day behaviorist credited with the technique of operant conditioning is B. F. Skinner. Some psychologists believe Skinner to be the most influential psychologist of this century. Skinner says that ambiguous inner forces like motives and conflicts are not needed to explain personality. All that's needed is to look at genetic endowment and reinforcement history since the environment with its reinforcements determines a person's behavior. "When a bit of behavior is followed by a certain kind of consequence, it is more likely to occur again, and a consequence having this effect is called a reinforcer."[11]

Skinner asserts that people have no free will. They are different from one another because they've grown up in different environments. "A child is born a member of the human species, with a genetic endowment sharing idiosyncratic factors, and he begins at once to acquire a repertoire of behavior under the contingencies of reinforcement to which he is exposed as an individual. Most of these contingencies are arranged by other people. They are, in fact, what is called a culture."[12] Believing that an individual is a lump of clay in the hands of the environment, Skinner describes a society in which people are manipulated by rewards and punishments in *Walden II*.

Social Learning Theory

Social learning theorists, although they too are behaviorists, believe that humans are more than mere robots with no free will. They are active reactors, not passive lumps of clay. Social learning stresses language, information processing, and planning. It attempts to integrate environmental variables with cognitive functioning to explain human behavior. Environment influences a person, but a person also influences the environment. Cognitive viewpoints influence the way people interpret behavior and respond to different situations. There is a reciprocal interaction between the person and the environment, and rather than being controlled by their environment, people are allowed to control their behavior.

Social learning theorists believe that there is a reciprocal interaction between the person and the environment.

Important variables to consider are the person's expectations concerning future outcomes and the value of different reinforcements that might occur in a given situation. Rotter, a noted social learning theorist, believes that behavior depends on what the person expects the outcome of an action to be and what those outcomes are worth.[13] The probability that a certain behavior will occur is determined by what the person expects as a reward and what the reward means to the person. General expectancies lead individuals to act in consistent ways. What expectations do you have? Do you want to be a supervisor? Do you want more money? How should you go about getting what you want? Is the promotion or raise (outcome) worth the effort?

Rewards and punishments are important, yes, but people learn in many ways. For instance, they learn through imitation, identification, and observation. Individuals learn to engage in behavior they see other people perform, and this is called observational learning or vicarious learning. Children learn sex roles, skills, manners, and values by imitating models they observe. People are more likely to imitate if those observed are reinforced. This observational learning occurs without external reinforcement and without the learner even performing the behavior.

Observational learning is an important concept in social learning theory and occurs without external reinforcement.

Behavior depends on situational variables and personal variables which are acquired through the social learning process. Situational variables include rewards and punishments and could be anything from a word of praise to an all-expense-paid trip to Trinidad. Some personal variables are competencies or skills like athletic ability or social ease. Others include expectancies and the subjective value of rewards mentioned earlier. Personal variables are different for each person and account for why people in exactly the same situation may respond differently.

Some factors considered important by social learning theorists are:

Competencies—skills and special abilities (leading, creating, singing).

Expectancies—expectations people have about what will happen in different situations.

Subjective values—the value attached to various outcomes—Is the money, the prize, or the prestige worth the effort?

Self Efficacy—the confidence someone has about what he can or can't do.[14]

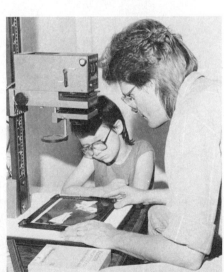

Like behaviorists, social learning theorists feel that behavior can change as environmental factors change.

Personality is situationally dependent, not stable across any situations or shaped by hidden motivation or predispositional forces. Since behavior can change as environmental factors change, social learning is an optimistic theory. Even an old grouch's disposition and personality can be improved by observational learning and proper reinforcements. Set a good example and reinforce him with praise when he imitates you.

Self Theory

Self theorists such as Abraham Maslow and Carl Rogers are humanists and reject the idea that people are influenced by mysterious primitive urges and repressed memories. Nor are they at the mercy of their environment. They are neither hedonists nor robots. Instead people are shaped by their own personal choice and own subjective view of the world and unique experiences in it. Positive aspects of the personality are emphasized, and a profound sense of respect for human nature is at the core of self theory. Rogers believes that "the innermost core of human nature is purposive, forward-moving, constructive, realistic, and quite trustworthy."[15]

Self theorists emphasize positive aspects of the personality.

The self is innate or inborn and is the most important structural construct in Rogers's theory of personality. His theory is called self theory since Rogers believes that the best vantage point for understanding behavior is from someone's internal frame of reference. Individuals have strong tendencies toward growth and are actively motivated to maximize their personal freedom or potential. Self theory is optimistic with respect to the capacity of people to accept responsibility, develop new skills, and behave in constructive ways.

Carl Rogers, influential self theorist, believes individuals to be strongly motivated to maximize their potential.

All behavior is energized and directed by the actualizing tendency, the very essence of life. The primary aim in life is to actualize, maintain, and enhance yourself to become the best that your inherited nature will allow. This actualizing tendency is illustrated by achieving or accomplishing something that makes life more enriching or satisfying—good grades, money, prestige, achievement in sports, and so on.

DEVELOPMENT OF THE SELF CONCEPT

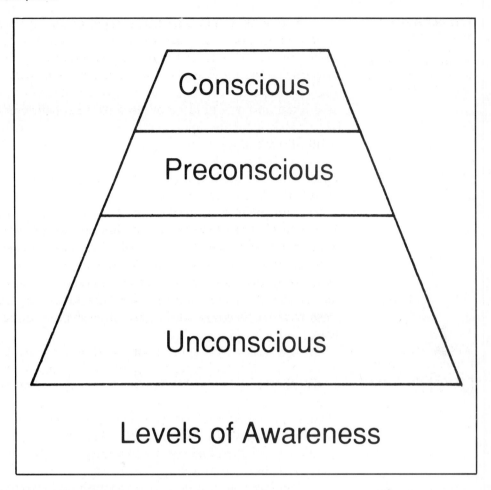

How do you feel about yourself? Are your bright? Dull? Average? Mean? Attractive? Your appraisal of yourself leads to self concept, an important aspect of Rogers's humanistic viewpoint, which determines how you act and view the world. It consists of judgments and attitudes about abilities, behavior, and even appearance. The ideal self is the concept you'd like to possess. People are motivated to reach the ideal self by reducing the discrepancy between our self-concepts and our self-ideal.

The self-concept comes about through:

1. Social interactions.
2. Comparison to others.
3. Personal feelings, thoughts, and behavior.
4. Statements of others.

People can reach their full potential and become self-actualized only to the extent that they can accept all their personal experiences as part of their self-concept. Rules, norms, and standards that tell people what is permissible, and people who scorn or ridicule others for not acting in desired ways can thwart the growth process, however. Persons need to feel liked and accepted regardless of their behavior. "I like you, but not your slack attitude about neatness" is a more positive statement than "You do such sloppy work! Can't you do anything right?"

Congruence is a fit among self concept, behavior, and thoughts.

Unconditional positive regard means that someone is loved and cared for regardless of looks, age, size, performance, or abilities. Conditional positive regard means that someone is cared for as long as she meets the needs or expectations of another. The child will do almost anything for positive regard—warmth, admiration, love, and acceptance—even if it means denying or rejecting parts of her own personality.

A person who has a strong sense of self and who has received unconditional positive regard is more likely to have congruence, a fit among self-concept and behavior, thoughts, and emotions. Inner feelings, awareness of these feelings, and expression of them click when a person has congruence.

TYPE AND TRAIT THEORIES

Ever been called the strong silent type? The bossy type? The athletic type? People are simply trying to categorize you according to your personality type. Types are really just clusters of traits, and Carl Jung and Gordon Allport are noted type and trait theorists, respectively.

Carl Jung, although associated with the psychoanalytic perspective, is responsible for the designations of introvert and extrovert. An introvert is a quiet, withdrawn person who values his or her own company while an extrovert is outgoing, bold, and enjoys the company of others. This is oversimplifying a bit, since there are degrees of introversion and extroversion. As mentioned earlier, some traits are situational. Maybe you are a shrinking violet among strangers but a blossoming rose among friends.

Gordon Allport is a trait theorist who regards that explanation of an individual's unique pattern of trait as the paramount goal of psychology. Each person's behavior derives from a particular pattern of personal traits. A "trait is a predisposition to respond in an equivalent manner to various kinds of stimuli."[16] Traits are enduring, produce consistencies in behavior, and account for the more permanent features of behavior. Since traits and the situation interact to produce behavior, the two components are interdependent. Traits are predispositions that make a person respond consistently over time and across situations.

Traits are predispositions that make a person respond consistently over time and across situations.

How many traits does a person have? To answer this question, Allport and a colleague catalogued some 18,000 words describing personal behavior. Some were physical (tall), some were behavioral (talkative), and some were moral (honest).[17] Not all of these traits are related to personality.

In addition, Allport says traits are classed as cardinal, central, and secondary. A cardinal trait is so pervasive that practically all of a person's activities can be traced to it influence. Such a trait cannot remain hidden in a person. Allport says it's like a ruling passion or master quality which few people have. A few who did have cardinal traits are Albert Schweitzer who had a "reverence for every living organism," Freud who had an obsessive interest in motivation, and Lincoln who had an honest nature.

Gordon Allport classified traits as cardinal, central, and secondary.

Less pervasive but still generalized dispositions of the person are central traits. If writing a letter of recommendation, you'd mention central traits like cheerful or hardworking. They're the tendencies that a person often expresses or shows which people around them readily notice. How many central traits does the average person have? The number of them is probably no more that from five to ten.

Secondary traits are dispositions that are less conspicuous, less generalized, and less consistent. Food preferences, attitudes, and situational differences are examples of secondary traits. The average person has a greater number of these. A person might be self-assured and confident in one situation and fearful and shy in another.

The major criticism of trait theory is that it describes rather than explains personality. It describes traits but gives no clue as to why a person is shy, aggressive, or generous. Also, observing traits in and of themselves implies too much. We see a person do such and such and surmise that he is gruff, shy, or aggressive based on limited observations. Traits should allow for the variability of a person's conduct.

In a work break area, one of the drink machines was known to be contrary. Sometimes the only way to receive a soft drink was to put the money into the machine and immediately begin to forcibly "attack" the drink machine by shaking it until the drink appeared. The contrariness of the machine and the behavior used to secure a beverage were common knowledge to all employees. One lady, however, a visitor to the break area, was visibly upset by seeing a worker shake the machine and later commented that the "attacker" seemed violent, hostile, and impatient. In reality, the person was a gentle, serene, and extremely patient man who just happened to know the formula for securing a Sprite.

IS YOUR PERSONALITY NORMAL?

After reading all this, you're probably wondering whether your personality is normal. It's difficult to define normality. It certainly doesn't mean an absence of problems. Normal people have problems, doubts, worries, fears, and anxieties. They worry about how they look, feel guilt about past deeds or thoughts, experience inadequacy, and get depressed.

So-called "normal" people have problems, doubts, worries, and anxieties.

Sometimes normality is a value judgment based on personal opinion. For instance, someone described as having a good personality often has socially effective traits. He is charming, considerate, thoughtful, witty, and entertaining. What do you mean when you describe a friend as having a good personality? It depends on your own value judgment about normality.

Cultural differences shouldn't be overlooked when attempting to describe the normal personality. In America, traits like competitiveness and assertiveness are admired, but there is a limit beyond which these characteristics might be considered abnormal. Fierceness, hostility, and aggression, although they occur, are not the norm. Among the Yanomamo people of southern Venezuela and northern Brazil, however, fierceness and violence are desired behaviors. The Yanomamo are a very warlike people who, with very little provocation, hit each other on the head with eight- to ten-inch clubs and administer wounds with spears and bows. Some of the older members of the tribe have several large angry scars on the tops of their shaved heads which they proudly display.[18] Americans might be aggressive, but we are amateurs compared to these explosively fierce jungle inhabitants.

Someone with a healthy personality is able to commit himself to relationships.

Does normal mean healthy? There is a correlation between mental health and normality and between physical health and mental health. Being psychologically and physically healthy enables a person to function well, and each brings about a feeling of well-being. Someone with a healthy personality is able to commit himself to relationships and to communicate feelings to others; he or she has an internal locus of evaluation, is open to new experiences, and is striving to fulfill inborn potential.

WHO AM I?

Adults of all ages have to try out many different roles to achieve a clear sense of identity. Larry Bugen suggests a simple exercise which should prove useful in exploring this aspect of development. Follow these instructions one at a time. Proceed to the next number only after the present one has been fully addressed.

1. Write down 10 different answers to the question, "Who am I?" You may respond in terms of your roles or responsibilities, the groups to which you belong (family, work group, church, etc.), your beliefs, your personality traits or qualities, and your needs, feelings, or behavior patterns. List only those things that would make a real difference in your sense of identity if lost.

2. Now that your list is complete, consider each item separately. Close your eyes and try to imagine what your life would be like if items on the list were no longer true. For instance, what would the loss of a parent mean to you if you wrote down "son" or "daughter"?

3. After you have reviewed items in this manner, rank order them in terms of importance. To determine the rank of each item, consider the adjustment required if you "lost" the item.

L. A. Bugen, *Death and Dying* (Dubuque, Iowa: William C. Brown, 1979).

From your reading about Carl Rogers's self theory of personality development, you know that how a person views and evaluates himself or herself greatly influences individual behavior. The self concept is a central feature of personality. Rogers suggests that in addition to the "actual self," there is also an "ideal self," which is what the person would like to be.

To help you appreciate the distinction between the actual and ideal self, complete the following exercise.

ACTUAL VERSUS IDEAL

Respond to the following adjective checklist by reading it quickly and making a check mark beside each item that describes you. Work quickly and do not spend too much time on each one. Be as frank with yourself as possible. Next, go back through the list and make a checkmark beside each item (in the second column) that describes the person you would like to be. Again, work quickly.

1. absent-minded	____ ____	24. headstrong	____ ____
2. anxious	____ ____	25. hurried	____ ____
3. artistic	____ ____	26. imaginative	____ ____
4. attractive	____ ____	27. impatient	____ ____
5. capable	____ ____	28. impulsive	____ ____
6. charming	____ ____	29. industrious	____ ____
7. clear-thinking	____ ____	30. ingenious	____ ____
8. clever	____ ____	31. initiating	____ ____
9. confused	____ ____	32. insightful	____ ____
10. courageous	____ ____	33. inventive	____ ____
11. dissatisfied	____ ____	34. irritable	____ ____
12. dreamy	____ ____	35. moody	____ ____
13. emotional	____ ____	36. nervous	____ ____
14. energetic	____ ____	37. original	____ ____
15. enterprising	____ ____	38. persevering	____ ____
16. excitable	____ ____	39. pessimistic	____ ____
17. forceful	____ ____	40. polished	____ ____
18. forgetful	____ ____	41. preoccupied	____ ____
19. gentle	____ ____	42. resourceful	____ ____
20. good-looking	____ ____	43. restless	____ ____
21. handsome	____ ____	44. tactful	____ ____
22. hard-headed	____ ____	45. wise	____ ____
23. hasty	____ ____	46. witty	____ ____

You might take a separate piece of paper and make three lists; first list those terms that you checked as characteristic of your self but not of your ideal, then those characteristic of your ideal but not yourself, and finally those for which you check both columns. The first list suggests those aspects of yourself that are not consistent with your highest standards. The second list is the way you would ideally like to be. The third list shows those traits that live up to your ideals. Do you believe this is an accurate description of your self-image?

Don Byrne and Kathryn Kelly. An *Introduction to Personality*, 3rd ed. (Englewood Cliffs, N.J.: Prentice Hall, 1981), p.103.

CASE STUDIES

Nedra Green

Nedra Green is puzzled. A dean at a small Eastern university, she is the supervisor of seven faculty members and two secretaries. One of those secretaries seems inexplicably low, and Nedra needs to get to the source of the problem.

Several months ago Nedra and two colleagues interviewed eight women for two secretarial positions after screening dozens of applications. Of the eight interviewed, the two who were hired, Donna and Linda, were clearly the most impressive. They seemed tailor-made for the school. Both were competent, intelligent, efficient, poised, and neat—real professionals. Their letters of recommendation were good, and they both had many years of applicable job experience. In fact, both women had worked in academic settings before and desired to do so again now that they had located in the area.

Their personalities were different, but in every other way, the two "administrative assistants" were equally qualified. Donna was outgoing, enthusiastic, and almost bubbly. Linda was also friendly and pleasant but seemed a little reserved. Nedra and her colleagues felt that this difference was because the applicants showed their interview nervousness in different ways. Since both applicants were equally capable, they were randomly assigned to the positions. Donna was hired to work with a few faculty members and Linda to work in the counseling center.

Although both jobs paid the same salary and involved similar work, the work areas were in different locations of the campus. One job involved typing outlines, tests, grants, and newsletters for the twelve faculty members and dean. The office for this position was away from the hub of activity, and for the most part, work was put into an "in-basket" for typing or filing. The other position was for the school's counseling center, often referred to as Grand Central Station. Students felt free to come in for academic, vocational, social, or personal counseling. If someone needed a resume typed, he dropped into the center. If a person had problems with her love life, finances, work, or courses, she came by the counseling center. The atmosphere was warm, caring, and noncompetitive. People were always around. The job in the counseling center called for typing resumes, letters, memos, and reports and for scheduling appointments.

After beginning the job, both women seemed content, and the quality of their work surpassed everyone's expectations. Not only did they both do their jobs, but they frequently took the initiative to go the extra mile. For example, when an employee retired, Donna offered to collect money for the gift and to assist in planning a farewell party. She seemed to thrive on the additional duty and actually looked forward to the task of collecting the money from other employees.

Lately, however, both women appeared downcast. Linda says she can't get anything done with people around all the time. She claims that the never-ending stream of visitors to the counseling center distracts her and prevents her from concentrating on her work. Donna, on the other hand, says she can't concentrate because of the constant quietness in her office. Donna finds the hum of the air conditioner oppressive and the distant sounds of human activity an ever constant reminder that she is nearly always alone. She never talks with anyone except at breaks or when a faculty member or Nedra needs to explain a special task. The poor woman seems to be languishing away.

1. Can you help Nedra out a little? What seems to be the basic problem? What should she do?
2. Could this and similar problems be prevented from occurring? How?

Sharon Smith

To the customer coming into the telephone company to pay a bill or request service, everything appears smooth and efficient. If John Doe were to linger a moment or two, however, he'd soon feel the tension filling the very air with electricity and realize that all was not well in Beaver Dam Telephone Cooperative.

Sharon Smith is a middle-aged woman who has been at the cooperative longer than anyone else and has begun acting as if that gave her special privileges. If someone comes in whom she doesn't like or if the customer has a complicated problem, Sharon beats a hasty retreat to the ladies' room where she stays 5, 10, or 15 minutes, until the person leaves. When she goes on her breaks, she stays for 20 minutes, 10 beyond the allotted time.

On special occasions such as holidays or birthdays, other employees bring cakes, candy, or cookies for everyone to snack on in the breakroom. For example, on Valentine's Day, one woman baked heart-shaped cookies, another baked a "love" cake, and a third brought red fruit punch. Sharon never contributes to these goodies but always eats more than her fair share.

The situation wouldn't be so intolerable if Sharon were a pleasant person, but she's not. Her personality is abrasive and obnoxious. She makes no attempt to be friendly unless there's some ulterior motive in mind. To make matters worse, Sharon and the office manager are old friends, and Sharon is always especially nice to her.

The other women grow more resentful every day. They resent the partiality Sharon receives and the manner in which she acts. They're afraid to say anything because of the relationship between Sharon and the office manager. Although the office manager is very conscientious and believes in a full day's work for a full day's pay, the other employees are wondering if perhaps she is unaware of Sharon's actions. Even if she did know, would the office manager take action?

1. Whose problem is this? Sharon's, the office manager's, or the other employees?
2. What do you recommend as a method to deal with this situation?

SUMMARY

The word "personality" originally referred to the masks worn by theatrical players in ancient Greek dramas. Holland believes that today individuals have three masks or faces: a social face, a personal face, and a real face. The social face is the one you wear in public, the way you act around others. Your personal face is the way you see yourself, and your real face is the way you really are.

Personality consists of enduring and unique patterns of behavior, enduring because characteristic ways of behaving will last throughout a lifetime and unique because of individual specialness.

Although personality, temperament, and character are often used interchangeably, Gordon Allport distinguishes among them. Temperament is the raw material, along with intelligence and physique, out of which the personality is fashioned. Character is an ethical concept and implies moral excellence. Personality refers to a person's social effectiveness.

There are numerous theories of personality to aid in our understanding of human behavior, some of which are psychoanalytic (psychodynamic), behavioristic, humanistic (self), and type and trait theories.

Sigmund Freud, the father of psychoanalytic thought, believed the unconscious mind to be instrumental in determining the personality. He believed that there are three levels of awareness: the conscious, the preconscious, and the unconscious. The conscious mind consists of one's present state of awareness, the preconscious is the available memory, and the unconscious contains unacceptable thoughts and sexual and aggressive impulses. Freud concluded that although troubling or upsetting experiences are repressed, they continue to make people feel guilt, doubt, shame, or insecurity.

The behaviorists concentrate on observable behavior instead of unconscious thoughts or stages of life. John B. Watson, the father of American behaviorism, emphasized environmental stimuli and the observable behavior or responses that occur in response to such stimuli.

Behavior, just like personality, is learned. According to the operant principle of B. F. Skinner, behavior are learned and continue to be displayed when they are positively reinforced. Behaviorists see personality as changing and adapting as situations change.

Social learning theorists, although they too are behaviorists, believe that humans are more than mere robots with no free will. These theorists attempt to integrate environmental variables with cognitive functioning to explain behavior and believe that there is a reciprocal interaction between the person and the environment.

Imitation, identification, and observation are important components of social learning theory. Both personal and situational variables determine behavior. Personal variables might include specific competencies and skills, while situational variables are rewards and punishments.

Self theorists like Carl Rogers believe that people are shaped by their own personal choice and subjective view of the world. Believing that individuals have strong tendencies toward growth, Rogers argues that the primary aim of life is to actualize and enhance yourself to become the best that your inherited nature will allow.

The self-concept which consists of judgments and attitudes about abilities, behavior, and appearance largely determines how someone acts and views the world. People can reach their full potential and become self-actualized only to the extent that they can accept all their personal experiences as part of their self concept. A person who has a strong sense of self and who has received unconditional positive regard is more likely to accept himself and experience congruence, a fit among self-concept and behavior, thoughts, and emotions.

Trait theorist Gordon Allport feels that behavior derives from a particular pattern of traits, predispositions that make a person respond consistently over time and situations. Traits can be classified as cardinal, central, and secondary.

Having a normal personality does not mean having no problems since "normal" people have doubts, worries, anxieties, insecurities, and fears. Most psychologists agree that there is a correlation between mental health and normality and between physical health and mental health since each enables a person to function well and each brings about a feeling of well-being.

KEY TERMS

Personality

Social face

Real face

Personal face

Gordon Allport

Temperament

Sigmund Freud

Psychodynamic theory

Conscious

Preconscious

Unconscious

John B. Watson

B. F. Skinner

Social learning theory
Observational learning
Situational variables
Personal variables
Self theory
Carl Rogers
Abraham Maslow
Self-concept
Unconditional positive regard
Conditional positive regard
Congruence
Trait theory
Cardinal trait
Central trait
Secondary trait

REVIEW AND DISCUSSION QUESTIONS

1. Apply Holland's three faces to your own personality. What are some aspects of your social face? How might your personal face differ from your friends' concepts of you? What might you see if you looked deeply inside yourself at your real face?

2. How can an understanding of personality development help in interpreting others' actions, attitudes, and feelings? What about your own behavior and thoughts?

3. Discuss the dynamic interplay among the conscious, preconscious and unconscious.

4. Compare and contrast the radical behaviorist perspective of personality development with the social learning viewpoint.

5. What are some specific situational and personal variables which might influence someone's career choices?

6. Describe self theory. Why is the self-concept such an important component of this theory? How can you enhance someone's self-concept?

7. From your reading of Allport's theory, what are some of your central and secondary traits? It might be interesting to get the opinion of someone who knows you well. Do you have any cardinal traits? Do you know anyone who does?

8. How would you describe a "normal" personality?

ENDNOTES

[1] SIGMUND FREUD, "Thoughts on the Business of Life," *Forbes*, January 27, 1986, p. 132.

[2] JOHN B. WATSON, *Behaviorism* (New York: W. W. Norton, 1970), p. 276.

[3] MORRIS K. HOLLAND, *Introductory Psychology* (Lexington, Mass.: D.C. Heath, 1980), pp. 323–324.

[4] STANTON PEELE, "The Question of Personality," *Psychology Today*, December 1984, pp. 54–55.

[5] DENNIS COON, *Essentials of Psychology: Exploration and Application*, 3rd. ed. (St Paul, Minn.: West, 1985) p. 410.

[6] GORDON W. ALLPORT, *Pattern and Growth in Personality* (New York: Holt, Rinehart and Winston, 1961), p. 33.

[7] Ibid., p. 31.

[8] COON, *Essentials of Psychology*, p. 433.

[9] WATSON, *Behaviorism*, p. 275.

[10] Ibid., p. 270.

[11] B. F. SKINNER, *Beyond Freedom and Dignity* (New York: Alfred A. Knopf, 1971), p. 27.

[12] Ibid., p. 127.

[13] J. B. ROTTER AND D. J. HOCHREICH, *Personality* (Glenview, Ill.: Scott, Foresman, 1975).

[14] SPENCER A. RATHUS, *Psychology,* 2nd ed. (New York: Holt, Rinehart and Winston, 1984), p. 364.

[15] LARRY A. HJELLE AND DAVID J. ZIEGLER, *Personality, Theories: Basic Assumptions, Research, and Applications* (New York: McGraw-Hill, 1976), p. 291.

[16] Ibid., p. 177.

[17] ALLPORT, *Pattern and Growth in Personality*, p. 353.

[18] NAPOLEON CHAGNON, *Yanamomo: The Fierce People*, 2nd. ed. (New York: Holt, Rinehart and Winston, 1977).

chapter 7

Motivation

After reading and studying this chapter, you will be able to:

1. Define motivation and explain why an understanding of "what makes people move" is important.
2. Distinguish between primary and secondary needs.
3. Describe the motivational process.
4. Explain Maslow's hierarchy of needs.
5. Give characteristics of a self-actualizing person.
6. Explain Herzberg's two-factor theory of motivation.
7. Discuss achievement, affiliation, and power as motivators.
8. Explain Vroom's expectancy theory of motivation.

Achieving good performance is a journey—not a destination.
Kenneth Blanchard and Robert Lorber[1]

MOTIVATION

"If you serve them ice cream first, they won't eat the spinach," or so says A. S. Mike Monroney.[2] Is he right? How do you get people to eat the spinach? To come to work on time? To work diligently? To get along with co-workers? To accept promotions? Few questions about human behavior are more frequently asked or more perplexing to answer than "What motivates people"?[3]

Understanding motivation is fundamental in establishing and maintaining relations with others.

Even if you don't at present have any aspirations of becoming a manager or supervisor, a study of motivation, of what makes people move, is helpful. A knowledge of what motivates others is fundamental in establishing and maintaining relations with other people, and it's absolutely essential to the practice of management. All of us have needs, and a knowledge of human needs and motives can increase understanding of yourself and others. Such an increased understanding will aid in solving problems, resolving conflicts, or simply developing tolerance for those whose behavior differs from your own. Knowing that every bit of behavior, no matter how small or insignificant, is motivated by some need gives you an advantage in working through, with, and for others.

WHAT IS MOTIVATION?

Motivation can be defined as an internal process that starts, energizes, and directs behavior toward achievement of a goal. Motivation is goal directed and derives from an individual's unique needs, values, desires, aptitudes, and experiences. It's the driving force, the impetus that drives a person to accomplish a goal, whether the goal is staying alive or acquiring material goods. In this chapter, after exploring the complexity of needs and the motivational process itself, we'll examine four major theories of motivation.

Motivation is an internal process that starts, energizes, and directs behavior toward goal achievement.

All humans have needs. They need to breathe, to rest, to eat. These primary needs are only part of the larger picture. People also need to feel accepted by a group, and to be loved and cared for by another. Humans are complex, though. It takes more than a good night's sleep and a few bowling buddies to motivate them. They search for more. They want recognition, appreciation, and the opportunity to fulfill a few dreams. "The key factors in a job are the sense of achievement one gets from doing the work, a sense of responsibility, the desire for a sense of purpose, and recognition for a job well done," states Pat Egan of Josten's, a Minneapolis-based designer and manufacturer of corporate and sports championship awards.[4]

PRIMARY AND SECONDARY NEEDS

Needs that motivate are classified as either primary or secondary. *Primary needs* are physiological and are necessary for physical survival. Breathing is necessary. So is eating. Try not drinking for a few hours and see how you fare. *Secondary needs* are social and psychological and are conditioned by unique experiences. An individual is aware of the clamoring of his primary needs because of a dry mouth or growling stomach, but secondary needs are not as obvious. A person may feel a vague discomfort, discontent, or dissatisfaction but is often unable to identify what is motivating him since secondary needs are needs of the "mind and spirit rather than of the physical body.... The secondary needs are the ones that complicate the motivational efforts of managers."[5]

Primary needs are physiological and are necessary for physical survival.

Understanding an individual's motives, the expression of her needs, is not as easy as you might think. What makes someone tick is very complex, and a person is not always reinforced by the same things all the time. All people of this great planet earth have exactly the same physiological needs, but these needs vary in intensity from person to person and even within the same person from day to day, hour to hour. Some people believe they "need" to sleep 10 hours a night or they'll be human wrecks, while others zip through life on 5 or 6 hours of sleep nightly. On a recent trip to Spain, the author saw firsthand that Spanish people "need" to rest 3 hours or so in the afternoon and don't need to eat their meal until nine or ten o'clock. Speaking of cultural differences and needs, American kids are conditioned to think of popcorn as a delicious after-school snack and may be surprised to learn that many Europeans consider corn as food fit only for pigs.

Interpreting secondary needs is especially complex since an individual is often not aware of her own motives. The idea that people are unconsciously motivated is widely accepted by not only psychologists but also by any one who works with people, especially managers. Few unhappy employees will pout and say, "You hurt my feelings; you've depressed my self-esteem," since he or she may not even be consciously aware of it.[6] Even if the person is aware of such motives, she is unlikely to express her feelings in such a childish manner, so instead she complains about salary or inadequate break time.

Since a person is often not aware of personal motives, interpreting secondary needs is especially complex.

Within a person, needs are subject to change. For example, if you were raised in an environment where independent thinking and autonomy were encouraged, the chance of your developing a strong need for achievement is increased. The person with a strong need for achievement, however, might temporarily put it on the back burner if his friends ostracize him because of a promotion or raise. Arthur Witkin, chief psychologist for Personnel Services Center in New York, states that a feeling of acceptance in the work group is almost as important as self-esteem in determining worker satisfaction.[7] Few people can tolerate the punishment of being excluded by peers.

Secondary needs

* are strongly conditioned by experience.
* vary in type and intensity among people.
* are subject to change with any individual.
* are often hidden from conscious recognition.
* are vague feelings instead of specific physical needs.[8]

In truth, primary and secondary needs are inseparable and always interact. The body affects the mind, and the mind affects the body. You'll see application of this concept in Chapter 13 on stress.

THE MOTIVATIONAL PROCESS

The motivational process really involves four steps.

1. Motive (unsatisfied need)
2. Tension (excitement)
3. Action (behavior)
4. Goal (relief of tension, satisfaction of need)

The person experiences a need, consciously or unconsciously, primary or secondary. The felt need creates tension or excitement. Tension motivates action or activity. Action results in the accomplishment of a goal or in the relief of tension.

Picture this:

An unsatisfied need creates tension or excitement within a person.

1. Ella experiences hunger pains. A quick glance at her watch indicates that it's noon. No wonder she's so ravenous!
2. Her hunger creates tension. Homeostasis, the body's state of equilibrium, is out of kilter. Blood sugar level is decreased. Ella feels weak.
3. As a consequence of internal tension, Ella is motivated to reduce the unpleasant stimuli by taking action. If devouring a double cheeseburger is not possible at the moment, maybe she can savor a life saver on the way to the lounge.
4. Food provides the relief of tension—at least temporarily.

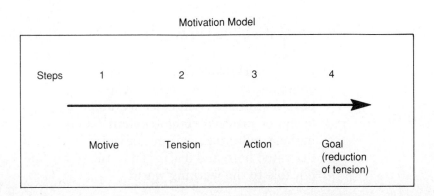

Motivation Model

Steps	1	2	3	4
	Motive	Tension	Action	Goal (reduction of tension)

MASLOW'S HIERARCHY OF NEEDS

One of the most popular and accepted theories of motivation is that of Abraham H. Maslow, a noted humanistic psychologist.[9] This theory, commonly referred to as Maslow's hierarchy of needs, proposes that all people have exactly the same needs which are satisfied in a certain order. Only satisfied needs motivate behavior, and once a need is satisfied, it ceases to motivate.

Maslow states that once a need is satisfied it ceases to motivate.

As the lower-level (physiological) needs are satisfied, the higher-level needs (social and psychological) become more important and demand the attention of the organism. In other words, needs are systematically satisfied as a person progresses up the ladder toward self-actualization. In general, people are motivated to satisfy physiological needs before concerning themselves with security or safety. After they feel somewhat secure, however, then humans yearn for a little brotherly (or sisterly) love from their fellow beings. Even feeling cared for is not enough. Once they receive affection and belongingness from others, people want their self-esteem enhanced by recognition, praise, and other forms of positive reinforcement before finally striving to reach their highest potential, self actualization. Maslow's hierarchy of needs, illustrated here and discussed in the paragraphs that follow, is easily applicable to the working world.

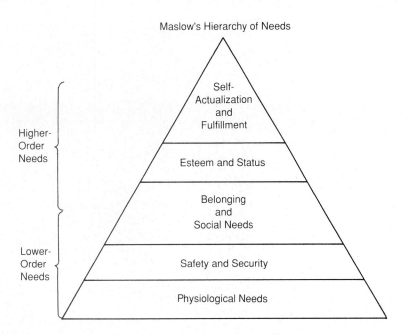

Maslow's Hierarchy of Needs

Physiological

At the lowest level in the hierarchy are the basic survival needs described as lower-order needs by Maslow. We all need certain physical needs satisfied before we can concentrate on anything else. Gandhi reportedly stated that it was useless to talk to a hungry man about anything but bread. A hungry person thinks about food, dreams about food, and can think of little else except how to satisfy the hunger drive.

Fortunately, in our society most jobs provide wages sufficient to provide for basic physiological needs. Your paycheck might not allow you to indulge regularly in caviar and champagne, but the average working person is not in the sad shape of Gandhi's hungry man. It's true that during the Depression, it was hard to survive, and workers were so preoccupied with keeping a roof over their heads and food on the table that they didn't have time to contemplate higher level needs. Things are different now. It's not as difficult to survive in the United States as it once was, and as a result, many workers feel they can call their own shots on a job or pick up their marbles and walk away to another one.

Before moving up the ladder of needs, think for a moment of how Maslow's lower order physiological needs can be satisfied at your own workplace. Are there vending machines with a variety of snack foods and hot and cold beverages? A cafeteria with a delicious assortment of entrees? Bathrooms and breakrooms? Is the temperature comfortable? Also, you probably don't have to look too far to find the water fountain, unless you work in Europe where water fountains are rare.

Safety and Security

When someone is successfully "making a living" and his physiological needs are being met, he begins to want a little security. Safety and

security needs must be met for a person to feel free from danger, uncertainty, and insecurity. A person thinks, "Sure, it's nice to be able to pay the rent today, but what about when I retire? What if I get laid off? Sick?" To satisfy security needs, employers offer pension plans, insurance policies, disability protection, and profit sharing. Employees are not just providing for today with their paychecks but are preparing for the future.

Safety and security needs provide freedom from danger, uncertainty, and insecurity.

Safety needs also refer to protection from actual physical harm. At work, someone might have to wear goggles, a special hat, or protective clothing. Also, unions and OSHA (Occupational Safety and Health Administration) have emerged to ensure that workers enjoy safe working conditions that reduce the chance of accidents, injuries, and even death on the job.

Finally, workers who value security aren't likely to desire a lot of change in their jobs. They're seemingly content doing the same old job year after year. Even though the tasks involved might be boring and unchallenging, at least they're known, familiar, and predictable and present no risk to the employee as a new job would. Managers hoping to motivate a security-oriented employee by offering a promotion might just be disappointed.

Safety and security needs extend beyond the workplace. People with strong needs in this area might stay in dull marriages, live in old familiar neighborhoods, buy smoke detectors for every room, and be "insurance poor." Don't bother asking such a person to go sky diving or mountain climbing. Watching Monday Night Football is safer.

Belongingness

"No man is an island entire of itself," said John Donne. We all have a need to see others and to be seen, to be included and accepted as part of the group. Affection needs don't mean that you need a big bear hug when you walk through the door, but isn't it nice to be spoken to? And doesn't it give you a warm feeling when someone says "Good morning, Ted. How's your lovely wife?" Fitting in, being part of a group, and being accepted are important and can't be overlooked in motivating people.

Many of our social needs are satisfied on the job. This should come as no surprise since some employees spend more time with co-workers at work than they do with members of their own family. Upon reflection, one co-worker realized that he had not actually talked with one of his children in four days, and yet this father perceived himself as a "family man."

Some employees foster belongingness needs by company-sponsored picnics, sports teams, and Christmas parties. Even without management intervention, workers interact. They exchange confidences during coffee breaks and share plans over lunch. They work in teams and on committees with co-workers. In fact, teamwork can motivate an employee with a desire to work as part of a team to be more productive. It's not surprising that many employees socialize after working hours because of attachments formed during their eight hours together.

Self-esteem

How do you feel about yourself? Do you feel likable, competent, and worthy of respect? Good. You probably have positive self-esteem. Esteem needs are the needs we all have for recognition, achievement, independence, and self-confidence. Workers today are more interested in personal job satisfaction than are workers of an earlier era. Recognition by the boss, the opportunity to participate in management decisions, and the feeling that one's work is useful are more important in motivating employees than are salary, fringe benefits, job security, and quality of supervision.

How can esteem needs be satisfied on the job? There are several ways, some of which are positive reinforcement, recognition, achievement, and participation.

Positive reinforcement is a rewarding, encouraging consequence given for desirable behavior and helps to assure that the behavior will be repeated. A pat on the back, a sincere compliment, or words of appreciation are a few examples of positive reinforcement. Regardless of position in the work organization, a person can influence the motivation of others by showing appreciation for their work, complimenting them on their accomplishments, and asking for advice because of their particular expertise on a subject.

Recognition is another way of enhancing a worker's self-esteem by acknowledging her contribution to an organization. Robert Sweet, owner of an award and design manufacturing firm says, "I don't care how successful employees are, there is something in a reward that touches all our lives. Money is important, but it's the extra things that companies do to make people feel good that is important."[10] He contends that how an award is presented is just as important as the honor itself. Outstanding performances should be recognized at luncheons or in-house gatherings in front of peers. Receiving a plaque in the mail is practically meaningless.

Achievement is experienced when employees are given challenging, meaningful jobs that utilize their resourcefulness and sense of responsibility. "People are willing and eager to push beyond the limits of their known capabilities when they face a challenging task and feel aware that they are expected to deliver."[11]

Workers need to participate in making decisions that affect their lives since a sense of powerlessness can stifle motivation. Employees need to be able to put in their two cents worth about choosing their vacation time or making physical changes in the work environment, for example. Ford Motor Company offers a good example of worker participation since it regularly solicits input from all workers. In fact, hourly workers provided 1,155 proposals for changes in design or production methods for three small trucks, and more than 700 proposals were adopted.[12]

A sense of powerlessness can stifle motivation.

Participation is characterized as ownership in *A Passion for Excellence* and means the employees' sense of being part of the company. Ownership, say the authors, turns workers on. It can be fostered by treating workers as members of a team, allowing them some control in their work, and letting them know what the company is all about. People who "own" the company and their jobs regularly perform a thousand percent better than the rest. A thousand percent better? Impressive, huh?

Self-actualization

At the top of the hierarchy is the need for self-actualization, the need to reach maximum potential, to become all that a person is capable of becoming. It involves setting goals, reaching them, and then setting ever more challenging goals. As Maslow so eloquently put it, "A musician must make music, an artist must paint, and a poet must write, if he is to be ultimately happy. What a man can be, he must be. This need we may call self-actualization."[13]

Eight Characteristics of the Self-actualizing Personality.

A self-actualizing person

The need to reach maximum potential is at the top of Maslow's hierarchy of needs.

1. fully experiences life in the present, the here and now instead of the there and then. Such a person doesn't focus excessively on the past or wish away days while striving toward future goals.
2. makes growth choices rather than fear choices and takes reasonable risks.
3. gets to know himself or herself. He or she looks inward to discover talents, values, meaningfulness.
4. strives toward honesty in interpersonal relationships. A self-actualizer strips away game play and facades, concentrating instead on self-disclosure, intimacy, and authenticity.
5. is assertive and self-expressive even in the case of occasional disapproval.
6. strives toward new goals and seeks to be the best he or she can be in the chosen life role. A self-actualizer doesn't give second rate efforts.
7. gets involved in meaningful and rewarding life activities and has peak experiences.
8. is open to new experiences and is willing to alter expectations and opinions; a self-actualizer says yes to life, to differences, to opportunities, to new paths.[14]

Some psychologists feel that there are no completely self-actualized individuals, but rather those who are self-actualizing. Such a person is more likely to have more "peak experiences," moments of grandeur, awe, or great happiness. An example of a peak experience might be the feeling you get when you make an A on a test, the exhilaration you feel when you win a tennis match, or the awe you experience when viewing a mountain or a sunset. Grandeur, beauty, order, and justice are important to self-actualizers.

To be what we are, and to become what we are capable of becoming, is the only end of life. Robert Louis Stevenson.

The satisfaction of these needs makes life fuller, richer. Unfortunately, in the working world many people do not achieve self-actualization for various reasons. Maybe job descriptions are too restrictive. Perhaps the job is boring and repetitious and impossible to improve. Then again, maybe management thwarts creativity and flexibility. There are, however, means of satisfying self-actualization needs off the job too, and a person with physical security, belongingness, and esteem needs satisfied doesn't need any hints as to the means. Have any ideas?

Maslow's theory does aid in our observation of motivation. Especially significant is the observation that once a need is satisfied, it ceases to motivate. If a worker's salary provides for his physiological and security needs, a nifty new pension plan is no great shakes. To control people, threaten their sense of survival and security since these are conditions to which most of us feel entitled. To truly motivate workers, however, social accomplishment and recognition should be encouraged since social acceptance and self-realization (actualization) are conditions to which they aspire.[15]

There are at least two considerations that limit the application of Maslow's theory. First, a person is complex and a number of needs operate within her at the same time. A person wants the new job (self-esteem) but doesn't want to relocate and leave familiar surroundings (safety). A runner is thirsty (physiological) but wants to finish the 10K race in 45 minutes and make a new personal record (self-actualization). Second, since the satisfaction of our needs is never completely final, we go up and down the hierarchy daily instead of "staying put" at one level.

HERZBERG'S TWO-FACTOR THEORY OF MOTIVATION

People do the darnedest things. Some work happily and productively under the most horrible of work conditions—dingy, drab rooms, uncomfortable temperatures, little status, and lousy supervision. Then again others who have fair and effective supervision, lavish fringe benefits, piped-in music, a clean and well-lighted workplace, and even company recreational facilities moan and groan. How do you make sense of such? Frederick Herzberg has a clue.

A discussion of motivation would be incomplete without an examination of Frederick Herzberg's motivation-maintenance model, sometimes referred to as the two-factor theory of motivation.[16] The gist of the theory is that the absence of hygiene (maintenance) factors creates dissatisfaction, yet the presence of such factors doesn't necessarily satisfy, much less motivate, workers. On the other hand, motivational factors motivate when present but don't cause dissatisfaction when absent. Are you thoroughly confused? Don't be. It's really a commonsense way of looking at motivation.

Hygiene or Maintenance Factors	Motivational Factors
Company policies and administration	Achievement
Supervision	Recognition
Salary	Work itself
Interpersonal relations	Responsibility
Working conditions	Advancement

Source: Frederick Herzberg, *Work and the Nature of Man* (Cleveland, Ohio: World, 1966), pp. 72–73.

Maintenance (hygiene) factors do not motivate people, yet if they are withdrawn, their absence creates dissatisfaction which often results in lowered productivity. "Hygiene" is a term borrowed from the medical profession and refers to factors that maintain but don't necessarily im-

Hygiene factors maintain the status quo rather than motivate.

prove health. Brushing your teeth helps maintain dental health, but the act won't cure a cavity. Hygiene factors on the job act much the same way in that they simply maintain the status quo.

Examples of hygiene or maintenance factors are salary, fringe benefits, working conditions, company rules and policies, and quality of supervision. These factors represent the basic benefits and rights that employees consider essential to any job. Consequently, most workers take salary and working conditions for granted. Maintenance factors are often referred to as extrinsic motivators since they aren't part of the job itself. Extrinsic motivators also correspond to Maslow's lower-level needs and take the form of pay, vacations, and job security. The fewer the possibilities for growth and fulfillment on the job, the greater the demand for maintenance factors.

The fewer the possibilities for fulfillment on the job, the greater the demand for hygiene or maintenance factors.

Speaking of growth and fulfillment, enter the motivational factors. These factors create satisfaction and increased motivation when present, and yet their absence doesn't always cause dissatisfaction. What satisfies you? When asked that question by Herzberg and associates, workers repeatedly voiced the desire for interesting work, the chance to grow, stimulation, achievement possibilities, and recognition. Aspects of the job itself were mentioned, not aspects of the working environment. Motivational factors motivate employees to achieve higher production levels and to feel more committed to their jobs. They are also called intrinsic motivators since they exist in the work itself. It is through intrinsic motivators that people satisfy self-esteem and self-actualization needs spoken of by Maslow.

When motivator factors are lacking, hygiene factors become increasingly important. Workers want more from their jobs than a paycheck and a retirement plan for all their time, effort, and loyalty, and when they don't receive that extra something, most employees ask for more fringe benefits—a bonus, a pay raise, new carpet, or a longer lunch break. Ironically, once a pay raise is granted or a bonus is rewarded, it quickly becomes an expected, taken-for-granted maintenance factor, most conspicuous by its absence. A big-bucks bonus at Christmas is great, but after the first year or so, the bonus causes an almost neutral effect—unless it's unexpectedly withdrawn by a Scrooge.

Herzberg contends that both hygiene and motivator factors must be present if employees are to be satisfied, productive, and motivated. Neither factor alone accounts for both satisfaction and dissatisfaction. In other words, job satisfaction and high motivation for work and job dissatisfaction and low motivation for work spring from different sources. Also, the relationship between maintenance and motivational factors can vary greatly. A person with a challenging job is more able to tolerate a gruff, irritable supervisor than is an individual with a boring job, regardless of the monetary reward.

Both hygiene and motivator factors are necessary for employees to be satisfied, productive, and motivated.

Some psychologists and educators see a similarity between Maslow's hierarchy of needs and Herzberg's two-factor model. For example, both men believe that salary, fringe benefits, and working conditions are only short-term motivators. More motivating in the long run are the higher-order needs such as the opportunity to use unique skills, the ability to participate in decision making, and the chance to be promoted.

Study the following chart and observe the similarities between the two theories.

Maslow	Herzberg
Self-actualization	Achievement Responsibility Work itself
Self-esteem	Recognition Advancement
Belongingness and affection	Interpersonal relations Supervision
Safety and security	Company policy and administration
Physiological needs	Salary Working conditions

ACHIEVEMENT, AFFILIATION, AND POWER

David C. McClelland believes that social motives are important in studying motivation.[17] The needs for achievement, affiliation (friendship), and power will be considered here. Achievement-oriented people gain satisfaction from the accomplishment of a task itself. Sure, they like rewards and probably wouldn't refuse a free trip to Hawaii, but they really do get turned on by solving difficult problems and by performing at their best. As a consequence of their hard work, high achievers have higher salaries and are more likely to be promoted than are others with similar opportunities. Such superstars often come from families where parents hold high expectations for their children.

Persons with a social need for affiliation have an extraordinarily high desire to be accepted by others and will conform to what they believe others want from them. Such individuals enjoy social interaction and actively seek the company of others. They're nice folks to have around since they attempt to iron out friction and tension.

Individuals with a higher need for affiliation desire to be accepted by others and will often conform to what others want from them.

Know anyone who loves to win arguments, to dominate situations, and to persuade others strongly in making decisions? Chances are this individual has a strong need for power. Having a need for power has both advantages and disadvantages. For instance, such a person could inspire feelings of confidence and ability in employees. On the other hand, using power to manipulate people or to make decisions affecting their lives without caring for their input is not always desirable.

Needs for achievement, affiliation, and power can all be useful in a work setting. It is important that the manager recognizes that all employees have different hot buttons and act accordingly. Workers with a high need for achievement should be given jobs and a chance to show they can perform them, for example. Those with a strong need for affiliation can be counted on to avoid conflict and contention while employees with a social need for power could inspire feelings of confidence in employees fearful of the inevitable changes that occur in the workplace.

VROOM'S EXPECTANCY THEORY

Victor Vroom is credited with developing another popular theory of motivation, the expectancy theory.[18] Unlike the three theories already discussed, Vroom's theory doesn't stress unsatisfied needs and motives. Instead it emphasizes that motivation and its resulting behavior are primarily the result of how an individual perceives a situation, what he expects from it, and what he thinks will occur as a result of certain types of behavior. The estimate of the probability of a specific outcome is what motivates someone to behave in a certain way.

A person is more likely to be motivated when she thinks that her efforts will result in a favorable performance which in turn will result in a desired reward. The word "desired" is important. The reward could be a raise, an outstanding evaluation, a promotion, or an A in a course, but if none of those rewards is desired by the person, they won't motivate her.

A person is more likely to be motivated when she believes her efforts will result in a favorable performance and earn a desired reward.

Generally speaking, whenever you've asked yourself the following questions, you were putting Vroom's theory into practice:

What's in it for me?

How much do I really want it?

How hard will I have to work to get this?

What are my chances of getting this reward (promotion, evaluation, raise, good grade, etc.) if I do what's required or requested?

Consider someone who's reviewing the work required for a course in communications. The thought processes involved in the expectancy theory might work something like this. "If I study two hours a day and write the optional research paper, will I get an A in this course? Will I have time to write the paper? Am I willing to give up social activities to spend extra time studying? Will writing the paper take too much time away from my other courses? Is an 'A' in a course outside my major really worth all of the extra work?"

By now you see that there is more to motivation than meets the eye. Many people oversimplify it and try to use a blanket approach to motivating others. They erroneously believe that all people are motivated by the same things at the same time. Motivation is a personal thing, and different approaches need to be applied to different personalities.

CASE STUDY

Rocky Mountain Aviation

A Rocky Mountain–based charter aviation firm had been experiencing high turnover among its employees. Within the past two weeks, two skilled mechanics had packed up their tools and left. Then, to top it off, one of the pilots quit without even giving notice.

"What's with these people?" asked Jim Berryman, the retired Air Force officer who had built the business from one plane to the present, multimillion-dollar operation. "I pay top dollar. Our work facilities are first class. I even give them three weeks' vacation a year. What more could they want?"

The personnel director, Myra Timmons, had a few ideas about why the employees quit. Myra had talked to each person on his or her last day of work—an "exit interview," she called it. As she reviewed the reasons these workers stated for quitting, there seemed to be a common thread: the workers felt they weren't appreciated.

"If only someone would say 'Thanks,' or 'Nice job, Bill' " said one mechanic. I'd work my heart out for this company. But no one ever says those kinds of things. I feel like a common grease monkey. I can get more satisfaction working on cars at a gas station than I get working on mil-lion-dollar airplanes here."

1. What levels of needs seem to be going unmet for the workers described in this case?
2. To what extent does management seem to be aware of employee needs and motivators?
3. Recommend some steps that might be taken to reduce this problem of employee dissatisfaction and turnover.

Source: Paul R. Timm and Brent D. Peterson, *People at Work*, 2nd ed. (St. Paul, Minn.: West, 1986), p. 43.

SELF-AWARENESS EXERCISE

This chapter focused on needs and wants which motivate individuals, and as an employee or manager, you were probably thinking of ways to put the various theories into practice on other people in your work environment. But what about yourself? What do you really know about what motivates you?

Read the following list of variables and then rank them in order of their importance to you. Put a "1" by what's most important, a "2" by the next important, and so on.

A. Good relationships with co-workers
B. Private, nicely furnished office
C. Personal secretary
D. Satisfying work

E. Individual responsibility
F. Creative work
G. Decision-making authority
H. Company car
I. Good rapport with supervisor
J. Company expense account
K. Fair supervisor
L. Recognition for ideas and work well done
M. Opportunity for advancement
N. Pleasant working environment
O. Above-average salary
P. Fair company policies

Look at the top five. Identify them as hygiene or motivator factors. Which do you have more of in the top five? What does this say about your needs at this stage of your career? Do you think these variables will change as your career progresses? Why?

Share your findings with classmates. Are their top five similar to yours? Different? How might you explain the similarities and differences?

Are you surprised that some classmates have different needs? What does the fact that some have different needs and wants tell you about the manager's challenge of motivating others?

Adapted from Richard M. Hodgetts, *Modern Human Relations at Work*, 3rd ed. (Chicago: Dryden Press, 1987), p. 69.

WHAT DO PEOPLE REALLY WANT FROM THEIR JOBS?

Is communication really clear in the workplace? Are managers accurately understanding the messages sent to them by employees? How can mangers motivate employees if they don't know what their needs and wants are?

While management and workers alike often profess to understand each other's motives, research demonstrates otherwise.

What follows is a list of items given to workers and their managers. The workers were asked to rank the variables on the list from most to least important. Their managers were asked to rank the same factors in the same way with one important difference. The managers were to rank the items as they believed the employees perceived them.

Before you read about the results, try the exercise yourself. After reading and considering all the factors carefully, rank them from most to least important from your personal viewpoint.

_____ Job security
_____ Full appreciation for work well done
_____ Promotion and growth with company
_____ Tactful disciplining
_____ Good wages
_____ Feeling "in" on things

_____ Interesting work
_____ Management loyalty to workers
_____ Good working conditions
_____ Sympathetic understanding of personal problems

Now look at the list as rated by employers and their employees. With whom do you most closely compare? Why do you think this is so? Why do you think there are so many differences between the two lists?

Employees		Employers
4	Job security	2
1	Full appreciation for work well done	8
7	Promotion and growth within company	3
10	Tactful disciplining	7
5	Good wages	1
2	Feeling "in" on things	10
6	Interesting work	5
8	Management loyalty to workers	6
9	Good working conditions	4
3	Sympathetic understanding of personal problems	9

SUMMARY

Understanding motivation, the "internal process that starts, energizes, and directs your behavior toward achieving a goal," is fundamental in establishing and maintaining relations with others.

Needs that motivate people can either be primary or secondary. Primary needs are physiological and are necessary for physical survival, while secondary needs are social and physiological.

According to the motivational process, a person experiences a need which creates tension or excitement. This tension motivates action which results in the accomplishment of a goal or in the relief of tension.

Abraham Maslow proposed that individuals have a hierarchy of needs to be satisfied. Lower-level needs like physical and safety needs are systematically satisfied as a person progresses up the ladder toward upper-level needs like self-esteem and self-actualization. Only unsatisfied needs motivate behavior, and once a need is satisfied, it ceases to motivate.

Frederick Herzberg's two-factor theory of motivation states that while the absence of hygiene factors such as salary, fringe benefits, and working conditions creates dissatisfaction, the presence of such factors doesn't necessarily satisfy, much less motivate, people. Motivational factors such as achievement, recognition, challenge of work itself, and advancement opportunity motivate employees to achieve higher production levels and increase organizational commitment. Herzberg contends that both hygiene and motivation factors must be present if employees are to be satisfied, productive, and motivated.

David McClelland suggests that understanding the social motives of affiliation, achievement, and power is important in the study of motivation. Knowing whether a person has a strong need to be accepted by others, a need to gain satisfaction from the accomplishment of the task itself, or a need to persuade others strongly in making decisions helps a supervisor to know how to motivate according to individual differences.

A final theory of motivation is Victor Vroom's expectancy theory which emphasizes how motivation and its resultant behavior are primarily the result of how an individual perceives a situation, what he expects from it, and what he thinks will occur as a result of certain types of behavior. Consequently, a person is more likely to be motivated when she thinks her efforts will result in a favorable performance, which in turn will result in a desired reward.

KEY TERMS

Motivation
Motivational process
Primary needs
Secondary needs
Abraham Maslow
Hierarchy of needs
Self-actualization
Frederick Herzberg
Two-Factor theory
Hygiene factors
Motivator factors
Extrinsic motivators
Intrinsic motivators
Needs for achievement, affiliation, and power
David McClelland
Victor Vroom
Expectancy theory

REVIEW AND DISCUSSION QUESTIONS

1. How can an understanding of "what makes people move" help you as a co-worker? A manager? A friend? How can a study of motivation aid in self-understanding?

2. Give examples of some of your primary and secondary needs. Contrast some of your secondary needs with those of a friend or a family member.

3. Discuss Maslow's hierarchy of needs as they affect a person throughout a typical day.

4. What are some characteristics of a self-actualizing person? What are some things you should do to place you on the path to self-actualization?

5. What are the basic differences between hygiene and motivator factors? What are examples of each? According to Herzberg, how can you best motivate people to achieve goals?

6. What are some different approaches you might use to motivate someone with a strong need for achievement as opposed to a person with a strong need for affiliation?

7. Why are blanket theories of motivation inefficient? Why do you think many employers persist in using such blanket applications?

8. How might Vroom's expectancy theory of motivation work for a person trying to get a promotion? Set personal or professional goals?

ENDNOTES

[1]KENNETH BLANCHARD AND ROBERT LORBER, *Putting the One Minute Manager to Work* (New York: William Morrow, 1984), p. 78.

[2]STAN KOSSEN, *The Human Side of Organizations*, 3rd ed. (New York: Harper & Row, Publishers, 1983), p. 134.

[3]"30 Ways to Motivate Employees to Perform Better," *Training/HRD*, March 1980, p. 51.

[4]MARGARET MAGNUS, ed., "Employee Recognition: A Key to Motivation," *Personnel Journal*, February 1981, p. 107.

[5]KEITH DAVIS, *Human Behavior at Work: Organizational Behavior* (New York: McGraw-Hill, 1981), p. 44.

[6]"How Bosses Get People to Work Harder," *U.S. News & World Report*, January 29, 1979, p. 63.

[7]Ibid., p. 64.

[8]DAVIS, *Human Behavior at Work*, p. 440

[9]A. H. MASLOW, *Motivation and Personality* (New York: Harper & Row, 1954).

[10]MAGNUS, "Employee Recognition," p. 103.

[11]EUGENE RANDSEPP, "Managing for Superperformance," *Office Administration and Automation*, February, 1983, p. 27.

[12]TOM PETERS AND NANCY AUSTIN, "A Passion for Excellence," *Fortune*, May 13, 1985, p. 26.

[13]A. H. MASLOW, *Motivation and Personality*, 2nd ed. (New York: Harper & Row, 1970), p. 46.

[14]A. H. MASLOW, *The Farthest Reaches of Human Nature* (New York: Viking Press, 1971).

[15]CHARLES ALDEN, "Incentives Can Unlock Self Motivation," *Sales and Marketing Management*, April 6, 1981, p. 92.

[16]FREDERICK HERZBERG, *Work and the Nature of Man* (Cleveland: World, 1966).

[17]DAVID C. McCLELLAND AND DAVID H. BURNHAM, "Power Is the Great Motivator," *Harvard Business Review*, March–April 1976, pp. 100–110.

[18]VICTOR A. VROOM, *Work and Motivation* (New York: John Wiley, 1964).

chapter 8

Morale and Job Satisfaction

After reading and studying this chapter, you will be able to:

1. Define morale.
2. Discuss several factors that influence morale and job satisfaction.
3. Discuss at least three methods of assessing morale.
4. List 11 methods of improving morale and discuss the merits of each as they apply to your job situation.
5. Discuss the advantages of maintaining high morale.

Without work all life goes rotten; but when work is soulless, life stifles and dies.

Camus

Job dissatisfaction is a malady that affects millions of American workers and costs billions of dollars in reduced output, shoddy workmanship, absenteeism, and even health problems and work injuries. In this chapter we will examine possible causes of worker unhappiness and investigate means of improving it.

William H. Franklin, Jr., management consultant and trainer, reveals that the average worker turnover rate in the United States is over 25 percent, which means that the entire work force is replaced every four years. In Europe, the rate is only half as high, and in Japan it is only about 5 percent. Americans also have the highest absentee rate in the free world (8 percent) and also the highest rate of work stoppages.[1] Is this anything to brag about? Is there something wrong with the American work climate?

In this chapter, we'll study the effect of morale and job satisfaction on the employee. After defining terms and exploring factors that affect morale, we'll examine several means of assessing job satisfaction. At the end of the chapter, several techniques of improving the work environment are suggested.

WHAT IS MORALE?

Job satisfaction refers to how people feel about their jobs and is determined by a host of variables ranging from how noisy their work areas are to having a "say-so" in matters that affect them. It's a composite of attitudes, feelings, likes, and dislikes that a person feels about his or her work. Job satisfaction refers specifically to feelings about the work itself, while morale reflects a worker's attitude toward both work and life in general. Morale is often described as a state of mind which affects attitude and willingness to work. Positive morale exists when workers know that their hard work and sacrifice are appreciated, recognized, and rewarded.

Morale is a state of mind that affects attitude and willingness to work.

Morale is an intangible concept, not easy to define, measure, or maintain. Nevertheless, since it is always present, whether high or low, it deserves a more specific definition. Kossen defines morale as "employees' attitudes toward either their employing organization in general or toward specific job factors such as supervision, fellow employees, and financial incentives in the atmosphere created by the attitudes of the members of an organization."[2] While morale is considered an individual characteristic, personal morale affects others with whom we come in contact. Morale is contagious.

Morale, whether high or low, is contagious.

In general, there is a relationship between morale and productivity, although this is not always the case. For example, employees could be happy because of their work-related social relationships, and they could be so busy socializing that they fail to produce, much less go the proverbial second mile. In addition, workers could be very productive even if their morale is low because they have bills to pay or because they are ambitious.

FACTORS AFFECTING MORALE AND JOB SATISFACTION

There are many factors that affect worker satisfaction and morale. Self-reports or worker satisfaction are related to the extent to which jobs provide "rewarding outcomes such as pay, variety in stimulation, consideration from their supervisor, close interaction with co-workers, an opportunity to influence decisions which have future effects on them, and control over their pace of work."[3] Compensation, consideration, and control are important, but there are other variables involved in job satisfaction as well. Those considered in this chapter are:

1. Employer (business, industry, organization)
2. Employee's personal life
3. Nature of the job
4. Work associates and peers
5. Supervision
6. Changing social values
7. Personal variables
8. Physical conditions
9. Relationship between effort and reward

Employer

The employer influences the employee's attitude toward his job in many ways. For instance, if the organization experiences a decline in the need for its services or products, morale could take a nosedive as people begin to worry about their job security. Additionally, if the business is perceived in the community as being dishonest or disreputable, the employee's attitude is more likely to be poor. Organizations don't have to take assaults on their reputations lying down. Harry Levinson, industrial psychologist, writes of a prominent chief executive who raised the morale of his employees by filing suit against a broadcast medium for false allegations about company products.[4]

People need to grow personally and professionally. Does the organization offer training, either in house or off the job site? Is there an opportunity for employees to take courses to help them improve in their jobs and pave the way for advancement? Speaking of advancement, does the employer provide the opportunity for aspiring candidates to take on more responsibility? If opportunities for education, advancement, and increased responsibility are available, are they available for all employees regardless of age, sex, race, religion, or national origin?

Company success and size are consistently paired with high morale.

Two factors that are consistently paired with high morale are company success and size. If a company is successful and wisely shares such information with its employees, these workers are more likely to have high morale. It seems that morale is higher in smaller organizations where a worker has a name and identity instead of just a number. How would you rate the morale of this steelworker?

You're not regarded. You're just a number out there. Just like a prisoner. When you request off you tell 'em your badge number. My number is 44-065. When your work sheet is sent in your name isn't put down, just your number. At the main office, they don't know who 44-065 is. They don't know if he's black, white, or Indian. They just know he's 44-065. Steve Dubi, Steelworker.[5]

Employee's Personal Life

An employee doesn't leave her personal life behind when she drives into the parking lot. Interests, activities, relationships, and experiences off the job can have an adverse effect on morale, experiences like a fight with a spouse, a sick child, a traffic jam, and even a nagging mother-in-law. It's hard to concentrate on work when worried or depressed.

Nature of the Job

The nature of the job itself can affect morale. The more workers are able to use their special skills, talents, abilities, and education, the higher their job satisfaction. Some jobs have become increasingly specialized and routine. Such specialization often leads to boredom, fatigue, dissatis-

faction, isolation, and even alienation. The length of the job cycle, how long it takes to perform a task without starting over, can affect job satisfaction. How long does it take to complete the cycle? A minute? A week? Several weeks? The shorter the cycle, the lower the satisfaction.

The more workers are able to use their special skills, talents, abilities, and education, the higher their job satisfaction.

To relieve boredom, many workers invent games or experiment with other techniques. John Runcie is a sociologist who spent five months working on an automobile assembly line and tells of many ingenious methods used to adapt to monotony. Runcie notes that what employees do is as individual as the workers themselves. Some pastimes were to sing, daydream, recite multiplication tables, gossip, trade jobs, or play games. One such game was hooting. "When a worker hoots at the top of his or her lungs, others pick up the cry and the hooting goes up and down the line until it dies out sometime later."[6]

Work Associates and Peers

Work associates and peers are significant in determining morale. Have you ever come to work enthusiastically ready to tackle whatever the eight-hour stint had to offer, only to be confronted with a down-in-the-mouth, complaining acquaintance? Then again it works both ways, and since morale is infectious, a cheerful, friendly co-worker can positively affect your morale.

Healthy competition and cooperation among co-workers can boost morale.

Whether a person is accepted by a work group is significant in determining morale. On-the-job friends are increasingly important in this era when people spend more and more time at work and less and less time at home. Informal groups in the workplace have a great influence over the behavior of employees. Others can offer companionship, support, and a sense of belonging. Is there unhealthy competition among co-workers, or is there healthy competition and cooperation. Is there backstabbing? A feeling of espirit de corps and camaraderie is a great morale booster.

Supervision

Many workers feel down and out because of ineffective or unfair supervision. When employees are left out of decision making, aren't appreciated for their contributions, or are made to feel insignificant, mere cogs in the machinery, a poor attitude often develops. "Managers who humiliate or mistreat employees and fail to communicate with them in constructive ways often contribute to the alienation of workers."[7] Some employees feel that they're classed "behind" the machinery in the eyes of management.

Supervisory style is a variable in job satisfaction. If a supervisor is an authoritarian leader who does all of the organizing, planning, and instructing in addition to commanding and demanding, he or she could create low morale within subordinates who desire a more democratic type of leadership. On the other hand, a manager who seeks feedback and participation from employees who want a strong decisive leader may be perceived as weak.

Changing Social Values

Social values have changed in the United States over the past 20 years. For example, the women's liberation and civil rights movements have made some women and other minorities more disgruntled over job-related conditions. Many women resent their limited career options and the attitude of society that women work only for "pin money." Equal employment opportunity legislation has improved discrimination somewhat, but in general women are still paid less than men for the same work, have fewer opportunities for advancement, and are concentrated in traditional female occupations such as teaching, nursing, and typing.

The quest for fulfillment satisfaction, and even "fun" at work reflect changing social values.

The fact that our nation has become more affluent and that it is not as difficult to survive physically as it once was has brought about changes in social values. Many people don't believe in work for work's sake anymore and are questing for fulfillment, satisfaction, challenge, and even "fun" at work. Do you think our forefathers came to work in search of fun and fulfillment? Probably not. Struggling to survive kept them too busy to ponder, "Is this all there is?"

At one time all an organization needed to do to make people loyal and satisfied was to offer decent pay and a secure job, but not anymore. Not content with a clean, pleasant workplace and adequate compensation, many employees now expect pay tied to performance, more say in what they do, and even perks such as health clubs and subsidized child care. These increased expectations reflect the changing social values of the nation.

The personality ethic stresses that the path to success is through other people; the character ethic emphasizes honesty, hard work, and prudence.

It's been suggested that the personality ethic prevalent today is important in shaping attitudes. This ethic stresses that the path to success is through other people. The value of developing a pleasing personality and getting along with others has, in some cases, replaced hard work, industry, diligence, prudence, and honesty, traits of the character ethic. The character ethic is more pronounced in those whose attitudes were partially shaped by the Depression and by the patriotic incentive to work during World War II.[8]

Personal Variables

Personal variables are too important to be overlooked when discussing job satisfaction. Such variables include age, sex, race, years of work experience, and personality.

Age

Morale is highest among older, more mature workers.

Survey after survey indicates that morale is highest among older, more mature workers. Schultz reports that only 25 percent of the workers between ages 21 and 29 report job satisfaction compared to 43 percent among workers from ages 45 to 64.9.[9] Why is this so? Younger people appear to have higher aspirations and want considerable personal fulfillment. More mature workers are influenced by the character ethic mentioned earlier. Also, it's believed that individuals become more mel-

low and accepting as they get older, especially if they free themselves from the "dream" spoken of by Levinson, youth's desire to leave a mark on the world.[10]

Sex

Research in sex differences in job satisfaction has been conducted, but findings are inconclusive. While it's true that women's earnings average only 70 percent of men's,[11] and while women face some discrimination mentioned earlier, some females don't seem perturbed by this. It's safe to say that there are probably two types of working women. One type is career oriented, while the other uses work to supplement family income, get out of the house, or socialize with others. It stands to reason that these two groups expect different things of their jobs.

Occupation is a factor that further complicates the question of female job satisfaction. Pink-collar workers, which include paraprofessionals in health care and other fields, waitresses, nurses' aides, and many office workers, usually experience pay and status dissatisfaction. Women in more prestigious, challenging fields are not as likely to report such dissatisfaction.

Race

Minority group workers are twice as likely to report job dissatisfaction as are whites.

Race affects satisfaction, especially since minority workers often face discrimination. Schultz reports that minority group workers are twice as likely to report job dissatisfaction as are whites regardless of whether the job is blue-collar, white collar, or management.[12]

Years of Work Experience

Unless an individual has been unemployed for an extended period of time, the older he is, the more job experience he has. Older, more mature workers generally have a more serious attitude toward the job and are more reliable and loyal. Furthermore, the longer someone works, the higher the job satisfaction.

When a person goes to work, the first year is called the honeymoon year. The worker is likely to be enthusiastic in spite of the fact that salary is low and responsibility is little. Things change, however, after a few years on the job, and many people change jobs after about five years in hopes of recapturing the lost enthusiasm. If a worker stays with the same company, morale does improve. The person probably evaluates the situation and decides that things aren't so terrible after all. By this time wages and other benefits seem too good to walk away from. After all, the grass only *looks* greener on the other side.

Instead of waiting it out, some people repeatedly job hop hoping to recapture that initial excitement in the perfect job. Moving from organization to organization puts such a person in a state of perpetual flux. For six months the individual is euphoric in anticipation of the challenges ahead, but later dissatisfaction invariably occurs as reality sets in. Chronic job hoppers experience not only personal costs to themselves, but costs in recruitment, hiring, and retraining to the company too.

Personality

Personality is a final personal variable. There are some people who are dissatisfied regardless of their work roles. These individuals are unhappy with other aspects of their lives as well and are often emotionally unstable. Vroom states that "the satisfied worker is, in general, a more flexible and better adjusted person who has come from a superior family environment, or who has the capacity to overcome the effects of an inferior environment. He is realistic about his own situation and about his goals. The worker dissatisfied with his job, in contrast, is often rigid, inflexible, unrealistic in his choice of goals, unable to overcome environmental obstacles, generally unhappy and dissatisfied."[13]

Someone with a low self concept is more likely to see others as rejecting and hostile.

Self-concept is a component of personality and refers to how a person perceives herself. This evaluation colors a person's perception of everything else. If an individual sees herself as unworthy, unlovable, and incompetent, she is more likely to see others as rejecting rather than accepting, hostile rather than friendly. Such an attitude is not left at home when the employee comes to work.

Physical Conditions

The physical environment contributes to morale. Is it too noisy to concentrate? Is the environment sanitary? Safe? Is there a place for employees to leave their personal belongings? "There is little else that is more damaging to morale than a work environment that is not well lighted, where equipment is not kept in good working order and where needed supplies or resources are absent."[14]

Relationship Between Effort and Reward

There is a relationship between attitude and the feeling that effort contributes to reward. Workers like to know that their hard work and

---

ARE PAY RAISES THE ANSWER?

Pay raises don't satisfy workers for long, a sociologist says. Rather than end discontent, a salary increase—no matter how large—merely intensifies the belief that we deserve more, finds a study of pay perceptions by John Mirowsky of the University of Illinois. And once we earn enough to cover our needs, we shift from trying to get by to trying to get ahead, which "by its very nature is always just out of reach."

Women see a bigger gap than men between their pay and what they consider fair, probably because females usually earn less. But employed wives feel less underpaid the more their husbands earn, while husbands feel more underpaid the more their wives earn. This reflects the traditional view that the husband should be the principal breadwinner.

Prof. Mirowsky suggests that since raises only whet the appetite for ever-greater boosts, workers should also seek other rewards.

"Labor Letter," *The Wall Street Journal*, January 20, 1987, p.1.

People need to know that their advancement is based on their skills and competence rather than office politics.

diligent efforts will be recognized and appreciated. If they feel that rewards in the way of promotions and raises are conferred upon people based on who's been there the longest or on who knows whom, cynicism and low morale are likely to develop. People need to know that their advancement is based on their skills and competence rather than office politics. Everyone doesn't want promotions, but the opportunity must be there and should be contingent on job performance.

ASSESSING MORALE

Managers should be on the lookout for signs of low morale. Too often the "powers that be" are so concerned with profits, machines, labor laws, and policies that they lose sight of the fact that maintaining high morale, a positive mental attitude, is an ongoing and vital process. An occasional pep talk or pump 'em speech provides only a temporary boost, a quick fix. Let's examine methods of assessing morale and job satisfaction and then ways of improving it when low.

Observation

Consistent absenteeism on Mondays and Fridays can indicate a morale problem.

There are many ways to determine whether morale is high or low. An observant person has only to keep his eyes and ears open to be aware of such signs as increased absenteeism, excessive tardiness, and a "don't care" attitude. Everyone is sick once in a while, but consistent absenteeism on Mondays and Fridays can indicate a morale problem. For example, GM assembly plants report that workers are more inclined to call in sick on Mondays and Fridays. The absenteeism runs as high as 20 percent and cost the company $1 billion yearly.[15]

I'VE ASKED ALL YOU GUYS HERE TO DISCUSS THE PROBLEM OF ABSENTEEISM

Frequent tardiness can indicate low morale too. A passive aggressive person might not verbally express his dissatisfaction, anger, resentment, or low morale either because he's not consciously aware of his feelings or because he's afraid that such an expression might result in dire consequences. Rather than express his true feelings, the worker comes in late, thereby passively expressing aggression or anger.

A passive aggressive person might express dissatisfaction and resentment by coming in late.

Speaking of the "don't care" attitude, an alert manager can pick up on all sorts of clues to low morale just by observing and listening. For example, an employee with bent back and furrowed brow is probably unhappy, especially if such is not her usual demeanor. Asking her what is wrong and then attentively listening might not straighten her back immediately, but knowing that someone genuinely cares affects attitude and mood for the better. Asking questions of employees and then listening patiently to their answers, problems, and concerns helps individuals grow in self-confidence, and a self-confident worker is more likely to be a satisfied, motivated, and productive one.

An excellent example of how a negative attitude can affect workmanship is provided by an angry worker on a Detroit assembly line. Dented door panels on cars coming off the assembly line were traced to an unhappy worker who was found hitting the passing cars with his fist. Talk about displacing anger and anxiety![16]

Records

Comparing one year's records of absenteeism, turnover, and production to another is one way of measuring morale.

There are other, perhaps more accurate, ways to measure morale and satisfaction than using eyes and ears. Managers have access to records of absenteeism, turnover, production, and safety. By examining these records and comparing one year's figures to another's, an observer can determine rises or declines. Incidentally, low turnover doesn't necessarily mean that everyone is happy. It could mean that disgruntled workers have no place else to go or that they can't afford to quit.

Surveys

Employee surveys are another way of measuring morale. Employees can be interviewed, presented with a questionnaire, or both. Interviews can be held with either current or existing employees. For obvious reasons, interviewing current employees has its drawbacks. Would you bite the hand that feeds you? Exit interviews are helpful in finding out employee attitudes toward the company, but even then some people are fearful of stating honest feelings and impressions, especially if such feelings could jeopardize a letter of recommendation.

Questionnaires are usually objective and anonymous. In some cases just administering a survey boosts morale, at least temporarily. Why? Maybe it gives people an opportunity to vent their suppressed feelings, or maybe it makes them feel important since management took the time to pay attention to them. Occasionally a questionnaire is given to help pinpoint problem areas and is followed by an interview to find out more details.

Simply administering a survey often boosts morale.

No matter what type of method is used to survey satisfaction, results should be reported to employees, and when possible, acted upon. If suggestions from workers can't be put into practice, they deserve to know why. A survey conducted by a Yonkers rug company indicated that employees felt underpaid. Although pay is no longer one of the major aspects of job satisfaction, it can be a cause of dissatisfaction if workers feel that they're underpaid. In this case it was impossible to pay more, so management allowed employees to find out on their own why wages couldn't be increased. Committees were formed to go around and learn about manufacturing costs and about the company's competition. The result? After seeing the expense involved from a management perspective, the employees volunteered to take a pay cut![17]

Survey results should be reported to employees and, when possible, acted upon.

IMPROVING MORALE

Finding methods to improve job satisfaction is a goal of progressive management. When people have no opportunity for growth and development, use only a portion of their skills, and experience no sense of belonging, it's not likely that they'll be satisfied with their jobs. Dissatisfaction leads to low morale which in turn leads to fatigue, boredom, sabotage, poor workmanship, and absenteeism.

Low morale leads to fatigue, boredom, sabotage, poor workmanship, and absenteeism.

What can be done to improve things? Following are several suggestions. Some of these suggestions are also recommended as ways to improve motivation. Motivation and morale are first cousins, not identical twins. Motivation propels someone, drives her to accomplish a goal. Morale is more of a mood, an emotion, an attitude, not an impetus to relieve tension, achieve a goal, or initiate some activity. A person with high morale, however, is often highly motivated as well.

MORALE ASSESSMENT FACTORS

Assessment Factor 1: Listen to the Humor. Healthy humor is a strong indicator of camaraderie, trust, and a positive sense of self. Unhealthy humor, filled with blatant hostility, deep cynicism or a cutting edge, thrives in organizations with low morale.

Assessment Factor 2: Tune into the Grapevine. Where there is high morale, people talk about the routine comings and goings and doings of people they know. In those organizations with low morale, however, the grapevine has a strong defensive quality and reflects the employees' needs to find out what the company is "up to now."

Assessment Factor 3: Be Sensitive to Complaints and Griping. There is always a baseline level of griping that exists in any organization, no matter how high the morale. In organizations with low morale, however, the level of complaining rises dramatically since virtually everyone is grumbling about something or other all the time.

Assessment Factor 4: Examine the Attrition Rate. It's a fact that good people stay in organizations where morale is high, but when morale is low, the attrition rate steadily increases. In companies with low morale, the organization is distrusted and consequently there is little "holding power" to keep good workers there.

Assessment Factor 5: Take a Close Look at Organizational Responsiveness. Does the organization listen to employees at every level down the hierarchy? Are legitimate complaints taken seriously and is something done about them?

Assessment Factor 6: Notice the Level of Employee Sickness. Low morale and high levels of employee stress go together, and chronic stress over time manifests itself in various forms of physical ailments. The number of sick days goes up as does an increase in health insurance usage by employees.

Assessment Factor 7: Get a Feel for the Number of "Mental Health" Days Taken. Mental health days are days off taken by employees who are not physically ill but who wake up to find that they just cannot face the office another day with its stress and frustration.

Bruce A. Baldwin, "The Magic of Morale," *Pace*, February 1986, p. 14.

Eleven Ways to Improve Morale

Many of the methods cited here fall under the umbrella of "job enrichment," a term which has become popular in recent years and can mean anything that alters or improves a job to increase satisfaction and motivation. Many managers now refer to job enrichment as quality of work life enrichment.

1. Job loading
2. Whole-job concept
3. Job rotation
4. Increased participation
5. Delegation

6. Flexitime
7. Positive reinforcement
8. Changes in physical environment
9. Improved communication
10. Job sharing
11. Adequate compensation

Job Loading

Job loading can be either vertical or horizontal. Vertical loading involves changing a job so that it is more challenging and meaningful. An example is to make a dishwasher responsible for keeping a record of broken and chipped dishes and for reporting such defects to the supervisor. Since horizontal job loading is simply giving more work at the same level, the dishwasher would be given more pots and pans to scour and scrub.

Whole-Job Concept

The whole job concept is also called job enlargement and increases the complexity of a job so that it appeals to the worker's higher-order needs. It's the opposite of "Taylorism," dividing work into small, specialized functions, often making the job routine and mechanized. The more skills and abilities a worker uses, the higher her job satisfaction.

Job enlargement increases the complexity of a job so that it appeals to the worker's higher-order needs.

A good example of a job enlargement, also called job redesign, is that of a telephone company who used the whole-job concept in compiling new telephone directories. The directories were usually compiled in assembly-line fashion involving 21 steps with each step performed by a different worker. What a bore. With job enlargement, each employee had the sole responsibility of compiling a complete directory. All 21 steps were combined into one task. Amazingly, turnover and errors dropped while productivity and job satisfaction increased.[18]

Job Rotation

In job rotation job tasks are rotated to relieve monotony and provide variety. A grocery store employee might bag groceries, stack shelves, order frozen foods, or check out groceries. To combat boredom, lifeguards at a waterpark could alternate watching the younger set at the kiddie pool with watching older swimmers on water slides or other attractions.

When supervisors don't rotate jobs, workers often do it themselves, especially on the assembly line. The supervisor is doing herself a favor by rotating jobs, since workers are then prepared to tackle other jobs when co-workers are out of work.

Participation

Letting employees participate in making decisions related to their work is helpful in raising morale. A GM plant located in Tarrytown, NY, which had the poorest quality record at the company—2,000 outstanding grievances against management, rising dealer complaints, and an unprecedented number of disciplinary and discipline notices—did a stunning turnaround. Workers and bosses who had constantly been at each other's throats began a small voluntary program of worker participation which later included 95 percent of the workers. Since the employees have been given a voice in their jobs, absenteeism has fallen by two-thirds, there are only 30 outstanding grievances, and disciplinary orders, firings, and worker turnover all show declines.[19]

Participative decision making is often helpful in raising morale.

Quality control circles are programs designed to improve communication between workers and management and to help employees feel more a part of company affairs. These are commonplace in Japan and have been implemented in many American firms as well. Benefits enjoyed include increased productivity, improved quality of products and services, improved communication, creation of openness and trust, and improved job satisfaction.[20]

Delegation of Responsibility

Delegating responsibility with the authority to make decisions improves morale of independent workers with a thirst for challenge. *A Passion for Excellence* relates instances of "the $8.95 syndrome." A prime example is of a first-line supervisor responsible for 25 to 35 people who had capital equipment worth up to $1 million and often up to $4 million

---

KEEPING THE WORKERS HAPPY

Every company likes to say it's concerned with employee welfare. Few come close to matching what the German chemical giants do to keep morale high. BASF offers workers a low-cost vacation and rest spa in the Black Forest and a company supermarket plus access to a company wine cellar. Not to be outdone, Hoechst has built a huge geodesic cultural center where it hosts concerts featuring big name stars. It also runs a low cost apartment rental program and helps employees buy houses with interest free loans up to $12,000 and unlimited 6% mortgages.

Wages are generally higher than in the U.S.; there a blue-collar worker packing pills gets about $12,000, a laboratory manager supervising three workers, about $49,000. Fringe benefits? Besides totally free, untaxed dental and medical plans (check-ups available at the company hospital) and generous year end bonuses, most retire at a pension that matches their final paycheck. Add it all up and the German wage-benefit package today is fully 50% above what the U.S. chemicals industry pays.

Before thinking of emigrating, realize that life is more expensive in Germany and less expansive. A four bedroom ranch style house fetches $300,000 in Frankfurt's suburbs, and a filet mignon runs from $8 to $11 a pound at the butcher's. The German mark simply doesn't buy as much in Germany as the American dollar buys in the U.S.

"Keeping the Workers Happy," *Forbes*, October 13, 1980, p. 161.

under his control. Without special permission, this responsible person didn't even have the authority to buy an $8.95 can of paint to clean up a work space.[21]

Flexible Working Hours

Flexitime is simply making a person's working hours more flexible. Changing hours can change mental attitude. Think about it for a moment. If you're a morning person, wouldn't it be nice to clock in at 7:00 and out at 3:00 instead of arriving at 11:00 and leaving at 7:00? Employees are happier and more productive if they have some say over the hours they work. Of course, there are many factors that would limit the application of flexitime. For example, golf course employees are not likely to be late sleepers since much of the work has to be done before the golfers arrive for tee time.

Positive Reinforcement

"Atta boy" is better than nothing, but specific, sincere expressions of praise and encouragement are greatly appreciated as forms of positive reinforcement, especially if employees are deserving of such. Even Mark Twain was not immune to the positive effects of flattery and reportedly said that he could live for two months on a good compliment.

Specific, sincere praise and encouragement are greatly appreciated by deserving employees.

The praise should be sincere. One golf course employee who later became a superintendent learned this lesson from his boss whose only praise was, "Great work, Max." This phrase was used repeatedly, with no specific mention of what work was great or what was so terrific about it. The employee felt that the compliment was insincere and virtually meaningless.

Since people are so complex, what works for one individual might have little effect on another. For instance, in attempting to try some positive reinforcement, an automobile industry offered a trip to Mexico for deserving shop foremen. One individual who won the all-expense-paid trip gave the trip to a co-worker because of the former's intense fear of flying. Another reward, for example, a television or a dinner in his honor, may have been more reinforcing.

Intermittent, specific, and unexpected reinforcement is most effective. Here's an example of the importance of immediate reinforcement. "At Foxboro, a technical advance was desperately needed for survival in the company's early days. Late one evening, a scientist rushed into the president's office with a working prototype. Dumbfounded at the elegance of the solution and bemused about how to reward it, the president bent forward in his chair, rummaged through most of the drawers in his desk, found something, leaned over the desk to the scientist, and said, 'Here!' In his hand was a banana, the only reward he could immediately put his hands on. From that point on, the small 'gold banana' pin has been the highest accolade for scientific achievement at Foxboro."[22]

Physical Environment

Changes in the physical environment can have an uplifting effect on morale. If a room is too stuffy and suffocating or too chilly and frigid, it's hard to do your best work. If the building is dirty, if the cafeteria food is tasteless, if the lighting is insufficient, or if the noise level is deafening, people will moan and groan. Don't assume, however, that lowering the noise level or introducing an attractive color scheme will put a smile on everyone's face. Job satisfaction is more complex than that. For example, a steady, familiar noise apparently does no harm to production, motivation, morale, or job satisfaction. The intermittent, unexpected burst of noise is another story, however, since the worker has to make a greater effort to maintain efficiency.

Since job satisfaction is so complex, lowering the noise level and introducing an attractive color scheme won't automatically lift everyone's spirits.

Since lighting, color, and music are often mentioned as important aspects of the physical environment, their effects on morale will be discussed briefly. Work is negatively affected by insufficient lighting but not necessarily morale. Remember the Hawthorne studies, when those happy workers had the lights so dim that they had to rely on their sense of touch to perform the job? Lighting is only a part of the story.

Attractive color schemes are pleasing to the eye, and some colors have actually been linked to different emotions. Red and orange excites while blue and green soothe us; red speeds decision making, and green encourages reflective thinking. Still, whether color actually enhances performance and satisfaction has yet to be proven.

For years there have been extravagant and often contradictory claims about the value of music in the workplace. Whether music enhan-

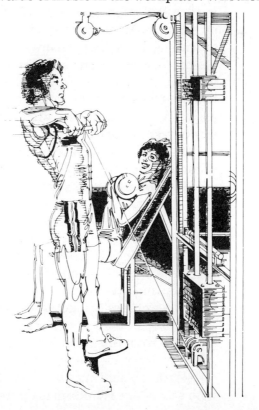

ces morale is dependent on the worker and on the job itself. We all have different preferences in music, and the question of what music to play is often a dilemma. Someone who enjoys classical music is not likely to perform at her best when forced to listen to country and western tunes preferred by co-workers. Additionally, music can sometimes be distracting, especially if the work demands concentration. In short, lighting, color, and music may be somewhat important in affecting attitudes, but the research is inconclusive.

The presence of fitness facilities seems to affect morale positively.

One change in the physical environment that appears to affect morale positively is the presence of physical fitness facilities. Exercise boosts productivity, and many firms have initiated physical fitness programs involving both educating employees about health education and then providing them with the means to improve their physical condition. Officials of the Battelle Memorial Institute, a private research organization, state that their employees who used the firm's fitness center averaged 2.8 days less absenteeism that did those who do not. Big deal, you might say. It is a big deal since reduced absenteeism resulted in a total savings of $150,000 per year.[23]

Improved Communication

Improved communication improves morale and motivation. Having to read the local newspaper to find out what's happening in their company alienates employees and hurts management's credibility. "In the know" employees feel better about the company and are more loyal.

In addition, listening supervisors indicate a caring attitude which in turn makes employees feel important and good about themselves. As an example, Monday through Thursday Wal-Mart's Sam Walton and top executives travel in company-owned planes, each aiming to visit a half-dozen stores every week. Walton chats with employees to find out what items and promotions are popular and helps managers to exchange ideas to solve problems.[24] Do you think he has a communication problem? No way. He communicates attention by his physical appearance, and workers know he cares.

Although it's easy to blame the boss and say that he or she doesn't communicate with employees, part of the burden for communicating lies with employees. Sometimes dissatisfied, complaining employees need to go to the boss and ask what they can do to make the job better for both of them. Keeping the boss informed and asking for direction is not apple polishing but an upfront method of working with a superior to obtain the best results for both of you—and for your company. Some bosses will be surprised by such a request, some will be perplexed over the employee's motives, and others might be relieved to be asked. Whatever the reaction, the workers will get a response and some useful information.

Job Sharing

With job sharing two people share one job. Picture this. A woman with school-aged children is distressed over leaving them at home in the afternoon, and yet she needs an outlet and a paycheck. A college student with morning classes and free afternoons who needs an income might be willing to work in the afternoons and pick up where the mother left off. With job sharing, the rapport of the individuals sharing the job is important so that one worker doesn't strive to outdo the other. "That cuts into your cooperation, and it's the cooperation that makes it flow," says Judy Kahn who shares a job in the office of an interior decorating business.[25]

Job sharing has its advantages for the employer, too. For instance, it saves on the payment of fringe benefits. More important, the workers are happier because of getting to choose their own hours. Mom isn't worried about children home alone and can concentrate more fully on her work. Also since job sharers are not as likely to be striving to the top, the work environment should be more cooperative than competitive.

Adequate Compensation

Well-intentioned job enrichment schemes sometimes fail when companies don't institute new pay practices with new job assignments. Many employees get perturbed when they feel they are not being paid in proportion to their increased work load. Enriched work isn't rewarding enough if employees feel that they are being taken advantage of.

Much has been written about whether salary is really that significant in determining job satisfaction. Adequate wages may keep employees satisfied but won't establish loyalty. Workers want saving plans, share-the-wealth bonuses, and profit-sharing plans. Employees in a sewing plant were told, "We can't give any higher wages, but is there any other way management can increase you job satisfaction?" The predominantly female work force said yes, that they wanted some sort of simple savings plan by which part of their wages were subtracted and put into a special account before the employees even saw the money. After weeks of being told how important they were to the company, the women were told that a payroll deduction was not feasible since payroll was done by computer, and the extra deduction would cost the employer approximately 5 cents per paycheck. Being told that their job satisfaction wasn't worth even 5 extra cents per month didn't do much for already sagging morale level.

If any of the techniques mentioned from vertical job loading to a fresh paint job are to work, they must be accepted by both workers and management who have a climate of trust and understanding between them. Trust is the main ingredient of any relationship and should be used to tighten the bond between employees and employers. If employees feel that employers are deliberately trying to manipulate them, job enrichment strategies are in vain. When morale is high, workers trust the company and its management since they know that it is sensitive to their needs and is concerned for their welfare and growth.

DESIGNING JOBS

In theory, job enrichment techniques sound like marvelous ideas. In practice, they are often difficult to implement. Sometimes it seems next to impossible to even formulate ways of improving the quality of work life—much less put them into practice. To give you a chance to apply what's been learned, follow these instructions.

1. Divide into groups of three to four people. Choose one particular job to study. It could be the present job of a group member, a future job for which one member is presently studying, or just a job from a career field someone is curious about. One stipulation is that this job is one which the group agrees could benefit from job enrichment. Another thing, before a job can be enriched, whether by job enlargement or any other method, someone has to have knowledge about the job requirements and description. Otherwise, how can improvement be made?

2. The group should develop a plan for job redesign that would help employee morale and productivity. The plan should be realistic enough to be accomplished without costing a fortune. Be specific. What exactly would you recommend? How would you carry it out? Why did you choose this method? Why do you think it will work?

3. Choose a spokesperson from the group to present the idea to the rest of the class. Although classmates may approve of part or all of your plan, you should be prepared for constructive criticism as well. Be ready to defend your plan.

4. Discuss whether job redesign is as easy as you thought it would be. What are some factors which make practice different from theory? What are some considerations you have previously not thought about.

Adapted excerpt, p. 184, from *Organizational Behavior* by Jane W. Gibson and Richard M. Hodgetts, copyright 1986 by Harcourt Brace Jovanovich, Inc., reprinted by permission of the publisher.

CASE STUDY

Janitors

Upon transfer to a new plant, an industrial relations superintendent found that, in addition to his other duties, 15 janitors reported directly to him. There was no foreman and observing the janitors for himself, the superintendent learned the 15 men indeed seemed to be lazy, unreliable, and unmotivated.

The new superintendent called a group meeting of all 15 janitors and began the meeting by saying that he understood that there were a number of housekeeping problems and that he didn't know what to do about them. He said that he felt the janitors were experts in the housekeeping area and asked if they would help him solve the problems. Deadly silence met the question, "Does anyone have a suggestion?" and the silence lasted for 20 minutes.

At last one janitor spoke up and told about a problem he was having in his area and made a suggestion. Soon others joined in, and the janitors were involved in a lively discussion while the superintendent listened and jotted down their ideas. The suggestions were summarized with acceptance by all at the end of the meeting.

After that first meeting, the superintendent referred any housekeeping problems to the janitors. When any cleaning equipment or material salesmen came to the plant, the janitors talked to them, not the superintendent. The janitors were given their own office where they could talk to the salesman. Also, regular meetings continued to be held so that problems and ideas could be discussed.

The behavior of the 15 men changed for the better. They developed a cohesive, productive team that took pride in its work. They appeared at work in clean, pressed work clothes instead of their previous grubby attire. It was not uncommon to see one or two janitors running floor tests to see which wax or cleaner did the best job. Since they had to make all the decisions, including committing funds for their supplies, they wanted to know which were the best. These men worked harder and more efficiently than ever before.

1. What do you think is responsible for this change in behavior?
2. What specific quality of work life techniques did the superintendent employ?
3. Can you think of other situations in which similar morale boosting principles could be employed successfully? Be specific.

Adapted from Paul Hersey and Kenneth Blanchard, *Management of Organizational Behavior*, 3rd ed. (Englewood Cliffs, N.J.: Prentice Hall, 1977), pp. 70–71.

SUMMARY

In this chapter we've examined signs of job dissatisfaction and morale and methods of assessing and improving both. Always present, morale is a state of mind that affects attitude and willingness to work. It's an individual characteristic, but since it's contagious, morale affects others with whom we come in contact.

Factors that affect morale are the employer, the employee's personal life, the nature of the job, work associates and peers, supervision, changing social values, personal variables such as age and race, physical condition, and the relationship between effort and reward.

Managers should be ever alert for signs of low morale. Methods of assessing morale and job satisfaction include informal methods of simple observation of frequent absenteeism, tardiness, and a "don't care" attitude to more formal means of studying personnel records and conducting surveys. Survey results should be reported to employees and, when possible, acted upon.

Since low morale can lead to fatigue, boredom, sabotage, poor workmanship, absenteeism, and turnover, progressive management has improving job satisfaction as one of its goals. Means of improving morale include job loading, the whole-job concept, increased participation, flexitime, positive reinforcement, improved communication, and job sharing.

Any method used singly probably will have limited success; perhaps several should be tried. If any of the techniques are to work, they must be accepted by both workers and management who have a climate of trust and understanding between them.

KEY TERMS

Morale
Harry Levinson
Social values
Personality ethic
Character ethic
Personal variables
Assessment methods
Job loading
Whole-job concept
Job rotation
Flexitime
Positive reinforcement
Job sharing

REVIEW AND DISCUSSION QUESTIONS

1. In your opinion, what is the relationship between morale and job satisfaction? Morale and productivity? Why are low morale and dissatisfaction such serious problems?

2. From your personal experience and observation, what are three of the most important variables involved in job satisfaction? Why did you choose these particular three?

3. What are some of the changes that have taken place in America that have influenced social values over the past 20 years?

4. Specifically, how can race, age, sex, and personality affect morale?

5. Of the techniques of morale assessment mentioned in your text, which do you believe to be the most effective? Why?

6. With a present or past job in mind, how could you use the whole-job concept and job rotation to improve job satisfaction?

7. Flexitime is useful in improving morale, but can you think of situations that might limit its application?

8. What is positive reinforcement? Think of several applications of positive reinforcement for various situations.

ENDNOTES

[1] WILLIAM H. FRANKLIN, JR., "What Japanese Managers Know That American Managers Don't," *Administrative Management*, September 1981, p. 37.

[2] STAN KOSSEN, *The Human Side of Organizations*, 3rd ed. (New York: Harper & Row, 1983), p. 253.

[3] VICTOR H. VROOM, *Work and Motivation* (New York: John Wiley, 1964), p. 174.

[4] HARRY LEVINSON, "When Executives Burn Out," *Harvard Business Review*, May–June 1981, p. 80.

[5] STUDS TERKEL, *Working* (New York: Avon Books, 1974), p. 716.

[6] JOHN F. RUNCIE, "By Days I Make the Cars," *Harvard Business Review*, May–June, 1980, p. 109.

[7] JEFFREY L. SHELER, "Why So Many Workers Lie Down on the Job," *U.S. News and World Report*, April 6, 1981, p. 71.

[8] "The Youngest Workers Care the Least," *Psychology Today*, October 1978, pp. 34–36.

[9] DUANE P. SCHULTZ, *Psychology in Use: An Introduction to Applied Psychology* (New York: Macmillan, Inc., 1979), p. 362.

[10] D. J. LEVINSON and others, *The Seasons of a Man's Life* (New York: Alfred A. Knopf, 1978).

[11] JUDY MANN AND BASIA MELLWIG, "The Truth About the Salary Gap(s)," *Working Woman*, January 1988, p. 61.

[12] SCHULTZ, *Psychology in Use*, p. 363.

[13] VROOM, *Work and Motivation*, p. 161.

[14] BRUCE A. BALDWIN, "The Magic of Morale," *Pace*, February, 1986, p. 16.

[15] SHELER, "Why So Many Workers Lie Down on The Job," p. 71.

[16] Ibid., p. 71.

[17] "How Bosses Get People to Work Harder," *U.S. News & World Report*, January 29, 1979, p. 64.

[18]ROBERT N. FORD, "Job Enrichment Lessons from AT&T," *Harvard Business Review*, January–February 1973, pp. 97–98.

[19]"Stunning Turnaround at Tarrytown," *Time*, May 5, 1980, p. 87.

[20]SUD AND NIMA INGLE, *Quality Circles in Service Industries* (Englewood Cliffs, N.J.: Prentice Hall, 1983), p. 7.

[21]TOM PETERS AND NANCY AUSTIN, *A Passion for Excellence* (New York: Random House, 1985), p. 244.

[22]THOMAS J. PETERS AND ROBERT H. WATERMAN, JR., *In Search of Excellence* (New York: Harper & Row, 1982), pp. 70–71.

[23]JOHN S. LANG, "America's Fitness Binge," *U.S. News & World Report*, May 3, 1982, p. 60.

[24]HOWARD RUDNITSKY, "How Sam Walton Does It," *Forbes*, August 16, 1982, p. 43.

[25]JEFF TRIMBLE, "Job Sharing: For Many, A Perfect Answer," *U.S. News & World Report*, August 23, 1982, p. 66.

chapter 9

Leadership

After reading and studying this chapter, you will be able to:

1. Define leadership.
2. Discuss trait theories of leadership.
3. Explain what makes a good leader.
4. Compare and contrast autocratic, participative, and free-reign leadership styles.
5. Discuss McGregor's X and Y theories of leadership.
6. Describe Kossen's "derived X."
7. Explain Ouchi's Theory Z.
8. Discuss Fiedler's contingency theory of leadership.

Leadership appears to be the art of getting others to want to do something you are convinced should be done.[1]

Vance Packard

Napoléon, Abraham Lincoln, Andrew Carnegie, Theodore Roosevelt, George Patton are all familiar names. They were all movers and shakers, possessors of that admired and sought-after quality, leadership. Is there something that sets such individuals clearly apart from ordinary mortals? Are leaders born or made? What are some traits of the ideal leader? Are there certain types of leadership that function well in one situation and fail miserably in another? The answer to these and many other questions will be explored in this chapter.

WHAT IS LEADERSHIP?

Leadership, the ability to get things done willingly and enthusiastically with and through other people, is not as mysterious as once believed. Many people confuse management with leadership, but the terms are not synonymous. Management is a practice; leadership is an art, a skill. Managers manage machines, money, and employees. Leaders lead people. Managers are expected to organize, plan, direct, and control activities and workers. Leaders have to influence others to follow in seeking personal and organizational goals and objectives. Leadership is an aspect of management that deals with people and behavior. Management includes leadership but also includes nonbehavioral functions that don't directly affect others.

Leadership is the ability to get things done willingly and enthusiastically with and through other people.

Mostly, leaders motivate. They help people find the best in themselves and then ask them to shine. They find and nurture champions, dramatize company goals, build skills, and spread enthusiasm. "They are cheerleaders, coaches, storytellers and wanderers. They encourage, excite, teach, listen, facilitate. Their actions are consistent. . . . You know they take their priorities seriously because they live them clearly and visibly; they walk the talk." [2]

Trait Theories

Believing that there existed a set of traits necessary for leadership success, scholars researched tirelessly for such characteristics. Ralph Stogdill concluded that the true leader exceeds the average member of his group to some degree in:

1. Sociability
2. Persistence
3. Initiative
4. Knowing how to get things done
5. Self-confidence
6. Alertness to, and insight into situations
7. Cooperativeness
8. Popularity
9. Adaptability
10. Verbal facility [3]

Trait theory of leadership doesn't provide adequate answers. There are thousands of people who are cooperative, persistent, and self-confident, and yet neither they nor their peers perceive of them as leaders. Obviously there is more to becoming a leader than having a few positive characteristics, especially when the foregoing traits are widely distributed in the population. Perhaps the difference is that leaders have developed these traits to a greater degree than others.

Leaders have developed positive leadership traits to a greater degree than others.

Take the characteristic of sociability, for example. Sayles contends that successful leaders have a large dose of interactional energy, the ability to talk with large numbers of people every day. They are capable of working long after the average person has grown tired of talking, arguing, and cajoling. Not only are they capable, but they are willing and anxious to work with others.[4]

Few consistent leadership traits have been identified. Before tossing years of research into the wastebasket, however, let's look at another set of traits believed to be essential to leadership success. Ross and Hendry conclude that effective leaders:

1. Are self-confident, well integrated, and emotionally stable.
2. Want to take leadership responsibility and are competent in handling new situations. They have a strong, almost obsessive, desire to be winners and are willing to pay the price for success.
3. Identify with the goals and values of the groups they lead.
4. Are warm, sensitive, and sympathetic toward other people and give practical, helpful suggestions. They don't just give lip service to a people orientation. Leaders get out of their ivory towers and mingle with others, listening to ideas, complaints, and suggestions.
5. Are intelligent in relation to other group members. Sure, there are group members who are more intelligent than the leader. He or she just exceeds the group average.
6. Can be relied on to perform leadership functions continuously. Inspiring and persuading others is not an on again, off again business.[5]

Leaders can be relied on to perform leadership functions continuously.

While it's true that early thinking suggested that anyone could be a leader if he or she possessed certain personality traits, intellect, and physical characteristics, we now know that this is not so. At one time it was believed that tall people made better leaders. But leaders actually come in all ages, sizes, shapes, and both sexes. Robert Townsend, author of *Further up the Organization*, offers a clue about spotting leaders when he remarks that "since most people per se are mediocre, the true leader can be recognized because somehow or other, his people consistently turn in superior performance."[6] In general, leadership is too complex to be reduced to a set of traits. As you'll see later in the chapter, other variables enter into the situation, variables such as the people involved and the task to be accomplished.

There are at least two qualities that inhibit leadership. Those qualities are fear and indecisiveness. Fear is a paralyzing emotion—fear

DO YOU HAVE WHAT IT TAKES?

Everyone has an influence in other people's lives. How great your influence will be is up to you. You might not be chairman of the board, night supervisor, or even an eensie teensie biggie at work, but you can still be a leader in your family, church, neighborhood, or softball team.

If you've got the qualities of caring, concern, courage, determination, commitment—and love, then you're leadership material, and somebody out there needs you. Maybe it's time you reached deep down for the potential you haven't even acknowledged exists.

The common denominators include:

1. *The ability to dream.* Leaders dream big dreams and have high expectations for themselves and for others. They also have the ability to instill those feelings in others.
2. *A positive attitude.* Leaders don't get bogged down by the petty difficulties of life or worry uselessly.
3. *A willingness to serve as an example.* Before they ask for commitment, leaders commit themselves. Before asking you to work hard, they work hard.

Reprinted with permission of The Saturday Evening Post Society, a division of BFL&MS, Inc. C 1984

of failure, fear of ridicule, fear of mistakes, fear of ostracism, fear of criticism. Fear keeps the manager or supervisor from acting assertively. There's no time for positive planning and goal setting when all the person's resources are being used to defend against fear.

Fear and indecisiveness inhibit leadership.

Concerning indecisiveness, "Nowhere is the lack of leadership more evident than when the boss won't decide on a crucial matter. . . . This does not mean that leaders always make quick decisions. On the contrary, they spend considerable time before deciding, but the point is that they do decide."[7]

Chester Barnard, a writer and former president of New Jersey Bell Telephone Company, agrees that the making of decisions is a burdensome task that many people try to avoid. "Offsetting the exhilaration that may result from correct and successful decision and the relief that follows the terminating of a struggle to determine issues is the depression that comes from failure or error of decision and the frustration that comes from uncertainty."[8] He feels, however, that decision making is a capacity that can be developed by training and experience.

So What Makes a Leader?

There are no magic formulas for leadership. However, it's agreed that all successful leaders have power, skills, and a vision.

Power

Leadership is not coercion, and yet it is a form of power, persuasive power. Power is the ability to influence other people and events. It's the way leaders extend their influence to others. Authority is granted from above, but power is granted on the basis of the leader's personality, activities, and situations in which he or she operates. The acceptance theory of leadership proposed by Barnard proposes that a manager's authority is ultimately derived from subordinates rather than from higher levels of management. A person without conferred power can become an informal leader on the basis of the power granted by the group.

McClelland and Burnham believe that the need for power is what makes the difference between a mediocre manager and a good manager. From their research of large companies, they found that the good manager has neither a high need for achievement nor affiliation. Managers with a high need for achievement end up doing much of the work themselves to feel that they've achieved or accomplished something, but a good manger delegates to others. This need for power is also greater than the need for affiliation, the need to be liked and to have friends.[9]

This need for power is not a desire to dominate others or to coerce them into working. Rather it's a need to influence others. Good managers are not coercive but persuasive. Two characteristics which keep them from becoming authoritarian are (1) a greater emotional maturity with little egotism and (2) a democratic, coaching managerial style.

Types of Power: Davis cites four types of power related to leadership: personal or referent, legitimate, expert, and political.[10] Let's take a closer look at these types.

1. *Personal or referent.* This is the power of personality. Words like "charisma," "personal magnetism," and "self-confidence" come to mind. This power causes people to follow the leader because their emotions tell them to do so.

2. *Legitimate.* This is position power or official power and comes from higher authority. It gives the leader power to control resources and to reward and punish others. People accept this leader because they believe it is desirable and necessary to maintain order.

3. *Expert.* This power comes from specialized training. It evolves from a person's knowledge and information about a situation and depends largely on education, training, and experience. It's an important source of power and shouldn't be overlooked.

4. *Political.* Political power comes from support of a group. It arises from a leader's ability to work with people and social systems to gain their allegiance and support. It develops in all organizations. To gain this power, there are a number of tactics like social exchanges and alliances of various sorts. After a period of time, trade-offs and social exchanges lead to an alliance in which two or more persons join in a power group to get benefits which they mutually want.

*Political power
comes from a
leader's ability to
work with people and
social systems to
gain their support
and allegiance.*

Another popular path to political power is to become identified with a higher authority and/or a powerful figure in the organization. "Anointing" is the term used by Sayles and means that a person's leadership can be authenticated by someone who already has status in the eyes of potential followers.[11]

Skill

Good leaders are knowledgeable. They have at least three types of knowledge or skill: technical, human, and conceptual.[12] Workers also expect their leaders to have organizational knowledge.

*Technical skills are
less important as the
leader rises in the
organization and
begins to rely more
and more on the
technical expertise of
subordinates.*

Technical skills are indispensable and are especially important at the lower levels of management. Workers expect their leader to know about the process or technique of marketing potato chips, teaching school, or selling cars before the will follow him or her willingly. This technical knowledge is less important as the leader rises in the organization and begins to rely more and more on the technical expertise of the subordinates.

Regardless of the level, the knowledgeable leader keeps abreast of changes in the profession instead of insisting on doing things the way they were done "back then." Technical skill is the most familiar to most people because it is the most concrete and because it is required of the greatest number of people. People are initially hired because of their technical skill.

Human skill is the ability to work effectively as a group member and to build cooperative effort among the subordinates. The person with highly developed human relations skill is aware of personal attitudes and beliefs about other people and is able to see the usefulness and limitations of these feelings. These human skills enable the leader to accept the existence of viewpoints and perceptions which are different from his own and to understand what others really mean by their words and actions. Such a person works to create an atmosphere of approval and security in which subordinates feel free to express themselves without

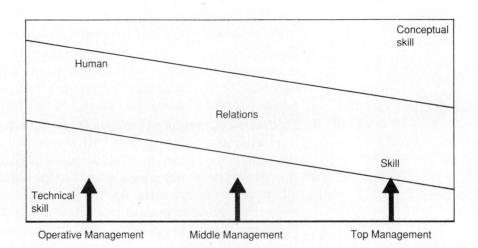

fear. Demonstration of human knowledge cannot be a "sometime thing" but a continuous activity.

Human relations skills are essential at all levels of management.

Human relations knowledge is of the utmost importance at all levels. To lead others, someone needs to understand what motivates behavior, how to communicate effectively, how to predict actions, and how people learn and use information. Leaders genuinely care about others. They want to know what makes them tick, what their ideas are, how they feel about change. They believe in treating people decently without mollycoddling them, and they realize that personal contact is effective and essential.

Many managers profess that people are important, their most important resource, and yet their actions say otherwise. Not so with Big Jim Daniell, chief executive of RMI, a subsidiary of U.S. Steel and National Distillers, an integrated producer of titanium products. This executive "spends much of this time riding around the factory in a golf cart, waving and joking with his workers, listening to them, and calling them by their first name—all 2,000 of them."[13] If this sounds a little corny to you, don't be so hasty in your judgment. For years the company's performance was substandard. Now because of the intense people-oriented program, Big Jim has managed about an 80 percent productivity gain. Everyone who knows him says he simply exudes care about his customers and his people. No one questions his leadership ability.

Achieving "followership" willingly is determined by a supervisor's actions toward subordinates. These actions or behaviors are fairness, consistency, and a demonstrated interest in workers. To demonstrate fairness, the leader should treat people as equally and impartially as possible and avoid socializing with some individuals more than others. Consistency and predictability are also important if workers are to know what a leader expects and how to conform. It's necessary also that the supervisor show interest in people by listening to work or personal concerns, giving credit when credit is due, giving support at difficult times, and giving constructive feedback on progress.[14]

Conceptual knowledge or skill deals with broader concepts. Conceptual skills are needed to think about unrelated ideas and to put them together to form new approaches. The higher a manager rises in an organization, the more he or she is confronted with ideas and concepts that are often vague. Instead of being concerned about the personal problems of a worker on the second shift or of a malfunctioning machine, the leader with conceptual knowledge is faced with problems of raising money, maintaining community support, and formulating long range goals. Broad experience, not specialization in one area helps to develop conceptual skills.

Conceptual skills are helpful in facing challenges of raising money, maintaining community support, and formulating long range goals.

Robert Katz states that "conceptual skill involves the ability to see the enterprise as a whole; it includes recognizing how the various functions of the organization depend on one another, and how changes in any one part affect all the others." Some people refer to conceptual skill as a person's ability, "the way he perceives and responds to the direction in which the business should grow, company objectives and policies, and stockholders' and employee's interest."[15]

Although often overlooked as an important type of knowledge, workers expect their leaders to have *organizational knowledge*. Employees want to know what's going on in the business. They are concerned with future changes in people, products, or the organizational structure itself, and they look to their immediate supervisor for such information. For instance, workers want to know who's in line for promotion or whether a new product line is being added, for instance. "People want to know as much as possible about their work environment, and not knowing hurts. It hurts their pride, insults their intelligence, arouses their fears, and results in counter-productivity.[16]

Vision

Remember the id mentioned in Chapter 6? The seething, boiling cauldron of repressed sexual and aggressive urges? Recent research indicates that the conflict among the id, ego, and superego is not as bitter within a leader as it is within the nonleader since the leader's superego or conscience isn't as bothersome as it is with some people. Since the leader has less energy invested in the superego, this frees him to concentrate on the ego ideal, the image of what he wants himself and his organization to be.[17]

The leader's vision gives him a sense of who he is, what he's after, and what he can incite others to strive for.

This *vision* is the leader's best motivational tool. It gives him a sense of who he is, what he's after, and a sense of what he can, by words and example, incite others to strive for. Because of his overriding commitment to the common goal, and because he's less hung up about his own aggressiveness and others', he can be utterly forthright in telling people when they're not performing up to the mark. The boss knows where the organization is going and is able to communicate his vision to others. He lets them know that he cares about it fervently and encourages workers to feel the same way and to strive for the same goals.

Rate Your Boss As A Leader

Score each characteristic from 0 to 10.
   He is

1. . . .available. If I have a problem I can't solve, he is there. But he is forceful in making me do my level best to bring in solutions, not problems.

2. . . .inclusive. Quick to let me in on information or people who might be useful to me or stimulating or of long-term professional interest.

_____

3. . . .humorous. Has a full measure of the Comic Spirit in his make-up. Laughs even harder when the joke's on him.

_____

4. . . .fair. And concerned about me and how I'm doing. Gives credit when credit is due, but holds me to my promise.

_____

5. . . .decisive. Determined to get at those little unimportant (how they are decided) decisions which can tie up organizations for days.

_____

6. . . .humble. Admits his own mistakes openly—learns from them, expects employees to do the same.

_____

7. . . .objective. Knows the apparently important (like a visiting director) from the truly important (a meeting of his or her own people) and goes where he is needed.

_____

8. . . .tough. Won't let top management or important outsiders waste his time or his people's time and is more jealous of his people's time than he is of his own.

_____

9. . . .effective. Teaches me to bring him my mistakes with what I've learned (if anything) and done about them (if anything). Teaches me not to interrupt with possible good news on which no action is needed.

_____

10. . . .patient. Knows when to bite the bullet until I solve my own problem.

_____

Total   *_____

*This is your boss's rating as a leader on a scale of 0 to 100. If it's below 50, look for another job.

Robert Townsend, _Further Up the Organization_, (New York: Alfred A. Knopf, 1984), pp. 249-251.

STYLES OF LEADERSHIP

All managers have to create a balance between decisiveness and participation. How he or she does so indicates a general leadership style. The styles are based on the type of control that the leader exercises and the resulting behavior toward group members. Is your boss the type who makes all decisions and then expects you to follow through without question? Then again, maybe your manager asks you for your input and thereby encourages you to participate in the decision-making process. There are three distinct styles of leadership: autocratic, participative, and free reign.

Autocratic

How a manager creates a balance between decisiveness and participation indicates a general leadership style.

An autocratic leader concentrates power, decision making, and responsibility in one person.

The *autocratic* or *authoritarian* leader leaves no doubt in anyone's mind as to who is in charge. This person runs a tight ship by setting all policy, making all decisions, and accepting total responsibility. Anyone working for an autocratic leader knows what is expected since assignments are clear. An autocratic leader concentrates power, decision making, and responsibility in one person.

An autocratic leadership style does have its advantages. It saves time and is very efficient. It might not suit your fancy, but for people reluctant to make decisions or accept responsibility, having an autocrat for an order giver is quite satisfactory. It makes them feel secure. Think about this. All our lives, we've taken orders from authorities like parents, teachers, principals, and law officers. We obey certain people in authority because we've been taught to and because it's easier. Some individuals get fed up with kow-towing to authority and rebel while others like it and are able to transfer that obedience to parents to obedience to employers.

An autocratic leadership style saves time, is efficient, and works well in crisis situations.

Another advantage of the autocratic style is that it works well in crisis situations in which decisions have to be made quickly and carried through without question. There's no time to ask Jane and Joe for their suggestions or to be concerned over having a consensus of opinion.

On the other hand, an autocratic or authoritarian style does have a few disadvantages. The main one is that the communication is one way, downward. The boss gives instructions but encourages no comments, questions, or complaints. Unfortunately, this leads to errors in thinking if people interpret things in a way not intended. Too, if some people within the group want to participate and accept responsibility, they feel thwarted and, consequently, dissatisfied. It is deadly for a leader to become isolated, and yet that's exactly what happens when he or she views communication as one way.

Participative

The *participative* leader asks for, even encourages, suggestions and ideas from employees. Such a leader feels that 2 or 10 or 200 heads are better than 1. The manner in which the participative leader handles upward communication determines whether she is *democratic* or *consultative*. If democratic, the manager lets the group members make the final decision. A consultative manager asks for input but makes it clear that the final decision will be made by the one in charge. Participative leaders request and expect constant feedback. "When people participate in making the decisions that affect their lives, they support those decisions more enthusiastically and try harder to make them work."[18] This is true even when the participants disagree with the decision.

There are advantages and disadvantages of a participative style of management. Sometimes efficiency and productivity improve when

A democratic leader lets group members make the final decision; a consultative leader asks for employee input but makes the final decision himself or herself.

people help make a decision or understand why it's been made. Consequently, job satisfaction, group cohesiveness, and improved communication often result. The better the communication, the more talent, expertise, ideas, and information the leader has access to.

On the other hand, participative leadership can be very inefficient and time consuming and can even result in the loss of managerial control. The one in charge must be certain of what he or she wants. He owes it to his people to use their ideas and suggestions when possible, or they'll grow resentful when constantly ignored.

Free Reign

Free–reign or *laissez faire* is a very "laid–back" style of leadership. The one in charge appears not to be. She down plays her "bossy" role and concentrates on providing information and resources to workers. The leader doesn't relinquish all control to the group but yet maintains only minimal control. In a sense the manager says, "Here are the goals. Here is the budget. Our deadline is December 8. Tell me what resources you need, and I'll secure them. If you need anything else, or if you encounter any problems or have any questions, call me. Otherwise, I expect results on the designated date."

The laissez faire leader downplays the "bossy" role and concentrates on providing information and resources to workers.

The advantage of a free–reign style is giving workers complete freedom to act. Many people operate at peak efficiency only if given such freedom and are motivated by freedom and challenge, especially people like researchers, scientists, writers, and sales representatives. Self–starters who don't need a lot of structure thrive and grow in such an atmosphere.

The main disadvantage to using free–reign style is that it's risky. The leader exercises little control, and yet the ultimate responsibility for success or failure falls squarely on his or her shoulders. The laissez–faire leader has to know subordinates very well indeed before giving such freedom. Before giving them freedom to act, the manager can answer certain questions positively. What are the abilities of subordinates? Can they be trusted? What are their dominant values?

Which Style Is Best?

The real art of leadership might be in being able to identify the most appropriate style in each circumstance. Since all the styles reflect personality, a person can't be expected to change personality, and yet he or she must be flexible when assessing the situation at hand. You'll understand more about assessing situations and applying management styles shortly.

A supervisor has to decide how he or she feels about subordinates before deciding on a management style.

Before deciding on a management style, the supervisor has to decide how she feels about subordinates, according to Cangemi et al. She either trusts and values people or she doesn't. "A positive attitude toward people is a prerequisite for a successful participative style of management. If a manager thinks subordinates are inferior in ability, desire, creativity, and holds them in low regard, it won't work. He can't get their trust and respect."[19] A manager who believes that people are capable, responsible, creative, and trustworthy is more likely to achieve success with a participative style of management.

McGREGOR'S X AND Y THEORIES OF LEADERSHIP

In the late 1950s Douglas McGregor developed the X and Y theories of management.[20] X and Y leaders have different viewpoints about human nature. The X leader believes that people are basically lazy and have to be goaded to work. This rather pessimistic view holds that people work only for money, have very little self–control, and have little or no commitment to organizational goals.

An X leader believes that people work only for money and have little or no commitment to organization goals.

The leader with a Y orientation is more positive. He or she believes that people get satisfaction from sources other than money, from the feeling of a job well done, for example. A Y leader determines and gives appropriate rewards and keeps the lines of communication open in the belief that workers will make the organization's goals their own. Here are assumptions of the two theories.

A Y leader believes that people get satisfaction from sources other than money.

Theory X

1. The average person has an inherent dislike of work and will avoid it if possible
2. Because of this dislike of work, most people must be forced, controlled, directed, or threatened with punishment to get them to put forth adequate effort toward the achievement of organizational objectives.
3. The average person prefers to be directed, wishes to avoid responsibility, has relatively little ambition, and wants security above all.

Theory Y

1. The expenditure of physical and mental effort in work is as natural as play or rest.
2. External control and threat of punishment are not the only means for bringing about effort toward organizational objectives. People will exercise self–direction and self–control to reach objectives to which they are committed.
3. Commitment to objectives is a function of the rewards associated with the achievement of those objectives.
4. The average person learns, under proper conditions, not only to accept but to seek responsibility.
5. The capacity to exercise a relatively high degree of imagination, ingenuity, and creativity in the solution of organizational problems is widely, not narrowly, distributed in the population.

6. Under the conditions of modern industrial life, the intellectual potentialities of the average person are only partially utilized.

The autocratic, X type of leadership is appropriate for many situations.

The X leader has a negative view of humankind. People have to be threatened before they'll perform. The X leader is often autocratic, but for some situations, the X type of leadership is needed. The X leader is production and task oriented instead of people oriented and uses the stick to motivate. Some X managers are really nice folks and have a paternal attitude that communicates itself as "Don't worry about a thing. I've made all the decisions about who's doing what and when and where and with whom. Papa's (or Mama's) going to take care of you."

The Y leader assumes that people are willing to give a full day's work for a day's pay. Work is not abhorrent or onerous but is as natural as rest or play. If people are treated with respect and dignity, they will respond in a positive manner.

One theory is not superior to the other in all situations. Theory Y, because of its optimistic outlook and its emphasis on the positive side of nature is used successfully in many cases. However, let's face facts. Some people really are lazy. Some people do have to be prodded, goaded, threatened, and directed. They like it. Too, there are some jobs you've done, are doing, or will do that aren't challenging, exciting, or enlightening. You do that job because you like to eat. So isn't it possible that even though you are a self–starter and a real go–getter that in some situations you might work better with an X leader, one that directs your work and reminds you of little details?

KOSSEN'S DERIVED X

Derived X leaders were once positive about subordinates but became pessimistic after being "burned" in the process.

Stan Kossen humorously contends that some managers have been "burned" because of their optimistic viewpoints and have consequently adopted a derived X leadership style.[21] These managers have tried to remain optimistic and positive about subordinates but have been "burned" in the process. It's similar, Kossen says, to being regularly ditched in love relationships. The person once felt good about true love, but after going through pain over and over, his or her position changed from optimistic to pessimistic, from positive to negative, from Y to X. The same holds true for managers. Here's Kossen's list of attitudes that can be derived from negative experiences with employees.

1. I want to feel that people are conscientious and find work a natural activity, but I've been burned too many times by some of my employees.
2. I've given my subordinates the chance to make decisions and to assume responsibility, but I've been burned too many times. They've simply taken advantage of me.
3. I've tried to create an atmosphere of growth and development for my subordinates by giving them the freedom to make mistakes and to fail, but I've been burned too many times. They haven't grown and developed; they've merely made mistakes and failed.

4. I've tried to get workers to participate in planning activities for achieving organizational goals, but I've been burned too many times. They're more interested in paydays than in accomplishing organizational goals.

OUCHI'S THEORY Z

X and Y lead to Z. Theory Z is not a combination of theories X and Y but rather a theory that combines characteristics of American and Japanese leadership practices. A (American style) and J (Japanese style) equal Z.[22] Before going through the alphabet, let's take a close look at this theory which stresses participative decision making, long–term employment, and nonspecialized career paths.

Theory Z combines characteristics of American and Japanese leadership practices.

The J style of leadership developed naturally according to the conditions in Japan of homogeneity, stability, and collectivism just as Type A adapted naturally to the conditions of heterogenity, mobility, and individualism in America. As william Ouchi, author of *Theory Z*, was describing characteristics of J management to a group of IBM executives, one of the executives remarked that his company used the same principles of management although it had not borrowed its style from the East. Ouchi's further research revealed that indeed many U.S. firms were not really J companies, but they weren't exactly typical A companies either. Rather, they were American organizations which had features similar to Japanese organizations. Some of these organizations include IBM, General Electric, Pillsbury, the U.S. Military, Texas Instruments, and Lockheed.

Theory Z stresses participative decision making, long–term employment, and nonspecialized career paths.

Although the Z companies have developed naturally in the United States, they have many characteristics similar to firms in Japan. Some of these characteristics include long–term employment and slow promotions, participative decision making, nonspecialized career paths, trust, close personal relationships and interdependence, and commitment on the part of management to its people. Let's examine each of these features a little more closely.

1. *Long–term employment and slow promotions.* Employees in the Japanese organization studied by Ouchi experience lifetime employment. Once hired, these workers, who comprise about 35 percent of the Japanese work force, are retained by the company until mandatory retirement at 55. "Promotions are entirely from within, and a person with 1, 5, or 20 years at one company will not be hired or even considered by another company." Z companies offer long–term but not necessarily lifetime employment. People tend to stay with one company since many of their skills are specific to that company and the worker can't readily find equally challenging work elsewhere. Promotions are from within as in the J companies, but a loyal worker doesn't have to wait 10, (yes, 10!) years as does his Japanese counterpart. Promotions are faster than in a typical J firm and slower than in a typical A firm.

2. *Participative decision making.* In a J company, collective decision making is practiced, even if it means getting 60 to 80 people to give their seal of approval. The group is responsible. In a Z company, decision making is also collective, but the ultimate responsibility still resides in one individual, not in the group.

3. *Nonspecialized career paths.* J and Z companies practice lifelong job rotation. Employees are provided with varied and nonspecialized experiences to broaden their career paths. They specialize in an organization, not necessarily in a technical field.

4. *Trust.* The Z company believes that without trust, any human relationship will inevitably degenerate into conflict. With trust, anything is possible. The egalitarian atmosphere implies that each person can work autonomously without close supervision since they are trusted.

5. *Close personal relationships and interdependence.* The organizational life is one of interdependence. All individuals rely on others. some have likened the interdependent Z company to an industrial clan.

6. *Commitment on the part of management to its people.* Z companies practice MBWA, management by walking around. Managers do more than sit in exclusive private offices making corporate decisions. The organization stresses direct hands–on participation of managers, not distant order giving.

FIEDLER'S CONTINGENCY THEORY

Fred Fiedler believes that anyone (yes, even you) can be a good leader in the right circumstances.[23] Contingent means "depends on," and since leadership success depends on the situation, Fiedler calls his theory the contingency theory of leadership. Situational components that spell success or failure are the setting itself, the characteristics of the people in-

---

SITUATIONAL COMPONENTS

Leader–member relations. Fiedler considers this component to be the most important. To what extent do the followers like, respect, and trust the one in charge?

Task structure. The more structured and defined the job, the more influence the leader has. Are goals clear? Are the tasks structured and defined or vague and undefined?

Position power. Because of their position, leaders have the authority to hire, fire, discipline, recognize, and reward. The more position power a person has, the more favorable the leadership position.

Fred E. Fiedler, *A Theory of Leadership Effectiveness* (New York: McGraw–Hill, 1967), pp. 22–32.

volved, the nature of the task to be completed, and the attitudes and actions of the one in charge.

Performance depends as much on the situation's favorableness as it does on the leader's ability to persuade and influence. Task–oriented leaders perform better in situations that are either very favorable or very unfavorable. In the most favorable situation, the group members like the leader and recognize him or her as having position power, and the task at hand is clearly defined (e.g., develop 50 widgets per hour). In the most unfavorable situation, the group members don't like the manager or supervisor, the task is not clearly defined, and the "followers" don't recognize the leader as having position power. The one in charge of situations very favorable or very unfavorable can afford to be a little bossy.

Sometimes situations aren't clearly favorable or unfavorable. Fiedler asserts that in situations of intermediate favorableness, the more successful leader is relationship oriented instead of task oriented. He or she succeeds not by bossing around but by building relationships. An example might be when the group likes the boss, are motivated to perform, and recognize the leader's power but are not sure of exactly what's expected of them.

Since people can't change their personalities and situations aren't made to order, the best thing to do is to try to match the right leader with the right situation at the right time. Find out to what extent the job situation will call for a strong work relationship and to what extent it will call for the completion of difficult jobs. A task–motivated leader works well in situations in which a task is either very easy or very difficult, and a relationship–motivated person leads best in a situation of moderate difficulty.

CASE STUDY

Sam's Leadership Style

After 15 years with the same company, Sam had been promoted from production manager at one of the company's plants to plant manager at another. He was competent, and everyone felt that he was a good choice for plant manager. However, there were some problems with Sam's management style in his new position.

Sam had a "natural" style of management, which began when he was on the line himself. The plant was new then, and its first manager had nurtured Sam's career and served as a model for him and all the supervisors who worked for him, especially in his consultative approach to employee relations. Although the plant had experienced tremendous growth since that time, plant supervisors still made major plant decisions by what might be called "town meetings" at which managers encouraged employee opinions and sought consensus on decisions.

Sam was proud of the high–tech assembly line he had installed, the outstanding productivity figures of his group, and of his people. When Sam walked by, his employees continued working but often paused to make friendly comments to their boss since they were genuinely glad to see him. When calling a visitor's attention to details of the production process, Sam always included a line worker in the demonstration by asking him to explain it. Sam praised their work, ideas, and contributions to the company. Things were rosy.

In his new job, however, Sam seemed to face a new labor grievance nearly every day, and relations with his supervisors were awful. He was operating the same way he always had, moving around the plant talking to his people and trying to work through problems with them, yet his management style wasn't working for him the way it had. For instance, while talking to a supervisor about the dangerous clutter in an area, the supervisor told Sam that the problem was a lack of people. Sam arranged to have an employee moved over to the supervisor's cluttered department, but the situation didn't change. This time the supervisor said the mess was because he had insufficient equipment.

Sam was frustrated, worried, and bewildered. His predecessor as plant manager had held the job for more than 10 years and retired with a reputation of having been a "tough cookie," feared as much by the supervisors under him as by his employees, a real X–oriented leader whose leadership style allowed little or no participation in decision making. The supervisors and workers were accustomed to such a style. Concerning Sam's democratic style, one supervisor said, "This one has to ask everyone what they think, what they need. If we know all the answers, they'd make us plant managers."

1. What is the basic problem creating Sam's inability to work with this group?
2. Do you think it's possible for Sam to change his leadership style? Why or why not?
3. How might an autocratic leader handle the "clutter" situation?
4. How does this case study illustrate the contingency theory of leadership?

Adapted from Marge Yanker, "Flexible Leadership Styles: One Supervisor's Story," *Supervisory Management*, January 1986, pp. 2–6.

SUMMARY

Leadership is the ability to get things done willingly and enthusiastically with and through other people. Leaders motivate others by helping them find the best within themselves and encouraging them to make maximum use of their abilities.

Scholars searched in vain for a set of traits believed to be necessary for leadership success. However, leadership is too complex to be reduced to possessing a few positive characteristics, especially since such traits are widely distributed in the population. Perhaps the difference between leaders and nonleaders is that the former have developed these traits to a greater degree than others. However, two traits that seem to inhibit leadership are fear and indecisiveness.

Successful leaders all have power, skills, and a vision. Power is the ability to influence other people and events and is granted on the basis of the leader's personality, activities, and situation in which he or she operates. The four types of leadership power are personal, legitimate, expert, and political.

Good leaders are expected to be knowledgeable. Three types of knowledge or skill they are expected to possess are technical, human, and conceptual. Technical skills are especially important at the lower levels of management and are required of the greatest number of people. Human skill enables the leader to accept the existence of viewpoints different from his or her own and is essential at all levels of management. More important at the higher levels of management, conceptual skill is needed to think about unrelated ideas and put them together to form new approaches.

The leader's vision gives him or her a sense of who he is, what he's after, and what he can incite others to strive for. It's known as the leader's best motivational tool.

How a leader creates a balance between decisiveness and participation determines his or her leadership style. The styles are autocratic, participative, and free reign and are based on the type of control that the leader exercises and the resulting behavior toward the group. An autocratic leader concentrates power, decision making, and responsibility in one person; the participative leader asks for, expects, encourages, and uses suggestions and ideas from employees, believing that people support decisions more enthusiastically if they have the opportunity to participate in making those decisions; the free–reign leader downplays the "bossy" role and concentrates on providing information and resources to workers.

Douglas McGregor developed the X and Y theories of management in the late 1950s. The X leader believes that people are basically lazy and have to be commanded, goaded, and threatened to work. Assumptions that people work only for money and have little or no commitment to organizational goals make Theory X a pretty pessimistic theory. The Y leader believes that people get satisfaction from sources other than money, and he or she gives appropriate rewards and keeps the lines of communication open. Underlying Theory Y is the belief that the expenditure of physical and mental effort in work is as natural as play or rest.

Feeling that some managers have been "burned" because of their optimistic viewpoints, Stan Kossen contends that they have developed a derived X leadership style. Such leaders tried to maintain Y assumptions but were repeatedly disappointed and let down by their subordinates.

Theory Z is a theory that combines characteristics of American and Japanese leadership practices and stresses participative decision making, long–term employment, and nonspecialized career paths. Trust, close personal relationships and interdependence, and commitment on the part of management to its people are other characteristics of Theory Z.

In his contingency theory of leadership, Fred Fiedler states that leadership success depends on three situational components: leader–member relations, task structure, and position power. Task–oriented leaders do best in situations that are either very favorable or very unfavorable as concerns situation components. However, in a situation of intermediate favorableness, the more successful leader is relationship oriented. Since people can't change their personalities and since situations aren't made to order, the best thing to do is to try to match the right situation to the right leader at the right time.

KEY TERMS

Leadership
Trait theories
Ralph Stogdill
Chester Barnard
Types of power
Technical skill
Human skill
Conceptual skill
Autocratic leader
Participative leader
Free-reign style
Douglas McGregor
X and Y leadership assumptions
Derived X
Stan Kossen
Theory Z
William Ouchi
Fred Fiedler
Contingency theory

DISCUSSION QUESTIONS

1. Think of three leaders you know. They could be in government, church, community, work, or even home leadership positions. Consider their traits and personalities. What does this say about trait theories of leadership?

2. In your opinion, what makes a leader? Is a leader the same as a manager? Why or why not?

3. Are there some traits that could exclude a person from leadership? What are they?

4. Choose one of your organization's leaders and discuss how this person demonstrates power, skill, and vision.

5. What are the four types of power relating to leadership? Name at least one leader who, in your opinion, has personal power. Do you consider one type more important than another? Which one?

6. Describe each of the types of skills needed by leaders. Which is more important at each of the different levels? Which skill is important at all levels? Why?

7. Discuss the difference between the autocratic, participative, and free—reign leadership styles. Is one style always preferable to another? Give examples of situations in which each style is preferable.

8. Describe both the X and Y theories of management developed by Douglas McGregor. Why is a leader's perspective about human nature important in applying X or Y assumptions?

9. List advantages and disadvantages of each leadership style.

10. What is Kossen's derived X theory? Give an example of its application . Have you seen it in operation?

11. What is Theory Z? List and briefly discuss some of the features of this theory.

12. What are the three situational components to be considered in Fred Fiedler's contingency theory? When should a leader focus on relationships? Task?

ENDNOTES

[1]VANCE PACKARD, "Thoughts on the Business of Life," *Forbes*, November 21, 1983, p. 356.

[2]TOM PETERS AND NANCY AUSTIN, *A Passion for Excellence* (New York: Random House, 1985), p. 324.

[3]RALPH M. STOGDILL, "Personal Factors Associated with Leadership: A Survey of the Literature," *Journal of Psychology*, January 1948, pp. 35–71.

[4]LEONARD R. SAYLES, *Leadership* (New York: McGraw-Hill, 1979), p. 224.

[5]MURRAY G. ROSS AND CHARLES E. HENDRY, *New Understanding of Leadership* (New York: Association Press, 1957), pp. 56–60.

[6]ROBERT TOWNSEND, *Further Up the Organization* (New York: Alfred A. Knopf, 1984), p. 123.

[7]T. HARRELL ALLEN, *The Bottom Line: Communicating in the Organization* (Chicago: Nelson-Hall, 1979), pp. 102–103.

[8]CHESTER I. BARNARD, *The Functions of the Executive*, 30th Anniversary Edition (Cambridge, Mass.: Harvard University Press, 1938-1968), p. 189.

[9]DAVID C. MCCLELLAND AND DAVID H. BURNHAM, "Power Is the Great Motivator," *Harvard Business Review on Human Relations* (New York: Harper & Row, 1979), pp. 341–356.

[10]KEITH DAVIS, *Human Behavior at Work: Organizational Behavior*, 6th ed. (New York: McGraw-Hill, 1981), pp. 132–133.

[11]SAYLES, *Leadership*, p. 40.

[12]ROBERT L. KATZ, "Skills of an Effective Administrator," *Harvard Business Review*, September–October 1974, pp. 90–102.

[13]PETERS AND WATERMAN, *In Search of Excellence*, p. 243.

[14]THEODORE L. HANSEN, JR., "What It Takes to Achieve Followership," *Supervisory Management*, November, 1984, pp. 22–24.

[15]KATZ, "Skills of an Effective Administrator," p. 93.

[16]WILLIAM G. OUCHI, *Theory Z* (New York: Avon Books, 1982), p. 158.

[17]WALTER KIECHELL III, "Wanted: Corporate Leaders," *Fortune*, May 30, 1983, pp. 135, 138, 140.

[18]JACK HALLORAN, *Applied Human Relations*, 2nd ed. (Englewood Cliffs, N.J.: Prentice Hall, 1983), p. 309.

[19]JOSEPH P. CANGEMI, CASIMIA J. KOWALSKI, AND JEFFREY C. CLAYPOOL, "*A Pragmatist's View of Participative Management*" (New York: Philosophical Library, 1985), p. 5.

[20]DOUGLAS MCGREGOR, *The Human Side of Enterprise* (New York: McGraw-Hill, 1960).

[21]STAN KOSSEN, *The Human Side of Organizations*, 3rd ed. (New York: Harper & Row, 1983), pp. 206–207.

[22]OUCHI, *Theory Z*, pp. 60–79.

[23]FRED E. FIEDLER, *A Theory of Leadership Effectiveness* (New York: McGraw-Hill, 1967).

chapter 10

Making Career Decisions

After reading and studying this chapter, you will be able to:

1. Discuss the significance of work.
2. Explain the impact of occupational choice on a person's total life-style.
3. List means of self–exploration relative to career choice.
4. Describe the *DOT*.
5. Explain the origin of values and how a knowledge of personal values can aid in career choice.
6. List ways of get information on careers.

Work consists of whatever a body is obliged to do. . . Play consists of whatever a body is not obliged to do.

Mark Twain

A man who has work that suits him and a wife whom he loves, has squared his accounts with life.

Hegel

Unless you belong to that elite group who does not have to work or unless you come into a financial windfall within the next few months, you will soon join forces with those in the world of work. You probably already have at least a part–time job while attending school. Then, again, you may be seeking a career change after years of working at a dead–end, boring, frustrating, or unsatisfying job. Making career decisions and finding jobs are repetitive activities that recur throughout life, so whether you're a teenager flipping hamburgers in a fast food restaurant or a more mature worker seeking a change, this chapter will help you in making your career choices.

Many people fail to realize the impact that a job can have on their lives. Not only can it affect your attitude about the job itself, but it can also affect your social/personal life during those hours away from work. "Too many people are so negatively affected by their jobs that their frustration and emptiness spoil their eating, recreation, family lives, sex lives, and relationships with friends."[1] Since work is central to life, let's explore its significance, its impact on you, your personal attributes related to career choice and development, and finally, sources of career information.

SIGNIFICANCE OF WORK

A job can affect your social and personal life.

Why work? What's so significant about it? Harry Overstreet says that we need only three things in life: something to do, something to hop for, and someone to love. Your job, if you put some time and thought into its selection, can provide satisfaction in all three areas. Murray Banks, a lecturer and psychologist, believes that we have four basic wants:

1. To live and be healthy
2. To have a feeling of importance
3. To be loved
4. To have a little variety[2]

Do you think that you could accurately assess your abilities and interests and match those to a career choice that would provide something to do, something to hope for, and someone to love? What about an occupation which would satisfy Banks's list of basic wants? Is there a career field in which you could get a feeling of importance, feel accepted by others, and enjoy variety and stimulation? You don't have to know yourself inside out. Some workers simply want a steady job and a comfortable income. However, since the most important influence on your life-style is your occupation, let's take a few moments to consider its impact.

IMPACT OF OCCUPATIONAL CHOICE

Consider the far-reaching influences of your occupational choice:

1. It can determine how much money you make and consequently your life-style. A life-style comprises a person's whole way of life, from the food eaten and clothes worn to the trips taken and interests pursued. Will you vacation with distant relatives and travel in the family car, or will you vacation at a resort and travel by air? Speaking of the family car, will it be a luxury automobile or a more basic model?

2. It can determine the neighborhood you live in, the type of dwelling you inhabit, and even where your children go to school. In turn, the education they receive and the peers and teachers with whom they interact will influence their futures.

Occupational choice can determine physical and mental health.

3. It can determine your physical and mental health. Work–related stress can play havoc with our overall feeling of health and well–being. Some jobs are physically more demanding than others. Some are downright dangerous. On the other hand, many jobs may be mentally or emotionally exhausting even though the individual exerts little physical effort.

4. It can determine who some of your friends are and with whom you will socialize. The workplace, whether factory, shop, office, or hospital, is an ideal setting for the development of friendship. Since people are spending more time at work and less at home, the water fountain is rapidly replacing the backyard fence as a gathering place.

5. It can determine your self–esteem. A person's self–concept, how he views himself, is tied in with what he does for a living, since his job as computer programmer, electrician, or air conditioner repairman is one of his primary roles. According to *Work in America*, "Doing well or poorly, being a success or failure at work is all too easily transformed into a measure of being a valuable or worthless human being."[3]

6. It can determine whether or not you are employed. By choosing an occupation in which employment is stable, you will increase the

Self–esteem is affected by occupation.

probability of being employed. Computer technology is expected to affect almost every job and almost every aspect of work. Not having at least a passing familiarity with computers will continue to be a disadvantage, especially in the business area. Many jobs in the automobile, steel, and rubber industries will vanish because of foreign competition and automation.

Career choice determines whether or not you will be employed.

Predicting the job market is risky business, but a new forecast by the Bureau of Labor Statistics estimates that by 1990 fast–food chains will add nearly 800,000 jobs, while the number of teachers will continue to drop. *Time* reports that in the next few years the economy will need 800,000[4] custodians and 425,000 truck drivers. "The business of America is service. . . . Today two–thirds of all people work in wholesale and retail trade, communication, government, health care and restaurants."[5] Examples of service jobs expected to expand are registered nurse, office clerk, and cashier.

7. It can determine what you do with your time, how your day is structured. "Work helps establish the regularity of life, its basic rhythms and cyclical patterns of day, week, month, and year. Time patterns become confused and disorganized without work since work provides a framework for activity."[6]

8. Finally, your occupation can determine the quality of your retirement years. Will they be bleak or beautiful?

A job is more than a way of making a living. It's a way of making a life. Your work is crucial to the quality of your life, so it is worthwhile to look at ways of finding out more about yourself. By understanding yourself as completely as possible, you will enhance the possibility of choosing a career you will enjoy and minimize job dissatisfaction and the accompanying Monday blues.

SELF-EXPLORATION

Hero worship, overestimation of abilities or of employment opportunity, and misconceptions regarding the nature of the work are common errors in choosing occupations.

People get into occupations for all sorts of reasons, some of them wrong. Hoppock cites the most common errors in choosing occupations as hero worship, overestimation of abilities or of employment opportunity, misconception regarding the nature of the work, and reliance upon recruiting literature and other biased sources of information.[7] Another factor is sheer ignorance. Many individuals are simply not aware of the diversity of jobs available, and even if they knew of the jobs, ignorance about how to find such an occupation is a problem.

Many people don't know what their special abilities are or how those abilities and interests can best be used in the working world. Before putting yourself in the job market, you have to get to know the product—yourself. Employers offer employment on the basis of what you can communicate to them about the unique skills and competencies you have to offer them, self–exploration will help you pinpoint those qualities that make you unique.

It is not uncommon for a person to "fall into" a job. Someone hears that Munger Industry is in need of welders, or his brother–in–law tells him of an opening in the neighborhood meat-packing plant. Most jobs, in fact, are filled through inside sources. Dubrin reports that 15 percent of jobs are filled through advertisements and unsolicited letters to employers, 5 percent are filled through employment agencies, and 80 percent are filled through the insider system.

Most jobs are filled through inside sources.

Securing jobs learned about from inside sources is evidently quite common and perfectly acceptable, but when a person gives little thought to his or her abilities, aptitudes, interests, or temperament in fulfilling the job requirements, job satisfaction is unlikely. So what if the job of sausage inspector in the meat-packing plant is landed if the employee had really rather prefer a job that involved work on the outside? One that allowed more time flexibility and offered more variety? What's really sad is the person who makes that decision and then compounds the initial occupational error by building a career from a job she lucked into but doesn't particularly like or feel suited for.

Correspondence develops when a person fulfills the requirements of the work environment and the work environment fulfills the requirements of the person.

When people fail to match their unique characteristics to a career choice, correspondence cannot develop. Correspondence can be described as the individual "fulfilling the requirements of the work environment, and the work environment fulfilling the requirements of the individual."[9]

Dictionary of Occupational Titles

A valuable tool to use in matching your needs, values, interests, and aptitudes to careers is the *Dictionary of Occupational Titles* (DOT) published by the United States Department of Labor. The DOT is simply a listing and description of jobs available in the United States; it defines and cross-indexes literally thousands of occupational titles. In fact, the 1977 edition of the DOT lists 20,000 job titles. It contains most, but not all, of the jobs available in America. To list them all would be well nigh impossible since new jobs are continually created while others become obsolete. In an effort to offer up-to-date material, the volume is revised every 10 or 15 years. Although the dictionary is a standard work in most libraries and career guidance offices, you may need the assistance of a career counselor to help you interpret the data.

The DOT defines and cross-indexes literally thousands of occupational titles.

This dictionary is somewhat complex and difficult to understand and is intended for use primarily by vocational counselors. However, the information contained in the dictionary is helpful for anyone choosing a first or second career. Each occupation is given a nine digit code number. The first three digits are called the occupational group. The second set of digits describes what workers do with people, data, and things since all jobs require a worker to function to some degree in relation to people, data, or things. The third group indicates the alphabetical order of titles within the six digit code group and serves to differentiate a particular occupation from another.

DOT JOBS

The variety of occupations listed in the *DOT* is staggering. The chances are excellent that you know someone who is a carpenter, a bus driver, a mechanic, a nurse, a salesman, and a lawyer but slim that you know a pigment pumper. Take a look at this small sampling of the jobs listed in the *DOT*, a truly fascinating volume.

Cloth printer
Printer roller handler
Log loader
Plastic tile layer
Quarry supervisor
Bridge operator
Production clerk
Gas welder
Diamond cutter
Electrical tester
Embossing machine tender
Fish drier
Christmas tree grader
Burner tender
Squeak, rattle, and leak repairer
Pigment pumper
Stencil cutter
Lens mounter
Seasoning mixer
Whizzer
Dogbather
Clip coater
Coat cutter

See anything interesting? Maybe not, but skim through the *DOT* on your own, and some occupation listed there is guaranteed to strike a responsive chord.

The 1965 edition of *DOT* lists six traits necessary for each of the occupations listed therein. As you read over them, think about these components in relation to your fantasy job.

1. Training time
2. Aptitudes
3. Interests
4. Temperament
5. Physical requirements
6. Working conditions

Training Time

All jobs require some training. Even unskilled work, though it may not require an advanced degree, requires that a person know and understand job duties. Jobs in skilled occupations such as tool and die maker require specialized skills and knowledge. Professional positions such as accountant require considerable knowledge and information. In general, the higher the occupational level, the greater the amount of formal education required.

Generally, the higher the occupational level, the greater the amount of formal education required.

Before flying out and getting more education, find out more information on job entry-level requirements. Find out what education is desired and what is actually accepted. Sure, some occupations require specific credentials, but others allow more flexibility. Talk to others employed in the field in which you are interested and find out precisely what training and education are absolutely positively essential. Also, don't assume that getting the degree will automatically open all the right doors. Be prepared to work at opening those doors with certain keys, your assets like aptitude and personality.

Aptitude

An aptitude is a talent or innate ability. Aptitudes included in the 1965 *DOT* are:

1. General learning ability
2. Verbal aptitude
3. Numeral aptitude
4. Spatial relations aptitude
5. Form perception
6. Clerical perception aptitude
7. Motor coordination
8. Finger dexterity

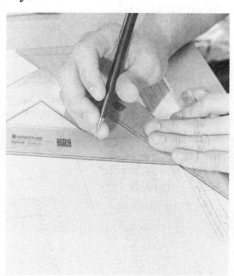

9. Manual dexterity
10. Eye, hand, foot coordination
11. Color discrimination

Aptitude is innate or inborn ability. All jobs require one or more of the foregoing aptitudes.

The DAT, Differential Aptitudes Test, is a useful tool for pinpointing an individual's most obvious abilities. Aptitude alone does not a happy worker make, however. Your finger dexterity may be outstanding, but if you have no interest in being a butcher, a candlestick maker, or watch repairman, you run the risk of being a disgruntled employee.

Let's examine the role of general learning ability or intelligence as it relates to career choice. David Campbell, author of *If You Don't Know Where You're Going You'll Probably End Up Somewhere Else*, states that the more complex the occupation, the higher your intelligence must be to succeed.[10] Complex occupations include nuclear physicist, medical researcher, and federal judge. Most workers in our society, however, have an average amount of intelligence. They sell cars, own their own businesses, work in hospitals and offices, and drive trucks. Campbell tells his readers that being average should not depress anyone since even those of us who are average still have a lot of control over our lives.

Some people with above-average learning ability work in average jobs for various reasons. Maybe they haven't had the opportunity to move into better jobs, have heavy family responsibilities, or haven't stretched themselves. Who knows? Maybe they're just lazy. Others who have great jobs but who have scored low on intelligence tests might have had unusual opportunities handed to them or might have applied themselves with unusual dedication.

Interest

Interest is related to aptitude although they are not always in complete agreement. You may have the aptitude to become a singer but lack the interest in practicing and attending rehearsals. Find something for your life's work that you really like to do; otherwise, you're probably never going to excel in it. As Thoreau said, "Do what you love. Know your own bone; gnaw at it, bury it, unearth it and gnaw it still."

It is believed that if a person has an interest in a career, she will persist in pursuing it even if her performance is mediocre or even marginal. Super and Crites cite four types of interests.

1. Expressed interests, specific interests made known by the person having them.
2. Manifest interests, those interests expressed by participation in activities.
3. Inventoried interests, estimates of your interests based on your responses to a large number of questions concerning your likes and dislikes.
4. Tested interests, interests indicated under controlled situations, not real-life situations.[11]

*Three types of
personal interests are
interest in people,
data, or things.*

Additionally, according to the *DOT*, there are three basic kinds of personal interests: interest in people, interest in data, and interest in things.

A person who is interested in people is likely to be friendly, outgoing, and concerned for others. She is involved in jobs such as minister, counselor, teacher, or social worker, which bring her closer to people.

An individual with a personal interest in data likes to be involved with numbers, facts, and written records. Data–oriented jobs require close contact with figures and other data and include bookkeeper, stockroom manager, proofreader,a nd computer programmer.

Someone who is more interested in things than in people or data enjoys jobs that require close contact with machinery and other "things." He or she is likely to be practical and objective and may be employed as a machine operator, a truck driver, a factory worker, a painter, or an auto mechanic.

Most jobs require a combination of people, data, and things. For example, a doctor is probably interested in people and is concerned for their physical and, sometimes, their mental health. However, he or she has to keep up with the latest medical findings (data) and be familiar with medical equipment (things). A machine operator may be thing oriented and still have an interest in other people.

There are several standardized tests for measuring interests. Some of the most widely used are the Strong-Campbell Interest Inventory, the Kuder Occupational Interest Survey, and Holland's Self Directed Search. A school or vocational counselor can recommend and administer the appropriate test to you. Discussing the results with a counselor will provide a base for your career planning. Such a discussion can stimulate your thinking and suggest areas of employment you never knew existed.

Temperament

Webster defines temperament as one's natural disposition or nature. Personality psychologist Gordon Allport refers to it as the hereditary aspect of a person's emotional nature, including his or her sensitivity, strength

and speed of response, prevailing mood, and fluctuations in mood.[12] Is it your nature to be calm and easygoing? Excitable and moody? It is useful to think of temperament as a facet of your personality. Temperament is not unchangeable, but it is believed to set limits on the development of personality.

A number of tests give insight into personality and temperament. The Meyers–Briggs Type Indicator indicates basic individual preferences that have far-reaching effects. The Minnesota Multiphasic Personality Inventory and the Guilford-Zimmerman Temperament Survey are inventories that can help one to become aware of temperamental traits. Additionally, since we do not always perceive ourselves as others do, sometimes it is beneficial to ask friends, co–workers, and family members about their concepts of our personalities.

John Holland, a psychologist who specializes in career life work planning, believes that "most persons can be categorized as one of six types. . . people search for environments and vocations that will permit them to exercise their skills and abilities, to express their attitudes and values, to take on agreeable problems and roles and to avoid disagreeable ones."[13] Holland's six categories and examples of each follow. Which type are you? For more information, see your counselor about an inventory called The Self–Directed Search.

Temperament is one's natural disposition or nature.

Six categories or "types" of people are realistic, scientific, artistic, social, enterprising, and conventional.

Realistic

A realistic person prefers activities involving the explicit, ordered, or systematic manipulation of objects, tools, and machines. Occupations include farmer, mechanic, carpenter, tool and die maker, and X–ray technician.

Scientific or Investigative

Investigative sorts like to observe and investigate physical, biological, or cultural phenomena. Laboratory jobs turn them on. They like to read scientific reports, work on new computer applications, read graphs, and solve problems. A investigative person might be a psychologist, a researcher, or a scientist.

Artistic

These creative types like work that involves free, unsystematized activities which create art forms or products. Occupations include dancer, singer, musician, writer, photographer, interior decorator, and actress.

Social

Social persons prefer jobs that inform, train, develop, care for, or enlighten others. A social person might teach, counsel, tend bar, style hair, or heal the sick.

Enterprising

Enterprising workers manipulate others to attain organizational or self-interest goals. They try to persuade others to do or buy something; you'll find such enterprising people working as business executives, fund raisers, politicians, and fashion merchandisers.

Conventional

Conventional workers enjoy such activities as keeping records, filling information, reproducing materials, and operating business and data processing machines. Careers chosen include accountant, typist, computer, bank teller, and payroll clerk.

Physical Requirements

All jobs have some physical requirements. The 1985 *DOT* lists six factors related to physical requirements:

1. Lifting, carrying, pushing, and pulling
2. Climbing and balancing
3. Stooping, kneeling, crouching, and crawling
4. Reaching, handling, fingering, and feeling
5. Talking and listening
6. Seeing

Since all jobs have some physical requirements, assessing your physical abilities and limitations is important.

With your chosen career in mind, assess your physical abilities and limitations according to the foregoing list. One young acquaintance revealed that she could never be a teacher because she felt physically unable and unwilling to talk and listen to others for hours on end. Jobs to scratch from your list if you can't stand on your feet all day are barber and retail salesperson. In addition, sometimes size, age, and sex should be considered. It will be difficult to be a top-notch sumo wrestler if you weigh in at 150 pounds. If you are considering a career change at mid-

life, being a professional baseball player or boxer is out. Jobs that require heavy physical labor are difficult for workers in their forties and fifties. While either sex can succeed as a pocket presser or pickler, rumor has it that men are better chefs and women are better secretaries. This is strictly a rumor! Times are slowly changing.

A worker today does not necessarily feel the pressure of 20 years ago to enter a traditional career role. However, while there are a few brave female welders and male nurses, most individuals continue to choose careers they believe appropriate for their gender. For example, women tend to be confined to and concentrated in a relatively small number of "female intensive" jobs—occupations in which more than three–fifths of all workers are female.[14] These jobs include secretary, child care worker, bank teller, telephone operator, registered nurse, and elementary school-teacher.

Working Conditions

Working conditions can be defined as the physical characteristics of the work environment. Is this a dangerous job? Will you be exposed to fumes, odor, or toxic substances? Will the job involve the day shift, or will you be required to work the so–called "graveyard" shift? "Bread is baked, milk is bottled, and pastry cooks arrive at restaurants before the sun rises. Truck drivers pound the highways at high speeds throughout the night, while police officers, ambulance drivers, and interns pick up the pieces of the celebrators who drink and drive. . . . Electric line workers repair broken wires in midnight blizzards, while short–order cooks in all-night restaurants stand ready to serve them when they can take time to eat."[15]

Working conditions are the physical characteristics of the work environment and should be considered seriously.

Will you be working outdoors or indoors? Will you be subjected to an excessive amount of noise, heat, or cold? Will you be working in cramped quarters with toxic conditions or in high places? Many jobs involve unpleasant physical conditions that workers must adjust to if they really desire that particular career. Consider the spot welder, Phil Stallings.

I stand in one spot, about a two– or three–feet area, all night. . . . The noise, oh it's tremendous. You open your mouth and you're liable to get a mouthful of sparks. (Shows his arms.) That's a burn, these are burns. You don't compete against the noise. You go to yell and at the same time you're straining to maneuver the gun to where you have to weld. . . . It don't stop. It just goes and goes and goes, I bet there's men who have lived and died out there, never seen the end of that line. And they never will—because its endless.[16]

You can read about working conditions and you can ask different workers about them, but until actually visiting a job site, it's difficult to imagine the heat of a hotel kitchen or the terrific noise of a boiler factory. Of working conditions, Hoppock writes that you need to see them, hear them, feel them, and smell them if you are to truly experience their importance. He quotes one of his students as saying,

During my first years in public health nursing, I had to visit a button factory and look for health hazards. I was amazed to learn the conditions under which people worked and to smell a terrible odor coming from a place where cows' hoofs were being processed for the making of the buttons. The smell was awful, but the visit was educational and memories of it will remain with me for the rest of my life.[17]

An understanding of your aptitudes, interests, and temperament is necessary in finding a suitable career. Discover your assets, all the things you have going for you, and develop them to the utmost. Talent is just a starting point; you've got to work that talent. Honest assessment of your general education background is beneficial also as is a knowledge of the physical requirements and working conditions of the job.

Values

A final factor considered to be crucial to career success, even though not listed in the *DOT*, is one's value system. Values comprise an underlying system of beliefs about what is important to a person. Values determine many facets of our behavior—where we work, our job performance, our attitude toward the job and co–workers, the food we eat, the movies we view, the way we spend our money, the company we keep, and even the leisure–time activities we pursue.

Our values develop from many sources, but the primary ones include the family, television, music, textbooks, peers, religion, life experiences, and schools. The family is especially important in instilling values and beliefs in the developing individual. Most people identify with parents or guardians by internalizing the adult role model's values and behaviors. Schools still teach reading, writing, and arithmetic, but they also teach the three R's of the "hidden curriculum": rules, routines, and regulations. Upon entry into kindergarten, a child learns discipline, order, obedience, cooperativeness, and conformity, skills needed for success in our society, whether someone becomes a lawyer, executive, secretary, assembly-line worker, or professional tennis player. It is difficult to measure directly the effects of the mass media, including television, radio, newspapers, magazines, movies, and records, but they are believed to be powerful socializing agents in the forming of values, especially when an average American watches television for over six hours a day.

GREAT AMERICAN VALUES TEST

Are your values in order? A national sample of American adults was asked to rank these 18 values in order of importance. To compare your value system with that of the typical U.S. citizen, rank the values in order of their importance as guiding principles in your life, from most important (1) to least important (18). A summary of the survey results appears at the end of the chapter.

_____ A Comfortable Life
_____ An Exciting Life
_____ A Sense of Accomplishment
_____ A World at Peace
_____ A World of Beauty
_____ Equality
_____ Family Security
_____ Freedom
_____ Happiness
_____ Inner Harmony
_____ Mature Love
_____ National Security
_____ Pleasure
_____ Salvation
_____ Self–respect
_____ Social Recognition
_____ True Friendship
_____ Wisdom

Sandra J. Ball–Rokeach, Milton Rokeach, and Joel Grube, "The Great American Values Test," *Psychology Today*, November 1984, pp. 38, 40.

Values comprise an underlying system of beliefs about what is important to a person.

Dr. Morris Massey states that knowing when a person was value processing (approximately 10 years of age) and what the dominant values of that time were are helpful in understanding that person.[18] Individuals value processing during the 1920s and 1930s are likely to have a strong sense of the Protestant ethic. They believe in hard work, perseverance, and thrift. On the other hand a younger worker value processing in the 1960s may have a different outlook. He wants growth, development, and fulfillment from his job, and if his occupation is too boring, too demanding, or too demeaning, he is more likely to switch jobs. However, the majority of young workers in America still believe in hard work and getting ahead. "If by work ethic—a very slippery term—we mean endowing

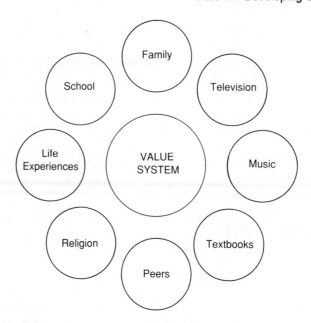

work with intrinsic moral worth and believing that everyone should do his or her best possible job irrespective of financial reward, then recent survey research shows that the work ethic in the United States is surprisingly sturdy, and growing sturdier."[19]

Primary sources of values include the family, television, life experiences, and school.

To illustrate how values might influence career choice, consider the following examples. An individual whose religious faith teaches abstinence from alcoholic beverages will not be likely to work in a brewery or to become a bartender. Someone committed to clean air and water is unlikely to find job satisfaction at a factory that dumps its waste into a river. If you are a physical fitness buff, you might be happy working in a health food store or a fitness center.

VALUES CLARIFICATION

Sidney Simon believes that all our decisions and actions are based on our beliefs, attitudes, and values. He has consequently designed a book of 79 value clarification activities formulated to help individuals become more aware of their life decisions as based on their own value systems. Examples of some of Simon's rank order exercises are as follows. Read the questions and rank the responses as first, second, and third choices.

1. Which would you most like to be?

   _____ Owner of a small business

   _____ Employee in a large corporation

   _____ Employee in a small business

2. Which would you least like to be?

   _____ A rifleman firing point blank at the charging enemy

   _____ A bomber on a plan dropping napalm on an enemy village

   _____ A helicopter pilot directing a naval bombardment of enemy troops

3. Which would you like to do most?

_____ Become a jet fighter pilot

_____ Become an astronaut

_____ Become a surgeon

4. Which would you least like to be?

_____ A prison guard

_____ A garbage collector

_____ An assembly line worker

5. Which do you like most?

_____ Math

_____ English

_____ Social studies

Sidney Simon, *Values Clarification* (New York: Holt, 1972).

GET THE FACTS

As crucial as it is to match your unique assets and interests to a career, finding out all the information about a particular job is beneficial too. To gather this information, look to the printed word, the spoken word, and your own personal experiences.

Printed Word

Printed information on careers abounds. It's inexpensive and easily accessible. Many individuals are not aware of the abundance of information available on careers. A quick glance around your college bookstore and library should be convincing. Among sources of the written word are:

> *Dictionary of Occupational Titles*
> *Occupational Outlook Handbook*
> *Occupational Briefs*
> *A Guide to Careers Through College Majors*
> *Encyclopedia of Careers and Vocational Guidance*

Printed information on careers is inexpensive and easily accessible.

Read whatever you can get your hands on about careers since the one you choose may save your life—literally. While reading occupational literature, ask yourself at least three questions:

1. Who wrote the material and why? Was the author's purpose to entertain? To recruit? Is it biased? Is the author reputable?
2. Where does the author live? Geographic restrictions have to be considered. The outlook in your area may be better or worse than in other areas.

3. When was the material written? Occupational literature becomes obsolete in a hurry as some jobs are phased out and others created. Jobs exist today that weren't even dreamed of thirty years ago while jobs once considered to be "sure things" have dwindled in number or disappeared. For example, increasing automation in automobile manufacturing is expected to limit the need for assemblers and welders in that industry.

Occupational literature quickly becomes obsolete as some jobs are phased out and others created.

The *Occupational Outlook Handbook* is published every two years by the U.S. Department of Labor and lists approximately 850 occupations. Each occupation is described in terms of nature of work, working conditions, employment training or other qualifications, average job outlook, earning, and related occupations. One school counselor describes the *OOH* as much "funner" than the *DOT*.

The *OOH* is definitely informative. For example, did you know that the service occupations are expected to grow faster than any other occupational group throughout the 1990s? Service jobs are projected to account for 9 out of 10 jobs between 1984 and 1995. These service occupations include barber, correction officer, and geriatric aide.[20]

Service occupations are expected to grow faster than any other occupational group throughout the 1990s.

And what about these informational tidbits? According to the *OOH*, employment in health occupations like health practitioner, nurse, dietician, pharmacist, and therapist is expected to grow faster than the average as population growth, especially the number of old people, increases the demand for health care. On the other hand, even though demand for food, fiber, and wood is expected to increase as the world population grows, the development and use of more productive farming and forestry methods is expected to result in declining employment in most agricultural and forestry occupations. Little or no growth is expected in the number of jobs for typists, while the number of jobs for computer and peripheral equipment operators is expected to grow much faster than the average for all occupations.

Interpreting Predictions of the *OOH*

If the statement reads,	The demand for workers may be
Excellent opportunities	Much greater than supply
Very good opportunities	Greater than supply
Good to favorable	About the same as the supply
May face competition	Less than supply
May face keen competition	Much less than supply

Read with discretion. And don't believe everything you read. To use the handbook effectively, the forecast should extend at least until the time you finish school. The predictions are hazardous, and the introduction to the *OOH* tells why. The number of job seekers and job openings constantly changes. Innovative practices and concepts create some jobs while eliminating others.

Job forecasts in the OOH should extend at least until the time you finish school.

Changes in size or age distribution of the population have to be considered. Post–World War II baby-boomers have influenced the job market since the mid 1960s and will continue to do so until the "babies" retire in Sun City. The children born to the postwar generation will necessitate greater demand for elementary education workers through 1995. Through the 1990s the chief cause of labor force growth will be the continued rise in the number and proportion of women who seek jobs. Women will account for more than three–fifths of the labor force during the period 1984–1995.

Changes in size or age distribution of the population greatly influence the job market.

Predicting the labor market needs is risky for many reasons, and the *OOH* predictions are somewhat conservative. Jobs created by simple turnover, people who stop work temporarily, individuals who re-enter the labor force, persons who transfer from other occupations, and retirement programs are a few of the factors leading to difficulties in projecting job market needs. Also, people just like you who read that there is an excellent chance of securing a job as a paralegal specialist or a dental assistant dash out to get appropriate training, and before you know it, job seekers face keen competition as the supply becomes greater than the demand.

Women will account for more than three–fifths of the labor force during the period 1984–1995.

Literature on jobs doesn't have to be technical. Studs Terkel interviewed thousands of American workers about what they did all day and how they felt about it. His findings are compiled in a fascinating book entitled *Working*, a book that everybody should read at least once. The following is an excerpt of Delores Dante's graphical description of being a waitress in a fashionable restaurant. The job is tense, tiring, and yet rewarding.

There is plenty of tension. If the cook isn't good, you fight to see that the customers get what you know they like. You have to use diplomacy with cooks, who are always dangerous. (Laughs.) They're madmen. (Laughs.) You have to be their friend. They better like you. And your bartender better like you too, because he may do something to the drink. If your bartender doesn't like you, your cook doesn't like you, your boss doesn't like you, the other girls don't like you, you're in trouble.

I want my hands to be right when I serve. I pick up a glass, I want it to be just right. I get to be almost Oriental in the serving. I like it to look nice all the way. To be a waitress, it's an art. I feel like a ballerina, too. I have to go between those tables, between those chairs. . . .I can do it with an air. If I drop a fork, there is a certain way I pick it up. I know they can see how delicately I do it. I'm on stage.

I tell everyone I'm a waitress and I'm proud. If a nurse gives service, I say, "You're a professional." Whatever you do, be professional.

It's tiring, it's nerve–racking. We don't ever sit down. We're on stage and the bosses are watching. If you get the wrong shoes and you get the wrong stitch in that shoe, that does bother you. Your feet hurt, your body aches.

"When the night is done, you're tired. You've had so much, there's so much going. . . You had to get it done. The dread that something wouldn't be right, because you want to please. You hope everyone is satisfied. The night's done, you've done your act. The curtains close.[21]

Spoken Word

Reading is beneficial, but speaking to a person directly involved in a specific job can be truly enlightening. Most workers are willing to talk with you about their jobs. When talking to this computer service technician, ironworker, or engineer, try to interview this person (if possible) at his workplace so that you can experience a more realistic view of his working conditions. Interview more than one person so your information won't be biased.

> *Most workers are willing to talk to you about their jobs, and speaking to someone directly involved in a specific job can be very enlightening.*

To get the information you are seeking, be certain to have some specific questions in mind. Ask the worker what she does all day. Ask her to give you the rundown of a typical day. Ask him what he likes most and least about his job. Inquire about how he got into that career in the first place and whether he'd choose it again. This is called informational interviewing, and a sample interview form is included at the end of this chapter. Through informational interviewing, an aspiring personnel manager nipped his career in the bud. He saw this occupation as people oriented and had visions of himself counseling people with personal and social problems. When a personnel manager informed the interviewer about the paperwork and all the federal and state guidelines involved in the job, the young man was able to see that being a personnel manager was not for him.

Do you think that you might want to be a service manager at an automobile dealership? An automotive technology student did. He made prior arrangements with such a service manager and followed him around for an hour or so. The observer found the service manager's job involved not only scheduling appointment, but also test driving cars, speaking to irate and demanding customers, motivating mechanics, and doing a certain amount of paperwork.

The student found that his mentor needed to be people, thing, and data oriented. Since a service manager must deal with the public, he has to be courteous, even–tempered, and primarily people–oriented. He also has to have an interest in both data and things. Innovations in the automotive industry make a knowledge of up-to-date information necessary. Since cars are classified as machinery (things), the manager must also be somewhat thing–oriented too.

Firsthand Experience

Before plunging head first into a career, get some firsthand experience. You could invest some of your leisure or vacation time in a part–time job as a teacher's aide, restaurant cook or machine tool operator to see if that's really for you. One young lady who had always wanted to be a nurse had a change of heart after working as a summer volunteer in a local hospital. Pharmacists really spend a lot of time counting pills, forestry

technicians do their work outside in all types of weather, air conditioner repairpersons crawl under homes and in attics, and any roofer can tell you that roofs are scorching during the long hot summer. Try out the job before you commit yourself to it.

Getting firsthand experience in a job during leisure or vacation time gives you the chance to see if it's really for you.

If you are already employed, why not try moonlighting to try out a new career area before plunging into it on a full–time basis. Where could you find the time? If you work 40 hours a week and sleep 56 hours a week, that still leaves 72 hours to use for other activities. Investing a couple of hours or so a day in a part–time job or working on the weekends in an area of interest can yield high results.

This time next year you could be a silver-tongued announcer, a beekeeper, a hypnotist, a claims adjustor, a pawnbroker, a private investigator, a square dance caller, a pet boarder, a sign painter, or even a weed commissioner, all job suggestions of Peter Davidson, author of *Moonlighting*.[22] All 200 moonlighting opportunities described by Davidson can be entered on a part–time basis and potentially develop into a full–time careers. If you decide moonlighting is for you, choose the activity that is most ideal for you in terms of your interests, abilities, available time, income requirements, energy level, and future goals.

INFORMATIONAL INTERVIEWING

For this activity, call up someone engaged in an occupation you want to know more about and tell the person that you would like to interview him or her about their work. Don't be shy or hesitant about asking for an interview since almost everyone likes to talk about his or her work to interested individuals. After all, it's flattering to be viewed as an expert.

Tell the person exactly why you are interviewing them. You might mention that it's because of a class assignment or simply because you are thinking of entering that occupation.

Think of specific questions you want to ask. Don't waste the interviewee's time and yours by idly chatting about this and that when there are certain things you want to know. The following are some possible questions you might consider asking, but feel free to add you own.

1. What is your job title?
2. Just exactly what do you do? Tell me about a typical day.
3. How long have you worked in your current job?
4. How did you decide on this occupation? Have you always wanted to do this?
5. What are some other occupations which you have considered?
6. What are some occupations that are closely related to this or that would require some of the same skills and abilities?
7. How did you get this job?
8. What do you like most about this job? Least?
9. Do you supervise other workers? Do you like or dislike that aspect of your duties?
10. Is there ample opportunity for employment in this job?
11. What about advancement for achievement-oriented people?
12. Do you get to use your creativity or special talents in this job, or do you feel unchallenged?
13. If you could, how would you change your job to make it more fulfilling?
14. From what you know about me, do you think I would enjoy a career in this field?
15. Do you expect this job to change in the next five year? Ten? How?

CASE STUDY

John's Diverse Careers

John Doyle has had a successful career that gets more and more interesting as time goes by. Quitting school in the eighth grade, he worked at odd jobs, including a stint in a grocery store, before enlisting in the Navy at age 19. While in the Navy, John served as a postal clerk, a job more glamorous than it sounds. Whether flying around in helicopters to deliver mail and sell money orders in Vietnam or dispatching letters and packages aboard an aircraft carrier, John found the job challenging and rewarding.

Because of his motivation and desire to improve himself, Chief Petty Officer Doyle not only took courses to finish high school but also studied air conditioning and heating, plumbing, automotive repair, and carpentry throughout his career. When asked why he studied those particular subjects, he replied simply that they were "practical."

While he was successful and satisfied with his Navy postal duties, John often remarked that he had always wanted to be a mechanic. Indeed, aptitude tests consistently indicated an innate talent for mechanical reasoning and administrative management.

After 20 years, John retired from the Navy and moved "back home." While doing subcontracting work on his own, he took a two–year course in heating and air conditioning at a local community college. After taking a state examination for the mechanical contractor's license, this military retiree landed a job as an air conditioning refrigeration mechanic at a large hotel. While working there, John then studied business administration for a year before his job interfered with study and class time.

Because of unexpected labor turnover, the job of mechanic turned into assistant chief engineer responsible for 30 ice machines, 356 window units, some 30 3–11-ton air conditioners, and cooking equipment in 2 big kitchens. In addition, John had six people reporting directly to him for assignments and instructions everyday. Despite the fact that his hours are sometimes long and uncertain, John finds this turn of events exhilarating.

When asked why he like the hotel engineer's job so much and what the similarities are (if any) between it and the 20 years as postal clerk in the Navy, John replies that both occupations are challenging, rewarding, and diverse. Repairing a faulty window unit gives him the same feeling of satisfaction as delivering a letter from home to a shipbound ensign. Being a "free spirit," he remarks that the variety of tasks facing him each day give him something different to look forward to.

1. Review the *DOT*'s six worker characteristics discussed in the chapter and relate each of them to John's career choices.
2. If you were a career counselor, what advice would you give John? Are there any other career fields you feel he should explore?
3. Would you consider John to be more aware of his unique traits and how to put them to optimal use than the average person? Why or why not?

SUMMARY

Work is central to life. The impact of your occupational choice on your life is tremendous. After all, half your waking hours are devoted to it. By making wise choices, you can improve the quality of life and also satisfy some basic needs like having something to do, something to hope for, and someone to love.

Occupational choice has many far-reaching influences. It can determine how much money you make and your subsequent life-style, the neighborhood you live in, your physical and mental health, the people you associate with, and your self–esteem. Whether or not you're employed, how your day is structured, and the quality of your retirement years are also influenced by occupational choice.

People get into occupations for many of the wrong reasons including hero worship, overestimation of abilities or of employment opportunity, misconceptions regarding the nature of the work, reliance upon recruiting literature, and ignorance about the diversity of jobs available. A final reason many people don't get into satisfying careers is because they don't know about their unique skills, interests, and abilities or how they can be best put to use in the working world.

The *DOT* (*Dictionary of Occupational Titles*) is a useful tool to use in matching needs, values, interests, and aptitudes to careers. It lists and describes jobs available in the United States.

One edition of the *DOT* lists six traits necessary for success in each occupation: training time, aptitudes, interest, temperament, physical requirements, and working conditions. To help you in choosing an occupation that will make the most of your unique skills and abilities, learn as much about yourself in relation to these traits. Values as a determinant of career choice are also often overlooked.

All jobs require some training, the degree depending on the occupational level. Since there is often a discrepancy between what education is required and what is actually accepted, find out from others in the field precisely what training and education are absolutely essential.

Aptitudes, talents, or innate abilities range from general learning ability and numerical aptitude to finger dexterity and color discrimination.

Interests can be expressed, manifest, inventoried, and tested. The *DOT* lists three kinds of personal interests: interest in people, data, and things. There are a number of standardized interest inventories designed to measure interest.

A person's natural disposition or nature is temperament, a facet of personality. Several tests are available to help you become aware of traits. John Holland, writer and psychologist, categorizes people as realistic, scientific, artistic, social, enterprising, or conventional and contends that careers exist to suit each type.

All jobs have physical requirements to be considered. Some jobs are more strenuous and involve lifting and carrying or climbing and balancing, while others might involve seeing, talking, and listening.

Working conditions, the physical characteristics of the work environment, are often overlooked in choosing an occupation but should be seen, heard, felt, and smelled to understand and experience their importance truly.

Values develop from many sources, among which are family, television, peers, life experiences, and school. As an underlying system of beliefs about what is important to a person, values determine many facets of behavior such as place of employment, job performance, and attitude toward the job itself.

Finding all the information available about a particular job is beneficial; this career information is primarily the printed word, the spoken word, and your own personal experiences.

The *OOH, Occupational Outlook Handbook,* is published by the U.S. Department of Labor and lists and describes approximately 850 occupations in terms of nature of work, working conditions, employment, training and other qualifications, average job earnings, and related occupations.

Speaking to a person directly involved in a specific job is enlightening. Since most people are willing to talk with you about their jobs, have some specific questions in mind and try informational interviewing. Investing some of your leisure or vacation time in a part–time job is a good investment of your time and lets you know if that occupation is really for you.

KEY TERMS

Harry Overstreet
Murray Banks
Correspondence
Dictionary of Occupational Titles
Aptitude
Temperament
Interest inventory
Gordon Allport
John Holland
Value system
Hidden curriculum
Protestant ethic
Occupational Outlook Handbook

REVIEW AND DISCUSSION QUESTIONS

1. Describe how career choice can satisfy Banks's four basic wants.

2. Discuss the far- reaching influence of your specific occupational choice. For example, how can a job as a secretary or electrician affect your physical and mental health?

3. What are some of the most common errors in choosing occupations? Tell of a friend or family member who chose a career because of one of those reasons and tell how this choice has affected the person.

4. What is the *DOT* and what are some advantages in using it?

5. When thinking of your fantasy job, think of the six traits necessary for occupations listed in the *DOT* and relate these traits to your job. For example, if your desire is to become a computer programmer, how much training time or education will it require? What types of interests are needed? What kind of physical requirements are there?

6. Distinguish between Super and Crites' four types of interests and give an example of each.

7. The *DOT* categorizes interest according to people, data, and things. Define the difference between these categories and describe a job for each.

8. From your knowledge of John Holland's six types of people, would you describe yourself as realistic, scientific, artistic, social, enterprising, or conventional? Why?

9. What are some of your dominant values? How do you think you acquired these values, and how have they affected your career choice thus far?

10. What are three primary sources of career information? What are some advantages of each? Where did you acquire most of the information about your present field?

ARE YOUR VALUES IN ORDER? SURVEY RESULTS

8	A Comfortable Life
17	An Exciting Life
7	A Sense of Accomplishment
2	A World at Peace
15	A World of Beauty
12	Equality
1	Family Security
3	Freedom
5	Happiness
11	Inner Harmony
14	Mature Love
13	National Security
16	Pleasure
10	Salvation
4	Self–respect

18	Social Recognition
9	True Friendship
6	Wisdom

ENDNOTES

[1]GERALD COREY, *I Never Knew I Had a Choice*, 2nd ed. (Monterey, Calif.: Brooks/Cole, 1983), p. 291.

[2]MURRAY BANKS, cassette tape of address to women's group about mental health.

[3]JAMES O'TOOLE, ed., *Work in America: A Report of a Special Task Force to the Secretary of Health, Education, and Welfare* (Cambridge, Mass): MIT Press, 1973), p. 5.

[4]JEREMY MAIN, "Work Won't Be the Same Again," *Fortune*, June 28, 1982, p. 61.

[5]RICHARD STENGEL, "Snapshot of a Changing America," *Time*, Sept. 2, 1985, pp. 17–18.

[6]O'TOOLE, *Work in America*, p. 8

[7]ROBERT HOPPOCK, *Occupational Information*, 4th ed. (New York: McGraw-Hill, 1976), p. 159.

[8]ANDREW DUBRIN, *Human Relations for Career and Personal Success* (Reston, 1983), p. 249.

[9]DONALD A. LAIRD, ELEANOR C. LAIRD AND ROSEMARY FRUCHLING, *Psychology, Human Relations and Work Adjustment*, 6th ed. (New York: McGraw-Hill Book Company, 1983), p. 73.

[10]DAVID CAMPBELL, *If You Don't Know Where You're Going You'll Probably End Up Somewhere Else* (Allen, Tex.: Argus Communications, 1974), pp. 65–68.

[11]DONALD E. SUPER AND JOHN O. CRITES, *Appraising Vocational Fitness* (New York: Harper and Brothers, 1962), pp. 378–380.

[12]GORDON ALLPORT, *Pattern and Growth in Personality* (New York: Holt, Rinehart and Winston, 1961), p. 34.

[13]J. L. HOLLAND, *Making Vocational Choices: A Theory of Careers* (Englewood Cliffs, N.J.: Prentice Hall, 1973).

[14]ROBERT PERRUCCI AND DEAN D. KNUDSEN, *Sociology* (St. Paul, Minn.: West, 1983), p. 291.

[15]HOPPOCK, *Occupational Information*, pp. 131–132.

[16]STUDS TERKEL, *Working* (New York: Avon Books, 1974), pp. 221–22.

[17]HOPPOCK, *Occupational Information*, p. 184.

[18]MORRIS MASSEY, *Who Are You Is Where You Were When*, (Farmington Hills, MI: CBS Fox Video, 1981).

[19]DANIEL YANKELOVICH, "The Work Ethic Is Underemployed," *Psychology Today*, May 1982, p. 5.

[20]U.S. Dept. of Labor, Dept. of Labor Statistics, *Occupational Outlook Handbook*, April 1982–83.

[21]TERKEL, *Working*, pp. 393–395.

[22]PETER DAVIDSON, *Moonlighting* (New York: McGraw-Hill, 1983).

chapter 11

The Job of Getting the Job

After reading and studying this chapter, you will be able to:

1. List sources of job leads.
2. Write an effective cover letter.
3. Explain the purpose of a resume.
4. Write an effective resume.
5. Describe the interview process and its purposes.
6. Give several "interview tips."
7. Understand the importance of follow–up activities.

Most people spend more time learning to play Monopoly than they ever spend learning to play the job market.

Richard Lathrop[1]

Once you have identified a career suitable for you, the job–finding campaign actually begins. Ah, the job hunt—it can be challenging, exciting, rewarding, frustrating, exhausting, and occasionally even exhilarating. Regardless of your age, sex, race, education, and experience, job hunting is a process you should tackle with a passion to succeed. Plan to work hard at it, for the harder you work, the shorter will be your duration of unemployment.

Research indicates that many talented people lose out in a competitive job market although they have excellent job skills. People need skills to *get* a job, not just skills to *do* a job. The job of getting the job will be a lot less frustrating if you develop job–seeking competencies.

With the belief that jobs don't necessarily go to the most qualified applicants but rather to those individuals who know how to get hired, in this chapter we'll closely examine the steps involved in a job–hunting campaign. Take a quick look at those steps:

1. Assess your abilities and interests (Chapter 10).
2. Explore sources of job leads.
3. Compose a positive cover letter.
4. Write a neat, effective resume.
5. Learn and rehearse interview skills.
6. Follow up your activities.

If these steps seem silly and fruitless to you, remember that your next job may very well determine the quality of your life for years—even decades. It will influence your productivity, overall attitude toward life, as well as your success in achieving self–actualization. You want this job to be an integral, exciting part of your daily life and challenge your abilities and creativity.

Realize that you are a unique person with certain abilities and attributes that you want to present and "sell" to a prospective employer. As such, you are a product in competition with other products. The way you as a product are packaged and marketed refers to your cover letter, resume, application form, interview skills and appearance, and follow-up activities.

JOB LEADS

Basically there are five sources of job leads:

Friends and Relatives

Most job openings are never advertised but are filled through the insider system. Employers fill these jobs with:

1. Friends or people recommended by their friends.
2. Friends of their employees.

3. People who have applied directly to them without knowing that any job opening existed.[2]

Most jobs are filled through the insider system.

Let as many people as possible know that you are looking for a job, and the more influential the individual, the better. Tell others what kind of work you're looking for and ask them for ideas and suggestions. Sociological factors such as contacts and the social groups in which a person is raised and with which he or she identifies help to determine which jobs are socially acceptable and available.

Want Ads

Newspapers and some professional trade journals advertise job openings. Follow the want ads diligently. Be sure to read them every day; otherwise, you could miss the very advertisement you were searching for. When an ad looks promising, respond to it promptly since a flood of other applicants probably see it as being just as promising.

Fewer than one in five jobs is filled through help wanted ads or employment agencies.

An open ad will give the name, address, and perhaps telephone number of the employer. Sometimes salary is mentioned. If the ad says that no experience is required, be cautious. The position probably offers low wages and/or poor working conditions. A blind ad uses only a box number or a telephone number. Most research indicates that blind ads are generally unrewarding to the job seeker. Fewer than one in five jobs is filled through help wanted ads or employment agencies; the more interesting, responsible, and highest-paying jobs are less likely to be advertised.[3]

School Placement Offices

Utilizing a school placement office is a primary and yet often overlooked method of finding a job. The personnel there have knowledge of local jobs as well as those in other geographical areas. The placement office is also

a place in which to gain experience in job–getting skills. Counselors can offer tips in writing cover letters and resumes. Some more progressive placement offices actually videotape role playing of the interview process so that hopeful job hunters have the opportunity to view themselves and pinpoint their strong and weak points. As mentioned in the preceding chapter, placement offices also administer interest and aptitude tests and have written material available on job availability, outlook, and income.

Employment Agencies

Individuals trained in personnel skills work at employment agencies to help match the right person to the right job. Such agencies may be public or private. Public agencies are operated by all states, and their personnel screen applicants and send them to prospective employers. The purpose of Job Service, the public employment service, is to "bring people to jobs and jobs to people." For this reason, state employment agencies provide employment counseling and aptitude testing. In most cases, future employees must pay a fee to a private agency for finding a job. The fees vary from agency to agency, but the charge averages from 20 to 50 percent of the first month's salary. The three main places in which private agencies advertise are newspaper ads, the Yellow Pages, and trade journals. Whether public or private, employment agencies serve employers better than employment seekers.

Personal Visits

Lathrop suggests that applicants go directly to the employers who have people on their payrolls doing the kind of work you want to do. Don't ask whether there are any openings. Go with the idea of convincing them that you should be the next person to hire when a job opens up. After all, someone could resign that very day. To take your aggressive approach a step farther, you might leave the employer a 3" x 5" card with your name, telephone number, and message stating, "The next time you need a really good employee, please call me."[4]

COVER LETTER

A cover letter is simply a letter that accompanies a resume. It allows you to explain why you want a certain job and to slant your approach toward that specific job.

The cover letter should be neatly typed and grammatically correct. When you are trying to get your foot in the door for a possible job interview, the cover letter and resume are all you have to represent you. The prospective employer does not have the benefit of being personally exposed to your diligence, discipline, and dynamic personality, so your letter has to reflect these traits. Be sure to use the person's name and title. Writing "Dear Sir" when Mrs. Hardee is the employer's name won't win you any points.

A cover letter allows you to explain why you want a certain job and to slant your approach toward that specific job.

Aim to be positive and somewhat forceful without being arrogant or boastful. Try to stress what you can do for the employer, a tactic which works well at all stages of your career. When composing the letter, ask yourself what you can say that will appeal to the self-interest of the person to whom you are writing. Is there anything you can do to help solve company problems, increase profits, or improve the person's chance of promotion? Finally, if you've done anything well or out of the ordinary (surely you have), you should mention this briefly.

```
Cover Letter A

Mr. John Doe
Marketing Outlet
Myrtle Beach, S.C.

Dear Johnny:

I read your ad in the paper that you needed a Manager Trainee, and I just
KNOW I would be good for the job. I'm sending along my Resume.

I am very good looking, honest, giggly—oh sometimes, I get mad and tell
someone off, but only if they need it—and I will work real hard.

How much do you pay? How much vacation does your company give? Do you
have coffee breaks—I really need one in the morning and in the after-
noon. How many holidays a year do you give off? I really like to be off
for Christmas to go and see my Mother and Daddy.

I'm still in school, but I'll soon be through. I made good grades, most-
ly A's. Now if you want to call me for an interview, I think I could come
in and talk to you on Tuesday between 4 and 6, or on Friday from 1 to 4,
I am really tied up most of the rest of the time. I really would like to
have this job.


Deanne Nease
```

```
Cover Letter B

Mr. John Doe
Marketing Outlet
Myrtle Beach, S.C.

Dear Mr. Doe:

Enclosed is my resume which I am sending to you in response to your ad
requesting applications for Manager Trainee of Marketing Outlet which
will open soon.

I am interested in learning more about your firm and the qualifications
necessary to be considered for the position. In May I will receive my
Associates Degree in business Management from the University of South
Carolina.

Honesty, good sense of humor, ambition, and good common sense are some
of my personal attributes, which I feel would be an asset to any firm
with whom I might become associated. I certainly believe in the adage "a
day's work for a day's pay" and am not afraid of hard work.

I wold appreciate the opportunity to meet with your personnel director
for an interview. Thank you for your consideration.

Sincerely,


Deanne Nease (Mrs.)
```

Cover Letter A was written by a former student and is designed to exemplify many of the "don'ts" of writing a cover letter. About the only thing right about the letter is its neatness. Its tone is flippant and immature, and its emphasis is on what the company can do for the applicant. On the other hand, Cover Letter B is the same letter—in revised form. The tone is self-confident and serious, and the emphasis is on how the applicant can help the company.

THE RESUME

Sooner or later someone will ask you for a resume. That someone could be a personnel director, a prospective employer, or even your present employer who needs to update her personnel files or who wants to consider you for a different position. Many people think resumes are only for white-collar workers, but this is definitely not so. Anyone who wants to show his or her strongest abilities and experiences to the best advantage needs to know how to write one.

A resume is an inventory of your work experience and education.

A resume is simply an inventory of your work experience and education. The primary purpose of a resume is obtaining a job interview, not a job. The resume shouldn't be overlooked as a tool in the job hunt, but you shouldn't rely solely on it to land that dream job. Some people send out dozens of resumes and then sit back with their fingers crossed waiting for an avalanche of job offers. Finding a job is a little more involved than that. Write that resume as professionally as possible, but since it's only part of "the hunt," plan to use it with other tactics.

There are basically four uses for a resume:[5]

* First, it can be used as a self-inventory. Writing down your work and educational history forces you to take stock of your pluses and minuses. Looking over it could remind you that you need to update your skills, for example.
* Second, a resume serves as an extended calling card to get you invited for an interview. Is it effective? Yes and no. If the organization is looking for a person like you and if you have tailored your resume to suit its specifications, then yes. Otherwise, your resume probably just gets filed along with dozens of others.
* Third, a resume serves as an excellent agenda during the interview process itself. The interviewer has her work made much easier if she knows what questions to ask, and during one of those inevitable awkward lulls, she can simply glance at your resume and say something like, "I see you worked at Gilmar Enterprises for two years. What did you like best about working there?"
* Finally, after the interview has taken place, the resume can serve as memory jogger for the employer, especially if a number of people have been interviewed, and she needs a memory refresher on some point.

Textbooks abound with suggestions to the resume writer. There is probably no one perfect way to prepare a resume since different individuals reading them have varying ideas about what is effective. Some readers prefer a one–page presentation and become irritated with two– or three–page resumes: others believe that a one–page presentation is entirely too brief. Some "experts" say limit it to one page for 10 years of work experience or less and two pages for more than 10 years.

Many employers prefer to see the job objective stated clearly on the resume. However, if you are sending out dozens of copies of your resume, it would be virtually impossible and very time consuming to type several resumes with different job objectives, not to mention expensive if you are paying to have it typed or printed. Many employers agree that it is acceptable to omit the job objective from the resume as long as it is included in the cover letter.

Some individuals prefer creative resumes. One young lady folded her resume like a pamphlet and entitled the outside, "The Story of My Professional Life." While a resume printed on a shocking pink shade of paper will surely be noticed, most resume readers agree that 8 1/2" x 11" white bond paper is preferred.

The resume should be factual, straightforward, neat, and relatively brief.

Fortunately, a number of guidelines do exist to aid you in preparing an effective resume. The resume should be factual, straightforward, and relatively brief. Always have the resume typed or printed—neatly. Neatness and organization are of the utmost importance. There should be no erasures, misspellings, grammatical mistakes, or errors of any kind. Remember that the cover letter and resume represent you. If either is smudged and disorganized, the reader may wonder about your sincerity in wanting the job and your ability to perform the job. Strive for eye appeal by using wide margins and double spacing between paragraphs.

Prepare a profile of your job experience, education, and personal information. A resume lists your work and educational experience in reverse chronological order. Some job hunters find it advantageous to list *and* describe their job duties, including dates of employment. A "Success on the Job" national survey made available from the Connecticut State Board of Education states that all work experience is important in the eyes of the employer when your experience is somewhat limited.[6] If you are a young or beginning worker, list all jobs, even baby sitting and lawn mowing. Although these jobs do not directly relate to the job for which you are applying, the fact that you worked at all indicates an acceptance of responsibility and a willingness to work. As you gain work experience, delete leaf–raking jobs from your resume and highlight those that portray you more favorably and that accent specific experience.

When listing educational experience, the last school attended should be the first on the list. In addition to the name of the school, give the type of degree or diploma earned and state your major area of concentration. Some individuals include awards, accomplishments, high class standing, foreign language ability, and extracurricular activities, although this is optional.

Personal information such as age, sex, religion, race, or marital status is not required in a resume.

Personal information such as age, sex, religious preference, and marital status is not required. It is unlawful for employers to request such information, since such knowledge may lead to discrimination in hiring. Most people, however, include a category comprised of personal information. If you do, never put anything negative that could cause you to be weeded out before you even have the chance to come for an interview. One applicant was screened out when the employer noted that her marital status was "separated." The employer decided that the applicant would be under emotional stress and not as able to fulfill her job responsibilities while going through such a traumatic experience. She never even had a chance to demonstrate her abilities. If you feel that your marital status might help you, put it in; if not, omit it entirely.

The question of whether or not to include references depends on personal preference. Many job seekers list three or four names of both friends and former employers or teachers. Avoid listing family members or others who might be guilty of the halo effect, a tendency to judge a person favorably because of one or two positive attributes. Sometimes when a person is held in high regard, negative traits are overridden by positive qualities such as attractiveness or a vibrant personality. Before listing a person's name as a reference, obtain his permission, since some people consider it an imposition to write a job reference. If you do not list references, simply state that references are available upon request.

In the accompanying examples of good resumes, notice that one mentions education first, while the other gives experience top billing. Remember that the eye travels to the upper two–thirds of a resume first. What is mentioned first depends on what you want to catch the attention of the prospective employer. Put education first if it's your best qualification so far or if it's an absolute must for the profession.

```
                          RANDOLPH G. BILLINGTON
                              Rt. 6, Box 287-B
                             Conway, SC 29526

POSITION SOUGHT:  MOTORCYCLE MACHINIST

EXPERIENCE:          Repaired and rebuilt Harley-Davidsons from 1978 to
                     present.

                     Operated small independent shop in 1983. Worked ex-
                     clusively on Harleys with very high rate of success-
                     ful repairs.

                     Acquired considerable experience rebuilding all Har-
                     ley-Davidsons' components including trouble shooting,
                     modifying, and customizing.

                     Gained experience supervising crews on construction
                     jobs.

EDUCATION:           Currently enrolled in Machinist Tool and Die Program
                     at Horry-Georgetown Technical College, Conway, SC.
                     Plan to graduate in May 198X.

                     Have taken courses in metals and heat treatment, draft-
                     ing, machine tool theory, numerical control, in-
                     dustrial psychology, English, and math. Maintained
                     4.00 average to date.

                     Anticipate further studies in welding, computer
                     numerical control, and tool and die making.

GOALS:               To become a proficient machinist and die maker. Con-
                     sidering a future in engineering. Consider myself in-
                     novative and resourceful. Would like to implement new
                     ideas in design and personnel management.

PERSONAL:            Date of Birth:       12/25/56
                     Height:              5'11"
                     Weight:              190
                     Health:              Excellent
                     Hobbies:             Camping, touring

REFERENCES:          Mr. Wayne Webb, Instructor
                     Machine Tool Technology
                     Horry-Georgetown Technical College
                     Conway, SC 29526
                     (803) 347-3186, Ext. 252

                     Mr. Phillip Freeman
                     Rt. 8, Box 27
                     Lumberton, NC 28516
                     (919) 738-1900

                     Mr. Doug Smith, Owner
                     Doug's Harley-Davidson Inc.
                     Florence, SC 29320
                     (803) 662-9145
```

APPLICATION FORMS

Application forms ask for much of the same information included on a resume. In addition, other questions pertaining to previous salary, health, draft status, and ability to travel are asked. Since it is difficult to remember dates, it is a good idea to have dates of school and employ-

```
                    DANIEL PRESTON MOORE
                   1404 SANDYGATE VILLAGE
              MYRTLE BEACH, SOUTH CAROLINA 29577
                      (803) 448-3937

OBJECTIVE:        To obtain a management position in the
                  hotel/hospitality industry.

EDUCATION:        Currently enrolled in the Associate Degree program at
                  Horry-Georgetown Technical College in the Hotel-Motel-
                  Restaurant program. Student government representative
                  for the HMR Department.

                  September 1975 to June 1979: Myrtle Beach High School.
                  Member of the Myrtle Beach High School Choir for four
                  years and the MBHS Madrigal Singers.

EXPERIENCE:       1985: Lands Inn Motel, Myrtle Beach, South Carolina,
                  Desk Clerk.

                  1983-1985: Globe Oil Company, D/B/A Starvin Marvin
                  Food Stores, Durham, North Carolina, Deli Manager.
                  Duties: Hired, trained, and supervised employees. Or-
                  dered stock and supplies, made bank deposits, prepared
                  invoices and daily reports. Studied profit margins and
                  improved operations. The Deli was operating at a loss
                  when I assumed my position as manager. I significant-
                  ly improved the Deli and operated it at a profit.

                  1981-1983: Grand American Presentations, Augusta,
                  Georgia, Sales Manager. Duties: Managed offices in
                  South Carolina and Georgia. Was promoted to manage of-
                  fices in Columbus, Macon, and Savannah, Georgia. Or-
                  ganized each of the offices from the beginning and
                  maintained them throughout. In Columbus, Georgia,
                  business collections rose approximately 30% over the
                  first year. I was working with the following nation-
                  al organizations at a state level: Mental Health As-
                  sociation of Georgia, American Council of the Blind
                  (South Carolina), Citizens for the Advancement of the
                  Physically Handicapped. My responsibilities included
                  bookkeeping, accounting, and payroll for these of-
                  fices. Maintained public relations with various local
                  organizations and people.

                  1977-1979: I worked at Dunes Cinema 1-2-3 as a con-
                  cessionist and soon became Assistant Manager.

                  1975-1977: Held various positions with restaurants. I
                  have learned the basic fundamentals of the food ser-
                  vice industry.

PERSONAL          I went back to school to receive an Associate Degree
PARAGRAPH:        and to establish a solid educational background to
                  manage and promote a business effectively on a steady,
                  profitable basis. I hope to further my education as
                  much as the economy and business trends demand to
                  achieve my goals and receive the benefits gained from
                  a successful career.

REFERENCES:       Available upon request.
```

ment written in a small notebook or on a card. Try to answer every question on the form as neatly as possible. Use a pen, and print all information, or, if possible, take the application form home and type the requested information. Poorly filled-out job application forms are a major reason for rejecting job applicants.

Sloppy resumes or job applications reflect negatively on a person.

Vice President, Public Relations
Newark, New Jersey

Haphazard completion indicates poor work attitude.

Supervisor
Baton Rouge, Louisiana

Why don't applicants realize that when they don't follow directions on a job application or do an incomplete or messy job, it's an indication of the kind of worker they will be?

Manager
Cleveland, Ohio[7]

THE JOB INTERVIEW

You have assessed your abilities, explored job leads, carefully composed and sent out cover letters and resumes. Now it's time for the acid test: the job interview. Employers surveyed by the Texas Advisory Council for Vocational–Technical Education indicate that five major reasons for ejecting job applicants relate directly to the job application process.

1. Little interest or poor reasons for wanting a job
2. Inability to communicate during a job interview
3. Personal appearance
4. Poor manners
5. Poorly filled out job application forms[8]

Additionally, a national survey of youth opportunity center counselors showed that the counselors felt that young people entering the labor market were handicapped in handling job interviews.[9] No doubt about it, the job interview is crucial, and if you are well prepared you will make a more positive impression.

Success in most endeavors begins with proper preparation, and the job interview is no exception. Do your homework thoroughly. Try to gather as much information as possible about the business or industry to which you are applying. This information can be gathered from company brochures, newspaper articles, and present and past employees. Being knowledgeable about the firm for which you are interviewing indicates a sincere interest in securing employment there. It is also helpful to find out how applicants are interviewed. Will there be a selection committee composed of several persons, or will there be only one interviewer?

Before the interview, try to gather as much information as possible about the business or industry to which you are applying.

Think through the interview procedure. Try to visualize who will be there. Where will everyone sit? How much distance will be between you? Put yourself in the seat of the interviewer and imagine how she will perceive you. Fantasize about possible questions and your brilliant, but not arrogant or boastful, answers. Decide how you want to come across and strive to make the fantasy become reality.

By permission of Johnny Hart and News America Syndicate.

Preparation also includes being familiar with the interview process itself. Become aware of questions frequently asked and formulate answers to those questions. For example, a question nearly always asked relates to why you are applying for a specific job. Naturally you want to have a more definite and positive response than, "I just thought it'd be kind of fun."

In *What Color Is Your Parachute?* John Bolles writes that the interview process is centered on four questions that the interviewer is just dying to know. If you formulate answers to those questions ahead of time, you stand a better chance of getting in the ballpark. Ready? The questions are:

1. Why are you here? Why have you chosen this particular place to come to instead of somewhere else? Have a good answer for this one. Never admit that you were just in the neighborhood or that you liked the landscaping or that you heard the firm had fabulous perks.

2. Precisely what can you do for me? What are your specific skills that you can use effectively if hired? What special knowledge do you have? Why should you be hired instead of someone else?

   Think positively here. A potential employer is not your benefactor. Remember that you have something to offer equal to any salary and fringe benefits you may be offered.

3. What kind of a person are you? What are some of your goals and aspirations? What are some of your dominant values? What do you do with leisure time? Are you outspoken? Agreeable? Motivated? Ambitious? Personal habits, personality traits, and interests are as important as your job skills.

4. How much is it going to cost me? How much money will it take to get you to sign on the dotted line? Bolles urges that you have a salary range in mind. Do some research ahead of time. Ask someone who already works there about her salary or ask a competitor.[10] Read the *OOH* for salary ranges.

Each occupation has a broad salary range depending on geographical region. Finding out what the range is in your area enables you to negotiate nearer the tip than the bottom of the range. If you ask for too much, you're out of the running. If you asked for too little, they might take you up on your low bid and figure they pulled one over on you. Then again, you might be screened out. Can a person who holds herself in such low regard actually be capable of carrying out the job duties?

Interview Preparation

Prepare some questions you may have about the job. Jot them down, or much to your sorrow, you'll forget them until five minutes after the interview. Possible questions include those relating to advancement opportunities, working hours, or specific job responsibilities. The interviewer may question your motives if you ask questions primarily about holidays, fringe benefits, and salary. However, if you are not told about these matters during the interview, it is permissible to inquire at the conclusion of the questioning period.

Preparation also pertains to your appearance. Look your best. It is important that your personal appearance is favorable. Appearance goes beyond pressed pants and polished shoes. Shampoo and style your hair. Trim and clean your nails. Make the most of what you have. Few people have perfect features, but that's no excuse to neglect grooming and hygiene.

Dress properly. Our attire tells others much about our taste, attitudes, and values since clothing tends to reflect our personalities. If your clothing is clean, neat, and appropriate, the interviewer is more likely to think that you are serious about wanting the job. If your clothes are soiled, unpressed, or disheveled, the interviewer may surmise that your sloppy appearance is indicative of the quality of your work. If they are too tight, too low, too short, or too flashy, she might wonder whether the inappropriateness indicates ignorance or immaturity.

There are no hard and fast rules about what constitutes appropriate clothing in every single situation. Use common sense. You don't need to wear a three-piece suit when applying for a job as sheet metal worker, but you can still dress neatly and create a good first impression. When applying for a job as an automobile mechanic, you don't want to look as though you are afraid of grease. Sometimes dress depends on geographical region. Based on research of more than 3,000 interviews with businesswomen, their co-workers, and superiors, and with top-ranking executives, John Molloy writes, "For any secretarial or clerical job, with the exception of those in the Deep South, the skirted suit is the best job-hunting outfit. In the South a conservative dress works better."[11]

Besides making a positive first impression, looking neat, clean, and well groomed gives you a psychological boost during the interview.

Personal appearance is important because it is invaluable in helping to make a favorable first impression. An added bonus is that a physical advantage can give you a mental advantage. Your self-confidence receives a boost when you feel that you look your best. Self-confidence will consequently help you with the "jitters" frequently encountered in stressful situations. A 1983 survey of employers revealed that 98 percent of those surveyed believed general appearance to be the first thing noticed in a prospective employee.

WHAT IS BEAUTIFUL IS SEX–TYPED: PUT AWAY THE DANGLING EARRINGS

Sex typing, the tendency of people to attribute certain stereotypical qualities to each sex, can negatively affect female employability. Looking too feminine can lessen the chances of a woman succeeding in a man's world.

In a study reported in *Psychology Today*, male and female corporate personnel consultants were asked to look at photographs and judge how qualified various attractive women were for jobs in corporate management.

In the first study, 16 personnel managers were shown photographs of women wearing various types of clothing, jewelry, hairstyles, and cosmetics. The more sex–typed or "feminized" the grooming styles, the less likely were personnel consultants to judge the women to be potential managers.

In a second study, they judged businesswomen photographed under two different grooming conditions: one very feminine and made–up, the other plainer and less sex typed. The more feminine style included long hair or hairstyles that concealed the face, soft sweaters, low necklines or ruffled blouses, dangling jewelry, and heavy makeup. Other "candidates" wore tailored clothes with a jacket, subtle makeup, and either short hair or hair swept away from the face.

The corporate personnel consultants made choices suggesting that the more feminine the appearance, the less competent the woman. Candidates groomed in a more feminine style were perceived to be less managerial, less intrinsically interested in work, less likely to be taken seriously by others, more illogical and overemotional in critical decision making, less financially responsible, sexier and more flirtatious in social relations with others, and less assertive than those groomed in a less sex-typed style. All this from a ruffled blouse and long hair?

The studies suggest that grooming style has a definite effect on whether women are sex typed and thus whether they are viewed as having good management potential. The message comes through loud and clear: looking too feminine can hurt a woman who wants to succeed in a man's world. The advice given in the "dress for success" books encouraging women to wear their hair short, use fewer cosmetics, and wear conservative suits is still valid.

Condensed from Thomas F. Cash and Louis H. Janda, "Eye of the Beholder," *Psychology Today*, December 1984, pp. 46–52.

The first thing I notice about a prospective employee is the manner in which the person is dressed. The correct clothing (clean and neat), the trim and combing of the hair, application of makeup (if female) are very, very important in first impressions.

Manager
Baton Rouge, Louisiana

Applicants with good skills have been turned down because of soiled and wrinkled clothing they were wearing.

Law Office Manager
Minneapolis, Minnesota[12]

Interview Tips

1. Try to get a good night's sleep the night before the interview. Otherwise you are not likely to appear enthusiastic and energetic. If you're feeling ill on the day of your interview, try to reschedule.

2. On the morning of the interview, one former personnel manager recommends skimming the newspaper to learn of newsworthy events going on in the world that day. Many interviewers make small talk before getting to specific job–related questions, and knowing that the Senate approved the tax reform bill helps you appear sharp and well informed.

3. Try to arrive a few minutes before time for the interview. Never be late! Upon arrival, learn the name of your interviewer if you haven't already done so. Greet the secretary pleasantly and give her your name and the position for which you are applying. Note the secretary's name; she (99 percent of all secretaries are female!) could be an ally in this campaign.

4. Bring an extra copy of your resume with you even though it should be referred to during the interview only if absolutely necessary. If needed, glance over the resume while waiting for your interview. A brief glance can refresh your memory on dates and places of employment and education and remind you of something you want to emphasize.

5. Let the interviewer make the first moves. Shake hands if the interviewer extends his or her hand. Shake hands firmly; limp, dishrag handshakes come from limp wimps. Sit down when asked to. You want to appear positive and confident, not aggressive.

6. Try to remain calm and at ease and yet attentive. Maintain eye contact throughout the interview since this indicates self–confidence, interest, and goodwill.

7. Do not smoke unless the urge is overpowering. Even then, ask the interviewer's permission before lighting up. Smoking at work is a serious issue in some organizations so unless you're positive about the company's position on smoking, why take a chance?

Maintaining eye contact and sitting up straight indicate interest, goodwill, and energy.

8. Sit up straight in your chair; don't slouch. Let your body language communicate interest and enthusiasm, not laziness or indifference.

9. Try to avoid nervous behavior or mannerisms. Many individuals nonverbally communicate nervousness by unconscious and purposeless mannerisms like foot tapping or pen clicking. Others may twirl their hair or fidget with their jewelry. Some interviewers deliberately place paper clips or a pen on the desk in front of an applicant to determine nervousness.

Desire for success coupled with fear of failure makes a certain amount of anxiety normal, even desirable. Positive anxiety acts as nature's stimulant and helps people to function at an optimal level. If you weren't at all nervous, you'd appear too laid back and nonchalant; if you're too uptight, well, you can pretty much visualize that performance. Strive for a happy medium between the extreme of casual nonchalance and excessive nervousness.

Your interviewer is probably a little nervous too, since his or her career is also on the line. After all, this person's supervisor is expecting the interviewer to hire an employee who will do a good job, who will fit in with others, and whose skills will benefit the company. So as not to be labeled incompetent by peers or supervisor, the person hiring you is under a lot of pressure to select just the right person.

10. Let the interviewer take the lead during the questioning period. To learn more about you, he or she will ask you a variety of questions. Most questions will relate to your job skills, education, and experience, but some questions will refer to your personal life. Finding out that an applicant enjoys jogging, gourmet cooking, or reading Western novels reveals something about that person. More and more employers realize that a "whole person" is hired, not just an eight–hour chunk.

    Most of the questions asked will be open ended. Instead of asking, "Do you like sports?" an interviewer may say something like, "Tell me about yourself. What do you like to do in your spare time?" Since the interviewer's goal is to learn more about you, you'll be encouraged to do most of the talking, maybe as much as 75 percent.

    Interviewers are prohibited from asking certain questions that refer to age, marital status, or religion. Sometimes they ask them anyway either because they don't know that such questions are illegal or because they hope you don't know they aren't lawful and will answer anyway. If you're asked such a question, you can answer it, or you can reply that since that question is not related to being a computer data processor or whatever position you're applying for , you don't wish to answer it. You might not get the job, but do you really want to work for an organization that wants to know all the details of your personal life?

11. Speak in a positive manner. Stress your special training or experience that will help you on this job. Your purpose is to sell yourself and your unique abilities to this employer without appearing boastful or conceited. Even if you are asked troublesome questions about past problems, turn a negative into a positive. It is unwise to try to hide a prison record or a drug problem. Instead, be honest and brief in your answers and then try to emphasize your good points and what you have to offer. The following questions serve as examples.

"I see you spent some time in prison. Could you tell me about it?"

"Well, I was very mixed up as a teenager. I became involved in a number of thefts and was sent to prison. That's a part of my past that I've managed to straighten out. I'm ready for work now and I'm looking forward to getting started in a job like this one."

"Are you sure someone your age can handle this job?"

"I know I appear young for the job, but I'm willing and anxious to learn."[13]

12. Do not criticize a former employer. A person who speaks negatively of a past employer might eventually say the same thing of the interviewer sometime in the future.

13. Ask your own questions toward the end of the interview. The interviewer will ask if you have any questions, and that is the time to inquire about hours, duties and even salary if those questions have not been addressed. Other possible questions may relate to a training period, a probationary period, overtime work, and promotional possibilities.

14. Follow the interviewer's lead when ending the interview. Stand when the person stands. Shake his or her hand and express appreciation for the time.

If you are offered the job and want it, then accept. If you need time to think it over, thank the interviewer for the offer and indicate a definite time that you will let him or her know of your decision. If, on the other hand, the interviewer cannot offer you the position, remain polite and positive. You could be offered a position later, or the interviewer could give your name to other employers. Ask to be kept in mind for future jobs.

FOLLOW–UP ACTIVITIES

A job campaign does not end with the interview. Do some follow–up activity. Most firms will only keep your application on active file for a limited period, and a simple phone call or letter keeps your file active and your interest obvious. It's much easier to keep an application alive than it is to start a new one. You don't want to be obnoxious and call the personnel office daily, but a phone call, visit, or follow–up letter to see if a decision has been made indicates a sincere interest in the position.

Many successful job hunters testify to the importance of sending a thank you note to the interviewer. Such a note indicates your sincere interest to the potential employer. It can also correct a faulty impression you might have made or add something you forgot to mention.

Since it's much easier to keep an application alive than it is to start a new one, call, write, or visit to indicate your continued interest.

Finally, resist the urge to become discouraged. Even if you don't get the job, look at the interview as a learning experience. Review the interview in your mind. What did you do right? Wrong? How would you rate your performance? Were you caught off guard by some unexpected questions? Is there something you left out? What about your appearance? Did you look your best? Were your clothes appropriate? The more often you go through the interview process, the more experienced and polished you will become.

If weeks, then months go by, and you're still unemployed, maybe you need to change your attitude about job hunting. Look at finding a job as a full–time job in itself. Everyday, five days a week from nine to five, devote yourself to finding a job.

Recently an acquaintance was yammering about low pay and unpleasant working conditions and complaining about the lack of available jobs. He insisted that he'd really been looking for something different, but as he talked, it became apparent that he had sent out three resumes, had two interviews, written two thank you notes, and made no follow-up phone calls. These activities took place over a three-week period and involved approximately five hours.

Contrast that with a committed job hunter who spends 8 hours a day, 5 days a week looking for a job. In three weeks, such a diligent seeker would have spent 120 hours in search of a job. Contrast that with the 5 hours spent by the acquaintance. Granted, an already employed person can't be expected to work 8 hours a day on finding another job, but there are lunch hours and after hours that could be put to good use. Weekends, holidays, and even vacation time can be used if finding another job is really top priority. Five hours isn't much of an investment if you really want another job, is it?

Different tactics work for different people. Some send out 50 resumes and get 40 interview invitations and 30 job offers. Some people don't do a thing. They hear about an opening from a friend of a friend and get the job without resume or formal interview. The most tried and proven method is go face to face as much as possible. Remember, for every successful job search, the common denominator is pursuing that desired job with a passion to win. It takes commitment and diligence. You have to keep at it.

Sample Interview Questions

Read the following interview questions and decide whether you think they are acceptable or unacceptable interview questions.

1. Are you married?
2. How many children do you have?
3. Have you ever been divorced?
4. What are the ages of your children?
5. What church do you belong to?
6. What is your marital status?
7. Are you planning to have children?
8. Are you now pregnant?
9. What does your husband (or wife) do for a living?
10. Can you arrange to have a reference sent from the pastor of your church?
11. Can you supply us with a copy of your birth certificate?
12. What is your religious affiliation?
13. How old are you?
14. Where were your parents born?
15. Have you ever been arrested for a crime?
16. What religious holidays do you observe?

17. If you get a job here, will it be a problem leaving your children at home?
18. Where were you born?
19. Can you furnish us with a photograph for the application?
20. You have to be under 40 years old to be eligible for our retirement plan. Is that a problem for you?
21. Can you describe your past work experience?
22. Would be you be available for overtime work on weekends?
23. Do you have any relatives employed by this company or its subsidiaries?
24. Have you ever worked under another name?
25. What schools have you attended?

The key to the validity of each answer rests on whether or not the question is truly job related. If it is found not to be, then it possibly falls within the category of discriminatory.

To test your answers, you would be correct if you checked "unacceptable" for questions 1–20 and "acceptable" for questions for 21–25. Remember that questions asked of an applicant must always relate specifically to the actual performance required for the job. The question must have relevance to the appropriate job standards selected for the position being filled. Caution areas involve questions regarding age, religion, marital status, and arrest records.

> Clark Lambert, *The Complete Book of Supervisory Training* New York: John Wiley, 1984, pp. 166 and 167.

More Sample Interview Questions

TYPICAL QUESTIONS ASKED BY INTERVIEWERS
The Job Interview. How To Be Effective.
Adkins Life Skills Program, 1975

Many of the questions that you will be asked during the interview can be answered more effectively if you know beforehand what they are and how you will respond to them. A number of questions often asked by interviewers are given below. Look them over and try to prepare answers for any that you think might be difficult for you to handle.

Let's start with questions about your work experience and education.

1. What job (position) are you applying for?
2. Do you want a permanent job or a temporary one? What hours are you available for work?
3. What job would you prefer? What kind of work do you like to do?
4. Have you had any experience with this type of work?
5. What other jobs have you had that are similar to the one you are applying for?
6. Tell me about the work you did on your last job. What were some of your work activities?
7. What did you like most about your last job? What did you like least about it?
8. Why did you leave your last job?
9. May I contact your last employer?
10. How does your past work experience relate to the job for which you are applying?

11. What special skills do you have? What tools, equipment, or machines can you use?
12. What qualifications do you have that will help you to do this job successfully?
13. What training have you had that prepared you for the duties of this job?
14. Which courses in school did you like best? Why did they appeal to you?
15. In what school activities did you participate? What did you enjoy most about them?
16. Which courses in school did you like least? What was there about these courses that made you dislike them?
17. Did you drop out of school? If so, why?
18. Have you attended any classes since you left regular public school? If so, what were they?
19. Do you have any educational plans? How would this job fit in with them?
20. Why do you think you would like to work for this company?
21. Do any of your friends or relatives work here?
22. What do you know about our company?
23. Are you satisfied with the salary we are offering for this job?

Interviewers are also interested in your work and interpersonal attitudes. Sometimes questions aimed at finding out about your feelings and attitudes are included during the discussion of your work history. Learn to recognize these questions and their purpose. Think about how you would reply to such questions.

24. What are your feelings about having to adjust to many different kinds of work situations? Would it bother you to have to move around among several departments?
25. How do you feel about having to work as part of a team?
26. What are your feelings about helping co–workers who have especially heavy work loads?
27. How do you feel about working overtime to complete a job?
28. How would you describe your relationships with past supervisors? With former co–workers?
29. Have you ever been discharged (fired) from a job? What were the circumstances?

Employers are often concerned with an applicant's physical ability to meet the work requirements. Here are some questions related to health and physical fitness that you should be prepared to answer.

30. Do you have any physical disabilities that may affect your work? If yes, give a brief description.
31. Have you ever had a serious illness or an injury? If so, describe it.
32. Have you ever been hospitalized for a nervous disorder?
33. When did you last have a complete physical checkup? Why did you have it? What were the results?
34. How many times were you absent on your last job due to illness or emergencies?

Keep in mind that one of the purposes of the interview is to give your prospective employer an opportunity to learn more about you. For this reason, you should be prepared to answer questions related to your personal and family life.

35. Tell me about yourself.

36. How long have you lived in this city? Do you plan to remain here?

37. What do you do in your spare time? What are your hobbies?

38. Do you drive? Do you have a car? What kind of a license do you have? Driver's? Chauffeur's? Have you ever been convicted of any traffic violations other than illegal parking? If so, what were they?

39. Have you ever been in jail or prison?

40. What is your military classification? (asked of male applicants)

41. Do you have any dependents? If so, who are they?

SUMMARY

The job hunt can be challenging, exciting, frustrating, and exhausting. Since your job determines the quality of your life for years, it pays to develop job–seeking competencies.

The steps involved in a job– hunting campaign include: assessing your abilities and interests, exploring sources of job leads, composing a positive cover letter, writing an effective resume, learning interview skills, and following up on your activities.

Four sources of job leads are friends and relatives, want ads, school placement offices, and employment agencies. Instead of relying exclusively on these old "stand–bys," Lathrop suggests going directly to the employers who have people on their payrolls doing the kind of work you want to do. Go with the attitude that you should be the next person to hire when a job opens up.

A cover letter is simply a letter that accompanies a resume and allows you to explain why you want a certain job. In addition to stressing what you can do for the employer, the cover letter should be neat, grammatically correct, positive, and somewhat forceful.

A resume is an inventory of your work experience and education, and its purpose is getting a job interview, not a job. There are basically four uses of a resume: a self–inventory, an extended calling card, an interview agenda, and a memory jogger for the employer after the interview has taken place.

Resumes should be neat, well organized, factual, straightforward, and relatively brief. Although personal information is often included, the resume is not meant to be an autobiography. Personal information such as sex, age, religion, and marital status are not required.

In addition to other questions pertaining to previous salary, health, draft status, and traveling ability, application forms ask for much of the same information included on a resume. As with the resume, neatness counts.

Being well prepared for the job interview will help you make a more favorable impression. To aid in your preparation, try to find out as much as possible about the business to which you are applying. Think through the interview procedure and try to visualize who will be there and what will take place. Become familiar with typical questions asked by interviewers, most of which center on four main concerns: Why are you here?

What can you do for me? What kind of a person are you? How much is it going to cost me?

Additional interview tips include preparing questions of your own, paying special attention to your appearance, being punctual, avoiding nervous behavior or mannerisms, and speaking in a positive manner.

A job campaign doesn't end with the interview. Since most firms will only keep your application on active file for a limited period, you need to call, visit, or send a follow–up letter to indicate a sincere interest in the position.

Even if you don't get the job, resist becoming discouraged. Try to look at the interview as a learning experience as you evaluate your performance and determine to become more prepared and polished. If unemployment persists, maybe you need to change your attitude about job hunting and think of it as a full–time job in itself.

KEY TERMS

Richard Lathrop
Cover letter
Resume
Halo effect
John Bolles
Follow–up activities

REVIEW AND DISCUSSION QUESTIONS

1. Of all the sources of job leads, which has been most productive for you in the past? Why do you think this is the case?

2. In what ways can a school placement office help you in a job search? Why do you think it is often overlooked as a method of finding a job?

3. Thinking of a job you now aspire to, tell exactly what you would do in following Lathrop's advice of going directly to the employer. What would you say? To who would you speak? How would you present your best qualities?

4. What are the four basic uses of a resume?

5. If you were advising someone on how to organize and write a resume, what are at least five points you would stress?

6. There are several things you can do to prepare for the job interview. What are at least three ways in which you prepare yourself ahead of time?

7. According to Bolles, what are four questions interviewers are just "dying to ask"? How would you answer those questions if being interviewed today?

8. Of all the interview tips listed in the text, which five do you consider to be the most important? Why?

9. Why does the job campaign not end with the interview? What kinds of follow–up activity would you engage in for your job?

ENDNOTES

[1] RICHARD LATHROP, *Who's Hiring Who* (Reston, Va.: Reston, 1976), p. 10.

[2] Ibid., p. 20

[3] CAROLYN HODGES PERSELL, *Understanding Society: An Introduction to Sociology* (Harper & Row, 1984) p. 382.

[4] LATHROP, *Who's Hiring Who*, p. 40.

[5] RICHARD NELSON BOLLES, *What Color is Your Parachute?* (Berkeley, Calif.: Ten Speed Press, 1982), pp. 171–174.

[6] "Success on the Job," national survey conducted by Watertown Chapter 3439, Future Leaders of America, Watertown High School, Watertown, Connecticut, 1983, p. 11.

[7] Ibid., p. 11.

[8] *Final Report of Statewide Employer Survey*, Austin, Tex., 1975.

[9] D.F. EGGERMAN, et al., "Problems in the Transition from School to Work as Perceived by Youth Opportunity Center Counselors," Center for Vocational Education, The Ohio State University, Columbus, Ohio, 1969.

[10] BOLLES, *What Color Is Your Parachute?* p. 233.

[11] JOHN T. MOLLOY, *Woman's Dress for Success Book* (New York: Warner Books, 1977), p. 109.

[12] "Success on the Job," pp. 107–108.

[13] WINTHROP R. ADKINS, "The Job Interview: How to Be Effective," *Adkins Life Skills Program* (New York: Institute for Life Coping Skills, 1975), p. 11.

chapter 12

Developing Good Work Habits and Getting Ahead

After reading and studying this chapter, you will be able to:

1. Set realistic, challenging goals.
2. Use time more efficiently.
3. Develop a more positive self–concept.
4. Discuss the importance of accepting challenges.
5. Explain the value of being persistent.
6. Explain why and how learning is lifelong.
7. Discuss what is meant by playing politics at work and how it can help an employee.
8. Explain how looking the part can contribute to career success.

There may be luck in getting a job, but there's no luck in keeping it.

J. Ogden Armour[1]

Congratulations! Because of your ability to sell someone on your unique combination of assets (aptitudes, experience, education, and interests), you landed the job you wanted. The painstaking efforts you took to write your cover letter and resume, the informational interviews you conducted, the time you spent learning about the organization itself, and the extra few moments you took with your grooming paid off. This is only the beginning, my friend. You can't rest on your laurels and become one of those people who quit looking for work as soon as they find a job. Not only do you have to keep your job, but you must also become all you possibly can. You owe it to yourself and to your employer.

Where do you want to be in 5 years? In 10? Many people fail to think about what they really want from their jobs and their lives. They don't plan their lives and end up doing pretty much the same old job year after year. That's fine for many individuals. However, if you're a person who wants more out of your job—money, growth, promotions, opportunity— you can't expect things to fall into your lap just because you're a super individual.

Ever wonder why some people who were hired after you were have passed you by? They make more money, have more responsibility, and get to do challenging work. Why is that? Is it luck? Were they at the right place at the right time? Are they related to the boss? Are they convincing apple polishers? Believe that if sour grapes are your favorite fruit. If not, then realize that "luck" is where preparation and opportunity collide. Busy yourself with preparation. Follow the guidelines suggested in this chapter and maybe you'll get lucky too. You're the one in control, the one in the driver's seat.

You, yes you, have to take steps to help ensure your success. Setting goals, managing your time, persevering, and striving for excellence are not meaningless phrases in the quest for success. Taking on challenges, developing your self–concept, and dressing for success are worthwhile activities that lead to professional growth. Letting others know of your aims and aspirations and softly tooting your own horn never hurt a ladder climber either.

SETTING GOALS

Before doing anything else, you have to set some goals. You have to know what you want out of life and work before starting out on your journey to success. *If You Don't Know Where You're Going, You'll Probably End Up Somewhere Else* is the name of an amusing, yet very informative book whose goal is to help you make the most of what you have.[2] There are many pathways leading to a fulfilling, successful life, but how will you know which one to choose if you don't know what you want? How can you get from here to there if you only kind of, sort of know what you want but haven't made any concrete plans? Or if you think you know what you want but haven't developed yourself sufficiently to open doors leading to the attainment of your heart's desire? Success in any venture doesn't just happen; it's planned. Set a few goals. Know where you want to go and end up there.

Principles of Goal Setting

"Syd's Wisecrack." A person without a milestone plan is like a fly buzzing on a window. There is an objective but no intelligent plan to get there. Sydney Love[3]

Goal setting is a phrase bandied about in all sorts of situations. People set goals to lose weight, improve their golf game, make more money, travel, spend more time with loved ones, and receive promotions. For a goal to be useful, there are some guidelines you must follow. Goals should be written down, specific, realistic, and time oriented.

Write them down

Dig a hole before you are thirsty. Chinese proverb.

It's important that goals be written down. Otherwise, a goal is only an idea, a pleasant thought. Taking pen in hand and jotting down your goal has at least two advantages: (1) it gives more structure to your vague, utopian idea, and (2) it increases your personal commitment. Writing is unfamiliar to many individuals, but it is necessary to make objectives tangible enough to give you direction. After writing your goals, you can study them, and consequently analyze, change, refine, and update them. Writing down your objectives is like saying, "There, I've done it. I've written them down. They're there in black and white, and now I have to get to work!"

Make them specific

To be effective, goals should be written down, specific, realistic, and time oriented.

Goals should be as specific as possible. People have hazy ideas of what they want to accomplish. One person wants to lose weight, one to be rich, another to see the world, and still another to have a happy family life. In fact, one person might have all four of these thoughts as goals.

The chances of achieving any of the goals are increased if the person setting them is as specific as possible. For instance, the odds of losing weight are improved by saying, "I want to lose one pound per week and fit into my size 34 pants within six weeks." Oh yes, having a game plan to lose a pound a week helps too. A game plan consists of activities to follow in reaching your goals. We'll get to that shortly.

Be specific. Want to see the world? The chances of seeing it all during your two–week vacation (on your salary) are between slim and none. Start with one place you want to visit. Yellowstone National Park, Williamsburg, Va., and Disneyworld are three great places to visit in the United States. If you yearn for foreign parts, pick a country and say, "I'm going to Spain in 1995," and start making plans accordingly. Do without a few luxuries and salt away a few dollars each payday. Tell people about your plans. Commit yourself. Buy some Spanish language tapes.

If you say you want a happy family life but are single, well, you have to give up your carefree, single status. If you're already married, you've learned that a happy family life doesn't just happen; you have to work at it. Set some goals—specific ones!

Make them realistic

It's imperative that your goals be realistic. From assessing your abilities, skills, intelligence, experience, and education in an earlier chapter, you have a pretty good idea of what you can and cannot do. Aim high, but don't set your yourself up for disappointment by attempting the impossible. In *How to Cure Yourself of Positive Thinking*, Donald G. Smith reminds readers that "some things are simply not attainable and the writer who says you can have whatever you want by pushing forward and driving all negative thoughts from your mind is telling you an out and out lie."[4] Read on; Smith's insight is refreshing, yet sobering.

> You cannot achieve whatever you set your mind to just by establishing a goal and working for it. If you haven't the mental capacity to pass the state bar, you can't be a lawyer. If you haven't the musical talent, you can't be a concert pianist. If you shoot in the nineties, you can't be a pro golfer. Accept it. You aren't good enough.

> We have all been spoon fed on the tales of people coming through under great adversity and doing something that people said couldn't be done. Unfortunately, we don't keep records of the millions of people who have tried something with the best and the most positive of intentions and failed completely; probably because they hadn't the ability to do it.

> Now that we have rid ourselves of the cruel delusion that we can do whatever we want to do, become whatever we want to be, even though we lack the intelligence, the training, the talent, and the physical ability, we can now proceed to the next step in the eradication of positive thinking. This is the realization that accomplishment is largely a cut and dried business, completely divorced from the realm of positive or negative thinking.[5]

Be realistic, yet ambitious. Some people are totally unrealistic. If they have the brain power, they lack the will power, the determination, and diligence to make things happen. What can you achieve with your own unique assets? While realizing that we all have limitations, don't aim at less than you are capable of becoming. It's no great feat if you aim too low and achieve your goal.

You need some time frame to follow in achieving your goals. To illustrate, one afternoon while talking with a young man of 22, it became evident that what he wanted within 10 years was to make a lot of money, do some traveling, and have a loving wife and two healthy, brilliant, adorable children. The future looked a little bleak since he had dropped out of college twice, ended a promising two–year romance, finally secured a job as a cashier at a convenience store after a brief period of unemployment, and had absolutely no idea how to make his goals become reality.

After being asked such questions as, "What will it take for you to get there?" ("there" being the attainment of dreams and goals) and "How exactly are you going to do it?" and "When are you going to start?" this young man realized that his chances of being where he wanted to be by age 32 were minimal unless he set some specific, realistic goals according to a time frame. He had some worthwhile and attainable long–range goals but no specific plan to achieve them.

Categories of Goals

According to David Campbell's categories, your goals are long range, medium range, short range, mini, and micro.[6] Take a peek at each category and think of some of your own goals.

Long-range goals concern your desired overall style of life–the type of job you want and the general situation you want to live in. Campbell cautions his readers not to use a lot of detail in setting long-range goals since change is inevitable, and you need flexibility to deal with it.

Long-range goals concern your future overall life–style and should be approached with flexibility.

Medium–range goals cover the next five years or so. What training or education do you need? You have more control over these goals and can easily tell whether change or modification is necessary. For starters, the 22 year-old just noted could go back to school, patch things up with his girlfriend, be an on–the–job job hunter, and save some money for education, travel, and investments.

Short–range goals cover one month to one year. A person can set these goals quite realistically and tell fairly soon whether or not she's reaching them.

Mini goals are goals covering from one day to one month. The shorter the time span, the more control over the goals. It's easier to decide what you're going to achieve this week and actually achieve it than it is to decide definitely what you're going to accomplish in five years. For example, you have more control over studying for two hours tonight, saving $10 from out of Friday's paycheck, or spending time with your child today than you do over events transpiring in March 1997 at 12:00 noon. You have more control over shorter hunks of time.

A successful life involves stacking smaller goals together to reach the long–range goals you really care about.

Micro goals cover the next 15 minutes to an hour, and Campbell states that these are the only goals you have direct control over. Even though they are modest in impact, micro goals are of utmost importance in your life since it is through these goals that you can achieve your long–range, larger goals. If you don't start working toward your long–range plan in the next 15 minutes to an hour, when will you? Sooner or later, you've got to pick 15 minutes and learn that new process, read that homework assignment, or make that phone call. Force yourself to make progress toward your micro goal, and your long–range goals will take care of themselves. Planning a successful life involves stacking smaller goals together in a way that increases your chances of reaching the long–range goals you really care about.

People need to reevaluate and reset their goals frequently.

Remember that goals aren't cast in concrete. People change, situations change. What you want in your twenties might seem shallow and meaningless in your thirties. You need some flexibility in your goal setting. Some people find that after achieving a long–sought–after goal, it doesn't seem nearly as important as it once did. No goal, once achieved, can sustain a person for very long. Does this ring of Maslow and his hierarchy of needs? People always need to evaluate and reset their goals since the world looks a little different as individuals gain experience and maturity.

A Game Plan

After writing down your goals, write down what particular activities you need to do to accomplish these goals.

The topic of goal setting would be incomplete without a brief look at a game plan to help you accomplish your objectives. Basically, after writing your long, medium, short, mini, and micro goals, write down what particular activities you need to do to accomplish these goals. If you want to make an "A" in an economics course, what can you do today to help you ace that course? If you want to exercise more, what can you do this morning? If you want a job that utilizes more of your skills, what can you do in the next hour to help you? You might be able to get a dozen or so activities for each goal. For example, to help you get a more challenging job, document an achievement, help a co—worker, or let someone know that you are interested in different work.

MANAGING YOUR TIME

Setting goals and managing time are behaviors that go hand in hand. People are always bemoaning a lack of time. They want to develop an interesting hobby, take a course, visit friends, read good books, spend time with their families, and get more accomplished at work. As soon as they have more time, these rushed, harried individuals are going to start these marvelous ventures.

The truth is that all people have exactly the same amount of time, 24 hours a day and 168 hours a week, but some people make better use of it than others. They manage and use their weekly allotment wisely, while others fritter it away in wasteful, useless activities. Time is life, and wasting time is wasting your life. What a sobering thought! Time is a nonrenewable resource. Once it's gone, it's gone forever, so grab those minutes today and use them to your advantage before they tick away.

The time management principles outlined here aren't designed to make you busy, busy, busy. To the contrary. It's important that you take time to smell the flowers, engage in idle conversation with your friends, gaze at the stars, listen to children's laughter, and watch a movie with no purpose but enjoyment on your mind. Don't be overly concerned with

making every minute count or with being superorganized. Just learn to use your precious time more effectively whether you're working or playing.

Set Priorities

When Charles Schwab was president of Bethlehem Steel, he gave Ivy Lee a challenge. "Show me a way to get more done with time," Schwab said, "and I'll pay you any fee within reason."[7] Would you like to know Lee's simple advice that earned him $25,000? He told Schwab to write down the most important tasks he had to do each day and to number them in order of their importance. Lee continued, "When you arrive in the morning, begin at once on number one and stay with it until it's completed. Recheck your priorities; then begin with number two. If any task takes all day, never mind. Stick with it as if it's the most important one. If you don't finish them all, you probably couldn't do so with any other method, and without some system, you'd probably never decide which one was most important. Make this a habit every working day."[8] Along with the generous check, Schwab sent a note telling Lee that the lesson was the most profitable he had ever learned. A cardinal rule in managing time is not necessarily finishing a task but making the most of your time.

A Cardinal rule in managing time is not necessarily finishing a task but making the most of your time.

Setting priorities is the utmost importance in setting goals. Do first things first. Getting your priorities in order is as basic as ABC, or at least that's what Alan Lakein professes in *Make the Most of Your Time and Your life.*[9] Make a list of all your goals, no matter how utopian or far out. To help you achieve these goals, whether long or short term, make a daily "To Do" list along the lines of Charles Schwab's. Keep the list visible. Plenty of well–meaning people say they have lists in their heads. Don't risk forgetting your goals and activities; write them down.

Making a daily "To Do" list and keeping it visible aids in time management.

Look over your list, and before starting on any activity, save yourself some time by seeing what you can delegate to someone else. After delegating what you can, simply write an "A" beside items of high value, a "B" beside those of medium value, and a "C" beside those of low value. Further break down these categories into "A-1," "A-2," "A-3," and so on. The "A" goals should be the real attention–getters on your list. When you ask yourself Lakein's question, "What's the best use of my time right now?" you should always get an "A" activity, preferably an "A-1." Anything else, according to Lakein, is a virtual waste of time.

Determine Activities

An "A" goal is an item of high value on your "To Do" list.

After establishing your priorities, determine what specific activities have to be done to accomplish the goal. An activity differs from a goal: the former is something you do, the latter is something you strive to attain. A goal is acquiring a more satisfying job; an activity is reading the want ads. List the activities, schedule them, and get started working toward that goal right away.

The average person doesn't always select "A" activities. He puts a lot on his list and gets a lot done, but many of the accomplishments are in the "C" category. You must set priorities! People often get bogged down in "C" activities because it gives them a feeling of accomplishment and because they're afraid or reluctant to tackle "A" activities.

A "C-Z" is an activity that can be postponed indefinitely without harm.

A "C-Z" is an activity that can be postponed indefinitely without harm. Some "C"'s deferred long enough become "C-Z"'s. Some examples of "C-Z"'s are washing the car when it looks like rain, shampooing your hair before going to the beauty shop, or taking a shower before going jogging. Say to yourself, "What can I not do?" If, as Lakein advises, you can let the filing, dusting, washing, and checking go one more day, you'll spend less of your precious time filing, dusting, washing, and checking.

The best possible use of your time is to tackle that "A." It's doubtful that you'll have a big hunk of uninterrupted time to handle that top priority activity. It's either overwhelming or unpleasant, so you tend to postpone it. An overwhelming "A" is something complex or time consuming like writing a research paper or painting your house. An unpleasant "A" is something like admitting a mistake to your boss, telling your boss she made a mistake, preparing an income tax form with several deductions, or reading six chapters for a test. Most people procrastinate rather than tackle overwhelming or unpleasant "A"'s.

Avoid Procrastination

Procrastination of "A"'s is deadly. Avoid it at all costs. There are many ways to fight procrastination, one of which is utilizing little bits and pieces of time as recommended by Lakein's Swiss cheese method.[10] That is, turn the overwhelming task into several short and easy tasks. Pretend that the "A-1" is a big hunk of Swiss cheese and proceed to punch holes in it. Get involved in instant tasks that take five minutes or less of your time. What are some instant tasks you can do to help you get ready for a big test? To write a term paper? To find another job? To get started on that major project? Just be sure that the instant task is easy and related to the overwhelming "A." Make a few holes in it, and the awesome task may turn out to be more simple than you imagined—or feared.

The Swiss cheese method of time management turns an overwhelming task into several short and easy ones.

Another suggestion for fighting procrastination is to use the "Well, as long as I . . ." technique suggested by Stephanie Winston in *The Organized Executive*.[11] There's nothing complex about this method. Simply say, "Well, as long as I'm standing at the file cabinet, I might as well file these letters," "Well, as long as I'm talking to the boss, I might as well mention my blunder." "Well, as long as I'm in the library, I might as well look in the card catalogue."

Creating a conducive atmosphere is also helpful for fighting procrastination. Are the materials you need convenient and accessible? If not, clear your desk or working area of everything not essential to the task at hand. Is the atmosphere too depressing, too distracting, too drab, or too noisy? If so, go somewhere else. Surroundings matter.

ROUND TUIT

If you've been saying to yourself, "I'm going to take a course, walk on the beach, watch a sunset, ask my boss for a raise, and do some life/work planning as soon as I can get a "round tuit," your troubles are over.

This illustration is a "round tuit." Cut it out, keep it handy, and you should have no more difficulties with procrastination since you now have a "round tuit."

This idea was borrowed from *The Three Boxes of Life* authored by John Bolles.

Creating a conducive atmosphere is helpful in fighting procrastination.

Winston also recommends that you consider the deadline factor. There are some people who perform optimally under pressure but can't seem to get going otherwise. As Samuel Johnson said, "When a man knows he is to be hanged in a fortnight, it concentrates his mind wonderfully."

Additional Tips

Say no

Learning to use that certain two letter word can save you untold amounts of time and frustration. When someone asks you to serve on a committee, steer a project, accept a promotion, or go somewhere you don't want to go, say no. Say it and don't allow yourself to feel guilty or anxious. Many adults "still have feelings of anxiety, ignorance, and guilt that can and are used effectively by other people to get us to do what they want, irrespective of what we want for ourselves."[12] You have the right to offer no excuses to justify saying no. Just say it and face the fact that no matter what you do, someone isn't going to like it.

Saying "no" can save untold amounts of time and frustration.

Sometimes people say yes when they want to say no and end up feeling resentment and anger. When questioned about why they didn't say no in the first place, they offer whining, mealy–mouthed excuses completely unworthy of any human adult, for example,

"He had me in a corner."
"I agreed to get rid of her."
"I didn't want to hurt her feelings."

Sometimes you owe it to other people to say no. Not saying it is unfair to them. Is it ethical to say yes to someone reluctantly and then not give the activity your best shot? Or what if you give it your best shot but are seething with resentment? Is it right to say that yes, you'll try, but then only try half way and end up failing? The person to whom you made the promise is likely to feel angry and see you as an untrustworthy, unreliable person.

Ask yourself what has to be done each day

There are certain things that have to be done everyday—eating, sleeping, dressing, undressing, shaving, curling hair, and driving to work are examples. Plan around these things and expect the unexpected. For instance, how long does it take for you to drive to work? What if there's an accident? What if you get behind a school bus? Plan for these interruptions, distractions, and crises.

Plan around certain tasks that have to be done everyday and then expect the unexpected.

You can work around those basic physiological needs of eating and sleeping. Is it really necessary to go out for lunch? If not, use your lunch hour more productively. Go for a walk. Read a news magazine. Meditate. Study.

Do you really need as much sleep as you get? If you sleep eight hours per night, you'll have slept 10 years by the time you're age 30. Ten years! What a waste of time, of life. Get up 15 minutes earlier or go to bed 15 minutes later and use that time effectively. Can 15 minutes make a difference? You bet it can. Fifteen minutes per day adds up to about 91 hours a year. Did you sleep through those 91 hours that you could have spent doing something you really wanted to do but didn't have the time? Remember, there's always time for the really important things.

Look ahead for the week

Reserve parts of the week for "A" projects, but be flexible. If you don't get to spend two hours learning how to use the new equipment, then reschedule.

Make use of waiting time

If you know you're going to the doctor, take your textbook. One acquaintance says she always gets in the longest line at the supermarket and makes use of her time by reading (devouring) a favorite magazine. While standing in line she's learned how to feed her family economically, improve her chances in the job market, apply makeup skillfully, and redecorate her living room. Contrast that with another person who stands there fretting and fuming with anger and frustration.

Make use of commuting time

There may not be a way to avoid spending 30 or more minutes going to work or school each day, but you can make those minutes count. Buy a foreign language tape to listen to in the car. Do isometric exercises. Rehearse an upcoming, important dialogue.

DEVELOP YOUR SELF–CONFIDENCE

Within each person there are vast possibilities that have never been realized. It's a sad but true fact that many people die with their music still in them, and this doesn't necessarily refer to frustrated singers, musicians, or composers. Within each person there is some special dream, some special talent that never comes to light. Why not? There are several reasons, one of which is a lack of self–confidence.

To achieve success in life and work, you need a boost of self–confidence. Often the way people perceive themselves as adults depends partially on the feedback they received as children from significant adults. For example, Leo Buscaglia, author of *Living, Loving, and Learning,* says that we tell little children what they are and who they are.

"If enough people tell you, "You are beautiful, you are beautiful, you are beautiful," you will begin to behave as beautiful. "You'll stand up straighter, you'll be prouder of yourself. But "You are ugly, you are ugly, you are ugly," will make you bend, become smaller and smaller, until you will become ugly. "You're wrong! You're stupid!"" will make you wrong and stupid."[13]

The way people perceive themselves as adults depends partially on the feedback they received as children.

It's possible to acquire self–confidence as an adult even if you weren't told you were beautiful as a child. Dr. Robert Schuller writes of four ways to increase your feelings of worth, feelings that you need to unlock the door to your future.[14]

1. If your self–confidence is so negative that you find yourself entertaining thoughts of suicide, seek professional help—immediately.

2. "Props" can be great confidence boosters. Get some flattering new clothes. Change your hairstyle. Lose 10 pounds. Consider cosmetic surgery. Few things make a person feel more confident and increase self–esteem than looking his or her best. Few individuals have ideal features, but that's no excuse for not doing the best you can with what you have. The media contain scores of helpful hints on fashion, exercise, diet, and cosmetics.

3. Surround yourself with positive friends. Who needs someone who sees the negative aspects of everything? Some people delight in telling you that it can't be done, that you're unrealistic, and that you've got your head in the clouds. Avoid them and find people to encourage and inspire you, not stifle you.

4. Take a chance. Use pluck. You've heard that nothing succeeds like success since you were a tot, and it's just as true now that you're an adult. Try something small that you feel positive about. Succeed and then set another goal. Rack up a few easy victories. The feeling of accomplishment will spur you on to yet greater heights and give you a feeling a confidence.

Visualize and actualize. Visualizing what it is that you want to do, imagining yourself playing that role, and then actually living the part develops self–concept. Do you want to be president of the company, owner of your own business, a master mechanic, or another Florence Nightingale? Visualize yourself engaging in actual behavior such as asking for a raise, suggesting an idea, or starting a conversation, and then do it. While engaging in the actual behavior, think of yourself as merely playing a part if you wish, but since feeling follows action, you'll soon begin to feel that part. It'll be you—part of your self–concept.

Shakespeare said that "There's nothing either good or bad, but thinking makes it so." Your mental response to circumstance can help or hurt you. If you see yourself as ignorant, unlovable, unworthy, incompetent, you're doomed to fail. Instead, look within and find what it is that makes you unique and celebrate that uniqueness. You're a special person. Think it. Visualize it. Believe it. Act it.

ACCEPT CHALLENGES

Change your thoughts and you change your world. Norman Vincent Peale

Say yes to life and to work. Don't stand on the sidelines shivering and thinking of the cold and danger, jump in. When in doubt, take the risk. Don't let negative thoughts, fear of failure, rejection, or criticism hold you back. There's no sin in failing to win, but there is in failing to try. If you aren't willing to take some risks, chances are that you aren't growing or progressing since there's no progress without risk. Leo Buscaglia believes that the word most conducive to continued growth is yes.[15] Say yes to life, to work, to differences, to opportunities, to relationships, to experiences.

You have to be willing to take some risks if you are to grow.

Many people say they're not smart enough, quick enough, old enough, or young enough to apply for that job, climb that mountain, get that degree, or accept that promotion. Realistically, in some cases these pronouncements are accurate. However, if you don't fit the bill today, will you tomorrow? It's doubtful. Go for it now, or you might regret it otherwise.

For all the sad words of tongue or pen, the saddest are these: "It might have been." John Greenleaf Whittier.

Sociologists and psychologists see applications of the self–fulfilling prophecy everyday. Basically what it means is that a person decides whether he'll blow the interview or not, get promoted or not, pass the test or not, and then works to ensure that the prophecy is fulfilled. I can't promise that predicting an "A" in a class will win you that "A," but your chances are better than if you set your sights on a "C." Think about it. What are some of your personal prophecies that have come true?

BE PERSISTENT

I know the price of success—dedication, hard work, and an unremitting devotion to the things you want to see happen. Frank Lloyd Wright

Once you've decided on your career path, stick with it and be willing to work hard. Many people don't actually fail; they just give up trying. Be persevering although it'll be difficult at times. Your supervisor may be overly critical, co–workers may be especially cantankerous, and your family may make special demands, but don't quit. Discipline yourself to stick with your goal until it's completed.

CONTINUE TO LEARN

Learning doesn't have to take place only between the ages of 5 and 22. It's a lifelong process. If you were having chest pains, would you go to a doctor who hadn't kept abreast of changes in the medical field? Would you trust your prized automobile to a shade tree mechanic? Probably not.

Learning is a lifelong process.

The message is clear. If you desire to succeed at life and at work, you have to stay informed. Do whatever it takes to keep your brain from getting rusty. Take formal courses. Read books and periodicals. Take advantage of seminars and workshops. Expose yourself to others who know more than you do. Not only does learning more about your field help you personally, but it also lets your boss and customers know that you have an interest in improving yourself.

Learning as much as you can about many topics makes you a much more interesting person.

Don't limit yourself to learning only the latest developments in your specific occupation. It's a big world out there. Broaden your horizons. Learn a foreign language. Improve your vocabulary. Learn more about the world of nature. Take piano lessons. Learning as much as you can about other topics makes you a much more interesting person. It also introduces you to other areas of interest which might lead to alternatives to work and leisure. One man who was at first mildly interested in the appearance of his lawn developed such an interest in landscaping that he eventually resigned from his job as a department store manager and started his own landscaping business.

PLAY POLITICS

Politics has been defined as the total complex of what goes on between people in society. Politics exists as long as there is more than one person. Don't doubt that it thrives in your workplace. It does. A little politicking can make your work more rewarding if you use it to a good purpose as a personal power. Many suggestions for success at work previously mentioned are forms of politics, but the following are even more specific.

1. Let others know of your plans and aspirations. One secretary was constantly frustrated by being passed over for promotion. She performed her job so admirably and cheerfully that her boss assumed that she was delighted in her position and had no idea that she was interested in moving ahead.

Politics exists as long as there is more than one person.

2. Keep a log of your accomplishments. It's easier to convince your order giver of your value and ability if you have concrete evidence. The reason for writing your accomplishments down is to compensate for your inaccurate memory. A written record helps to substantiate your claim that you contributed or grew in some way. If you leave it up to your boss to keep a record for you, then you deserve exactly what you get.

3. Consider getting a mentor, a person who teaches, coaches, and counsels others on their way up. Find someone in a higher place in your organization and learn from him or her. If you don't have access to

a mentor, DuBrin suggests that you "grab a shooting star."[16] There are only so many high ranking people around to take an interest in you, so instead cultivate a relationship with someone who already has a sponsor or mentor. Become a protege of a protege. As that person moves up, so will you.

LOOK THE PART

Pay attention to your attire and grooming. Few businesses or industries are satisfied with employees who are chronically or excessively sloppy or poorly groomed. "Appropriate" is the key word. It's sheer folly to wear a three–piece suit to repair air conditioning units or install carpet, but you do need to be neat, clean, and well groomed. John Molloy, author of *Dress for Success*, suggests that you use clothing as a tool right along with your education, experience, and aptitudes since "you are your product and you must dress accordingly."[17]

Molloy suggests using clothing as a tool along with education, experience, and aptitudes.

Molloy doesn't believe in written dress codes since they tend to create problems and intrude on an employee's privacy. An unwritten code is acceptable, however, and is established by example and sound psychology. If dressing for success appeals to you, look around and above you at the people who have the jobs you'd like to have and dress accordingly. People who look successful receive preferential treatment in about all of their social and business encounters, whether it's in ordering a hamburger or in explaining instructions.

You want specifics, right? Okay, here are a few. Molloy contends that most men should not wear facial hair in the business world. If a man *has* to have a mustache, it should be moderate—no handlebars or pencil stripes. Goatees should be strictly avoided since people don't trust or

---

JOURNEY PREPARATION

For any journey, there has to be preparation since good planning can make the difference between a successful trip and a disaster. Pack the following items;

A helmet for knocks
A cushion for falls
Earplugs for gossip
A hammer to nail down promises
A gavel to command attention
A box to pick up pieces
A key to open closed minds
A hatchet to open closed doors
And a friend for the good times and especially for the bad times

Adapted from Natasha Josefowitz, *Paths to Power* (Reading, Mass.: Addison–Wesley, 1980), p. 23.

believe men with goatees.[18] If you want more specifics, read Molloy's book. He's also written one for women, and both are informative and interesting.

Looking physically fit is also important in your "success look." Looking well rested and trim gives you a slight edge over the competition. It's unfortunate but true that discrimination against overweight people is practiced frequently. "Fat people do not advance as far in the world as slender ones . . . salaries of fat people are lower than those of thin people with the same training and experience."[19] Push away that pineapple cheesecake and take a brisk walk instead.

Looking physically fit is also important in your success look.

There you have it. Let's hear no more talk about being slighted, ignored, overlooked, passed over, or taken for granted. Forget the broken promises, ungiven credit, and unsought ideas. Read, study, and apply the guidelines suggested in this chapter. Don't bother whining about your lack of education, your overbearing boss, your nagging spouse, your low IQ, or your social class. They're just alibis for your laziness or lack of motivation.

Eradicate that "poor me" mentality that says "What's the use of even trying?" After all, you're the one in control of your success. Lee Iacocca, who began his life as the son of an immigrant and who is now one of the country's most powerful and successful executives says, "Apply yourself. Get all the education you can, but then, by God, do something! Don't just stand there, make something happen. It isn't easy, but if you keep your nose to the grindstone and work at it, it's amazing how in a free society you can become as great as you want to be.[20]

When you show up for work on time, give an honest day's effort, are loyal to your employer, and accept an agreed-upon salary for your contribution, then you and this employer are even. To be paid more, you must become more valuable to your employer by exerting a little extra effort, showing extra enthusiasm, working extra hours, and assuming extra responsibilities. "In a nutshell, you go the extra mile which is one stretch of highway where there are never any traffic jams."[21]

THE LIFE CYCLE

This exercise involves constructing a "lifeline" that will help you to understand better the stages of career and personal development. Instead of letting your life "just happen" in a random, haphazard manner, this lifeline should help you to develop it in a more systematic way.

1. Draw a horizontal line from left to right across the middle of a piece of paper. Label your birth date on the far left of the line, a projected death date on the far right, and today's date at the appropriate place on the line.
2. Fill in the left side with important events from your childhood and adolescence. You might include a family move, the birth of a sibling, a memorable birthday, or your first date, for example.
3. Now fill in important events that have taken place more recently like your first job, a marriage, a divorce, an award, or a personal accomplishment.

4. Leave the past behind and project yourself into the future. What would you like to have accomplished in your career during the next 5 years? The next 10 years? By the time you are 60? By the time you die? Do the same thing for your personal life.

5. This lifeline should help you identify where you are now and what you'd like to achieve before your career and life are over. Can you attain the objectives you set for yourself? If so, then put your plans to work. If not, then reevaluate.

6. Compare your lifeline with those of your classmates and share what you have learned from this exercise.

ARE COLLEGE KIDS NAIVE?

According to a study mentioned in a recent article in *The Wall Street Journal*, today's college kids are naive about the workplace.

Catalyst, which fosters careers of women, says a survey of 377 male and female undergraduates finds that students hold the "somewhat unrealistic view they can succeed at work the same way they succeed at school, through superior performance, enthusiasm and self–confidence. In the students' opinion, these are all more important than getting along with the boss, having a helpful adviser, working long hours, or playing—or dodging—office politics.

"Knowing the ropes, being a team player, and other important workplace concepts are not part of students' consciousness," Catalyst says. "For employers to elicit a truly superior performance, they may need to teach new recruits about these concepts."

Employers also have something to learn: New workers—men and women—want more time off for families.

Labor Letter, *The Wall Street Journal*, May 12, 1987, p. 1.

CASE STUDY

Matthew Clyburn

Matthew Clyburn is a fellow aged twenty filled with youthful enthusiasm and high hopes for the future. In his second year of college, Matthew maintains a high grade–point average, has an active social life, and now, to add to his already full life, he has a job in a men's clothing store. True, it's only an after–school job that involves four days a week, but on Saturdays the four hours stretch into eight. He sees the job as but a stepping-stone to financial success. Sure, his girlfriend was pretty upset about his not being able to go on the picnic with her on Sunday, but after all, he has to study sometime. Still, Matthew is a little down on himself since this weekend is a big one and he hates to miss out on all the fun.

Matthew is pondering his goals and wondering how to achieve them and make the most of his time. He wants to be a millionaire by the time he's 30 although he's not quite sure how he is going to achieve it. He wants to maintain his high academic standing, but it's going to be difficult to study while working and playing too. He's a popular fellow with lots of friends, and he hates to let his social life become nonexistent. His girlfriend Marilyn is already hurt and angry that he spends so much time with the guys, and Matthew knows these next few months are going to be rough ones for their relationship.

1. Are Matthew's goals realistic and attainable?
2. Can you suggest medium– and short–range goals to help Matthew achieve his objectives?
3. What time management techniques can you suggest to Matthew that would enable him to accomplish all his activities?

SUMMARY

You owe it to yourself and to your employer to develop yourself to become all you possibly can. To ensure your success in your career you have to think about what you really want from your job and your life and then plan accordingly.

Steps to take in planning a successful life include setting goals, managing time, taking on challenges, developing your self–concept, and dressing for success. In addition to these activities, letting others know of your aspirations, playing politics, and finding a mentor are other ways to grow on the job.

To be effective, goals should be written down, specific, realistic, and time oriented. Goals can be long range, medium range, short range, mini, and micro. After writing goals, you need to write down specific activities needed to accomplish these goals.

Time management principles teach how to use time more effectively. One important principle is setting priorities and writing them on a daily "To Do" list. Items on the list should be categorized as having high, medium, or low value. After establishing priorities, determine the activities necessary for attaining the goal.

Since procrastination is a real problem in accomplishing goals, try Lakein's Swiss cheese method and the "Well, as long as I . . ." technique. Creating a conducive atmosphere and considering the deadline factor are also helpful.

Additional tips for using time effectively are saying no, asking yourself what has to be done each day, looking ahead for the week, and making use of waiting and commuting time.

To achieve success in life and work, you need a boost of self–confidence. As an adult, you can improve your self–confidence by using "props," surrounding yourself with positive friends, taking on challenges, and using visualization.

Since there's no progress without risk, you can't let negative thoughts or fear of failure or criticism hold you back. You have to believe in yourself and say yes to life, work, opportunities, relationships, and experiences.

Although some people frown at the word "politics," it thrives in every workplace and can make your work more rewarding if you use politics wisely. You should let others know of your plans and aspirations, keep a log of your accomplishments, and find a mentor.

Looking the part means that you should pay attention to your attire and grooming. Use clothing as a tool right along with your education, experience, and aptitudes.

Following the guidelines in this chapter will assist you in being paid more and/or advancing on your job. Your career is much too important to develop haphazardly, and you are the one who is ultimately in control of its success or failure.

KEY TERMS

David Campbell
Long–range goals
Medium–range goals
Short–range goals
Mini goals
Micro goals
Time management
Alan Lakein
"A-1" activity
"C-Z" activity
"To Do" list
Swiss cheese method
"Well as long as I . . ." technique
Leo Buscaglia
Robert Schuller
Visualization
Self–fulfilling prophecy
Politics
Mentor
John Molloy

REVIEW AND DISCUSSION QUESTIONS

1. What are some advantages in setting goals? What are at least four requirements for effective goals?

2. Define each of David Campbell's five categories of goals. How do all these categories work together in achieving a successful life?

3. While making a "To Do" list is a common activity, some people still don't manage time well. What advice would you give such a person?

4. What are several ways of fighting procrastination? How is each effective? Give examples. Which would work best for you? Why?

5. How can self–confidence contribute to achieving your goals? Can self–confidence be increased? How?

6. Why is it important to accept challenges in your work and personal life? To be persistent in achieving your goals?

7. Cite evidence to show that learning doesn't take place just between the ages of 18 and 22? Give an example of someone you know who, as an adult, improved his or her life by education.

8. What is the self–fulfilling prophecy? Can you think of a personal example in which you have worked (unconsciously) to make your prophecy about yourself come true?

9. If you have a part–time job right now, what could you do specifically in playing politics? How can playing politics help you?

10. Why is it important to pay special attention to attire and grooming as you aspire to career success? What is meant by the phrase, "Clothing is a self–fulfilling prophecy"?

ENDNOTES

[1] J. OGDEN ARMOUR, "Thoughts on the Business of Life," *Forbes*, July 4, 1983, p. 196.

[2] DAVID CAMPBELL, *If You Don't Know Where You're Going, You'll Probably End Up Somewhere Else* (Allen, Tex.: Argus Communications, 1974).

[3] SYDNEY F. LOVE, *Time Management* (Englewood Cliffs, N.J.: Prentice Hall, 1978), p. 266.

[4] DONALD SMITH, *How to Cure Yourself of Positive Thinking* (New York: Seemann, 1976), pp. 59–61.

[5] Ibid., pp. 60–61.

[6] CAMPBELL, *If You Don't Know Where You're Going*, pp. 36–40.

[7] R. ALEC MACKENZIE, *The Time Trap* (New York: AMACOM, 1972), p. 39.

[8] Ibid., pp. 38–39.

[9] ALAN LAKEIN, *Make the Most of Your time and Your Life* (New York: New American Library, 1979).

[10] Ibid., pp. 128–133.

[11] STEPHANIE WINSTON, *The Organized Executive* (New York: W. W. Norton, 1983), p. 169.

[12] MANUEL J. SMITH, *When I Say No, I Feel Guilty* (New York: Bantam Books, 1975), p. 22.

[13] LEO BUSCAGLIA, *Living, Loving and Learning* (New York: Holt, Rinehart and Winston, 1982), p. 43.

[14] ROBERT H. SCHULLER, *You Can Become the Person You Want to Be* (New York: Pillar Books, 1976), pp. 56–59.

[15] LEO BUSCAGLIA, *Love* (New York: Ballantine Books, 1972), p. 151.

[16] ANDREW J. DUBRIN, *Human Relations for Career and Personal Success* (Reston, Va.: Reston, 1983) p. 301.

[17] JOHN MOLLOY, *Dress for Success* (New York: Warner Books, 1976), p. 143.

[18] Ibid., p. 120.

[19] CAMPBELL, *If You Don't Know Where You're Going*, p. 106.

[20] LEE IACOCCA, "Iacocca," *Readers Digest*, July 1985, p. 208.

[21] ZIG ZIGLAR, *See You at the Top* (Gretna, L.: Pelican, 1977), p. 308.

chapter 13

Stress

After reading and studying this chapter, you will be able to:

1. Define stress.
2. Describe the GAS.
3. List several symptoms of stress.
4. Discuss five causes of stress.
5. Discuss four types of conflict.
6. Identify several stress reduction techniques.
7. Describe several defense mechanisms and their role in alleviating stress.
8. Discuss the importance of stress reduction at work.

Stress has surpassed the common cold as the most prevalent health problem in America.

AMA, 1978

Jangling telephones, demanding bosses, impossible deadlines, irritating co-workers, irate customers, and boring jobs can all lead to stress. So can positive experiences like promotions and raises. Many people believe that stress is caused only by anxiety, conflict, and frustration when, in fact, any change can elevate blood pressure, accelerate breathing, and tense muscles. Even a vacation is a stressful experience for some people. Since stress is such a timely topic, read on to discover its effects, symptoms, causes, and finally, methods of dealing with this prevalent health problem.

WHAT IS STRESS?

Stress can be defined as the demand placed on a person to adapt, to adjust, and to cope or simply the "rate of wear and tear on the body."[1] Some stress is beneficial and can keep you alert, occupied, fully functioning and can actually enhance your life. This optimal amount of stress is called *eustress*. However, if stress is too intense, prolonged, or mismanaged, your psychological and physiological defenses are weakened. A person can only withstand so much pressure before *distress* and eventually *disease* occur.

HOW DOES STRESS AFFECT YOU?

Stress is the demand placed on a person to adapt, adjust, or cope.

Regardless of the type of stress experienced, the physiological changes within the body are the same. Asking for a raise or parachuting from a plane make you feel about the same, since both increase respiration, perspiration, heart rate, blood pressure, and blood clotting. These changes occur in a pattern called the *fight or flight response*, and when used appropriately, this response enables a person to escape a threatening situation by fighting or fleeing. When this response is elicited frequently in someone who can't fight or flee—cope in some appropriate way—the resulting stress is believed to be an underlying cause of disease, including high blood pressure, heart attacks, and strokes.[2]

The fight or flight response enables a person to escape from a threatening situation.

Hans Selye, founding father of stress research, labeled the body's response to stress as the general adaptation syndrome, or GAS.[3] The GAS consists of three stages:

1. Alarm reaction
2. Resistance stage
3. Exhaustion stage

A stressor, which is a stress-producing event or person, triggers the alarm reaction that arouses the body and prepares it for fight or flight. Listed in Table 12–1 are characteristics of the alarm reaction. These reactions are short term, but if the stress is not reduced or managed, you enter the resistance stage in which your body's arousal level is still greater than normal, though not as elevated as when in the alarm reaction. At this time your body attempts to repair any damage and to restore lost energy. Finally, if the stress is not dealt with adequately, you enter the exhaustion stage of the GAS.

Excessive stress invites illness.

Selye believes that "disorders of adaptation" are the result of continued stress. They are not so much the direct results of an external event as they are the consequences of the body's inability to cope with these events by adequate adaptive reactions. These disorders range from hives, migraine headaches, and allergies to heart disease, high blood pressure, and peptic ulcers. Excessive stress actually invites illness! Stress is now known to be a "major contributor, either directly or indirectly, to coronary heart diseases, cancer, lung ailments, accidental injuries, cirrhosis of the liver, and suicide—six of the leading causes of death in the U.S."[4] Stress also plays a role in aggravating such diverse conditions as multiple sclerosis, diabetes, genital herpes, and even trench mouth.

Table 12-1 Characteristics of Alarm Reaction

Increased respiration rate
Increased heart rate
Increased blood pressure
Tensed muscles
Secretion of adrenaline
Shifting of blood away from the skin
Slowed digestion
Release of sugar from liver
Increased blood coaguability

SIGNALS OF STRESS

Stress creates expensive problems for employers.

Stress not only affects individuals and their physical well being, but it also creates problems for employers since most people spend about one-third of their lives at work. These problems include increased absenteeism, tardiness, reduced productivity, low morale, high turnover, and

---

SIGNALS

As you can see, stress can have some negative effects on workers and their employers. Look over the following signals of stress to see if any apply to you. Which have you observed in yourself? In others? An increase in the intensity or frequency of symptoms may indicate a troublesome stressor in your life.

Two Dozen Stress Signals

_____ Accident prone	_____ Legal drug use increase
_____ Crying	_____ Migraine headaches
_____ Dry throat and mouth	_____ Nausea
_____ Floating anxiety	_____ Pounding heart
_____ Fatigue	_____ Queasy stomach
_____ Grinding teeth	_____ Restlessness
_____ High-pitched laughter	_____ Speech problems
_____ Increased physical problems	_____ Trembling and tics
_____ Insomnia	_____ Weight loss or gain
_____ Irritability	_____ Extrasensitivity to pain
_____ Jitteriness	_____ Yelling
_____ Keen awareness of sound	_____ Zealousness beyond reason

---

high accident rates. The expenditures for heart attacks, ulcers, and other stress–related problems are staggering, and much of that cost is paid by employers. High levels of stress also contribute to drug and alcohol abuse, which also tug on employer purse strings. Problems with alcohol abuse alone are estimated to cost U.S. business in excess of $30 billion a year in absenteeism, paid sick benefits, and loss of productivity.[5]

CAUSES OF STRESS

Recognizing causes of personal stress is the first step in dealing with it.

Are you convinced that perhaps that nagging headache could be related to stress? Just what are some of the stressors in your life? Recognizing causes of your personal stress is the first step in dealing with it.

Change, anxiety, frustration, and conflict are major sources of stress, both on and off the job. In addition, some people are more likely to suffer the adverse effects of stress because of their personalities. We will examine each of these sources and identify specific stressors in both your professional and personal life.

Change

Major causes of stress are change, anxiety, frustration, conflict, and personality.

We live in an ever-changing society. Job skills become obsolete, and we have to learn new methods and skills or change jobs. Supervisors get promoted or retire, and we have to adjust to a new management style and personality. Whether it's a new job, a new spouse, or a new residence, change is the common denominator.

Life changes are inevitable, even desirable. Variety is the spice of life, right? Too much spice, however, can have a souring effect. Thomas Holmes and Richard Rahe attempted to measure the impact of life change events in the late 1940s and 1950s. The result is the increasingly popular Holmes and Rahe scale shown here.

Life Event	Life Change Units
Death of one's spouse	100
Divorce	73
Marital separation	65
Jail term	63
Death of a close family member	63
Personal injury or illness	53
Marriage	50
Being fired at work	47
Marital reconciliation	45
Retirement	45
Change in the health of a family member	44
Pregnancy	40
Sex difficulties	39
Gain of a new family member	39
Business readjustment	39
Change in one's financial state	38
Death of a close friend	37
Change to a different line of work	36
Change in number of arguments with one's spouse	35
Mortgage over $10,000	31
Foreclosure of a mortgage or loan	30
Change in responsibilities at work	29
Son or daughter leaving home	29
Trouble with in-laws	29
Outstanding personal achievement	28
Wife beginning or stopping work	26
Beginning or ending school	26
Change in living conditions	25
Revision of personal habits	24
Trouble with one's boss	23
Change in work hours or conditions	20
Change in residence	20
Change in schools	20
Change in recreation	19
Change in church activities	19
Change in social activities	18
Mortgage or loan of less than $10,000	17
Change in sleeping habits	16
Change in number of family get-togethers	15

Change in eating habits	15
Vacation	13
Christmas	12
Minor violations of the law	11

T. H. Holmes and R. H. Rahe, "The Social Readjustment Scale," *Journal of Psychosomatic Research*, (1967), 213–218.

As you can see, 100 stress points are given for death of a spouse, 73 for divorce, and 65 for marital separation. Evidently marriage and its support is important as a way of life to the approximately 5,000 asked to rate the life events. Work changes are significant also. Changes in responsibility are worth 29 points, and trouble with one's boss is worth 23 life change units.

What about your own life events? Are you curious about your predisposition to medical and mental problems? Read the list and total the life change units "earned" during the past year.

Holmes and Rahe found that 8 out of 10 individuals with more than 300 life change units developed medical problems while only 1 of 3 people with fewer than 200 developed similar problems. The ailment could be short term, like an upset stomach, or long term like ulcers. Keep in mind that this research is only correlational, not experimental. In other words, a high number of life change units is related to physiological and psychological disorders, but other explanations are possible.

Also, no change occurs in isolation. Just think of the ramifications associated with a spouse beginning or ending work. Sure income is increased, but a portion of it may be utilized for transportation, appropriate clothing, and child care. Acquiring these necessities is stressful. Too, stress comes about from role overload of both husband and wife. Marriages in which both spouses work appear to be subject to more conflict. More and more working wives are in a double bind, facing urgent demands both from the family and the job. The double bind puts great stress on the mother and, as a result, on her marriage and on her entire family.

Think for a moment of the changes experienced on your job. Do any of the following sound familiar?

1. Change in work area or environment
2. Change in job duties or responsibilities
3. Changes in supervision
4. Change in method or time of payment
5. Change in company policy

Workers who are able to dictate the style and pace of their work experience less stress.

It is interesting to note that workers who feel a lack of control over changes that affect them experience more stress than do those able to dictate the style and pace of their work. "Telephone operators, waiters, cashiers, and others whose work makes substantial psychological demands but offers little opportunity for independent decision making are the worst off."[6] Powerlessness and lack of control are even more stress-producing when combined with conflicting or unreasonable demands. Surprisingly, top executives with more power and autonomy, actually have fewer heart attacks than do midlevel managers.

Concerning changes in supervision, firms that routinely rotate managers as a type of training create a state of constant change for workers since the employees have continually to adapt to new personalities, different expectations, and new management styles.[7] When a new manager is being broken in, some workers are so apprehensive that being disliked by the new boss that their performance on the job suffers.

Anxiety

Anxiety is a feeling similar to fear, except that you don't know what you are afraid of. You fell uneasy and experience a sense of foreboding. Although you are aware of feeling tense, worried, nervous, and moody, you don't knw why. Some anxiety on the job is good and aids in your top performance. This positivive anxiety ensures that you arrive at work on time, show respect for your boss, and give a day's work for a day's pay.

Too much anxiety, however, interferes with planning, thinking, and performing. For example, industrial surveys indicate that exposure to noise increases self-reported anxiety and emotional stress. Workers habitually exposed to high-intensity noise show increased incidence of nervous complaints, nausea, headaches, instability, argumentativeness, sexual impotence, and anxiety.[8] Wow! Before complaining to your boss about the noise in your work area, however, realize that noise is only part of a package of problems and that solving the noise problem won't solve all the others.

Charles Spielberger described two types of anxiety: trait and state.[9] People who have trait anxiety are chronically uptight and worried, even under the best of circumstances. This uneasiness is an aspect of their personalities. On the other hand, state anxiety is temporary and is triggered by a particular event or person. A job interview gives you just cause for experiencing state anxiety.

Trait anxiety is a personality characteristic; state anxiety is situation specific.

There are several causes of anxiety. Perhaps these are stressors in your work and social life that you are unable to pinpoint. Maybe Freud was right in proposing that anxiety results from unconscious conflict. Impulses, painful memories, sexual and aggressive urges, shameful experiences, and even fears are seething in your unconscious mind. It could even be that you have an especially excitable nervous system. What are specific sources of anxiety in your life? What makes you feel worried and nervous?

A performance evaluation?

Giving a speech?

An abrasive co-worker?

Unpleasant physical environment?

A company-sponsored social function?

High managerial turnover?

Frustration

Being prevented from attaining a goal or motive causes frustration, another primary cause of stress. Your behavior can be thwarted by both people and things, even yourself. For instance, in setting your goals you may be unrealistic in assessing your abilities and your limitations. If you aspire to become a supervisor within six months and yet you have little experience and no prior training in management, it is unlikely that you will reach your goal. The world of work demands that people tolerate a certain amount of frustration, be willing to set realistic, attainable goals, and delay gratification:

> It's not the large things that
> send a man to the madhouse . . . no
> it's the continuing series of
> small tragedies
> that send a man to the madhouse
>
> . . .
> not the death of his love
> but a shoelace that snaps
> with no time left. . . .Charles Bukowski

Other stressors act simply as annoyances. Getting in your car to come to work only to discover an empty gas tank is frustrating. A talkative co-worker creates frustration when such a person prevents you from concentrating on your work. All people experience these frustrating occurrences, and most of the time we are able to tolerate them quite well. However, an imminent deadline piled atop an empty gas tank, a talkative co-worker, a misplaced report, and an irritating boss lead to stress. Do you have any particularly frustrating people or events in your life?

> A dead-end job with no hope of promotion
> A boring routine job that fails to stimulate you or utilize your ability

Lack of resources (money, time, education)

Work overload—too much to do in too little time

Lack of ability

Contact with a stress carrier—a person who creates stress within another

Physical limitations and health problems

Conflict

A certain amount of conflict is inevitable.

We are social beings. Since we live and work with other people, it is inevitable that conflict occasionally arises. Conflict, a fourth source of stress, does not necessarily mean "fight" in the traditional sense. It refers to a battle within you when faced with incompatible needs, demands, or opportunities. Four types of conflict have been identified.

1. Approach-approach
2. Avoidance-avoidance
3. Approach-avoidance
4. Double approach-avoidance

Approach-Approach

An approach-approach conflict is the easiest to resolve and indicates a choice to be made between two desirable alternatives. Suppose you have a choice of being transferred to one of two or three desirable locations. The salary, job duties, and chances for promotion are identical. What will you decide? How?

Decisions on a smaller scale affect us daily. It's payday, and you need your paycheck. On the other hand, the day promises to be beautiful and sunny. Should you go to work, or should you take a day of accumulated leave time and go fishing? The work ethic prevails and you go to work. At lunch, do you choose apple pie or cherry, two of your favorites? Do you dine with Mary or Carol? Both are pleasant and likable.

Avoidance-Avoidance

An avoidance-avoidance conflict involves two undesirable choices.

When confronted with two undesirable choices, you have an avoidance-avoidance conflict to resolve. You cannot avoid both alternatives, so you choose the lesser of two evils. Imagine that you are a supervisor and that one of your employees has a problem with alcohol abuse. You've spoken to this individual before, and even though the chronic imbiber has promised not to let drinking interfere with his work, he often comes to work late, bleary eyed, and irritable. The quality of his work has declined, and yesterday this individual left work early without a word to you. You dread the confrontation and yet you cannot continue to tolerate the problem behavior. What do you do?

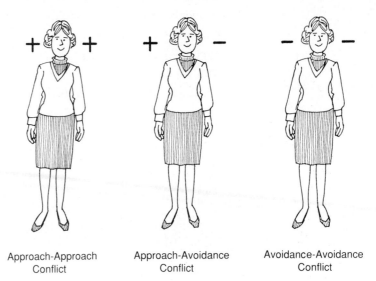

Approach-Approach
Conflict

Approach-Avoidance
Conflict

Avoidance-Avoidance
Conflict

Approach-Avoidance

In an approach-avoidance conflict, the choice is attractive and unattractive at the same time. You want it but don't want it, or you want it but are afraid of disappointment, failure, or rejection. You want to be supervisor, but what if you can't handle the pressure of being the only female "foreperson" in the automobile assembly plant? Also, while you might enjoy the increased salary and prestige of being in a supervisory position, how would you feel about being separated from your friends? As with the other conflicts, an approach-avoidance conflict is one that is found several times a day. The conflict could have far-reaching consequences as in deciding careers, promotions, or spouses, or the conflict could be relatively minor as in choosing whether to jog on a dreary, misty morning or stay inside and feel fat and lazy.

Double Approach-Avoidance

A double approach-avoidance conflict is the most complicated and the most stressful. In this type of conflict, each choice has both desirable and undesirable aspects. A successful salesperson with job security and fringe benefits galore becomes dissatisfied with his cushy job, but realizes that to become the accountant he has always dreamed about, will require four years of college. The sales job is safe, secure, and profitable, but it is also unchallenging and boring. Being an accountant is an attractive possibility, but going to college is not. What if this supersalesperson turns out to be a sorry student?

A double approach-avoidance conflict is the most complicated and most stressful.

A certain amount of conflict is unavoidable. Vacillating between choices, postponing decisions, and in some cases even refusing to decide whether to go or not to go, apply or not apply, speak or not speak causes anguish or stress.

Personality Type

Because of their personalities, some people are more predisposed to stress and stress-related disorders than are others. Cardiologists Meyer Friedman and Ray Rosenman identified Type A and B behavior patterns.[10] Type A individuals are highly competitive, ambitious, and impatient. Urgency is a Type A trait behavior as a Type A person feels there is never enough time to do the things that need to be done and want to do more and more in less and less time. Type As make lists and lists of things to do and always strive to be more competent in everything they attempt. Often, these individuals show an easily aroused hostility.

A sense of time urgency is a trait of Type A behavior.

Type A's are highly successful. They make high grades and lots of money, but these hard-driving individuals pay the price by having a greater number of physical ailments than do Type Bs. In fact, Type A behavior is often called *coronary-prone behavior* because Type A people are likely to have more heart attacks than are those who do not.

Type B people are more interested in the quality of life than in the quantity of things they accomplish. Such a person is more aware of personal capabilities than concerned about what peers and superiors think of his or her actions. These individuals can relax more easily than can their Type A co-workers. They enjoy leisurely pursuits like hobbies or sports, and although they take their jobs seriously, a Type B person seldom brings work home. It's true that Type As bring home more money while the Type Bs are smelling the flowers and reciting their mantras, but the more relaxed B's are likely to live longer and suffer fewer physical problems.

ARE YOU A TYPE A?

1. Do you accentuate various key words in your everyday speech even when there is no real need?
2. Do you always move, talk, and eat rapidly?
3. Do you feel an impatience with the rate at which most events take place? For example, do you attempt to finish the sentences of persons speaking to you before they can?
4. Do you frequently strive to do two or more things at the same time? Do you listen to someone talk and continue to think about an irrelevant subject? Eat your breakfast and drive?

5. Do you find it always difficult to refrain from talking about those subjects which interest or intrigue you? If unable to bring the conversation around to your interests, do you only pretend to listen while remaining preoccupied with your own thoughts?

6. Do you almost always feel vaguely guilty when you relax and do absolutely nothing for several hours to several days?

7. Do you no longer observe the more important or interesting or lovely objects in your environment?

8. Are you so occupied with getting the things worth having that you don't have time to become the things worth being?

9. Do you attempt to schedule more and more in less and less time?

10. Do you find yourself compelled to challenge other Type As?

11. Do you resort to certain characteristic gestures or nervous tics; for example, clench fist, bang head on table, grind teeth, or clench jaw?

12. Do you believe that whatever success you have enjoyed has been due in large part to getting things done faster than your peers?

13. Do you find yourself evaluating your own and others' activities in terms of "numbers"?

Adapted from Meyer Friedman and Ray H. Rosenman, *Type A Behavior and Your Heart*, (New York: Random House, Inc./Alfred A. Knopf, Inc., 1974), pp. 82–85.

Speaking of personality types, stress affects individuals differently. Getting a promotion may trigger self-doubt and depression in one person, encourage growth and development in another, and have a neutral effect on a third. People who are "hot reactors," those who overrespond to everyday stressors in ways that may damage the heart and blood vessels, can get into trouble. Robert S. Eliot, the cardiologist who coined the term "hot reactor," says that such people "burn a dollar's worth of energy for a dime's worth of stress."[11]

STRESS REDUCTION TECHNIQUES

A certain amount of stress is positive, desirable, and even pleasurable. The aim of a stress-reduction plan is not to eliminate stress but to control its negative effects. No single approach works for every person. Read the following suggestions and select your personal strategy.

Experiment with Meditation

Several varieties of meditation exist for the thousands of individuals who practice this ancient art of narrowed awareness. Transcendental meditation (TM) is a popular and relatively simple technique involving only a few easy steps known as the relaxation response. This response is not only useful in treating stress-related diseases but may also be helpful in their prevention.

1. Find a quiet spot.
2. Get into a comfortable position and relax.
3. Close your eyes.
4. Concentrate on a *mantra*, a word or phrase like "om" or "one" or "calm." If words don't relax you, try visualizing a pleasant scene.
5. Adopt a passive attitude. Allow yourself to drift and cast off worrisome thoughts.

Try Progressive Relaxation

Progressive relaxation is another relaxation response used to both treat and prevent diseases linked to stress. Using the relaxation response lowers the metabolism of the body. Heart and breathing rates decrease, blood flow to the muscles stabilizes, and blood pressure falls. How is progressive relaxation done? It's easy. Set the scene for relaxing. Lower the lights. Recline on a bed or couch at a time when you are unlikely to be disturbed. Now follow the activity instructions to tense and relax muscle groups alternately throughout your body.

RELAXATION OF HANDS, ARMS, CHEST, AND BACK

1. Select a quiet area where you can lie down. Lie in a comfortable position on your back. Place your hands at your sides. Close your eyes and take a deep breath slowly.
2. Clench the fist of your preferred hand. Increase the tension in your arm as much as you can. Think about how this feels. Concentrate on your arm. Now relax your arm and let your fingers straighten out.
3. Repeat the same procedure with your other hand.
4. Take a deep breath and exhale slowly. Make your body feel as limp as you can.
5. Place your hands on the surface you are lying on. Push down as hard as you can. Concentrate on your hands, chest, and back, as these are the areas you will feel tension in. Notice the tension in both arms. Relax your arms so that the tension is released. Repeat this step once.
6. Take a deep breath and exhale slowly. Make your body as limp as you can.[12]

Breath Fully and Deeply

Inhale through your nose and notice that your abdomen balloons out as your lungs fill with oxygen. Breath in s-l-o-w-l-y and exhale tension. More on this?

Engage in Biofeedback

Biofeedback is a system to make you more aware of what is going on inside of your body. A machine gives "feedback" to a person on muscle tension, blood pressure, and skin temperature, and the person learns to relax and consequently lower the stress response.

Biofeedback makes you more aware of what's going on inside the body.

You don't have to use expensive equipment to go to a mental health center to experience the positive effects of biofeedback. Patricia Taylor of Sumter Area Technical College has experimented with biofeedback in her psychology classes with some very promising results.

To make instruction for control and experimental groups as similar as possible, Taylor personally taught both groups, used the same lectures and transparencies for the groups, and gave identical unit tests to both groups upon completion of each unit of study. The only difference in the treatment of the experimental and control groups was the use of biofeedback training for the experimental group. Participants engaging daily in biofeedback sessions prior to lectures and prior to unit tests had mean scores seven points higher than did the control group at the end of the quarter. Furthermore, the experimental subjects also reported reduced tension, increased confidence and improved self-esteem, improved concentration, increased ability to remain calm under stress, and slowing of the natural aging process.[13]

Express Your Emotions

Scream. Shout. Cry. Smile. Laugh. Hug someone. Pent-up emotions and hostility are unhealthy.

Communicate

Talk it out. Complain directly to the person you believe to be responsible for your present unhappiness instead of holding a grudge, feeling resentful, or worrying others with your complaints.

Think and Act Positively

Don't say, "I don't know whether I can get up to go to work today." Instead say, "I'm lucky I can get up and go to work today." Do something nice for someone or pamper yourself. You deserve it!

Avoid Stress Carriers

Stress carriers create stress in others.

These are people who create stress in others although they may not be experiencing it themselves. Stress carriers complain, whine, moan, groan, tear things down, tell hard-luck stories, and act helpless. Who needs them?

Increase Your Physical Activity

Walk. Jog. Ride a bike. Go fly a kite. A study conducted by John Greist of the University of Michigan revealed that "running relieved depression caused by major changes in peoples lives."[14] Regular exercise is very helpful since it burns off the potentially harmful physiological effects of the fight or flight response, allowing the person to react in the way nature intended.

Get Enough Sleep

If you are suffering from insomnia, consider the possible causes and act accordingly. Drinking too many cola drinks or too much coffee might be keeping you awake since caffeine acts as a stimulant. Don't resort to sleeping pills or other depressants as they disturb normal sleep patterns. Tryptophan, an amino acid found in such foods as turkey, cottage cheese, and milk, acts to fight insomnia. By the way, tryptophan is available at most health food stores.

Pay Attention to Your Diet

You're an adult and you don't need a lecture on the four basic food groups or advice about decreasing your consumption of refined sugar, salt, and saturated fats. You might, however, need to be reminded that how you eat is as important as what you eat. Eat slowly, calmly, and quietly. Make meals special occasions. Avoid eating quickly in a noisy, rushed environment. One person revealed that she frequently ate in her kitchen while standing over a garbage disposal since she didn't have time to sit down and eat. Is that healthy?

TEST YOUR NUTRITION IQ

Being an adult is no guarantee that you know everything there is to know about nutrition. Knowing the facts about vitamins, minerals, health, and nutrition is a must for a person desiring to control the possible harmful effects of stress.

An often-heard lament of doctors is that Americans eat foods high in fat, sugar, and salt but low in carbohydrates. These lopsided dietary habits lead to medical problems such as stroke, heart disease, headaches, obesity, and high blood pressure.

How much do you really know about nutrition? Test your knowledge by indicating whether the following statements are true or false.

_____ 1. Watermelon tastes good, but its nutritional value is practically nil.

_____ 2. Five or six mini meals a day may be just as healthful as three larger ones.

_____ 3. Spaghetti with meat sauce is more nutritious than lasagna.

_____ 4. Skim milk is more nutritious than American cheese.

_____ 5. Processed foods should be removed from your diet.

_____ 6. Taco salads are both delicious and surprisingly nutritious.

_____ 7. Caffeine has been linked to birth defects

_____ 8. While baked potatoes provide needed carbohydrates and minerals, unfortunately they are high in calories.

_____ 9. Coconuts are low in fat.

_____ 10. Bananas contribute to a person's proper fluid balance and muscle tone.

ANSWERS

1. False. Watermelons taste good, look good, and are good for you. They contain iron and are rich in vitamins A and C.

2. True. You're probably a lot more alert and productive after a 300-calorie meal than a 1,000-calorie one.

3. True. Spaghetti has 30 percent less fat, 40 percent less cholesterol, and 25 percent less sodium than lasagna.

4. True. American cheese is loaded with sodium and saturated fat, both of which contribute to heart disease and high blood pressure.

5. False. Processing some foods has made then safer and more nutritious—pasteurized milk, for example.

6. False. The deep-fried shell, the beef, the sour cream, and the cheese all add up to fat. Delicious, yes. Nutritious, no.

7. True. Research indicates that caffeine, a drug used in coffee, tea, and many cola drinks, may cause birth defects.

8. False. While a four-ounce baked potato has only 80 calories, it provides complex carbohydrates and minerals. The butter, sour cream, and cheese add the fat and calories.

9. False. Surprisingly, coconuts are high in saturated fat and are harmful to the heart.

10. True. Bananas are high in potassium, an element found in every body cell, and potassium provides a counterbalancing action with sodium.

Find a Support System

Find someone to care, to listen, to share sadness and disappointment, joy and success. Does misery really love company, or does company prevent misery? *Time* magazine quotes a thrice laid-off employee who was remarkably well adjusted. His secret? He said, "I've got a loving wife and go to church every Sunday."[15]

Take Control of Your Life

Take time to talk to small children, listen to a friend without interrupting, watch a sunset, sigh, take a bubble bath, listen to music, and yes, smell the flowers. If your private life doesn't allow you that control, make some changes. Get a new life!

I think people ought to do what they want to do, what else are they alive for?[16]

DEFENSE COPING

There are other means of coping with stress that a person uses unconsciously. Freud says our egos are fragile and need protecting, and defending our egos against anxiety is the purpose of the defense mechanisms. These mechanisms are quite normal and acceptable. They only become problems when used excessively and are the only means used to cope with stress.

The text that follows presents a few of the most common of the defense mechanisms. Do you recognize any of them in yourself? In your co-workers or family?

Rationalization involves making excuses for failures or disappointments.

Rationalization is probably the most common of the defense mechanisms. The person simply makes excuses for his or her disappointments, failures, or unsatisfactory behavior. An individual does not get the promotion he wanted but rather than say he was evidently not the right person for the job, he might say, "It's just as well because I really didn't want to give up time with my family."

Repression is unconscious; suppression is conscious.

Repression is unconscious forgetting. There are things which would worry or hurt individuals if those thoughts or memories were allowed into consciousness. To prevent unhappiness, people repress or forget anxiety–provoking thoughts, impulses, and experiences. Sexual and aggressive thoughts are the ones most typically repressed.

Many individuals confuse suppression with repression. *Suppression*, however, is conscious, deliberate forgetting. Someone makes a conscious decision not to dwell on or think about a distressing subject.

Reaction formation is repressing material and insisting that the opposite is true.

Reaction formation actually involves two processes. First, the person represses whatever is bothering her and then insists that the opposite is true. Someone who is overly sweet and polite could actually be seething with repressed hostility and anger.

Projecting unconscious undesirable feelings onto others is called projection.

All people have unacceptable impulses or thoughts that they don't want to admit to. They repress them and project the undesirable feelings onto other people in much the same way that a movie projector projects an image onto a screen. Projecting these feelings onto someone else is called *projection*. An unconsciously hostile person might say that others don't like him instead of vice versa because admitting his own hostility would create anxiety. Saying "He's out to get me," justifies hostility toward another.

Regression is returning to an earlier way of behaving when under stress. You've probably seen this defense mechanism on several oc-

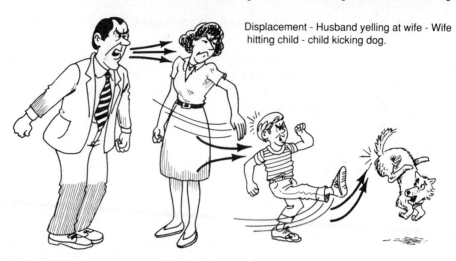

Displacement - Husband yelling at wife - Wife hitting child - child kicking dog.

casions. A person gets angry about having to work overtime and slams a door, pouts, or has a temper tantrum.

Denial is just what it sounds like. The person denies sources of danger or the reality of an unpleasant situation. Here's an example given by Harry Levinson.

> Suppose a plant superintendent has five years to go before reaching retirement age and his boss suggests that he pick a successor and train him. But our plant superintendent does not select a successor despite repeated requests from the boss. He cannot "hear" what the boss is saying. He may be forced to select such a man. When the time for retirement arrives, he may then say to his boss that the boss really did not intend to retire him. He cannot believe the boss will compel him to leave. This behavior reflects a denial of the reality of the situation because the ego had difficulty accepting what it regards to be loss of love (status, esteem, and so forth).[17]

Displacement is the transferring of a response from one object to another. A classic example is of a man who gets reprimanded by his boss. Instead of expressing angry feelings to the boss, the worker yells at his wife who spanks the children who kick the dog who chases the cat.

STRESS REDUCTION AT WORK

A healthy worker is a more productive and efficient worker. To reduce the approximately $125 billion or more spent on health care for employees, many companies are establishing stress reduction programs and policies. Management efforts in stress reduction range from exercise facilities and meditation classes to relaxation breaks and alcohol and drug abuse programs. One progressive company gives "rest breaks" for the employees to fantasize, yawn, stretch—in a word, rest! Recognizing that relaxation, exercise, and biofeedback cannot solve every problem, many companies provide a counseling service for troubled employees who need to "talk it out."

Most employers agree that whatever can be done to reduce worker stress should be done. Because the majority of adults in the United States spend half their waking hours at work (outside of weekends), the workplace is a logical environment to alleviate stress. Whether stress is the responsibility of the organization or the individual makes no practical difference. Too much stress is costly to both the employee and to the employer.

An excellent example of organizational participation is Tenneco, Inc., in Houston. Fifteen hundred employees of the organization are taking part in computer-monitored programs, including stress management, nutrition counseling, and cardio-pulmonary resuscitation classes. Tenneco provides everything but the shoes—lockers, showers, whirlpool baths, steam rooms, saunas, towels, and uniforms. Since the corporation sees fitness as a part of the job, it adjusts employee schedules to allow time for workouts before, after, or during office hours.[18]

HOW VULNERABLE ARE YOU TO STRESS?

The following test was developed by Lyle H. Miller and Alma Dell Smith, psychologists at Boston University Medical Center. Score each item from 1 (almost always) to 5 (never), according to how much of the time each statement applies to you.

_____ 1.   I eat at least one hot, balanced meal a day.

_____ 2.   I get seven to eight hours sleep at least four nights a week.

_____ 3.   I give and receive affection regularly.

_____ 4.   I have at least one relative within 50 miles on whom I can rely.

_____ 5.   I exercise to the point of perspiration at least twice a week.

_____ 6.   I smoke less than half a pack of cigarettes a day.

_____ 7.   I take fewer than five alcoholic drinks a week.

_____ 8.   I am the appropriate weight for my height.

_____ 9.   I have an income adequate to meet basic expenses.

_____ 10. I get strength from my religious beliefs.

_____ 11. I regularly attend club or social activities.

_____ 12. I have a network of friends and acquaintances.

_____ 13. I have one or more friends to confide in about personal matters.

_____ 14. I am in good health (including eyesight, hearing, teeth).

_____ 15. I am able to speak openly about my feelings when angry or worried.

_____ 16. I have regular conversations with the people I live with about domestic problems (e.g., chores, money, and daily living issues).

_____ 17. I do something for fun at least once a week.

_____ 18. I am able to organize my time effectively.

_____ 19. I drink fewer than three cups of coffee (or tea or cola drinks) a day.

WELLNESS PROGRAMS FOR EMPLOYEES

In White Plains, New York, PepsiCo brings in specialists from the community to lecture on health care topics such as injury prevention. Also, classes are offered on such topics as stress management and interpersonal communication.

Phillips Petroleum Co. in Bartlesville, Oklahoma, has a 75,000-square-foot facility that contains a swimming pool, bowling lanes, softball and soccer fields, weight rooms and locker areas. Over 6,000 of the 7,500 employees pay annual dues of under $20 to use the facilities.

Johnson Wax in Racine, Wisconsin, has its main fitness center in the middle of a 146-acre company park. Tennis courts, a football field, a driving range, a miniature golf course, cross-country ski trails, an archery range, and a pond for canoeing provide outdoor fun. Inside the building are a 20,000 foot gymnasium, a jogging track, three racquetball and two squash courts, two weight rooms, treadmills, rowing machines, and stationary bicycles. Tennis anyone?

Scherer Bros. Lumber Co. in Minneapolis makes the pursuit of an unhealthy life-style a bit more difficult. Candy, caffeinated coffee, and cigarette machines were ripped out and replaced with fresh fruit dispensers. Free, nutritious lunches, low in salt and fatty foods, were offered to office employees. Finally, Scherer Bros. pays two hours straight time each month to any worker who hasn't missed a day of work.

Dale Feuer, "Wellness Programs: How Do They Shape Up?" *Training*, April 1985, pp. 25–34.

_____ 20. I take quiet time for myself during the day.

_____ TOTAL

To get your score, add up the figures and subtract 20. Any number over 30 indicates a vulnerability to stress. You are seriously vulnerable if your score is between 50 and 75 and extremely vulnerable if it is over 75.

> "Vulnerability Scale" from the *Stress Audit*, developed by Lyle H. Miller and Alma Dell Smith. Copyright 1983, Biobehavioral Associates, Brookline, MA, reprinted with permission.

DEFENSE MECHANISMS

Indicate the defense mechanism illustrated by placing the appropriate letter next to the statement. Use the following code.

A. Repression
B. Regression
C. Reaction formation
D. Rationalization
E. Displacement
F. Projection

_____ 1. Soldiers exposed to traumatic experiences in concentration camps during war-time sometimes had amnesia and were unable to recall any part of their ordeal.

_____ 2. The mother of an unwanted child may feel guilty about not welcoming her child. As a result, she may try to prove her love by becoming overindulgent and overprotective of the child.

_____ 3. The habitual drinker may insist that he really doesn't care much for the taste of alcohol but feels that he is obliged to drink with friends "just to be sociable."

_____ 4. Mrs. James can't understand why her husband has been so grumpy and irritable for the past week. It certainly isn't her fault that he didn't receive the anticipated promotion at the factory.

_____ 5. The majority group of a culture may blame all the various ills of society on a small minority group. This is a process termed "scape-goating" and is a factor in racial and religious prejudice.

_____ 6. Joan has discovered an amazing coincidence in relation to her attendance at school. Every time a test in Spanish is scheduled, she oversleeps and arrives at school too late for the class.

_____ 7. Margaret is convinced that she received a "C" in her chemistry class instead of an "A" because of widespread cheating by her fellow students. She is sure that she must be as capable in the chemistry course as in her other subjects.

_____ 8. It is possible that smokers have graduated from the earlier stages of thumb-sucking and pencil-chewing, either of which would be acceptable behavior in adult society. Smoking is a socially acceptable outlet for the oral need.

_____ 9. It is typical for the person who is most difficult to convince in an argument to say that everyone else is stubborn.

_____ 10. Mr. Martin carried around a letter in his coat pocket for weeks. The note which he somehow neglected mailing was an invitation to his mother-in-law to visit the family for several months.

R. Kellogg, _Simulation/Gaming/News_, (January 1976), pp. 13–16.

CASE STUDY

Bud Morgan

Bud Morgan needs help with a problem. Two years ago he developed a sore on the palm of his hand. At first Bud wasn't too concerned about it since he noticed the sore the same week that his storage shed had been muddied by a septic tank overflow. Since his hand didn't heal, however, Bud reluctantly paid a visit to the doctor. His doctor said that the problem was an allergic reaction, prescribed an antibiotic, and injected steroids to combat the allergy.

The treatment seemed to work until six weeks later when the sore appeared and started to spread, covering his hands and beginning to eat the skin under his fingernails. Another costly trip to the doctor resulted in some hand creams, more antibiotics, and another shot of steroids.

LITTLE HASSLES

Do the little things in life get you down? Little things like being stuck in traffic, arguing with a spouse, or running out of checks when your cart is filled with groceries? Recent evidence indicates that disagreements, disappointments, accidents, and unpleasant surprises are more closely linked to our moods and our health than the major misfortunes of life.

The popular Holmes and Rahe research indicates that the big events in our lives like death of a spouse or unemployment are major causes of stress that can lead to physical illness. However, Richard Lazarus believes that events which occur in our everyday transactions with the environment may add up to more grief than life's major stressful events. The more frequent and intense the hassles, the poorer the overall physical and mental health.

Hassle studies were first conducted with a small, homogenous group comprised of white middle-aged, middle-class Protestants with above-average income and education. Of the total, 86 percent were married. With this group, hassles turned out to be much better predictors of psychological and physical health than were major life events.

Some of the criticisms of the Holmes and Rahe chart include

* The events may not be relevant ones for some people, like students, the poor or elderly, or working moms.
* Simply adding up the life change units without taking into account the particular content of changes can be inaccurate. How does the person appraise the change? How well or poorly does he cope with them? Loss of a job might actually be evaluated as a plus if it helps someone find greener pastures. Parents might actually sigh with relief when children leave home.
* Changes are important, but what about the chronic conditions of day-to-day living like boredom, continuing tension in a family relationship, lack of occupational progress, or isolation and loneliness.

Major life events like death of a spouse or divorce are significant, but could they be worsened by the daily hassles they produce? Consider the ripple effect of life changes. For example, what are some of the changes and adjustments that accompany a wife returning to work or a son or daughter leaving home?

Like major events, how hassles affect a person depends on personality, coping skills, and how the day has gone. For instance, when under pressure petty annoyances have a greater effect. "Psychological stress resides neither in the situation nor the person; it depends on a transaction between the two. It arises from how the person appraises an event and adapts to it."

Richard S. Lazarus, "Little Hassles Can Be Hazardous to Health," *Psychology Today*, July 1981, pp. 58–62.

Two years, two dermatologists, and dozens of prescriptions later, Bud's skin problem was still getting worse. His hands looked as though a fungus had taken over, and the bottom of his feet had the same symptoms. He and his wife Donna were constantly trying to find a cure for this mysterious allergy. Was it soap? Was it detergent? His shoes? Was it a rare and incurable dermatitis. Bud refused the allergy tests that the doctors were trying to get him to take. He was constantly embarrassed, frustrated, and in pain.

A couple of interesting things happened. Bud and Donna moved to another area. Compared to their previous location, they were in heaven. Fewer people "dropped in" unexpectedly, and the atmosphere was cozy and homey. Surrounded by trees, their new home was serene and tranquil. A lake was within walking distance, and the Moores found themselves looking forward to their daily walks around the lake. Bud found that he didn't have to use his ointment nearly as often, and one day his "leprosy," as he called it, had disappeared.

Trouble was brewing in the Morgans' paradise. Bud started hearing rumors that his company was going to be sold. He had been employed by Smith and Jones Sales and Service, based in Noname, Nostate, for the past 10 years. The franchise unit that he worked for could be closed, sold, or transferred into a branch of the main corporation at anytime without notice.

Bud had never been able to express himself openly and was not able to communicate his fears, worries, and doubts with his wife. He has a tendency to let all his problems get bottle up inside. Donna knew that he was troubled about something as evidenced by his unusual moodiness, irritability, and brooding. They were both alarmed when Bud's skin condition recurred and was worse than ever.

Even though they were concerned about money. Bud and Donna felt that they just had to get "away from it all." The couple decided to join their families in another state for Christmas. They were very excited to be flying together for the very first time, especially on Christmas Eve and thought the whole adventure to be romantic. For weeks, they discussed their trip and shopped for just the right gift for all the relatives from the hard-to-please Aunt Carolyn to the man-who-had-it-all Uncle Michael. When they boarded the plane, the oddest feeling came over them as they realized that Bud's hands were smooth. Later they discovered that so were his feet! They had a marvelous seven days, but when they landed back in Noname, Bud's skin problem was back.

1. What was Bud's problem? Could it be stress related?
2. What treatment(s) would you recommend?

SUMMARY

Stress, the demand placed on a person to adapt, to adjust, or to cope is a timely topic in today's world. The optimal amount of stress is called eustress and can actually enhance a person's life. If stress is too intense, prolonged, or mismanaged, however, psychological and physiological defenses are weakened.

Physiological changes take place within the body in response to stress. These changes occur in a pattern identified by Hans Selye as the general adaptation syndrome, which as three stages: alarm reaction, resistance stage, and exhaustion stage. Continued stress in the exhaustion stage can lead to diseases of adaptation such as hives, allergies, heart disease, high blood pressure, ulcers, and headaches.

Causes of stress include change, anxiety, frustration, conflict, and in some cases, personality. Although life changes are inevitable and usually desirable, they require adjustment. Holmes and Rahe have developed a scale measuring life change units and their relation to physical illness.

Anxiety, a second cause of stress, is a feeling of dread and foreboding. While some anxiety is positive and aids in top performance, too much anxiety interferes with planning, thinking, and performing.

Frustration occurs when one is prevented from attaining a goal or motive. The world of work demands that people tolerate a certain amount of frustration, but knowing its cause can alleviate its negative effect.

Conflict occurs when a person is faced with incompatible needs, demands, or opportunities. The four main types are approach-approach, approach-avoidance, avoidance-avoidance, and double approach-avoidance.

People with Type A personality are more predisposed to stress and stress-related disorders, particularly heart problems. These individuals are competitive, ambitious, and impatient.

The purpose of stress-reduction techniques is to reduce the negative effects of stress. The old saying "different strokes for different folks" applies to these techniques. Some people experiment successfully with meditation and relaxation techniques while others try biofeedback, physical exercise, or a positive mental attitude to combat stress.

Defense mechanisms are unconscious means of controlling stress. A few of these are rationalization, repression, reaction formation, regression, denial, and displacement.

Since a healthy worker is a more productive and efficient one, most employers agree that what can be done to reduce worker stress should be done. Management efforts in stress reduction range from exercise facilities and meditation classes to relaxation breaks and alcohol and drug abuse education programs.

KEY TERMS

Stress

General adaptation syndrome

Eustress

Hans Selye

Stressor

Anxiety

Frustration

Conflict

Type A personality

Meditation

Progressive relaxation

Biofeedback
Rationalization
Repression
Suppression
Reaction formation
Denial
Displacement

REVIEW AND DISCUSSION

1. Explain the general adaptation syndrome and its relationship to physiological disorders.

2. How can stress create problems for employers? What are some advantages of stress reduction techniques at work?

3. What are some ways in which companies can help individuals cope with stress? Be creative. If you were a manager, what would you do.

4. What are four major sources of stress? What specifically about your life can you put under each category?

5. Give examples of trait and state anxiety. How can anxiety be positive? Give an example.

6. Give examples of each of the four conflicts discussed in your text. Discuss conflict as a cause of stress.

7. Imagine that you're a supervisor and one of your employees is a definite Type A. You want him to succeed. After all, when he succeeds, you do too. Yet you see that his constant striving is affecting his health. What do you say to him about causes, consequences, and cures?

8. What are at least six ways of coping with stress?

9. Observe your own and your family members', co-workers', and friends' behavior. What defense mechanisms are most common? Give examples.

ENDNOTES

[1] HANS SELYE, *The Stress of Life*, rev. ed. (New York: McGraw-Hill, 1976), p. 1.

[2] HERBERT BENSON AND ROBERT L. ALLEN, "How Much Stress Is Too Much?," *Harvard Business Review*, September-October, 1980, p. 87.

[3] SELYE, *The Stress of Life*, p. 38.

[4] CLAUDIA WALLIS, "Stress: Can We Cope?" *Time*, June 6, 1983, p. 481.

[5] CHARLES E. SHIRLEY, "Alcoholism and Drug Abuse in the Workplace," *Office Administration and Automation*, November 1984, p. 25.

[6] WALLIS, "Stress: Can We Cope?," p. 52.

[7] ROBERT A. BRYMER, "Stress and Your Employees," *The Cornell H.R.A. Quarterly*, February 1982, p. 64.

[8] SHELDON COHEN, "Sound Effects on Behavior," *Psychology Today*, October 1981, p. 42.

[9] C. D. SPIELBERGER, *Anxiety and Behavior* (New York: Academic Press, 1966).

[10] MEYER FRIEDMAN AND RAY H. ROSENMAN, *Type A Behavior and Your Heart* (Greenwich, Conn.: Fawcett, 1974).

[11] LYNN LAMBERG, "How to Break the Stress Chain," *Working Woman*, May 1985, p. 93.

[12] ANTHONY F. GRASHA, *Practical Applications of Psychology*, 3rd ed. (Boston: Little, Brown, 1987), p. 459.

[13] PATRICIA TAYLOR, "Biofeedback as a Means of Reducing Test Anxiety," unpublished research paper, December 1985.

[14] BARRY L. REECE AND THONDA BRANDT, *Effective Human Relations in Organizations*, 2nd ed. (Boston: Houghton Mifflin, 1984), p. 387.

[15] WALLIS, "Stress: Can We Cope?," p. 50.

[16] JAMES BALDWIN, "Sonny's Blues," *Going to Meet the Man* (Garden City, New York: Doubleday, 1965).

[17] HARRY LEVINSON, *Emotional Health: In the World of Work* (New York: Harper & Row, 1964), p. 34.

[18] JOSEPH BENHAM, "Where Fitness Is Part of the Job," *U.S. News and World Report*, May 3, 1982, p. 61.

chapter 14

Personal Problems at Work

After reading and studying this chapter, you will be able to:

1. Discuss how personal problems can affect work performance.
2. Define depression.
3. Discuss three theories of depression.
4. Explain what is meant by burnout and describe its symptoms.
5. Discuss the various problems involved in substance abuse at work.
6. Define addiction.
7. Distinguish between categories of drugs by identifying their effects and symptoms.
8. List the stages of alcohol dependence.
9. Discuss employee assistance programs.
10. Differentiate between different types of counseling.

In a real dark night of the soul, it is always three o'clock in the morning.
F. Scott Fitzgerald

Personal problems are no respecters of age, occupation, sex, or race. Lumberjacks get depressed now and then; so do sales clerks and librarians. Accountants, secretaries, machinists, computer data processors, and chefs all suffer from burnout occasionally. Chief executives and assembly line workers alike sip wine, snort cocaine, or pop pills to alter mood, induce pleasure, or reduce displeasure.

Depression, burnout, and substance abuse are problems in the workplace.

Throughout their lives, people experience loss, change, inadequacy, fear, and rejection. How they adjust depends on myriad factors ranging from support groups to basic emotional "hardiness." Since depression, burnout, and drug and alcohol abuse are recognized as problems in the workplace, we'll examine these three problems and review types of help and counseling available for the troubled worker. Pay close attention, for the symptoms described could be your own—or you buddy's.

DEPRESSION

Depression is the common cold of mental illness.

Ever had the blues? Sure you have. Depression is so common that it's frequently called the common cold of mental illness. It's estimated that 15 percent of all adults suffer from a depressive disorder in any single year and that at any one time 2 to 4 percent of the population has impaired functioning due to depression.[1] Getting the blues is so common that many psychologists feel that it's the most prevalent health problem in the United States today.

Definition

Depression affects your body, thoughts, feelings and behavior.

Depression is a common psychological problem characterized by feelings of hopelessness, worthlessness, and sadness in response to real or imagined loss, failure, or misfortune. It affects more than mood; your body, thoughts, feelings, and behavior are also affected by depression. Symptoms include a loss of interest in many activities, inability to concentrate, reduced activity level, loss of sexual drive and appetite, lowered aggression, loss of enthusiasm, fatigue and lethargy, and sleep disturbances.

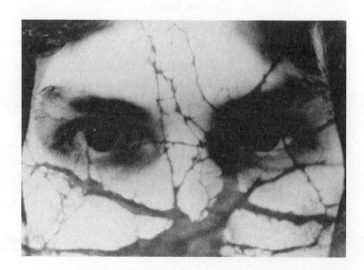

"Depression can turn the best employees into the worst."[2] At work the depressed person can't concentrate or make decisions, his initiative and productivity may be lowered. Work seems to require a lot of effort and the person sometimes asks, "Is it worth it?" He just can't seem to get going. In severe cases, the employee may not be able to work at all.

Depression is often associated with a negative situation like divorce, loss of a job, demotion, or death of a loved one, but it can also be linked to positive changes. For example, a person who's just received a promotion or landed a promising new job could feel a letdown. Achieving that promotion or new job helps provide force and direction, so feeling a little down after reaching goals is typical. Also, when you get a promotion, you're not one of the guys or gals anymore; you're the boss. You gain the power and prestige but lose the comraderie. Many people who get a much desired and sought-after job think, "Oh, wow, I've finally landed the biggie," and then don't understand why they feel blue. They weren't aware that a job is more than just a job. It's part of a complex system comprised of many variables like the fellow employees, the physical environment, and the philosophy of the company.

Depression can be linked to both positive and negative changes in your life.

Everyone feels this "dark night of the soul" from time to time. We've all felt down, sad, listless, withdrawing, and disinterested in people and events. However, when a person just can't shake it, when she always feels that the world is a gray, sterile place, then the depression may be extreme, even abnormal, especially if it lasts a long time and prevents the person from functioning normally. The severely depressed person may neglect personal appearance and hygiene and suffer motor retardation in which movements like walking are slow. At this stage suicide becomes a real possibility since the person sees no hope and reflects, "Why go on? Things are never going to be any better for me."

Theories of Depression

Since depression has such far-reaching effects, psychologists have formulated several theories to explain its occurrence. Recall that the goals of psychology are to explain, control, and predict behavior. It's possible for all of us, not just psychologists, to predict what causes this sad feeling state (dysphoria) and to control its symptoms and effects. The major theories of depression are biological, psychoanalytic, learning, and cognitive.

Biological

Depression with a biological source responds well to drug therapy.

Many psychologists believe that depression has a biological basis. Their research indicates that it is linked to the lack of certain neurotransmitters, chemical substances that carry messages. Other psychologists contend that depression runs in families and think that it might be associated with inherited genetic structures. This doesn't mean that you're doomed to grimness if you've got a history of it in your family. It just means that you're more predisposed to depression than are others with different genetic structures. Depression with a biological or endogenous source responds well to drug therapy which alters body chemistry.

Psychoanalytic

As you probably guessed, the psychoanalytic theory of depression emphasizes unconscious thoughts. Childhood experiences predispose certain people to become depressed when they experience frustration, loss, or failure. Remember the oral stage of personality development which occurs during the first year of life? Freud believed that a child receiving insufficient gratification of needs during this stage develops low self-esteem and high dependency. When such a person later suffers a loss or failure in her personal, social, or occupational life, she may regress somewhat to the oral stage by becoming dependent and by feeling hostility toward those who could gratify dependency needs. When the person is unable to express this inner hostility, anger turned inward occurs and develops into self-hate and depression.[3]

Repressed childhood anxiety resurfaces when adult is experienced.

Here's another way of looking at the psychoanalytic theory of depression. When someone suffers loss of a loved one or of self-esteem during childhood yet fails to show feelings of hostility, anger, and sadness, those same repressed feelings may occur in later life when the individual suffer a loss that reminds him or her of the first one. When as a child you lose a family pet or a loved one, it arouses considerable anxiety. The anxiety is pushed out of consciousness, but later can cause depressions when other losses that symbolic of the earlier one occur. Your sweetheart leaves you, and you respond with the same feelings that surrounded the childhood loss.

Learning Theories

Learning theorists believe that when little positive reinforcement exists in the environment, depression can result. If someone doesn't get enough love, recognition, praise, or other rewards, he gets depressed. If a person finds social interaction fruitless, he begins to avoid people and withdraw from contacts. Being alone often leads to brooding and can actually intensify the depression. It's a vicious cycle. If someone stops engaging in activities that might lead to positive outcomes, how can he get better? Life seems to lose its zip and the person loses vigor. He gets sad and cries a lot. He complains. People start avoiding him. Who wants to be around a sullen, self-pitying complainer? The person feels even more worthless after being avoided and excluded. Research indicates that people who are depressed make others feel hostile and anxious.[4]

Depression can result when there is little positive reinforcement in the environment.

How can life lose its reinforcing value? It's simple. What if a person works hard on a project at work and is not reinforced. Not only is she not offered a promotion, but she doesn't even get a teensy-weensy raise—not even a "Great work, Lynn," from the supervisor. A person can shrug it off for a while, but if it happens again and again and again, depression can occur since work offers no reinforcement.

People who are depressed make others feel hostile and anxious.

Another learning theory is that of *learned helplessness*, in which a person believes that she has no control over the stresses, strains, and traumas of life. The loss or failure itself is not what causes the depression but the feeling that the person has no control over the situation. An individual learns through experience that he is helpless in controlling traumatic experiences and therefore feels hopeless and helplessness in responding to certain events. Learned helplessness and the accompanying depression could be situational. If an individual blames the blues on the situation, then the depression is milder. The feeling is that when the situation changes, feelings will change for the better.

Feeling little or no control over situations can lead to depression.

The concept of learned helplessness developed from Seligman's experiments with dogs. A dog was first placed in a cage from which it was impossible to escape and then was given electric shock. The dog yelped and tried to escape the trauma, but since there was no escape, the animal soon ceased in its efforts. Later when the dog was placed in the same situation except with an escape possibility, the dog was much slower to escape than were animals who had never been shocked. The dog had learned that its behavior was fruitless and stopped trying.[5] Some people act the same way in that they give up trying to cope when past efforts have failed.

Cognitive Theory

Cognitive theory concludes that depressed people often have negative thoughts about themselves and about their world. Therefore, they believe that changing someone's thoughts will help with depression. For example, Beck has shown that depression-prone people often set very high goals for themselves, and when they fail to reach these goals, they blame themselves.[6] Instead of realizing that the goal was unreachable, the depressed person says, "I'm stupid. I'm a failure for not meeting that quota."

People with faulty cognitions magnify their personal faults and overlook their positive qualities.

People with faulty cognitions overgeneralize from failure and focus on the negative side of things. "Since I didn't' reach the quota, I probably won't be able to do anything else. Everybody knows what a loser I am. No one wants to associate with me." Some people just seem to think in a "distorted, irrational, and negative way."[7] They misinterpret events, magnify their personal faults, and overlook their positive qualities.

SHAKING THE BLUES

If depression is mild, there are several things you can do to lessen its impact. Choose a few strategies from the following list. If the depression is more severe and you just can't shake it, get some professional help.

Choose action over inaction.
  * Take a walk.
  * Exercise.
  * Go shopping.
  * Call a friend instead of waiting for the friend to call you.

Increase participation in enjoyable activities.
  * Work on a hobby.
  * Get involved with others.
  * Go out to eat in a nice restaurant.
  * Read a good book.

Change your thoughts.
  * Don't downplay your accomplishments.
  * Don't "catastrophize" your problems.
  * Don't belittle your efforts.
  * Think positive.

BURNOUT

All of us have days when we think of shutting off the alarm and sleeping in instead of going to work. That's human nature. However, when a person dreads going to work because of unhappiness and frustration regularly, day after day, that's job burnout, according to Larry Cherniss, an expert on job stress.[8] Job burnout occurs when a person who has been experiencing a high level of stress hasn't been able to cope with it. Cherniss sees burnout as a reaction to a stressful job. Even though burnout was first recognized as affecting such workers as teachers, police officers, and executives, it's now known to exist in many careers.

Burnout is much more intense than stress.

The symptoms of stress and burnout are similar, but burnout is much more intense. It is defined as the depletion of physical and mental resources caused by striving to reach some unrealistic job related goals. Symptoms include "chronic fatigue, job boredom or cynicism, an unfulfilled need for recognition, less commitment, moodiness, poor concentration or forgetfulness, and certain physiological changes such as high blood pressure."[9]

Emotional and physical exhaustion is also apparent in the burned-out worker. A person feels that he just can't go on any further. A "major defining characteristic is that people can't or won't do again what they've been doing."[10] They resent demands made by others, and they get angry with themselves for complying with such demands.

All people experience stress from time to time, but not all people develop burnout. Just the same, it can happen to anyone who has to endure boredom, confusion, tension, and the feeling that they have no control over their work lives. Are you a candidate? Burnout candidates differ from stress sufferers in at least three ways:

1. They predominantly experience stress caused by job-related stressors such as hazardous working conditions or job function ambiguity. Family or personal problems coupled with the work factors increase the likelihood of burnout.
2. They tend to be idealistic and/or self-motivated achievers. Burnout is rarely a malady of the underachiever.
3. They tend to set unattainable goals. Goal setting is important, but if a goal isn't there to reach, or if it's there but out of reach, it's frustrating. After people consistently put out a lot of effort without getting results, they feel angry, helpless, depleted—burned out.[11]

Burnout is rarely a malady of the underachiever.

What can you do if you recognize some of the symptoms of burnout in yourself? Basically, the methods used to combat stress are also useful in treating burnout. Additional means include listing priorities, setting attainable goals, altering stressful working conditions, and possibly making a career change.

DRUGS AT WORK

Drug and alcohol use and abuse in the workplace is a growing problem reflecting national drug use patterns. The Research Triangle Institute, a respected North Carolina business-sponsored research organization, drug abuse cost the U.S. economy $60 billion in 1983, nearly 30 percent more than the $47 billion estimated for 1980. The National Council on Alcoholism has found that six percent of the working population is burdened by serious drinking problems.[12] Further evidence indicates that 1 of every 16 people in the modern work force is developing a serious alcohol problem that is probably being overlooked by their work associates and managers. While no one really knows precisely how pervasive substance use on the job is, federal experts estimate that between 10 per-

---

SECRETARY BURNOUT: SURVIVAL OF THE FITTEST

Secretaries are no exception to the trauma of burnout. As a group, they are unique in terms of job pressures and responsibilities and the stress that can result from them. Here are some of the factors believed to contribute to burnout in secretaries:

No control. Secretaries assume that they have little or no control over their working environments and job atmospheres. The author reminds her peers that they are responsible for their job attitude. Since secretaries have more responsibilities and technological skills than at any other time in their professional lives, they should take advantage of their position instead of letting it take advantage of them.

Perfectionism. By the very nature of their jobs, secretaries must daily juggle job duties, rank assignments, and remember a million details—all this while smiling pleasantly and answering a phone that never stops ringing.

The solution is to learn to let go when necessary and to say no when necessary. Secretaries should try to invent shortcuts and timesavers for themselves and for their organization by learning and practicing effective time management. When they've done all that can be done, secretaries have to learn to *let it go*.

Job Satisfaction. Secretaries who don't experience job satisfaction or who aren't getting recognition and well–deserved praise should consider going outside of the actual working environment for reinforcement. Suggestions include taking time off to attend professional seminars and workshops, taking courses to enhance feelings of self-esteem and to help as stepping stones in job advancement, and joining professional organizations. It's gratifying to brainstorm with peers who have similar frustrations.

Secretaries are an integral part of an organization, and the profession doesn't need another burnout casualty. "Remember," concludes this executive secretary, "the choices are yours."

Reprinted from *P.S. for Professional Secretaries*, by permission of the publisher: Bureau of Business Practice, 24 Rope Ferry Road, Waterford, CT 06386.

Six percent of the working population is burdened by serious drinking problems.

cent and 23 percent of all U.S. workers from the shop floor to the executive suite use dangerous drugs at work.[13]

Employee drug use is of increasing concern to management since the costs can be astronomical. Problems with drugs contribute to loss of productivity, absenteeism, paid sick benefits, and theft. Additional costs include reduced efficiency, lateness, faulty decision making, increased accidents, impaired morale of co-workers, friction among workers, early retirement, premature disability and death, personnel turnover, loss of skilled and valued employees, and the added costs of insurance and substance abuse programs. That's not all. When intangible costs like time expended by a supervisor or co-worker(s) in dealing with the affected employee and the repercussions on the family and friends of the affected employee are thrown in, the total costs are grossly underestimated.[14]

The costs of employee drug use can be astronomical.

The statistics surrounding drug abuse are misleading and probably somewhat inaccurate. There's a conspiracy of silence surrounding the alcoholic person. Family and friends convince themselves that "good old Joe" really doesn't have a problem. Too, neither supervisors nor employees are aware of many of the signs of drug use and abuse. If the odor of alcohol can't be detected, it's often assumed that the person isn't abusing drugs.

There is often a conspiracy of silence surrounding the alcoholic employee.

Another factor leading to the inaccurate statistics is that management is sometimes looking for bizarre Jekyll and Hyde behavior, but unfortunately by the time drug use affects work, the employee's job performance, personal problems, and physical condition are worsened. Finally, there is a secretive aspect to both legal and illegal drug use and a taint of criminality about the use of illegal drugs such as cocaine and marijuana which makes their use harder to detect.

Assistance should be offered to employees who are willing to seek it.

Some people just don't care or are reluctant to recognize the problem. As long as Henrietta is doing her job and is not making a nuisance of herself, many employers feel that drug use is none of their concern. Some psychologists refer to this as the Dixie cup attitude. Keep an employee around until he begins to leak and then dispose of him just as you would a paper cup. Such an attitude is unfortunate. Assistance should be offered to employees who are willing to seek it. An attitude of caring and concern is good for all concerned. It's beneficial for the worker since she feels that she's not such a loser after all. It's good for morale of other workers to know that management looks after its own. The community sees this concern on the part of management, and the company's image is enhanced.

WHO USES DRUGS?

Who are the drug and alcohol abusers? Are they bleary eyed maniacs who consistently come in late, hung over, irritable, and unkempt? No. Substance abusers are executives and blue collar workers. They're rich and poor, male and female, young and old. Some researchers feel that legal prescription drugs dominate the drug scene. Women are more likely to use and have problems with mood drugs, and two of every three mood drug prescriptions are written for women, especially anti-anxiety drugs for women in the 40 to 59 age range.[15] Alcoholics are more likely to be beer drinking men who are separated, single, and divorced (in that order) and who have no religious affiliation.[16] Heroin is a drug that disproportionately affects the poor, and cocaine is more exclusively a drug of the middle class and wealthy.[17]

Cocaine appeals to achievement–oriented people.

Your boss may even have a drug problem. Steven Flax reports that executives abuse prescription drugs, cocaine, and even heroin.[18] Alcohol is still probably the most abused substance, but its incidence seems to have leveled off while illegal drug use is mounting. Cocaine use among executives is growing since it seems more suited to their life-style and instead of dulling the senses, enhances them. Cocaine appeals to achievement-oriented people by making them feel that they can accomplish anything. Executives have more money and more privacy so it's easier for them to use drugs on the job. After all, they don't have to ask permission to go to the bathroom like some workers and are even protected by their associates who cover for them and by a private secretary who screens visitors. Executives don't fear drugs the way some people do since they're accustomed to feeling masterful and don't see drugs as threatening.

Why do workers turn to drugs? Sometimes people use drugs to give them pep and sometimes to help them relax. Others use them to forget emotional pain, ease physical aches and pain, get through an eight-hour stint of mind-dulling work, handle the stress of managerial duties, or mask insecurities. People like drugs and their effects and are willing to take social, legal, psychological, physical, and financial risks to enjoy them.

ADDICTION DEFINED

A person must experience tolerance, psychological dependence, and physical dependence for addiction to take place.

Although it is common to hear someone say that she's addicted to certain drugs like caffeine, addiction is related to actual physical dependence. For drug addiction to take place, three conditions must be present: tolerance, psychological dependence, and physical dependence.

Tolerance means that the person needs increasingly greater amounts of the drug to achieve the same effect. If you're a teetotaler, a few sips of wine might lower your inhibitions, but a person who drinks alcoholic beverages frequently will require a glass or two or three of wine to experience the same relaxed feelings.

Psychological dependence means that the user feels that the drug is necessary to maintain psychological and emotional well-being. When deprived of the substance, the smoker or pill popper will feel no painful physical withdrawal symptoms such as convulsions or nausea, but the person may be powerfully affected psychologically and feel an intense craving for the drug.

Narcotics and depressants have the potential for physical addiction.

Many substances create tolerance and psychological dependence within the indulger, but not all drugs create *physical dependence*. When this occurs, a person's body has become so accustomed to the substance that painful and sometimes fatal withdrawal symptoms occur if the drug is withheld. Withdrawal symptoms include extreme shaking, severe sweating, convulsions, and even death. *Narcotics* and *depressants* have the potential for physical addiction, but it is easy to become psychologically dependent upon other categories of drugs.

CATEGORIES AND EFFECTS OF DRUGS

*Psychoactive drugs
can alter mood,
perception, attention,
behavior, and
self-control.*

Many people point an accusing finger at a young person smoking marijuana or at a Yuppie snorting cocaine without realizing that they too could be using and possibly abusing drugs. Such people aren't being hypocritical, just ignorant. Many Americans think of alcohol to relax them or Valium to calm their nerves as nondrugs, but in fact they are both powerful drugs with the potential for addiction. All these drugs are psychoactive, substances capable of altering attention, mood, perception, behavior, and self-control (See Table 14-1). To aid in understanding, let's take a brief look at the various categories of drugs.

Narcotics

*Narcotics are derived
from the opium
poppy.*

Narcotics are those drugs derived from the opium poppy and are very addictive. Although many individuals use the word narcotic to include all drugs, narcotics refer specifically to opiates, which include opium, morphine, heroin, codeine, and other synthetic narcotics such as demerol and methadone.

*Methadone is used to
treat heroin addiction.*

Morphine was introduced around the time of the Civil War in the United States and was used to deaden the pain of wounded soldiers. Addiction occurred quickly and addiction to morphine became known as the "soldier's disease." *Heroin* was claimed to be the "hero" of drugs since it was believed to be less addictive than morphine from which it was derived. However, heroin is powerfully addictive as well as illegal. *Methadone* is a man–made or synthetic narcotic used to treat heroin addiction. While it acts more slowly than does heroin and does not provide heroin's thrilling rush, methadone is the drug of choice for people who are unwilling to undergo withdrawal symptoms or to live without drugs.

MINI DRUG TEST

Before studying the material about drugs in this chapter, give yourself a little pretest. Label the following drugs as depressants (D), narcotics (N), hallucinogens (H), or stimulants (S).

_____   1. Alcohol

_____   2. Nicotine

_____   3. LSD

_____   4. Heroin

_____   5. Amphetamines

_____   6. Cocaine

_____   7. Morphine

_____   8. Codeine

_____   9. Demerol

_____   10. Valium

_____   11. PCP

Table 14-1
Drugs, Their Effects and Recognition

Drug Family	Examples	Effects	Recognition
Narcotics	Heroin, morphine, codeine, methadone, demerol	Drowsiness, euphoria, psychological and physical dependence	Drowsiness, stupor, constricted pupils, needle marks or sores, presence of drugs or paraphernalia
Depressants (sedatives)	Barbituates, tranquilizers, alcohol	Relaxation, depressed reflexes, euphoria, psychological and physical dependence	Slurred speech, disoriented behavior, constricted pupils, presence of drugs or paraphernalia
Stimulants	Cocaine, caffeine, amphetamines, nicotine	Intense stimulation; excitability, nervousness, euphoria, psychological dependence, psychological and physical dependence for nicotine	Excited, erratic behavior, dilated pupils; can become paranoid; presence of drugs or paraphernalia
Cannabis	Marijuana, hashish, "hash" oil	Similar to alcoholic intoxication; disoriented behavior, possible psychological dependence; changes in perception, illusions, hallucinations; may cause psychosis	Sluggish, intoxicated behavior, smell of burning rope, drugs or paraphernalia
Hallucinogens	LSD, peyote, certain mushrooms	Changes in perception, hallucinations; may cause psychosis	Bizarre behavior, dilated pupils, trance-like state, incoherent speech; panic may occur
Inhalants	Solvents, anesthetic gasses, aerosol propellants	Similar to alcoholic intoxication; psychological dependence possible; death from suffocation may be a side effect	Excessive nasal secretions, smell of solvent, drunken behavior, paraphernalia including bags, solvent soaked rags, and aerosol cans

Depressants

Minor tranquilizers include valium and librium.

Depressants slow the action of the central nervous system and are addictive drugs. Some commonly used depressants are barbiturates, tranquilizers, and alcohol. *Barbiturates* are also known as sedatives and are often used to calm people or to induce sleep. They have many medical uses like relieving anxiety and tension, deadening pain, and treating epilepsy and high blood pressure. When used in combination with alcohol, barbiturates are particularly dangerous. Excessive dosages can intoxicate and cause drowsiness, motor impairment, slurred speech, and mental confusion just like alcohol. Since barbiturates are so rapidly addictive, many doctors instead prescribe *minor tranquilizers* such as valium and librium for anxiety and tension.

Alcohol is America's drug of choice.

Alcohol is clearly America's drug of choice. Some 70 percent of the adult population are regular users of alcohol though not all become serious alcoholics.[19] the substance is completely legal and has little or no stigma attached. It's a tranquilizer you can enjoy without a prescription. A man could be characterized as a wimp swallowing tranquilizers but a real man guzzling alcohol. Society remains tolerant of drinking even after it has passed the moderate stage.

Long-term effects of alcohol include cirrhosis of the liver, brain disorders, heart disease, and high blood pressure.

Since it's a depressant, alcohol slows the activity of the central nervous system. It lowers inhibitions, dulls aches, relaxes nerves, and brings about feelings of elation. People feel euphoric and sociable after a drink or two. If alcohol sounds too good to be true, that's because it is. The beverage has some negative effects. Since it impairs, cognitive functioning, people become intoxicated and speak incoherently, experience reduced motor coordination, and become overconfident and sometimes obnoxious. Long-term effects include cirrhosis of the liver, brain disorders, heart disease, and high blood pressure.

Problems with alcohol surface in the workplace.

Problems with alcohol surface in the workplace. "Today it is recognized that the largest subpopulation of alcoholic persons are those whose alcohol abuse is associated with or occurs at the place of employment."[20] Since 1980, the number of people who are alcoholics has increased by 8 percent, to 12 million, according to the National Institute on Alcohol Abuse and Alcoholism. More than any other ailment, alcoholism breeds absenteeism, high medical bills, and reduced work quality. North Carolina's Research Triangle Institute estimates that alcoholism cost the U.S. economy $117 billion in 1983.[21]

The greatest amount of alcoholism is found at the height of a person's career.

Alcoholics are not skid-row bums. At least 70 percent of them reside in respectable neighborhoods, live with a spouse, try to send their kids to college, pay taxes, and continue to perform more or less effectively at their jobs. The greatest amount of alcoholism is found at the height of a person's career between the ages of 35 and 55.[22] It takes its most severe toll among workers who have gained experience, are skilled at what they do, and in whom the employer has a vested interest.

Stimulants

Stimulants stimulate. They excite the central nervous system and include amphetamines, cocaine, caffeine, and nicotine. Stimulants are medically prescribed to treat narcolepsy and to counterattack overdoses of depressants. People use them to stay awake and to improve mental or physical performance. Workers who need energy, truck drivers who have to drive long distances, and students who need to stay awake to study for a psychology test use stimulants.

ARE YOU HAVING PROBLEMS WITH ALCOHOL?

The following test questions are used by Johns Hopkins University Hospital in deciding whether or not a patient is having a problem with alcohol. Take a few minutes and answer them honestly.

* Do you lose time from work due to drinking?
* Is drinking making your home life unhappy?
* Do you drink because you're shy with other people?
* Is drinking affecting your reputation?
* Have you ever felt remorse after drinking?
* Have you gotten into financial difficulties as a result of drinking?
* Do you turn to lower companions and an inferior environment when drinking?
* Does your drinking make you careless of your family's welfare?
* Has your ambition decreased since drinking?
* Do you crave a drink at a definite time daily?
* Do you want a drink the next morning?
* Does drinking cause you difficulty in sleeping?
* Has your efficiency decreased since drinking?
* Is drinking jeopardizing your job or business?
* Do you drink to escape from worries or trouble?
* Do you drink alone?
* Have you ever had a complete loss of memory as a result of drinking?
* Has your physician ever treated you for drinking?
* Do you drink to build up your self-confidence?
* Have you ever been to a hospital or institution on account of drinking?

The test concludes with the statement: "If the answer is affirmative to any one of the questions, there is a definite warning to watch your drinking. If the answer is affirmative to any two, the chances are that you have a problem and should stop drinking. If the answer is affirmative to three or more, you are definitely in trouble and it is probably too late for prevention. You need help."

Joseph F. Follmann, Jr., *Alcoholics and Business: Problems, Costs, Solutions* (New York: AMACOM, 1976) pp. 37 and 38.

High doses of amphetamines can cause nausea, vomiting, high blood pressure, and strokes.

Amphetamines are physically dangerous drugs, and drug tolerance increases rapidly. High doses can cause nausea, vomiting, high blood pressure, and even strokes. Amphetamines can also lead to behavior that mimics paranoia, a disturbance in which a person is convinced that people are out to get him. Feeling suspicious of others sometimes leads to violence against imagined persecutors. Amphetamines don't actually produce energy but rather borrow from the body's available energy sources. Borrowing from this energy supply over and over again can lead to symptoms ranging from tooth grinding to cerebral hemorrhage.

Cocaine has been called the marijuana of the 1980s and is the newest drug being used by young, employed Americans. *Newsweek* reports that the "plain fact is that cocaine abuse is the fastest growing

---

STAGES IN ALCOHOL DEPENDENCE

1. *Prealcoholic Symptomatic Phase (social drinking).* Drinking begins to serve the function of releasing tension. When tension increases, so does the amount of alcohol needed to reduce it. The change from occasional to frequent drinking may take several months to two years.

2. *Prodromal.* This stage is marked by the onset of blackouts and memory losses. The drinker may show few if any signs of intoxication and can carry on conversations and not remember them later. The following signs are likely to occur:
   a. Surreptitious drinking—sneaking around
   b. Preoccupation with alcohol—will there be enough at the party?
   c. Avid drinking—gulping the first couple of swallows
   d. Guilt feelings about drinking behavior
   e. Avoidance of reference to alcohol in conversations

3. *Crucial Phase.* The person experiences a loss of control over drinking and is unable to control the drinking once it has begun. However, the drinker can still control whether he or she will drink or not and has considered going on the wagon. The individual begins to rationalize drinking behavior and is still struggling to maintain employment. At this time hospitalization for an alcohol-related problem might occur.

4. *Chronic.* The alcoholic has extended drinking bouts and may suffer delirium tremens, hallucinations, medical complications, and the loss of tolerance for alcohol. The person has little or no control over either starting or continuing to drink.

James C. Coleman, *Abnormal Psychology and Modern Life*, 5th ed. (Glenview, Ill.: Scott, Foresman, 1976), pp. 420–424.

---

drug problem in America for adults and school-age children alike."[23] After alcohol, cocaine is the second most popular drug in use with perhaps 500,000 to 750,000 Americans using it daily.[24] People aren't convinced that it will hurt them, probably because many who snort coke belong to a generation presented with a somewhat benign picture of drugs.

The effects of cocaine, the drug which comes from the leaves of the coca plant, include confidence, euphoria, alertness, power, and well-being. From 1886 to 1906 Coca Cola contained the real thing, but today the only "life" Coke adds is from caffeine and sugar. One main difference between it and amphetamines is that cocaine effects last only from 15 to 30 minutes while amphetamine effects last several hours.

Cocaine affects include increased confidence, euphoria, alertness, power, and well-being.

The cocaine user appears witty, alert, and confident. Cocaine is becoming a popular drug to use at work for at least two reasons.[25] Because of the sensation-enhancing effect of the substance, cocaine often gives users the false feeling that they can do their jobs better and faster. Cocaine is also easy to hide. It is usually snorted rather than smoked and does not give off an odor as marijuana does. Some users take the drug right in front of their co-workers without being detected by emptying a squeeze bottle containing medication for sinus congestion and refilling the bottle with cocaine.

Cocaine use can have medical, psychological, and social consequences.

Symptoms of abuse and dependency include loss of control, exaggerated involvement, and continued use despite adverse consequences.[26] The user is unable to stop cocaine use and experiences irresistible urges and cravings for the stimulant. He fears distress without the drug and prefers it to food, sex, family, and friends. Types of adverse consequences can be medical, psychological, and social. The snorter suffers fatigue, insomnia, headaches, and nose problems. Sometimes the cartilaginous wall between the nostrils is destroyed. Psychologically, the person experiences personality changes, is irritable and often depressed, becomes more withdrawn, and has difficulty with memory and concentration. Problems develop with the user's relationships and job and/or career.

Cocaine has not been proven to be physically addictive, but it's such a rewarding drug that users quickly develop a strong psychological dependence. After the exhilarating effect wears off, the snorter feels depression that can only be relieved by snorting more of the drug. Hence, the cycle begins. People who use cocaine regularly lose interest in paying bills, keeping sweethearts, going to work, or looking presentable. Nothing matters but the drug.

Caffeine is found in coffee, tea, cola drinks, and chocolate.

Caffeine is a stimulant that speeds up heart activity and promotes the release of stomach acid. It reduces fatigue and increases alertness and is contained in coffee, tea, cola drinks, chocolate, and many nonprescription drugs. Caffeine is not really considered a problem at work since it's not illegal. However, many health conscious Americans have realized that caffeine can be hazardous to their health and are opting for decaffeinated beverages.

Nicotine is also a stimulant and is found mainly in tobacco. Now considered to be an addictive drug, withdrawal often causes headaches, sweating, cramps, insomnia, and a strong craving for cigarettes. Smoking is not perceived as serious a problem in the workplace as alcoholism or cocaine, but it has been shown to be physically harmful. The link between cancer and tobacco has been firmly established. It also contributes to heart disease, emphysema, and birth defects. Cigarette smoke is also harmful to nonsmokers who have to inhale the secondhand smoke. People trapped in close quarters with smokers show increased levels of carbon monoxide in their blood, and this is one of the many reasons why nonsmokers have begun complaining about the smoking habits of their smoking co-workers.

Cannabis Derivatives

Cannabis derivatives are derived in one form or another from the hemp plant, Cannabis sativa. *Marijuana* and *hashish* are the most common members of this drug family. In moderate doses they produce intoxicating effects similar to those caused by alcohol, but larger amounts can produce disordered behavior.

Marijuana and hashish are the most common members of the Cannabis sativa family.

The main active substance is THC, a hallucinogen that alters sensory impressions. THC accumulates in the fatty tissues of the body, especially the brain and reproductive organs. At first marijuana makes the person feel euphoric and relaxed. But it impairs short-term memory and slows learning. For the workplace, it's crucial to remember that the possession and use of marijuana are illegal, so the drug can be quite costly in terms of a career.

The long-term dangers of smoking marijuana are inconclusive. However, some of the proven health hazards are that marijuana smoke is irritating to the lungs and can cause chronic bronchitis in regular users. Since it has many chemical components similar to tobacco smoke, many scientists suspect a link between marijuana and lung cancer. Also, marijuana temporarily lowers sperm production and causes an increased number of abnormal sperm in male smokers.

Hallucinogens

Hallucinogens can produce bizarre changes in perception.

Hallucinogens are capable of producing bizarre changes in the way in which individuals perceive the world about them. Included are *mescaline, LSD,* and *PCP.* These drugs bring about hallucinations or disturbances in perception. Users see things that aren't there and hear voices and sounds that aren't there. They also experience altered time and space perception. They might step out of a five-story window thinking the ground is but a step outside of the window.

Inhalants

Inhalants are those drugs that contain volatile chemicals whose fumes produce intoxication when inhaled. Their use is more popular among younger adolescents.

EMPLOYEE ASSISTANCE PROGRAMS

Increasing awareness of drug use and abuse at work has led to the development of employee assistance programs (EAPs). Many of these programs were set up in the 1970s for workers suffering from alcoholism and have since been expanded to include drug abusers. Some of the larger corporations have in-house programs, while other businesses refer their employees to outside agencies.

EAPs established for treatment of alcoholics now treat drug abusers as well.

Many businesses have no adequate policy for dealing with employee substance use. However, increasing numbers of employers are interested in taking steps to cope with the problems arising from drug use. The feeling is that the employer owes the employee, especially an honorable and long-standing employee, the obligation of at least one attempt to rehabilitate himself. It's more economical to help an employee who has been on the job for a number of years than it is to hire and train someone to replace him.

It's more economical to help a long-standing employee than it is to hire and train a new one.

The treatment of workers with substance disorders is complex and involves skills, patience, and understanding. The first step in dealing with the drug problem is to establish a firm and fair policy which might include letting the employees know that those caught using or selling illegal drugs will be fired and that those who admit their problem and who desire rehabilitation or counseling will be helped. Sometimes the mere threat of losing a job can help since a job is such an important facet of someone's life. The situation boils down to two choices for the troubled employee. He or she either has to seek assistance or accept appropriate discipline, perhaps even dismissal, early retirement, demotion, or suspension without pay. In other words the person has to seek rehabilitation, or her job is in jeopardy.

Workers with substance abuse problems are often found to choose between a job and rehabilitation.

Since drug use is expensive, potentially dangerous, and sometimes illegal, employers feel that it can't be condoned in the workplace. Many workers, on the other hand, feel that their privacy is being invaded when an employer attempts to interfere with personal habits. However, since some drugs continue to affect people for days, even weeks, it's felt that a worker is accountable on Monday morning for what he does on Saturday night. Consequently, many large employers have begun testing their employees for drugs—the U.S. military, for example.

Since the burden of controlling drug use falls more and more on the shoulders of the affected enterprises, consider the following suggestions for controlling drug use at work.[27]

Drug policies should be spelled out clearly and specifically.

1. *Establish and communicate a clear policy on drug use.* It needs to spell out the drug policy clearly and specifically so employees know exactly where they stand. Employees need to understand health and safety risks caused by drugs and dangers posed in the workplace by drug abuse.

2. *Be sure to enforce the policy.* Establishing a policy is one thing, and enforcing it is another. Since Shell Oil feels that work on the oil rigs is too important to be taken for granted, the company conducts random searches of employees crews on the rigs as they go on and off duty. Spot searches on the rigs themselves are conducted by private security agencies with canine units, and undercover people are planted in the work force to discover and obtain evidence of on the job drug use.

3. *Provide education and accurate information about drugs.* Employees need to know the legal, physical, and psychological effects. How do certain drugs affect behavior and coordination? How do certain drugs affect behavior and coordination? How will they affect workplace performance while working on the assembly line, driving a forklift truck, or dealing with customers? Ford provides treatment facilities and detoxification units and access to outpatient clinics, hospitals, and group therapy for its employees.

4. *Anticipate problems.* Many employees resent the company telling them what they should do in their free time. What many don't realize is that leisure-time drug use spills over into worktime problems.

   For example, marijuana's THC stays in the bloodstream several days, even weeks, and can affect job performance.

COUNSELING

There are at least two circumstances in which you are permitted to offer emotional first aid.

Emotional disturbances like depression and burnout involve impairment of relationships with others and reduction of job satisfaction and efficiency. Drug abuse does too. When do you as a co-worker or supervisor step in and volunteer to help? In *Emotional Health: In the World of Work*, Harry Levinson says that there are at least two circumstances in which you are permitted to offer emotional first aid. One of those is when the troubled worker asks you as a friend, thereby making his problem your business. The other is when his job performance may be impaired, especially if you are the supervisor responsible for the quality of the job performance.[28]

When to Help

Even if a person does not approach you and inform you of his problems, there are many signs that indicate that a person needs help. Levinson says that the person's unusual manner may be overemphasized. A quiet person may become even more withdrawn than usual. On the other hand, there could be a radical change in behavior. An orderly and controlled person may begin to drink too much. The quiet person mentioned earlier could become noisy and aggressive. There are other obvious signs of distress. The person may be restless, agitated, unable to concentrate, jittery, panicky. Even an unprofessional eye can spot these symptoms of suffering.[29]

What can you do if a co-worker comes to you with a problem?

As a listener, do not offer quick advice or make light of a person's discomfort.

1. You can act as a friend. Permit the distressed person to feel that it is all right to talk about the problem.
2. Listen, really listen to the person, since that implies that you are willing to help him and that you respect him as a worthy human being. Levinson cautions that listening is difficult but that talking about an emotional problem is sometimes even harder. As a listener, be a sounding board and do not make light of the person's discomfort, offer quick advice, or make decisions for the person. Listening has powerful effects on the speaker since he is able to release the feelings that have been held in and ease their pressure. Talking to another somehow magically clarifies and dissipates feelings and helps to restore the person's confidence in others.[30]
3. Realize that since you are not a psychotherapist or counselor, you may need to refer the person to a professional, especially if the problems are intense, severe, or of prolonged duration.

Types of Counseling

Means of dealing with a problem range from drug therapy to talk therapy. Dozens of approaches are available, and the appropriate one depends on many variables such as the cause of the problem, the nature of the problem, and the emotional makeup and attitude of the person. Although an in-depth look at the therapeutic methods available is beyond the scope of this text, it is useful to be familiar with the terms "directive," "nondirective," and "cooperative counseling."

Directive counseling is the traditional means of counseling and is called directive since the counselor directs "the form, flow, and the content of the exchange between the counselor and counselee."[31] It's the easiest type of counseling available, is very efficient, and requires little skill. For these reasons, directive counseling is probably overused at work.

Directive counseling is very efficient and requires little skill.

Directive counseling is not difficult to practice. A counselor asks questions, makes a diagnosis based on the responses, and gives advice or reassurance. While most professional counselors prefer that people solve their own problems instead of depending on the counselor or friend or supervisor, there are times when a more direct approach is needed. For example, maybe a worker needs reassurance that she is doing the right thing.

Nondirective counseling is also known as client-centered therapy, a type of counseling popularized by Carl Rogers. The counselor does not direct the client with advice at any time, and the person being counseled determines what will be discussed. The hope is that if the person is allowed to talk freely about his or her problems, insight into motivation behind feelings and behavior will be gained. Employees who have a real desire for mental health and who are willing to talk freely about themselves have a greater chance of success with this type of counseling. While nondirective counseling is quite effective, it can also be very time consuming and costly.

Nondirective counseling can be time consuming and costly.

A client-centered therapist feels that the client is an important person and tries to feel empathy and to create a warm permissive atmosphere. The counselor actually tries to see the world through the eyes of the troubled person. It's a very caring type of counseling, and the counselee is treated with unconditional positive regard. No matter what is said, the counselor remains caring and concerned instead of judgmental, evaluative, or condemning.

The nondirective listener avoids being judgmental, evaluative, or condemning.

No advice is given. If the person were to say, "Well, what do you think I should do?" the counselor would more than likely say something like, "What do you think you should do?" The rationale is that people are responsible for their own behavior and will solve their own problems once the problems are recognized fully. Advice is easy to give, but then the person with the problem would return to the counselor or similar substitute with the next problem and the next and the next instead of depending on himself.

Counselors use active listening techniques such as paraphrasing and clarification. In paraphrasing, the counselor may repeat a statement of the client's in her own words rather than that of the client. Also, the counselor may make a statement such as "You seem to be feeling annoyed with Myrtle over this situation" and wait for the client's response. This is clarification. At all times the client is encouraged with appropriate nonverbal and verbal responses. For example, the counselor will nod or frown or say, "I see," during the interchange.

*Paraphrasing and
clarification are
techniques used in
active listening.*

By blending the best of directive and nondirective counseling techniques, *cooperative counseling* seeks to establish a cooperative exchange of ideas to help solve a person's problems. It combines many advantages of the other types of counseling while avoiding their disadvantages. Many individuals feel that directive counseling is neither helpful nor progressive and that nondirective counseling is both expensive and time consuming.

Neither counselor nor counselee directs the process. Instead each participant contributes his or her own unique knowledge and perspective to the problem-solving process. The cooperative counseling process begins by using the listening techniques of nondirective counseling. However, as the interview progresses, participative (cooperative) counselors may play a more active role than nondirective counselors. For instance, they might offer opinions, personal knowledge, or insight. They might even discuss the situation from their broader organizational knowledge, thereby giving a counselee a different view of the problem.

CASE STUDIES

The Depressed Draftsman

Brian Harris works in a telephone company as a draftsman. You and he have been working together for nearly four years. Although the relationship started out as strictly work related, you and Brian have become friends. Common interests in sports, particularly racquetball and tennis, have led to many enjoyable off-the-job contacts.

Lately Brian has seemed a little down. He's moody, depressed, and preoccupied. Since you work together so closely, you feel certain that whatever is troubling him is not work related. Still, the "problem" is affecting his work performance. He's having trouble concentrating and sometimes has to be told things as many as three times before he understands. Brian is quite intelligent; it's as if his mind is elsewhere. You want to help him because he's your friend, but you don't want to appear snoopy or meddling.

At lunch you overhear Ralph and Henry, co-workers, discussing Brian's strange behavior. Ralph lives next door to Brian and through information gleaned from Brian's wife and children, Ralph has an idea of what some of the problem may be. He too wants to help, but he doesn't know exactly what to do. As Ralph tells it, here are a few of the things on Brian's mind:

* His property taxes are past due, and he has no money to pay them.
* His car insurance is due.
* One of his daughters need braces.
* His house needs reroofing.
* His wife lost her job and is pessimistic about finding another one.
* His father is ill and may move in with them.

1. What should you do? Following Levinson's guidelines, would it be appropriate to talk to Brian about his problems?
2. If he does open up and talk to you what will you do and say? Will you offer him money? Slap him on the back good-naturedly and tell him that things can't be all that bad? Tell him all of your problems? Try some counseling?
3. If you decide to counsel him, what method would be most effective? Why?
4. Role play a counseling session using the method you think best.

The Restaurant Manager's Dilemma

Kevin Barker is the restaurant manager in a large international hotel chain. Things are going smoothly for him except for one little problem—his assistant manager seems to have a drinking problem that is interfering with his job performance. At least, that's what Kevin suspects; he has no real proof that strong spirits account for Bob Brown's behavior.

The assistant manager is capable and competent and has tremendous potential in the restaurant business. He's people oriented, is considered to be an outstanding gourmet cook, and has a knack for running a business too. Lately, however, the other employees have noticed changes in Bob's behavior and appearance. Up until now, the manager was the only one aware of the declining job performance and was able to carry Bob's load and rationalize for Bob's slackness.

Usually early for work, lately Bob has been arriving at the last moment, leaving the details of setting up to anyone and everyone else. Usually immaculately groomed and wearing clean, pressed black pants, white shirt, and dark tie, Bob now appears for work looking disheveled and unkempt. During the evening when Bob is needed either in the kitchen or on the floor, he seems to have mysteriously disappeared. Sometimes he's sitting at a table socializing with the patrons, and once he was spotted at the restaurant bar. Whether he was drinking on the job is uncertain, but his job performance has definitely suffered, and Kevin suspects a problem with alcohol. This places Kevin in a dilemma, for he feels that Bob has great promise potential and hates to lose him.

1. After reading the guidelines in this chapter, what would you do if you were the manager?
2. Have you had a similar job experience? If so, how was it handled?

BURNOUT ACTIVITY

Dedicated, dynamic perfectionists are more likely to experience burnout than their more "laid-back" co-workers. However, personality is only part of the picture. The work environment is a crucial factor in contributing to burnout.

Committed goal-oriented people who work in an environment which does not appreciate or support their dedication and zeal are prime candidates for burnout.

What about you? Are you a potential burnout victim? Are you a success-oriented person? Have you found your job to be as rewarding as you expected it to be? Read over the following statements and check the ones that are true of your organization.

_____ 1. Employee complaints and grievances are generally ignored.

_____ 2. Although unlawful, discrimination because of race, sex, and age is practiced.

_____ 3. Employers give little or no positive feedback.

_____ 4. There is a distinct division between organizational levels.

_____ 5. The work itself is dull, repetitive, or unchallenging.

_____ 6. Management expects work above and beyond the call of duty without additional compensation or reward.

_____ 7. Management expects perfection from employees.

_____ 8. Employee feelings are not taken into consideration when decisions are made that affect their work.

_____ 9. Occasional playfulness is considered unprofessional and taboo.

_____ 10. There are frequent changes in policy without time to evaluate the original policy.

_____ 11. The comfort (or discomfort) of the physical environment is not considered to be important to management.

_____ 12. Partiality, favoritism, and inconsistency is common in policy enforcement.

While this checklist may not be complete, it does include many of the workplace descriptions cited by burned-out employees as being factors contributing to their problem. Although not scientifically foolproof, if you checked as many as five statements, you could be headed for burnout, especially if you are idealistic, committed, and success oriented.

BECK DEPRESSION INVENTORY

Read each of the statements in each item and then circle the number beside it that best describes the way you feel right now. The higher your total, the greater the likelihood that you are depressed.

1. 0 I do not feel sad.
   1 I feel sad.
   2 I am sad all the time and I can't snap out of it.
   3 I am so sad or unhappy that I can't stand it.
2. 0 I am not particularly discouraged about the future.
   1 I feel discouraged about the future.
   2 I feel I have nothing to look forward to.
   3 I feel that the future is hopeless and that things cannot improve.
3. 0 I do not feel like a failure.
   1 I feel I have failed more than the average person.

    2 As I look back on my life, all I can see is failure.

    3 I feel I am a complete failure as a person.

4. 0 I get as much satisfaction out of things as I used to.

    1 I don't enjoy things the way I used to.

    2 I don't get real satisfaction out of anything anymore.

    3 I am dissatisfied or bored with everything.

5. 0 I don't feel particularly guilty.

    1 I feel guilty a good part of the time.

    2 I feel quite guilty most of the time.

    3 I feel guilty all of the time.

6. 0 I don't feel disappointed in myself.

    1 I am disappointed in myself.

    2 I am disgusted with myself.

    3 I hate myself.

7. 0 I am no more irritated now than I ever am.

    1 I get annoyed or irritated more easily than I used to.

    2 I feel irritated all the time now.

    3 I don't get irritated at all by the things that used to irritate me.

8. 0 I don't feel I look any worse than I used to.

    1 I am worried that I am looking old or unattractive.

    2 I feel that there are permanent changes in my appearance that make me look
      unattractive.

    3 I believe that I look ugly.

9. 0 I don't get more tired more than usual.

    1 I get tired more easily than I used to.

    2 I get tired from doing almost anything.

    3 I am too tired to do anything.

10. 0 My appetite is no more worse than usual.

    1 My appetite is not as good as it used to be.

    2 My appetite is much worse now.

    3 I have no appetite at all anymore.

A. T. Beck, (1967). *Depression: Causes and Treatment* (Philadelphia: University of Pennsylvania Press, 1967), pp. 333–335.

SUMMARY

Depression, burnout, and substance abuse have been recognized as major problems in the workplace. These personal problems are no respecters of age, occupation, sex, or social class. In the workplace, these problems have an astronomical price tag and have been linked to personal turnover, lowered productivity, impaired morale of co-workers, increased absenteeism and tardiness, increased accidents, and increased cost of insurance benefits.

Depression, frequently called the common cold of mental illness, is experienced as feelings of sadness, worthlessness, listlessness, disinterest in others, and withdrawal from others and activities. Depression is more than just a bad mood and affects a person's body, thoughts, and behavior. Severely depressed people neglect personal appearance and hygiene and might consider suicide.

There are several theories of depression. The most common ones include biological, psychoanalytic, learning, and cognitive theories. While biological explanations focus on studies which indicate that depression may have a biological basis, psychoanalytic theorists turn their attention to the unconscious mind. Learning theories concentrate on the environment as a cause of depression, and some even believe that people learn to be helpless in overcoming problems. Cognitive theories focus on the depressed person's faulty cognitions or thoughts.

Job burnout is the depletion of physical and mental resources caused by striving to reach some unrealistic job goal. Symptoms include chronic fatigue, job boredom, less commitment, poor concentration, and certain physiological changes such as high blood pressure.

Drug and alcohol use and abuse in the workplace is a growing problem reflecting national drug use problems. The stereotype of bleary-eyed drug addicts who consistently come in late, hung over, irritable, and unkempt is inaccurate. Substance abuse is not always easy to detect and may affect workers from the shop floor to the boardroom.

Tolerance, psychological dependence, and physical dependence are necessary for drug addiction to take place. While many substances create tolerance and psychological dependence, only narcotics and depressants have the potential for physical addiction.

There are six major categories of drugs: narcotics, depressants, stimulants, cannabis derivatives, hallucinogens, and inhalants.

Because of the problems and costs of substance abuse, many companies have set up employee assistance programs to help employees with drug- and alcohol-related problems The rationale is that it's more economical to help a long-standing and loyal employee than it is to hire and train a new one.

Whether the personal problem is depression, burnout, substance abuse, or conflict in relationships, having someone to listen can help. Harry Levinson offers guidelines to improve listening and suggests that the practice clarifies and dissipates feelings and helps to restore the troubled person's confidence in others.

There are three types of counseling frequently used in a work situation: directive, nondirective, and cooperative. In directive counseling, the easiest type, the counselor (listener) directs the flow and content of the interchange. In nondirective counseling, the counselor doesn't direct but rather encourages the speaker to determine what will be discussed. The nondirective listener is neither judgmental or evaluative. Cooperative counseling blends the best of directive and nondirective techniques as the participants each contribute his or her own unique knowledge and perspective to the problem-solving process.

KEY TERMS

Depression
Theories of depression
Learned helplessness
Faulty cognitions
Burnout
Tolerance
Physical addiction
Psychological dependence
Narcotics
Depressants
Stimulants
Hallucinogens
Inhalants
EAPs
Harry Levinson
Directive counseling
Nondirective counseling
Cooperative counseling

REVIEW AND DISCUSSION

1. What are some causes of depression? What are some symptoms? How can depression affect someone's work?

2. Contrast the four perspectives as to the causes of depression. What about you? Do you get depressed? Which theory seems more appropriate in your situation?

3. What are some symptoms of burnout? Why do you think it happens more frequently to high achievers?

4. What are some reasons why dug use is so difficult to detect? What are some fo the hidden costs of drug use?

5. What three conditions are necessary for addiction? How do these conditions relate to popular drugs like nicotine, cocaine, and alcohol?

6. What are some steps to follow in setting up an employee assistance program? How do you feel about such programs? Do you feel that they are an invasion of an employee's privacy? Do you feel that employer's should focus more on education, testing, or treatment?

7. What are some signs of emotional distress? How can you help a troubled co-worker or friend?

8. Compare and contrast the three counseling techniques in the chapter. What are the advantages and disadvantages of each?

ENDNOTES

[1] S. K. SECUNDA AND OTHERS, *Special Report 1973: The Depressive Disorders*, (Washington, D.C.: U.S. Government Printing Office, 1973). DHEW Publication No. 739152.

[2] MILDRED G. PRYOR AND MITCHELL KEITH GOLDEN, "The Depressed Employee," *Supervisory Management*, October 1984, p. 14.

[3] MORRIS K. HOLLAND, *Using Psychology: Principles of Behavior and Your Life* (Boston: Little, Brown, 1985), pp. 175–176.

[4] J. COYNE, "Depression and the Response of Others," *Journal of Abnormal Psychology*, 85 (1976), 186–193.

[5] M. E. P. SELIGMAN, "Depression and Learned Helplessness," in R. J. Friedman and M. M. Katz, eds., *The Psychology of Depression: Contemporary Theory and Research* (Washington, D.C.: Winston-Wiley, 1974).

[6] A. T. BECK, *Depression: Clinical, Experimental, and Theoretical Aspects* (New York: Harper & Row, 1962).

[7] MARK G. MCGEE AND DAVID W. WILSON, *Psychology: Science and Application* (St. Paul, Minn.: West, 1984), p. 404.

[8] "Job Burnout: Growing Worry for Workers, Bosses," *U.S. News & World Report*, February 18, 1980, pp. 71–72.

[9] OLIVER I. NIEHOUSE, "Controlling Burnout: A Leadership Guide for Managers," *Business Horizons*, July-August 1984, p. 81.

[10] HARRY LEVINSON, "When Executives Burn Out," *Harvard Business Review*, May-June 1981, p. 76.

[11] NIEHOUSE, "Controlling Burnout," pp. 81–82.

[12] JANICE CASTRO, "Battling the Enemy Within," *Time*, March 17, 1986, p. 53.

[13] Ibid., p. 53.

[14]JAMES A. BELOHLAV AND PAUL O. POPP, "Employee Substance Abuse: Epidemic of the Eighties," *Business Horizons*, July-August 1983, p. 31.

[15]DAN DAERCHER, "The Uses and Abuses of Mind Altering Drugs," *Better Homes and Gardens*, May 1983, pp. 83–90.

[16]JOSEPH F. FOLLMANN, JR., *Alcoholics and Business: Problems, Costs, Solutions* (New York: AMACOM, 1976), pp. 14–15.

[17]"What Is Our Drug Problem?" *Harper's*, December, 1985, pp. 39–51. Article based on a discussion with Mark Danner, senior editor acting as moderator.

[18]STEVEN FLAX, "The Executive Addict," *Fortune*, June 24, 1985, pp. 24–31.

[19]"What Is Our Drug Problem?" p. 41.

[20]BELOHLAV, "Employee Substance Abuse," p. 30.

[21]CASTRO, "Battling the Enemy Within," p. 58.

[22]FOLLMAN, *Alcoholics and Business* pp. 14, 16.

[23]TOM MORGAN AND OTHERS, "Kids and Cocaine," *Newsweek*, March 17, 1986, p. 58.

[24]"What Is Our Drug Problem?" p. 41.

[25]CASTRO, "Battling the Enemy Within," p. 54.

[26]CHARLES E. SHIRLEY, "Alcoholism and Drug Abuse in the Workplace," *Office Administration and Automation*, November 1984, p. 90.

[27]PETER B. BENSINGER, "Drugs in the Workplace," *Harvard Business Review*, November-December 1982, pp. 48–60.

[28]HARRY LEVINSON, *Emotional Health: In the World of Work* (New York: Harper & Row, 1964), p. 220.

[29]Ibid., p. 222.

[30]Ibid., pp. 223–227.

[31]JACK HALLORAN, *Applied Human Relations: An Organizational Approach*, 2nd ed. (Englewood Cliffs, N.J.: Prentice Hall, 1983), p. 169.

chapter 15

Prejudice and Discrimination

After reading and studying this chapter, you will be able to:

1. Define prejudice and discrimination.
2. Explain how prejudice is acquired.
3. Explain the disadvantages of discrimination.
4. Discuss racism, sexisms, and ageism as forms of discrimination.
5. Discuss equal opportunity legislation.
6. List ways of overcoming prejudice and discrimination.

Come to think of it, the one burning ambition in my life is to live long enough to become an old man.

Lewis Grizzard[1]

Take a look around you. What do your co-workers, supervisors, subordinates, classmates, neighbors, and friends look like? Chances are that they're dissimilar in many ways. Some are young and energetic while others are mature and mellow. Some are male and others are female. Skin color, size, shape, and general overall appearance differ greatly too.

Part of the American experience is being confronted with others whose religion, culture, race, life-style, and national origin differ from your own. Instead of capitalizing on these differences, however, many individuals let prejudice and discrimination negatively affect their attitudes and behavior. A prejudiced person who can't open his eyes and mind to the benefits of getting to know those who are different is at a distinct disadvantage.

DISADVANTAGES OF PREJUDICE AND DISCRIMINATION

If there were less discrimination, the labor force could be better used, and more contributions to society could be made.

From a social standpoint, getting rid of discrimination has a host of benefits and few, if any, disadvantages. The labor force could be better used, families could enjoy more earning and purchasing power, and more contributions to society could be made. America is called the land of opportunity, a land in which getting and keeping a job are means of participating in the culture. People who work have higher self-images and a more enhanced social status than those who are denied employment based on discrimination.

Prejudice and discrimination deny a business or industry of the talent, creativity, and energy of people who are "different."

On an organizational level, prejudice and discrimination can be quite costly. Because of equal employment opportunity (EEO) laws, everyone making a hiring, promoting, evaluating, demoting, or firing decision should realize that such a decision might be second guessed by a judge or jury in an antidiscrimination suit. "Stakes can be high. In addition to legal expenses, an employer losing a suit could face a court order to hire the plaintiff, pay all accumulated back wages and—when willful discrimination because of age is proved—pay double damages," says Peter Panken, a lawyer specializing in representing management in labor and employment laws.[2] Discrimination is also costly in that such a practice denies a business or industry of the tremendous talent, creativity, and energy of people who are "different."

In this chapter prejudice and discrimination are defined, and their possible causes are explored. The prejudices felt and the discrimination demonstrated are multiple and varied. Everyday people miss out on job opportunities and promotions because someone in a decision-making position dislikes people with big noses, people who have "funny" accents, people who smoke, or people who wear makeup. These types of discrimination are difficult to prove and aren't as big an issue as racism, sexism, or ageism, the three types of illegal discrimination faced at work. Finally, the chapter offers methods of alleviating negative stereotypes and ignorance which lead to blatant discrimination.

WHAT ARE PREJUDICE AND DISCRIMINATION

Prejudice is an attitude; discrimination is behavior which demonstrates prejudice.

The word "prejudice" has its roots in the Latin word *prejudicum* and means "prejudging people without knowledge of their personal qualities." Doob defines it as a "highly negative judgement toward a group, focusing on one or more negative characteristics that are supposedly uniformly shared by all group members."[3] Prejudice usually has a negative aspect, but it can also have a positive orientation. A person could be prejudiced *toward* an individual or group and regard them favorably. For our purposes, prejudice refers to an unfavorable opinion *against* members of racial, ethnic, or social groups.

If prejudice is an attitude, then discrimination is the behavior that demonstrates a preconceived judgment about others. It includes any kind of behavior in which people are treated unequally because of the categories into which they are neatly boxed, regardless of their individual attributes and interests. Examples of discrimination range from racial slurs and ethnic jokes to sexual harassment and actual bodily harm. Discrimination leads to segregation, reduces the life changes of some while improving others, and generates resentment and hostility.

Although the attitude and the act usually interact, they don't necessarily have to. Because of legal requirements, for example, a bigoted employer may not be allowed to demonstrate prejudiced feelings and avoid a day in court. On the other hand, a person completely free of prejudice (Is there such a saint?) may avoid socializing with minority co-workers because of group pressure from his or her "in-group." Most of the time, however, prejudice and discrimination are mutually reinforcing.

DO YOU REALLY KNOW THE FACTS?

What do you really know about prejudice and discrimination? Before reading any further in this chapter, test yourself. Read the following statements and decide whether they're true or false. The answers are given on the following pages.

1. Requiring a high school diploma for a custodial job could be a form of discrimination.
2. The emergence of women and other minorities has complicated black unemployment.
3. Asian Americans are twice as likely as native-born Americans to be college graduates.
4. The American Indian high school dropout rate is twice the national figure.
5. The majority of all women over 16 are in the labor force.
6. Women have less education and work experience than men.
7. Older workers have higher absentee and turnover rates than do younger employees.

8. Age has a detrimental effect on manual workers over age 40.
9. Evidence supports the stereotypes that link age with senility and incompetence.
10. Men between age 20 and 40 comprise the majority of those in protected groups.

1.	True	6.	False
2.	True	7.	False
3.	True	8.	False
4.	True	9.	False
5.	True	10.	False

After being hired, minorities face continued discrimination by not being promoted as often, not being selected for training, and being paid less than members of the majority group.

Job discrimination manifests itself along the entire continuum from hiring and firing. Many employers are reluctant to hire individuals because of color, age, origin, and the "shape of their skin." Once hired, these minorities face continued discrimination by not being promoted as often, not being selected for training, and by being paid less than members of the majority group. For example, even though Asian Americans have surpassed the educational achievements of the average American and have the highest average income of any major racial or ethnic group in the United States, they are still paid less than whites at comparable levels of education. Asian Americans earn 88 percent of the income that whites with the same education and occupation earn.[4]

HOW PREJUDICE IS ACQUIRED

Most reasonable people agree that discrimination that develops from prejudice is harmful and negative. Society's members who are avoided, excluded, ridiculed, harassed, and harmed suffer emotional and psychological damage. Too, those treating people unequally and unfairly are harming themselves since discrimination hampers team-building efforts and cooperation needed on the job.

Discrimination is such a waste! Minorities can add energy, creativity, and a different cultural viewpoint. Older workers can offer wisdom and stability that often accompany maturity. In the hopes of discovering means for overcoming discrimination, let's look at some of the causes of prejudice, the attitude that often leads to discrimination. The theories discussed are psychological, social, and economic.

Psychological Theory

One psychological explanation is that of psychoanalytic theorists like Freud and Jung, who believe that prejudice is a form of projection, a defense mechanism in which a person represses (forgets) unpleasant or unacceptable thoughts and projects them on to someone else, much like a movie projector projects an image onto a screen. Projection helps a person to alleviate anxiety and guilt. In others we see the laziness, fear, anger, lust, and greed that reside within ourselves. "It's not me who's lazy and didn't get the job done" you insist, "but Vukmanovich, the foreign kid."

A scapegoat is blamed for problems for which he or she is not responsible.

Another similar psychological explanation is the scapegoat theory. A scapegoat is a person who is blamed for problems although in reality he or she had nothing to do with the problem. "It is not we ourselves who are responsible for our misfortunes, but other people." In our common speech we recognize this failing in such phrases as "whipping-boy," "taking it out on the dog," or "scapegoat."[5] Easily recognizable minority groups are more likely to be scapegoats since they are relatively powerless and can often be seen demonstrating some despised activity or trait.

Scapegoating is a form of displacement.

Scapegoating is really a form of displacement. A frustrated person can't react aggressively because the source of frustration is unavailable or because it might be dangerous and foolhardy to do so. For instance, you might feel the urge to hurt your boss but are thwarted from doing so because of negative consequences that you will surely have to pay. Therefore, you displace your aggression toward a group such as Hispanics or blacks.

The authoritarian personality is submissive to authority figures and has contempt for those in a lower status.

A final psychological theory proposes that prejudice develops more readily in persons having an authoritarian personality.[6] Such persons are uncritically submissive to authority figures, follow conventional standards, prefer rigid categories, and are preoccupied with dominance and submissiveness as the basic forms of human interaction. They have contempt for those in a lower status, like strong, controlling people, and prefer pat solutions to problems. This personality often follows a harsh, disciplined childhood in which children unquestionably follow the rules set down by their parents and are subject to violent and arbitrary whippings and beatings.

Social Theory

There are social theories to explain the development of prejudice. The most popular of these is the social learning theory. According to this theory, people acquire prejudice just as they acquire other values like patriotism and honesty. A newborn baby knows no hate, but as a child matures, prejudices are learned from parents and other significant people such as teachers and friends.

Children model after their parents. They identify with them and imitate their behavior, including their attitudes. It's a part of the learning process, yet the child may be completely unaware of the attitudes and feelings being developed. It's learned in informal day-to-day contacts and experiences. Children listen. They observe. They read. Indeed, society itself as portrayed through media teaches prejudice.

GENDER ROLES: A MINI TEST

Many of our ideas about what constitutes appropriate masculine and feminine behavior originate from childhood experiences. Observing parents in their day-to-day lives is crucial in the development of gender roles an sexual stereotypes. What went on in your home? What kinds of models were your parents?

Quickly answer the following questions and reflect on the significance of your responses.

1. When you went out, who drove?
2. Who was more likely to ask, "Where are my socks/stockings?"
3. When the car needed repair, who took it to the garage?
4. Who did the laundry? The dusting? The vacuuming?
5. Who knew where to find the thermometer?
6. Who knew where to find the pipe wrench?
7. Who watered the house plants?
8. Who watered the lawn?
9. When you went on a trip, who packed the suitcases?
10. When you went on a trip, who packed the car?

Adapted from J. Doyle's *Sex and Gender: The Human Experience* (Dubuque, Iowa: William C. Brown, 1985), p. 271.

Stereotyping develops through social contacts. It's a term discussed in the chapter on communication and refers to a process in which a group is judged according to the behavior of a few of its members. Stereotypes

Stereotyping is a process by which a group is judged according to the behavior of a few of its members.

are overgeneralizations. Often, people categorize and then observe instead of vice versa. Actions of one group member are seen as typical for all group members. Since stereotypes develop over a period of time and since a lot of people share the same ones, they are extremely difficult to overcome.

Unfortunately, stereotypes often lead to Merton's self-fulfilling prophecy. Discussed in Chapter 7, there are two types of prophecies. The first type is when someone makes his or her own predictions about personal behavior and unconsciously works to make these predictions come true. The second type takes place when expectations of one person influence another's thinking and behavior. If a woman is treated as emotional, a black as lazy, and a senior citizen as senile, those people will begin to perceive of themselves as emotional, lazy, or senile and begin to act accordingly.

A member of a minority group is denied employment because of a lack of ability or experience, both of which could be acquired on the job. Since this denial then deprives the person of possible training and experience, the prophecy becomes true. When minorities fulfill our prophecy, we rub our chins and smugly say, "Aha, didn't I tell you so? What else can you expect from a woman? A Mexican American? An Indian?" Interestingly, the victims of prejudice and discrimination often hate themselves rather than the discriminating group since they've been influenced by the self-fulfilling prophecy.

POPULAR STEREOTYPES

Here are some of the popular, but untrue, stereotypes. Are you guilty of any? Are you the victim of any?

Blacks—happy go lucky, lazy, ignorant, pleasure loving, superstitious
Women—weak, scatterbrained, sensitive, less committed to career, emotional
Jews—intelligent, shrewd, grasping
Handicapped—unreliable, accident prone, clumsy
Irish—stupid, quick tempered, witty
Italians—impulsive, passionate
American Indians—drunken, shiftless

Economic Theory

There is a correlation between the degree of competition of two or more groups and the prejudice felt toward each other.

Economic theory should be considered as a major contributor to prejudice. When too many people compete with each other for jobs, educational opportunities, promotions, and so on, scarcity of the preceding results. There is only so much pie to go around, and everyone wants at least a sliver. As the pieces get smaller and smaller, competition and prejudice develop. There is a direct correlation between the degree of competition of two or more groups and the prejudice felt toward each other.

If there are simply not enough jobs to go around, and if someone can be singled out, the prejudice against that group develops and grows. As a recent example look to sunny Miami with its large Hispanic population and note the anti-Cuban sentiment there. Cubans, who have done better economically than all other Hispanics, are resented by many young blacks who feel that the Cubans are "messing us up . . . taking the bread out of our mouths."[7] Some argue that competition for jobs can encourage employers to disregard poor working conditions and reduce wages, but this is certainly no benefit for the minority worker. It might even increase feelings of ill will between minorities if one group is willing to work for low wages while another is not.

TYPES OF DISCRIMINATION

The variation within groups is as great as the diversity between them.

All humans are guilty of prejudging others before all the facts are known. Based on limited information and lack of exposure, many, yes even you, hold stereotyped beliefs against someone because of group membership. One of the most persistent myths about race, sex, and age is that certain abilities or traits are characteristic of a group. In reality, the variation within groups is as great as the diversity among them.

People are treated unfairly and unequally for many reasons. Discrimination based on color, national origin, sex, and age, though illegal, is still evident in the workplace. Since racism, sexism, and ageism are problems in many work environments, let's concentrate on these three types of discrimination. A person who belongs to more than one minority group, such as an older woman, is said to suffer double jeopardy.

Racism

Racism is prejudice based on skin color, race, or national origin.

Racism is prejudice based on skin color, race, or national origin. A race is a category of people who are socially defined as distinct because of inherited physical characteristics. An ethnic group is a category of people who are distinct because of cultural characteristics handed down from generation to generation, characteristics like language, religion, and customs. The terms, though not synonymous, are difficult to separate.

The racial groups victimized today include blacks, Hispanics, Asians, and native Americans. Since equal employment opportunity (EEO) laws prohibit discrimination based on race, overt discrimination is not as prevalent as it was 20 years ago. There are still ways in which employers and employees alike discriminate, however. One example is tokenism, the practice of hiring a few "token" women, blacks, Hispanics, or handicapped workers to comply with the letter, if not the spirit, of the EEO laws. Thinking, feeling tokens are aware of their "show" status and resent it.

*People don't get along because they fear each other. People fear each other because they don't know each other. They don't know each other because they have not properly communicated with each other.
Martin Luther King, Jr.*

Our nation is comprised of a number of races and ethnic groups, and most have been gradually assimilated into American industry and society. Racial groups most readily incorporated are those of Northern European descent whose physical appearance and culture allow them to be less "different" and more readily accepted. On the other hand, there are others whose obvious physical and cultural differences prevent them from becoming a part of the mainstream of American society. Not only are they often not allowed to participate in social benefits America offers, but they are also hindered from making contributions of their own. Since racism is one of the major forms of prejudice, let's examine at least four of the groups briefly: blacks, Hispanics, Asian Americans, and native Americans.

Blacks comprise approximately 12 percent of the total U.S. population. Because of centuries of prejudice, the American black has experienced inequities in both educational and employment opportunities. Despite progress, a wide gap in the economic position of whites and blacks exists. The median income of a black family is only 55 percent of that of a white one, and "the unemployment rate for blacks is more than twice that for whites."[8] When the economy goes into a recession, the unemployment rate for young blacks rises faster than it does for any other group.

Exclusion from lack of opportunity lingers on. Timm and Peterson contend that black youth unemployment is "the most basic and persistent of all the economic problems facing blacks in the U.S." and believe that early youth unemployment leads to lifelong economic disadvantage.[9] Black unemployment has recently been complicated by the emergence of increasing numbers of other minority groups like women and Hispanics. Employer efforts to help black workers with their problems have helped other minority workers as well.

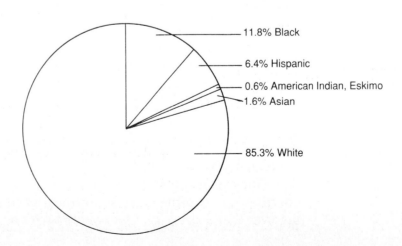

11.8% Black

6.4% Hispanic

0.6% American Indian, Eskimo

1.6% Asian

85.3% White

Black unemployment has recently been complicated by the emergence of increasing numbers of other minority groups.

Why haven't blacks done as well as some of the more recent immigrants? There are several explanations. One is many blacks' lack of fundamental job skills and work values. Many are unaware of skills needed to be successful on the job, skills known to middle-class white workers. Also, many blacks don't have the advantage of the "buddy system" of finding a job. Many jobs are found through employed buddies who hear of an opening, and whites are more likely to be aware of and to use this system. However, networking among black professionals is yielding career benefits.[10] Blacks also suffer from lower education levels, although this is changing. From 1960 to 1982 the average number of years of education for blacks increased from 8.0 years to 12.2[11]

It's impossible to discuss the black situation without looking at their history. "No other people came to America in chains. Unlike other groups that experienced spasms of prejudice that lasted a few decades, blacks have faced generations of racism."[12] Their plight cannot be discussed without looking at slavery, exploitation, and deprivation. Blacks have been here since the founding of the nation and have roots deeper than other ethnic and racial groups, and yet they were actually legally segregated from other groups until President Truman abolished segregation in the armed forces.

Differing greatly among themselves, *Hispanics* are people from Puerto Rico, Mexico, Cuba, and other Central and South American countries. The word Hispanic itself refers to people of white, black, Indian, and thoroughly mixed ancestry who come from countries which have little in common except historical conditions, the Catholic religion, and the Spanish language. Also in common are traditional virtues like devotion to God, to family, and to work.

At the present Hispanics comprise approximately 6 percent of the U.S. population. Some analysts predict that because of their high fertility rate and young median age, they will comprise 18 percent of the population of the United States in 50 years.[13] If so, Hispanics will outnumber blacks and people of English, German, French, Italian, or any other single ethnic background, to become the largest American minority.

Hispanics suffer from poor education, a lack of job skills, and a language barrier.

Hispanics suffer from poor education, a lack of job skills, and a language barrier. Hispanics over the age of 25 have completed only 10.3 years of school compared to the 12.5 years for whites.[14] The lower educational level has led to employment in low-paying jobs like migrant work. The Spanish language is a handicap in the labor force and is an almost insurmountable problem in school. Even so, the day may arrive when America is a bilingual country, and knowledge of a second language would be advantageous to your career.

Asian Americans are the latest victims of discrimination and accounted for approximately 1.5 percent of the American population by 1980. Asian Americans are Japanese, Chinese, Filipinos, Vietnamese, and other Asians. Demographers predict that the Asian population is likely to double by 2010.[15]

Many Asians feel that they are victims of racial prejudice. Highly educated Asians often find job hunting a humbling experience when they discover that degrees that took years to complete are suddenly meaningless in this land of opportunity. The picture is not totally bleak, however, since educational and occupational opportunities have enabled numbers of Asians to achieve success in professional careers like law and medicine.

Asian Americans are represented far beyond their population at virtually every top ranking university.

Of all the other immigrants to this country, Asian Americans are represented far beyond their population at virtually every top-ranking university and are speedily climbing the American economic ladder. Except for the Indochinese, the new Asian arrivals are at least twice as likely as a native-born American to be college graduates. Asians are also well represented in the ranks of managers and professionals.

No one denies that Asian Americans have enhanced the nation's talent pool. A demographer at Rand Corporation in Santa Monica, California, said, "They are the most highly skilled of any immigrant group our country has ever had."[16] Why? How? What is their secret? The reasons are many. The fact that many Asian Americans are permitted entry to the United States because of a desirable vocational background is part of the fascinating puzzle. In addition, Asians have it easier than some immigrants since they often come from urban middle-class backgrounds. Also, they place a high premium on education and hard work. To many of them a 40-hour workweek looks like child's play. Their diligent labor pays off since the median income for the Asian group as a whole exceeds that of American families in general.

Native Americans are high in unemployment, health problems, and alcoholism, and low in wealth and education.

Unfortunately, the *native Americans* have not fared as well as the Asians. "After more than a century of federal supervision and dashed hopes, the first Americans find themselves still at the bottom of the ladder—high in unemployment, health problems and alcoholism, low in wealth and education."[17] They comprise only 0.5 percent of the total American population, nearly half of whom live in Oklahoma, Arizona, California, and New Mexico. Shunned, ridiculed, and resented by Americans whose ancestors would have starved had the Indians not taught them to plant corn and to fish, they exist in poverty on reservations.

Many native Americans leave reservations hoping for a better life in the city. Once there, they unfortunately find the same poverty they left behind, especially since they often lack job skills and an adequate education. Urban Indians usually blend in with the rest of the urban poor rather than congregate in recognizable native American neighborhoods.

Often the city-dweller is in a no-win situation. Not only does he suffer culture shock at the fast-paced city life compared to slower paced reservation life, but he also is often cut off from family and friends who could provide psychological, financial, and emotional support.

Native Americans are the most disadvantaged group in America today.

Native Americans are the most disadvantaged group in America today. The per capita income is less than 60 percent of the American average. The male unemployment rate is three times the national average, and the dropout rate from high school is twice the national figure.[18] Those are pretty sobering statistics. Perhaps more than any other minority, native Americans have remained unassimilated into the mainstream of American society. They are one of the smallest and poorest racial groups, a people torn between two cultures, one destroyed and one unwelcoming.

Sexism

Sexism is discrimination based on gender.

As more and more women enter the work force, sexism, discrimination based on gender, has become a major issue in society and at work. Sexism is based on widely held beliefs about the abilities, traits, and behavior of men and women and can limit the opportunities to choose a preferred career and life-style. It's shown by vulgar jokes, low salary, low-status jobs, and no promotions.

Because the Woman's Liberation Movement created an awareness of the restrictions based on gender, many men have also claimed to be victims of sexism. As a result, today there are a few male nurses and secretaries, but not many. It seems that throughout life the male sex role is more narrowly defined than is the female role. In childhood, girls proudly profess to be tomboys, but few boys admit to being sissies.

Sexual harassment is physical or verbal conduct that creates an offensive or unpleasant work environment. Demeaning and also now illegal, it includes offers of job favors in return for sexual favors, jokes or sexual innuendos, and unnecessary sexual contact that is suggestive or lewd. It can happen anywhere, no matter what the job. Female executives, tellers, receptionists, and cashiers all fall prey to harassment. Men also suffer from sexual harassment, though not as frequently.

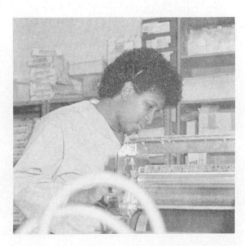

LET'S GET RID OF "THE GIRL"

Wouldn't this be a great year to take one giant step forward for womankind and get rid of "the girl?"

Your attorney says, "If I'm not here just leave it with the girl."
The purchasing agent says, "Drop off your bid with the girl."
A manager says, "My girl will get back to your girl."

What girl?

Do they mean Miss Rose?
Do they mean Ms. Torres?
Do they mean Mrs. McCullough?
Do they mean Joy Jackson?

"The girl" is certainly a woman when she's beyond her teens. Like you, she has a name. Use it.

The majority of women over 16 are in the labor force.

Women constitute a majority of the world population yet are treated like a minority group and are excluded from political and economic power. Although women comprise over 40 percent of the labor force, they are still victims of discrimination. The majority of all women over 16 are in the labor force, in fact in 1983 the U.S. Department of Labor reported that over 50 percent of adult women were working. The numbers are predicted to increase, and the Bureau of Labor Statistics estimates that in 1995 the labor participation rate of women will average about 60.3 compared to 53.7 percent today.[19]

American women are indeed pursuing different life-styles from those of their mothers and grandmothers. Many have taken off their aprons and donned "dress for success" apparel. Increased education and participation in the labor force has changed female attitudes about marriage and the family. Total life-style is different. Women are having fewer children and are spending less time at home and more on the job.

Some positive changes have occurred, but there is still a wage gap since a woman's labor, even though she may be performing the same job as a man with the same skill level and responsibility, is not considered as valuable. In fact, the gap between the earnings of men and women has widened, not narrowed. Sources differ in the figures, but in general, the average woman can expect to earn around 70 cents to every male dollar earned.[20] It s no secret that the average starting salary for women college graduates is roughly equal to the average starting salary for men high school graduates. Furthermore, only 2 percent of women earn $30,000 a year compared to 21 percent of men.[21]

Why does this happen? As in all prejudice, the social learning theory has a lot to do with it. We know that what determines masculinity and femininity vary from culture to culture and believe that sex role acquisition is at least partially culturally determined. For example, anthropologist Margaret Mead describes a tribe of people called the Tchambuli whose sex roles seem almost exactly opposite of the so-called traditional male and female roles. The women are the family breadwinners and are very impersonal, dominant, and businesslike. While the women are out securing food for their families, the men are caring for the children, gossiping, and waiting to cook the food found by the women. The men don't rebel at their lot in life, for it's all they know.[22]

Why does sexism persist? Whose fault is it? Employers say it's not theirs. "They prefer to blame it on the secretarial schools, the news media, the misguided guidance counseling, the long legacy of women having to take second place in the employment world. And what's more, they continue, women are not equal; look at their average height, weight, strength, home responsibilities, reduced capabilities when pregnant, etc."[23] This type of faulty reasoning perpetuates itself, and men who generalize about women's capabilities often contribute in preventing women from reaching their potential.

Women and men have both learned and accepted the sexual stereotypes, and a lifetime of conditioning is hard to uncondition. Attitudes that take years to develop don't disappear overnight. Women have to learn a lot new rules of organizational life that men know about and take for granted, rules like team playing. Also, women have had fewer sexual role models with whom to identify. The top dogs were men. Finally, females don't know about the opportunities available to them. When and if they get to high positions, sometimes they don't know how to trust their own judgment, make decisions, or exercise authority.

DISTRIBUTION OF OCCUPATIONS

The distribution of women and men by occupations is very uneven, and some jobs are occupied almost exclusively by men and others by women. Women comprise the following percentage of workers in the selected occupations. As you can tell, women's jobs are among the lowest paying and least prestigious; nor do they provide opportunity for upward mobility.

99.2% of all secretaries
95.6% of all nurses
95.9% of all domestic help in private households
92.0% of all bank tellers
82.4% of all elementary school teachers
3.4% of all college and university teachers
14.8% of all physicians, medical and osteopathic
15.4% of all lawyers and judges
5.7% of all engineers
96.6% of all typists

Statistical Abstracts of the United States, 1984 (Washington, D. C.: U.S. Government Printing Office, 1984), pp. 419–420.

Sex roles and gender identity seem to be a more basic cognitive category than the work role.

Sex roles and gender identity seem to be a more basic cognitive category than the work role. Sex role expectations are carried over into the workplace. Society insists that a person's sex makes a difference in "virtually every domain of human experience."[24] Consequently, a person is often characterized as a man or woman first and as a welder or secretary second. Furthermore, we notice someone's gender first and remember it long after we've forgotten other traits. Gender roles spill over into the workplace since many women feel more comfortable with stereotypically female roles and since some men are content with that arrangement.

Myth or Fact?

Myth: Women have a higher turnover rate than men.
Fact:

Regardless of sex, people with more education and skills stay on the same job longer.

True and false. Who's being discussed? Managers or receptionists? It's true that turnover rates are higher for women, but is it because they're women or because of the low-paying job that offers little satisfaction or advancement? Turnover rates are lower in better jobs. Kossen suggests that many people are guilty of statistical discrimination, "making of prejudgments about a person's potential performance in a higher level job based upon statistical results in a lower level job."[25] The fact is that people with more education and skills stay on the same job longer than do those with less, regardless of sex.

Myth: Women work only for pin money, for the little extras of life.
Fact:

Because of continuing increases in the nation's rates of divorce and unwed motherhood, many children will be reared at least temporarily in single-parent families. The mother is most often the single parent, and there's a correlation between families headed by single mothers and poverty. Women provide money for rent, food, and clothing—the necessities, not the luxuries—in many cases.

Women are the primary source of support for more than 10 million households, and in two-income families full-time working wives bring home 40 percent of the total earnings. Single mothers are working because they want to feed their children. Many married mothers are working for the same reason.

Myth: Women have less education than men.
Fact:

According to the U.S. Census Bureau women earned 50 percent of the Bachelor's degrees awarded in 1980, and both sexes completed 12.8 years of school.

WHAT'S YOUR MIND SET

Many women are often guiltier of having sexist attitudes than men. Again, these are attitudes they've acquired through the socialization process. The authors of *The Managerial Woman*, Henning and Jardin, say that men and women bring to the workplace entirely different mind sets, a mind set that gives men an immediate advantage as they move into management positions.[27] A mind set is an image that a person unconsciously conveys to others. A few examples from the book will illustrate.

1. Women are more likely to make later career decisions. A woman may be 10 years into her "career" before she makes a conscious commitment to long-term advancement.
2. Women have a sense of passivity. If they achieve success in a work area, they feel that "it just happened" or "someone did it for me."
3. They emphasize individual self-improvement as the most critical factor determining career advancement, and there are many self-improved women just "waiting to be chosen."
4. Definition of jobs differ between the sexes. For women, it's a way of making a living and for men it's a set of responsibilities to be met or an assignment to be fulfilled. Men and women both see a career as a means of growth and fulfillment, but men take the feeling a step farther and see it as a series of jobs in a path leading upward.
5. Men find it difficult to separate personal goals and career goals while women actively strive for separation.
6. In a subordinate role women center on the concept of themselves and men on the expectation of his boss. A women says, "Take me the way I am," and a man says "The boss can make me or break me."

   The authors aren't suggesting that women become more like men but that they should perceive of themselves as thinking people, assessing what's in it for them, what they really want, how to go about getting it, and what the costs and rewards of getting it are going to be.

Myth: Women have less work experience than men.

Fact:

Women are gaining experience rapidly. The Rand Organization projects that by the year 2000, a 40–year–old working woman will have 5.7 more years of work experience than her counterpart had in 1980.[26] Sure the cost of employing them will rise, but so should the benefits to the economy.

Myth: Women have no emotional stamina. They cry and get upset too easily.

Fact:

Not true. There's no proof that women are more emotional than men. It is unquestionable, however, that their conditioning as children is different. Little girls actually get reinforced for crying and grow to believe that it is perfectly acceptable, whereas little boys are taught to "dry up those tears and act like a man." The sexes are equally emotional, but they express their emotions differently.

Things are changing for women as they are for men, and more changes will occur as they gain work experience and education. They need to change their concepts of themselves and men need to also—if sexism is a problem. Many women find a nurturing, caring, typically female role to be quite satisfying, and bearing children to be future citizens is an admirable goal for any person regardless of sex. In the workplace, however, "Removing the barriers that prevent women from realizing their full potential is of critical importance for the stability, growth, and competitive position of American business."[28]

Ageism

Ageism is discrimination against individuals between the ages of 40 and 70.

Ageism is discrimination against individuals because of age, especially those between the ages of 40 and 70. Maybe the realization that you too will eventually become an older man or woman will help you see the harmful effects of ageism. Consider the fact that "Ageism is the only common prejudice in which those who hold it eventually wind up as the members of the group that they stereotype."[29]

With the life expectancy today around age 74, ageism is a form of discrimination which is very likely to affect you personally. Societies differ. The Japanese revere and respect their older citizens, but here in America older people are often treated with little dignity or respect. Attitudes and actions must change as the numbers of mature Americans increase. The baby-boomers of the post-World War II years will swell to the size of the over-65 population and bring about changes in the society as they have throughout their lives.

Interestingly, many people respond to ageism by thinking of wise and gray senior citizens, but ageism is particularly apparent to people in their forties. Women who've stayed at home with their children have a difficult time entering or reentering the work force, since their skills are likely to be outdated and since they have no recent experience. Men and women experiencing a midlife reassessment and subsequent job change are more likely to experience job discrimination than workers in their twenties and thirties. Also people who retire after 20 years in the military, workers whose jobs are replaced by technology, or employes who get laid off have a difficult time finding employment. From age 40 on, job changing and job hunting can be a nightmare for these people who are too young to retire and too old to rehire.

Chronological age is an invalid and illegal way of measuring a person's potential.

Chronological age is an invalid and now illegal way of measuring a person's potential. Age is a relative concept, and the nature of the job can influence appropriate age. Professional football players are old at 30. So are some fashion models. On the other hand, corporate presidents, Supreme Court justices, and U.S. presidents consider 30 to be young and relatively inexperienced.

It's impossible to overgeneralize about older people. They're just as heterogeneous and diverse in their membership as are teenagers or people in their thirties. They differ in their sex, race, religion, national

origin, marital status, ethnic group, and life experiences. The only thing they have in common is having lived for a long number of years.

When you look at the facts, there is not much actual evidence to support the stereotypes and prejudices that link age with senility, incompetence, and lack of worth in the labor market. Most are not arthritic, senile old codgers who live in the past. There's no proof that age always has a detrimental effect on capabilities. Biological years can't be discounted, but age is influenced by other factors as well. Heredity, life-style, use of alcohol and drugs, diet, and emotional and psychological strength are all factors that contribute to age. Is the person active? Does he or she eat properly? Does she exercise? Does the person smoke? Does she have a support group? Are they active and involved? Some 65-year-olds are tireless while some 25-year-olds are tiresome.

People are living longer and want to work for a number of reasons. They want to feel productive and useful as contributors to society. You don't have to look far to see the contribution of the elderly in society in arts, industry, and government. Sigmund Freud and Jean Piaget were productive psychologists into their eighties, Grandma Moses didn't begin painting until she was 76, and Dr. John Rock developed the birth control pill at 70. Also, because retirement pensions are fixed and don't keep up with changes in the economy, the older person often needs employment to get by and to meet financial obligations. Some don't even have pension plans and must rely on social security benefits which are minimal. Finally, older Americans need to be seen and to see others. Social contact and interaction are important at any age but especially for an older person whose family are living their own lives, perhaps in another part of the country.

Obsolescence and job change are major fears of older workers.   The graying work force has some problems other groups don't have. As job conditions change, younger people are more likely to relocate. Often motivated by security, many older people don't want to leave their communities and face uncertainty. They've seen the big city lights, thank you, and prefer their own, familiar surroundings. Obsolescence and job change are major fears of older workers. They don't want jobs with less pay and prestige. No one does, but an older worker is often forced into such a situation if earlier-acquired job skills are obsolete.

Looking for today's jobs with yesterday's skills and education hurts many older people. Developing new skills is a frightening experience, especially if a young know-it-all is doing the training. A woman who had been a secretary in a hospital for nearly 20 years felt that a change of scene was needed as she approached middle age. Finding a satisfying job with skills from the 1960s was difficult until the woman was trained to use a word processor. She's lucky. Many middle-aged and older workers are hesitant to enter retraining programs, and many employers are reluctant to train them.

Some employers feel that older workers don't have as much to offer or as many years to work. Not training and hiring older people is a tremendous waste of human resources. Some younger workers have been heard to say that you can't teach an old dog new tricks. That's absolutely erroneous. You can teach an old dog new tricks, but often they don't care to learn. Many older workers have no interest in learning new skills since they are not motivated by advancement. Reaction time is increased, but older people are still quite capable of learning.

WHY HIRE AN OLDER WORKER?

From his study of older people on the job, Jeffrey Sonnenfield presents research findings which indicate advantages in hiring and retaining older workers. He admits that workers staying on the job may be different somehow in their skills or interests in that they have managed to stay on the same job. Still, the findings indicate greater reliability among older workers and suggest that those who stayed on the job are the most competent.

* Older people seemed to have achieved superior standing among sales workers and to have remained higher performers. Reports from insurance companies, auto dealers, and large department stores suggest that age is an asset, if a factor at all, in performance.

* Age has little effect on manual workers. In several studies, performance seemed to remain fully steady through age 50, peaking slightly in the thirties. The decline in productivity never seemed to drop more than 10 percent from peak performance. Attendance was not significantly affected, and the separation (quits, firings, layoffs, discharges) rates were high for those under age 25 and very low for those over 45.

* Older workers studied (clerical) in government and private industry found no significant difference in output because of age. Researchers found that both female and male older workers had attendance records equal to those of other workers, as well as lower rates of turnover.

* Polaroid found that those who remain on the job after age 65 tend to be better performers. Even among older workers whose jobs entail physical demands, high performance is maintained.

Jeffrey Sonnenfield, "Dealing with the Aging Work Force," *Harvard Business Review*, November–December, 1978, pp. 88-89.

Older workers have low absentee and turnover rates.

There are many advantages in hiring an older worker. They have a lot of experience and maturity. They are probably less costly to an organization since their absentee and turnover rates are actually lower than those of a younger person. Older workers show more wisdom, are more helpful, and perform their duties with few personality clashes, according to Banker's Life and Casualty Company. The company has a tradition of retaining top executives, clerks, and secretaries through their sixties, seventies , and eighties.[30]

Additional Types of Prejudice

The three types of prejudice covered in this chapter are the most prevalent in our society, and there are laws to combat discriminatory behavior toward a person because of race, sex, or age. There are many, many other types of discrimination not covered by legislation, however, that affect individuals day after day. Employees and employers alike show discrimination toward people because of their height, size, physical appearance, and manner of dress, to name a few. This type of discrimination, though unfair, is hard to prove. *Time* reports that discrimination against corpulent adults can be blatant and cites an example of a 250-pound woman who is an executive assistant in a New York hospital who was once told to withdraw a job application because she would be "an assault to the eyes of the director." "Even when they are hired, the overweight contend that they are often passed over for promotions and raises."[31]

MEANS OF OVERCOMING PREJUDICE AND DISCRIMINATION

Exposure

There are means of overcoming prejudice and discrimination. Some of these means depend on an individual, others on the organization. Because of laws passed in recent years, changes have begun. Have they

---

HISTORY OF MAJOR ANTIDISCRIMINATION LEGISLATION

1954—Supreme Court orders schools desegregated.

1963—Equal Pay Act passed requiring employers to provide equal pay to women and men who perform "comparable work." This was amended by the Fair Labor Standards Amendment of 1974.

1964—Civil Rights Act passed and was later amended by Equal Employment Act of 1972.

1967—Age Discrimination Act passed to protect workers age 40 to age 65. This was amended in 1978 to protect workers from age 40 to age 70.

1973—Rehabilitation Act passed requiring federal contractors to take affirmative action to hire and advance handicapped persons.

1978—Pregnancy Discrimination Act was passed that provided equality in employment for women who are able to work during pregnancy.

helped? Somewhat. Legislation got the ball rolling, but it's difficult to legislate values and attitudes. "I may have to hire or to work with one of 'those people,' but I don't have to associate with them" is a widespread attitude. That's too bad, since sometimes association with someone "different" is an enlightening experience as you realize that people are not really so different after all. Exposure is educational since contact with others can make you aware of the fallacy of your thinking. Unfortunately, the people who need most to change their bigoted attitudes are often the least likely to avail themselves of the opportunity to do so.

Legislation

Let's look at the featured legislation in a little more detail. Title VII of the 1964 Civil Rights Act prohibits discrimination by employers on the basis of race, color, age, religion, sex, or national origin. All aspects of employment, from recruitment and hiring to training and promoting, are covered by this law. The EEOC (Equal Employment Opportunity Commission) is the agency primarily responsible for enforcing Title VII. It processes charges of discrimination brought by people and helps organizations to establish and implement affirmative action plans. The commission can also require employers to file reports on the numbers of minority workers holding various types of jobs.

Groups protected by federal EEO laws are called protected groups.

EEOC provides equal opportunities and is supported by local, state, and federal EEO laws. In some cases the laws prohibit discrimination against the handicapped. It gives equal access to jobs for those who want to work and who are willing to develop themselves to perform the job successfully. Since the laws are designed to protect certain people, the groups are called protected groups. There are literally millions in these protected groups since most workers can claim discrimination in one form or another.

Affirmative action programs are required for companies contracting with the federal government, all public employers, and all federal agencies.

Affirmative action (AA) refers to positive efforts on the part of employers to increase employment opportunities for groups inadequately represented in a firm's labor force. The existence of an AA program indicates that an organization is making an effort to recruit, hire, promote, and provide education opportunities for members of minority groups. Its goals are to rectify past alleged discrimination and prevent its occurrence in the future. These programs are common and usually follow established timetables. Affirmative action programs are required for companies contracting with the federal government, all public employers, and all federal agencies.

Have the laws helped? Much progress has been made, but there are still problems, especially concerning subtle forms of discrimination. Also, because of legislation, many people have complained of reverse discrimination, a form of discrimination against a person in a majority group. For example, many men between age 20 and age 40 feel that people in the protected groups have been protected at their expense. They remind employers that the solution to ending discrimination against some shouldn't result in practicing it against others.

It's to our advantage to go beyond simply tolerating those perceived to be different because of race, ethnic background, sex, or age. We should accept and even welcome the differences so as not to waste human potential. In general, Americans are more tolerant of diversity. The moral and social climate in this country is more favorable than at any other time for eliminating discrimination against people and for providing a climate that will meet their needs for esteem and growth.

CASE STUDY

Barbara Stalvey

Barbara Stalvey is a librarian who has a tough decision to make. She needs a library assistant to catalogue and check out books, equipment, audiovisual aids, and other materials and to assist library patrons with their requests. These requests might range from helping a child find a book on anatomy to aiding an adult in use of the card catalogue or setting up a filmstrip. Sometimes some typing is required although this is rare since the library employs a secretary. The job is a full-time position calling for night work two nights per week and paying $5.50 per hour.

Twenty-seven people applied for the job, and the librarian has narrowed the selection down to four. Maybe you can help Barbara make her decision after looking at brief sketches of the remaining four applicants:

Rose Green is a 50-year-old white female who's held a similar position on a part-time basis in a school for three years. Rose applied for the job because she needs full-time employment. A full-time job would enable her to quit her moonlighting job at the local pizza palace. She has an Associate's degree in Business Administration which she completed only two month's prior to applying for the library assistant's job.

Rose is divorced, has two children and one grandchild at home, and has had a variety of work experience, including being a waitress, teacher's aide, and school lunchroom attendant. She's pleasant and somewhat low-key and quiet during the interview.

Samantha King is a 24-year-old black female with an Associate's degree in secretarial science. Samantha is presently employed as a secretary in a large city library and has been there ever since she graduated from college four years ago. While in college, she was employed as a work-study student in the financial aid department.

Samantha now desires to relocate to be near her fiance. As soon as she can get a job, she plans to marry and make Oak City her new home.

The applicant is very attractive, well-dressed, self-assured, and almost aggressive in the interview. Her competence is quite obvious.

Lavinia Mickel is a 34-year-old white female presently employed as a salesperson in a department store. She applied for the job in response to a want ad in the newspaper. Lavinia completed one year of college before getting married and starting her family. She now has two children, ages 11 and 13. Although the applicant worked part-time while in college and has done volunteer work for the hospital, the salesperson's position is the first Lavinia has held since her marriage 13 years ago. She devoted herself to being a full-time wife and mother until her children began to develop their own interests and became less dependent on their mother.

Lavinia is personable, outgoing, and vivacious. Although she's never worked in a library, she's very bright and could easily learn the job duties. In the job interview, the applicant expressed a love of learning and a desire to grow.

Gary Wofford is a 62-year-old white male retired from the U.S. Army. After retirement, Gary used the G.I. Bill to get a Bachelor's degree in English. He then started his own business, a successful bookstore. Although the bookstore did quite well, Gary found that he didn't like the pressure and paperwork involved in running a business. He opened the bookstore to be around people and books and didn't enjoy inventories and invoices.

Gary appeared gruff and "no nonsense" at first meeting, but his stiff manner was really just a facade for a very friendly, pleasant, and delightful man. Gary receives his military pension and has some money invested from the sale of his bookstore. He really wants the job, not just for the money, but for personal satisfaction as well. He feels that he would be an asset to the library and isn't reluctant to say so.

Does Barbara have a dilemma or not? Keeping the equal opportunity laws in mind, whom would you choose? Why?

SUMMARY

Prejudice means prejudging people without knowledge of their personal qualities: discrimination is any behavior that demonstrates that preconceived judgment. If prejudice and discrimination could be removed, the labor force could be better used, families could enjoy more earning and purchasing power, and more contributions to society could be made.

Discrimination manifests itself along the entire continuum from hiring to firing. Once hired, minorities face continued discrimination by not being promoted as often, not being selected for training, and being paid less than members of the majority group receive.

Three theories explaining the causes of prejudice are psychological, social, and economic.

Using projection and blaming scapegoats are two examples of psychological theories. Another psychological explanation suggests that prejudice develops more readily in persons having an authoritarian personality.

The most popular of the social theories is the social learning theory which proposes that people acquire prejudice just as they acquire other values like patriotism and honesty. Stereotyping, a process in which a group is judged according to the behavior of a few of its members, is a key concept of this theory.

The basis of economic theory is that there is a direct correlation between the degree of competition of two or more groups and the prejudice felt toward each other.

Three types of prejudice often encountered in the workplace are racism, sexism, and ageism.

Racism is prejudice based on skin color, race, or national origin. The racial groups most victimized today are blacks, Hispanics, Asians, and native Americans.

For centuries American blacks have experienced inequities in both educational and employment opportunities, and today black unemployment has been complicated by the emergence of increasing numbers of other minority groups such as women and Hispanics.

Hispanics, people from Puerto Rico, Mexico, Cuba, and other Central and South American countries, continue to suffer from poor education, a lack of job skills, and a language barrier.

Asian Americans, the latest victims of discrimination, have a brighter future than do other minority groups, since educational and occupational opportunities have enabled many to achieve success in professional careers such as law and medicine. Reputed to be the most highly skilled of any immigrant group our country has ever had, Asian Americans place a premium on education and hard work.

As the most disadvantaged group in America today, native Americans are high in unemployment, health problems, and alcoholism, and low in wealth and education.

Sexism, discrimination based on gender, is based on widely held beliefs about the abilities, traits, and behavior of men and women. Sexual harassment is any unwanted verbal or physical conduct that creates an unpleasant work environment.

Although women comprise over 40 percent of the labor force, they are still victims of discrimination. Some positive changes have occurred, but there is still a age gap between the earnings of men and women. Things will change for the better for women as they gain work experience and education and change their concepts of themselves.

The social learning theory provides one explanation for the development and persistence of sexism. Too, women have to learn many new rules of organizational life that men already know about and take for granted. Finally, women have had fewer sexual role models to identify with and have been unaware of opportunities available to them.

Gender roles spill over into the workplace since many women feel more comfortable with stereotypically female roles and since some men are content with that arrangement.

Many unfounded myths about women in the workplace include the following: (1) women have a higher turnover rate than men, (2) women work only for pin money, or the little extras in life, (3) women have less education and work experience than men, and (4) women have no emotional stamina.

Ageism is discrimination against individuals between the ages of 40 and 70. Chronological age is an invalid and illegal way of measuring a person's potential. There is little actual evidence to support the stereotypes and prejudices that link age with senility, incompetence, and lack of worth in the labor market.

People are living longer and want to work for a number of reasons. They want to feel productive and useful as contributors to society, they need employment to meet financial obligations, and they need social contact with others.

The graying work force has some problems that other groups don't have. They're looking for today's jobs with yesterday's skills, and developing new skills can be a frightening experience. Also older workers are not as likely to relocate as are younger people when job conditions change.

Advantages in hiring an older worker are that they have experience and maturity, they have lower absentee and turnover rates, and they perform their duties with fewer personality clashes.

Means of overcoming prejudice and discrimination can be individual, organizational, and legislative. Particularly important in combating discrimination is Title VII of the 1964 Civil Rights Act, which prohibits discrimination by employers on the basis of race, color, age, religion, sex, or national origin. All aspects of employment from recruitment and hiring to training and promoting are covered by this law.

The EEOC is the agency primarily responsible for enforcing Title VII and is supported by local, state, and federal laws. Affirmative action refers to positive efforts on the part of employers to increase employment opportunities for groups inadequately represented in a firm's labor force. Laws have helped, but there are still problems concerning subtle forms of discrimination and claims of reverse discrimination.

KEY TERMS

Prejudice
Discrimination
Equal Employment Opportunity Commission
Psychological theory of prejudice
Social theory of prejudice
Economic theory of prejudice
Scapegoat
Gordon Allport
Authoritarian personality
Stereotypes
Racism
Sexism
Sexual harassment
Statistical discrimination
Racism
Ageism
Hispanics
Affirmative action
Civil Rights Act
Antidiscrimination legislation

REVIEW AND DISCUSSION QUESTIONS

1. In your opinion, what are some disadvantages of prejudice and discrimination?

2. Briefly discuss each of the three theories of prejudice outlined in the chapter. Which do you think accounts for more prejudice? Why?

3. Discuss the disadvantages of the four types of racism in the chapter. What are the other types with which you are familiar?

4. Why is sexism more an issue today than it was 20 years ago?

5. What are some reasons for removing ageism from the workplace?

6. Give examples of equal opportunity legislation. How have the laws helped? Why is it to your advantage to become familiar with the laws?

7. What are some ways of overcoming prejudice and discrimination?

8. What are some common stereotypes about various groups of people? How do you think these particular stereotypes developed?

9. What is a protected group? Do you think some people in these groups are sometimes protected at the expense of others? Give an example.

ENDNOTES

[1]LEWIS GRIZZARD, *Kathy Sue Loudermilk, I Love You* (Atlanta, Georgia: Peachtree Publishers, Ltd., 1979), p. 317.

[2]PETER M. PANKEN, "The Road to Court Is Paved with Good Intentions," *Nation's Business*, June 1985, p. 45.

[3]CHRISTOPHER BATES DOOB, *Sociology: An Introduction* (New York: Holt, Rinehart and Winston, 1985), p. 235.

[4]DAVID B. BRINKERHOFF AND LYNN K. WHITE, *Sociology* (St. Paul, Minn.: West, 1985), p. 248.

[5]GORDON W. ALLPORT, *The Nature of Prejudice* (Reading, Mass.: Addison-Wesley, 1954), p. 244.

[6]T. W. ADORNO AND OTHERS, *The Authoritarian Personality* (New York: Harper & Row, 1950).

[7]RICHARD STENGEL, "Resentment Tinged with Envy," *Time*, July 8, 1985, p. 56.

[8]ALEX THIO, *Sociology: An Introduction* (New York: Harper & Row, 1986), p. 233.

[9]PAUL R. TIMM AND BRENT D. PETERSON, *People at Work* (St. Paul, Minn.: West, 1982), p. 327.

[10]*The Wall Street Journal*, October 12, 1984.

[11]U.S. Bureau of the Census, *Statistical Abstracts of the United States: 1985* 106th edition (Washington, D.C.: U.S. Government Printing Office, 1985).

[12]STENGEL, "Resentment Tinged with Envy," p. 56.

[13]CARY DAVIS, "The Future Racial Composition of the U.S.," *Intercom*, 1985, pp. 8–10.

[14]AARON BERNSTEIN, "The Forgotten Americans," *Business Week*, September 2, 1985, p. 55.

[15]WILLIAM R. DOERNER, "To America with Skills," *Time*, July 8, 1985, p. 42.

[16]Ibid., p. 43.

[17]STEVE HUNTLEY, "America's Indians: Beggars in Our Own Land," *U.S. News & World Report*, May 23, 1983, p. 70.

[18]DOOB, *Sociology*, p. 255.

[19]KAREN PENNAR AND EDWARD MERVOSH, "Women at Work," *Business Week*, January 28, 1985, p. 83.

[20]JUDY MANN AND BASIA MELLWIG, "The Truth About the Salary Gap(s)," *Working Woman*, January 1988, p. 61.

[21]Women's Bureau, Office of the Secretary, U.S. Department of Labor, *Job Options for Women in the 80's* (Washington, D.C.: U.S. Government Printing Office, 1980), p. 5.

[22]MARAGARET MEAD, *Sex and Temperament in Three Primitive Societies* (New York: William Morrow, 1935).

[23]RICHARD PERES, *Dealing with Employment Discrimination* (New York: McGraw-Hill, 1978), p. 34.

[24]BARBARA A. GUTEK, *Sex and the Workplace* (San Francisco: Jossey-Bass, 1985), p. 17.

[25]STAN KOSSEN, *The Human Side of Organizations* (New York: Harper & Row, 1983), p. 358.

[26]PENNAR AND MERVOSH, "Women at Work," p. 82.

[27]MARGERET HENNIG AND ANNE JARDIN, *The Managerial Woman* (Garden City, N.Y.: Anchor, 1977), pp. 11–34.

[28]JANICE CASTRO, "More and More, She's the Boss," *Time*, December 2, 1985, p. 66.

[29]ROBERT PERRUCCI AND DEAN D. KNUDSEN, *Sociology* (St. Paul, Minn.: West, 1983), p. 162.

[30]JEFFREY SONNENFELD, "Dealing with the Aging Work Force," *Harvard Business Review*, November–December 1978, p. 89.

[31]ANASTASIA TOUFEXIS, "Dieting: The Losing Game," *Time*, January 20, 1986, p. 55.

GLOSSARY

Affirmative Action: Positive efforts on the part of employers to increase employment opportunities for groups inadequately represented in a firm's labor force.

Approach-Approach Conflict: A conflict having two equally desirable or attractive alternatives.

Approach-Avoidance Conflict: A conflict with both positive and negative qualities.

Autocratic Leader: Leader who concentrates power, decision making, and responsibility in one person.

Avoidance-Avoidance Conflict: A conflict with two undesirable alternatives.

Behaviorism: School of psychological thought emphasizing the behaviors that occur in response to environmental stimuli.

Biofeedback: A system to make a person more aware of body processes such as heart and respiration rates.

Boss Management: Process of making work more enjoyable and productive for both employer and employee.

Broken-Record Technique: An assertiveness technique that involves being persistent and repetitive without getting irritated or angry.

Burnout: Depletion of physical and mental resources caused by striving to reach unrealistic job related goals.

Cardinal Trait: A trait so pervasive that practically all of a person's activities can be traced to its influence.

Central Trait: Generalized disposition or tendency of a person.

Character Ethic: Ethic demonstrated by hard work, industry, diligence, prudence, and honesty.

Civil Rights Act of 1964: Act prohibiting discrimination based on race, color, age, religion, sex, or national origin.

Conceptual Skill: Ability to see the enterprise as a whole and recognize how the various functions of the organization depend on one another.

Conditional Positive Regard: Caring for someone as long as he or she meets the needs or expectations of another.

Conflict: State resulting from being faced with incompatible needs, demands, or opportunities.

Congruence: A fit among self-concept, behavior, and thoughts.

Connotation: Subjective meaning of a word.

Conscious: Present state of awareness which contains sensory information, thoughts, and daydreams.

Contingency Theory: Leadership theory emphasizing leader-member relations, task structure, and position power.

Control Group: In an experiment, the group receiving no special treatment.

Cooperative Counseling: A blend of directive and nondirective counseling that seeks to establish a cooperative exchange of ideas.

Correlational Research: Method of scientific investigation that identifies and studies the relationship among variables without showing cause and effect.

Correspondence: A condition that develops when the individual fulfills the requirements of the work environment and the work environment fulfills the requirements of the person.

Cover Letter: Letter accompanying a resume allowing the person to explain why he or she wants a certain job and to slant the approach toward that specific job.

"C-Z" Activity: A low-value activity that can be postponed indefinitely without harm.

Decoding: Interpreting thoughts and ideas of the sender of a communication message.

Denial: Defense mechanism in which the person denies sources of danger or the reality of an unpleasant situation.

Dependent Variable: A variable presumed to be affected by the independent variable; in an experiment, the one that may change in response to manipulation of the independent variable.

Denotation: Literal dictionary definition of a word.

Depressants: Drugs such as alcohol and tranquilizers that depress the central nervous system.

Depression: Common psychological problem characterized by feelings of hopelessness, worthlessness, and sadness in response to real or imagined loss, failure, or misfortune.

Derived X: Stan Kossen's humorous spinoff of Theory X that contends that derived X leaders were once positive about subordinates but became negative after being "burned."

Directive Counseling: Traditional means of counseling in which counselor directs the form, flow, and content of the exchange between counselor and counselee.

Discrimination: Behavior that demonstrates prejudice.

Displacement: Defense mechanism in which a response is transferred from one subject to another.

DOT: *Dictionary of Occupational Titles*, a listing and description of jobs available in the United States.

Double Approach-Avoidance Conflict: The most complex of the conflicts; a conflict in which a person has to choose between two alternatives, both of which have positive and negative qualities.

Downward Communication: Formal communication channel that carries information on policies, job duties, and expectations from the top executive down to the lowest-level employee.

EAPs: Employee assistance programs that seek to identify and treat employee with problems which may affect work performance; originally set up for treatment of alcoholics which now treats drug abusers as well.

EEOC: Equal Employment Opportunity Commission. Agency primarily responsible for enforcing Title VII of the 1964 Civil Rights Act.

Ego: Personality structure that evolved from the id and operates according to the reality principle.

Emblems: Gestures that directly suggest specific words or phrases such as a beckoning gesture of the hand.

Emotional Barriers to Communication: Those barriers to communication which are private and difficult to remove. Examples are stereotyping, hostility, preoccupation, and self-concept.

Empathy: Feeling with someone, putting oneself in another's place to better understand him or her.

Encoding: Translating thoughts and ideas into symbols for transmission.

Eustress: Optimal amount of stress that keeps a person alert, occupied, and fully functioning.

Expectancy Theory: Theory that states that motivation is greater when someone believes one's efforts will result in a favorable performance and earn a desired reward.

Experimental Group: In an experiment, the group receiving the independent variable.

Experimental Method: A research method in which an investigator manipulates one or more independent variables to observe the effect upon the dependent variable.

Expert Power: Power that comes from a person's knowledge and information about a situation and depends largely on education, training, and experience.

Extrinsic Motivator: Motivators such as sick leave, dental plans, or paid vacations that can be enjoyed only off the job.

Faulty Cognitions: Incorrect or faulty thinking in which a person overgeneralizes from failure and focuses on the negative side of things.

Flextime: Making working hours more flexible.

Fogging: An assertiveness technique that helps a person to cope by offering no resistance or hard psychological striking surfaces.

Follow-up Activities: Phone calls, visits, or letters made or sent to interviewer after a job interview has taken place.

Formal Communication: Communication that moves along both vertical and horizontal lines along official paths dictated by job function and the organizational hierarchy.

Free-Reign Style: Leadership style that downplays bossy role and concentrates on providing information and resources to workers.

Freudian Slip: A slip of the tongue that indicates an unconscious thought.

Frustration: A state resulting from being prevented from attaining a goal or motive.

General Adaptation Syndrome: Body's response to stress, which includes the alarm reaction, the resistance stage, and the exhaustion stage.

Good Fairy Syndrome: Attitude that problems can somehow be swept away if the right Good Fairy waves the magic wand.

Grapevine: Informal communication channel that operates along both vertical and horizontal lines and that helps to satisfy workers' social needs of belongingness and helps to clarify formal communication.

Hallucinogens: Drugs capable of producing bizarre changes in the way in which individuals perceive the world around them.

Hawthorne Experiments: Efficiency studies undertaken at the Hawthorne Western Electric plant in the late 1920s that led the way for the human relations movement.

Hawthorne Effect: Any improvement in worker performance that is the by-product of attention and feelings of self-worth.

Hidden Curriculum: Rules, routines, and regulations that are taught in schools in addition to the "three R's."

Hierarchy of Needs: Abraham Maslow's theory that proposes that needs are systematically satisfied as a person progresses from lower-level needs to higher-level ones.

Horizontal Communication: Formal communication occurring among co-workers, managers, departments, and divisions on the same level.

Human Skill: Ability to work effectively as a group member and to build cooperation and effort among subordinates.

Human Relations: Process in which both management and workers are brought into contact with the organization in such a way that the objectives of each are achieved. Also, a term applied to organizational behavior early in its history.

Hygiene Factors: Maintenance factors such as company policies and administration, salary, and working conditions.

Id: Personality structure present at birth that acts according to the pleasure principle.

Illustrators: Gestures and expressions that reinforce the verbal message.

"I" Message: A three-part technique used in reporting feelings to someone without criticizing, complaining, condemning, or judging.

Independent Variable: Treatment given to the experimental group involved in scientific research.

Intrinsic Motivator: Motivators that benefit the person while on the job such as interesting or challenging work.

Ideation: First step in the communication process; also referred to as developing an idea.

Informal Communication: Communication patterns that emerge from social interactions of people who work together.

Informal Groups: Groups arising in the workplace that strongly influence organizational effectiveness and meet a variety of individual needs not met by the formal organization.

Interpersonal Communication: Communication that takes place between people.

Intimate Distance: Distance extending from touch to 18 inches reserved for close, private encounters.

Intrapersonal Communication: Communication that takes place within a person such as thoughts, ideas, and fantasies.

Job Loading: Changing a job to make it more meaningful and challenging.

Job Rotation: Process of rotating jobs to relive monotony and provide variety.

Job Sharing: Two people sharing the same job.

Kinesics: Body language consisting primarily of gestures, facial expressions, and posture.

KISS Formula: "Keep it simple, stupid" or "Keep it simple and straightforward."

Language Barriers to Communication: Barriers to communication such as foreign words and phrases, technical jargon, complex words, ambiguous terms, and connotation differences.

Leadership: The ability to get things done willingly and enthusiastically through other people.

Learned Helplessness: Theory of depression in which a person believes that he or she has no control over the stresses, strains, and traumas of life.

Legitimate Power: Also called position power; power granted by a higher authority.

Long-Range Goals: Goals concerned with overall life–style, including the type of job you want and the situation you want to live in.

MBWA: Management by walking around.

Meditation: Ancient art of narrowed awareness that involves the relaxation response.

Medium-Range Goals: Goals that concern the next five years or so.

Mentor: Someone in a higher place in an organization who teaches, coaches, and counsels others on their way up.

Micro Goals: The only goals a person has direct control over and which cover 15 minutes to 1 hour.

Mini Goals: Goals that cover one day to one month.

Morale: Attitudes toward an employing organization in general or specific job factors such as supervision, fellow employees, and financial incentives.

Motivation: An internal process that starts, energizes, and directs behavior toward achieving a goal.

Motivational Process: A process involving four steps: (1) motive or unsatisfied need, (2) tension or excitement, (3) action or behavior, and (4) goal achievement or relief of tension.

Motivator Factors: Factors that create satisfaction when present and include achievement, recognition, and advancement.

Narcotics: Addictive drugs derived from the opium poppy. Examples include opium, morphine, heroin, codeine, and synthetic narcotics like demerol.

Naturalistic Observation: Observing the organism in his or her natural environment.

Need for Achievement: Need to gain satisfaction from the accomplishment of a task itself.

Need for Affiliation: Need to be accepted by others.

Need for Power: Need to dominate situations and strongly persuade others in making decisions.

Nondirective Counseling: Client-centered counseling in which the counselee determines what's to be discussed. No advice is given, and the listener is nonjudgmental and nonevaluative.

Nonverbal Communication: Messages communicated by gestures, posture, clothing, vocal cues, distance, and facial expressions.

Norms: Behavior expectations that express the collective values of a group and provide guidelines for member behavior.

Object Language: Artifacts such as hairstyle, dress, cosmetics, and jewelry that give messages to others about personality, age, role, socioeconomic status, and group membership.

Observational Learning: Learning through imitation, identification, and observation.

Occupational Outlook Handbook: Publication of the U.S. Department of Labor that lists and describes approximately 850 jobs in terms of nature of the work, working conditions, employment training, job outlook, average earnings, and related occupations.

Open-Door Policy: The practice of the supervisor leaving the door open for employees with questions, suggestions, complaints, and ideas.

Organizational Knowledge: Knowledge of what's going on in the business concerning people, products, and organizational structure.

Paralanguage: All oral aspects of language except the words themselves; pitch, tone, volume, and quality are examples.

Parallaction: A type of pseudointeraction in which people appear to be having a communication exchange, yet there is no involvement with each other.

Participative Leader: Leader who asks for suggestions and ideas from employees; can be democratic or consultative.

Personality: A person's enduring and unique pattern of behavior.

Personal Distance: Distance from 18 inches to 2 feet, which includes a variety of conversations from personal to newsy, formal to informal.

Personal Face: The way you see yourself.

Personal Power: Power of the personality associated with expertise, ability, expertise, or the strength of one's personality in persuading others to follow.

Personal Space: Imaginary 2-foot bubble surrounding you and keeping you at a distance from others.

Personal Variables: Competencies and skills like athletic ability or social ease.

Personality Ethic: Ethic that stresses that the path to success is through other people, through getting along with others and developing a pleasing personality.

Physical Addiction: A situation in which the body has become so accustomed to a drug that painful and sometimes fatal withdrawal symptoms occur if the drug is withheld.

Physical Barriers to Communication: The least complicated of the communication barriers, including noise, distance, poor hearing, furniture arrangement, lighting, and temperature.

Political Power: Comes from support of a group, from the leader's ability to work with people and social systems to gain their allegiance and support.

Politics: Total complex of what goes on between people at work, specifically, ways in which they gain and use power.

Positive Reinforcement: Reinforcement such as praise that follows a behavior and serves to strengthen the likelihood of the behavior being repeated.

Preconscious: A person's available memory that acts as a bridge between the conscious and unconscious.

Prejudice: A negative judgment toward a group that focuses on one or more negative characteristics supposedly shared by all group members.

Progressive Relaxation: A relaxation response used to both treat and prevent diseases linked to stress.

Protestant Ethic: The endowing of work with intrinsic moral worth; attitude demonstrated by the belief in hard work, perseverance, and thrift.

Psychological Dependence: A situation in which a user feels that the drug is necessary to maintain psychological and emotional well-being.

Primary Needs: Physiological needs necessary for physical survival.

Proxemics: Use of space in nonverbal communication.

Psychodynamic Theory: Personality theory that concentrates on the dynamic interplay and struggle within the unconscious mind.

Psychology: Scientific study of human and animal behavior.

Public Distance: Distance of over 12 feet used in public speaking situations.

Pure Research: Research gathered for the sake of adding to the body of scientific information.

Quality Circles: Small group of workers doing similar work who meet and discuss work-related problems.

Racism: Prejudice based on skin color, race, or national origin.

Rationalization: Common defense mechanism in which the person makes excuses for his or her failures, disappointments, or unsatisfactory behavior.

Reaction Formation: Defense mechanism in which the person represses disturbing material and insists that the opposite is true.

Real Face: The way you really are.

Reductionism: Breaking down of tasks to maximize efficiency.

Regulators: Nonverbal messages such as nodding the head that regulate the communication of others.

Repression: Unconscious forgetting.

Resume: An inventory of work experience and education whose purpose is to obtain an interview.

Reverse Discrimination: Discrimination against someone not included in a protected group.

Role Expectation: How we expect ourselves and others to act based on perceptions of roles such as stenographer, father, teacher, or minister.

Scapegoating: A type of displacement in which someone is blamed for problems for which they are not responsible.

Scientific Management: Scientific means of improving worker efficiency and productivity.

Scientific Method: Process of formulating a hypothesis, gathering and analyzing data, and applying research to describe, explain, predict and control behavior.

Secondary Needs: Needs of the mind and spirit rather than of the physical body. Needs that complicate the motivation efforts of managers.

Secondary Trait: Dispositions that are less conspicuous, generalized, and consistent than central traits.

Self-Actualization: The need to reach maximum potential, to become all that a person is capable of becoming.

Self-Concept: Mental picture of what we believe about ourselves that develops from social interactions, comparisons to others, personal thoughts, and statements of others.

Self-fulfilling Prophecy: Situation in which a person creates or causes the outcomes that he or she expects.

Self Theory: Carl Rogers's personality theory that emphasizes positive aspects of the personality such as a person's strong tendency toward growth.

Sexism: Discrimination based on gender.

Sexual Harassment: Physical or verbal conduct that creates an offensive or unpleasant work environment.

Short Range Goals: Goals covering the next one month to one year.

Situational Variables: Rewards and punishments.

Social Learning Theory: A type of behaviorism that attempts to integrate environmental variables with cognitive functioning to explain human behavior.

Social Distance: Distance of 4 to 12 feet recognized as the appropriate space for people conducting business.

Social Face: The face you wear in public that changes according to the impression you want to make.

Statistical Discrimination: Making prejudgments about a person's potential in a higher-level job based on statistical results in a lower-level job.

Stereotyping: Process in which a group is judged according to the behavior of a few of its members.

Stimulants: Drugs such as amphetamines, cocaine, nicotine, and caffeine that excite the central nervous system.

Stress: The demand placed on a person to adapt, adjust, or cope; the rate of wear and tear on the body.

Stressor: A stress-producing event or person that triggers the alarm reaction.

Superego: Personality structure that represents your conscience and acts according to the morality principle.

Suppression: Conscious forgetting.

Survey: Type of scientific investigation in which people are questioned in a personal interview or by a questionnaire.

Swiss Cheese Method: Method of turning an overwhelming or unpleasant task into several short and easy tasks; time management technique used to avoid procrastination.

Technical Skill: Person's knowledge and ability in any type of technique or procedure.

Telecommuting: Creating, processing, and distributing information by use of a computer terminal or word processor.

Temperament: Hereditary aspect of one's emotional nature or personality.

Territory: One's own space, which is generally immovable and usually separate from the person.

Theory Z: Theory combining characteristics of American and Japanese leadership practices such as participative decision making, long-term employment, and nonspecialized career paths.

"To Do" List: Lists of daily goals that should be written down, visible, and prioritized.

Tolerance: Needing more and more of a drug to achieve the initial effect.

Trait Theory: Based on belief that each person's behavior derives from a particular pattern of personal traits.

Trait Theory of Leadership: Theory assuming that there is a set of traits necessary for leadership success.

Two-Factor Theory: Herzberg's motivation-maintenance model of motivation.

Type A Personality: Coronary-prone personality type characterized by competitiveness and a sense of time urgency.

Type Theory: Based on belief that traits cluster together to form a personality type.

Unconditional Positive Regard: Caring for someone regardless of looks, age, size, performance, or abilities.

Unconscious: Part of the mind that contains sexual and aggressive impulses as well as repressed memories, feelings, and emotions.

Upward Communication: Formal communication channel that carries suggestions, complaints, or questions from workers at all levels to the top executive.

Value System: An underlying system of beliefs about what is important to a person and that determines many facets of behavior.

Whole-Job Concept: Also called job enlargement; increases complexity of a job so that it appeals to higher-order needs.

X Leadership Type: Leader who believes that people work only for money and have little or no commitment to organizational goals.

Y Leadership Type: Leader who believes that the expenditure of physical and mental effort in work is as natural as play or rest.

Index